HISTORICAL DICTIONARIES OF RELIGIONS,
PHILOSOPHIES, AND MOVEMENTS
Edited by Jon Woronoff

Historical Dictionary of
New Religious Movements

George D. Chryssides

Historical Dictionaries of Religions,
Philosophies, and Movements, No. 42

The Scarecrow Press, Inc.
Lanham, Maryland, and London
2001

SCARECROW PRESS, INC.

Published in the United States of America
by Scarecrow Press, Inc.
4720 Boston Way, Lanham, Maryland 20706
www.scarecrowpress.com

4 Pleydell Gardens, Folkestone
Kent CT20 2DN, England

British Library Cataloguing-in-Publication Information Available

Library of Congress Cataloging-in-Publication Data

Chryssides, George D., 1945–
    Historical dictionary of new religious movements / George D. Chryssides.
        p. cm. — (Historical dictionaries of religions, philosophies, and movements ;
        no. 42)
    Includes bibliographical references and index.
    ISBN 0-8108-4095-2 (alk. paper)
        1. Cults—Dictionaries. 2. Cults—History—Dictionaries. I. Title. II. Series.
    BP601 .C47 2001
    291'.046—dc21   2001034196

⊗™ The paper used in this publication meets the minimum requirements of
American National Standard for Information Sciences—Permanence of
Paper for Printed Library Materials, ANSI/NISO Z39.48-1992.
Manufactured in the United States of America.

To my former teacher
Professor Howard J. N. Horsburgh
who taught me not to be dismissive of
unpopular or implausible opinions

Contents

Editor's Foreword

New religious movements (NRMs), or "cults" to some, are an amazingly variegated group. Some are theologically conservative, others radically innovative; some reach forward to a remote future, others back to the distant past. They may stick to one broad religious tradition or mix several, their approaches to morality and ethics often have little in common, and their religious practices and organization are equally eclectic. In addition, some NRMs have waxed and attracted numerous adherents, while others have waned and could disappear. There is no way of summing them up in a few simple pat phrases. And that is why this *Historical Dictionary of New Religious Movements* is so useful. It just presents and describes and then leaves readers to draw their own conclusions.

But this is not as simple as it sounds. Readers of this latest volume in the religion series will immediately be impressed by the enormous amount of research needed just to present and describe the more significant new religions. There are approximately four hundred in this one volume, coming from dozens of countries, each with its distinctive characteristics. Each has its own entry and perhaps another on its founder. There are also numerous entries on salient aspects of NRMs and broader traditions as well as key persons and writings. While the dictionary provides a handy reference to the parts, the whole is treated more comprehensively in an introduction which examines the genesis and growth of new religious movements as a category. The chronology tracks their growth over time, and the bibliography directs interested readers to more specialized and complete sources.

It is already difficult to present and describe one religion, how much more so to introduce four hundred? It obviously took a long time for the author to accumulate the information, something George D. Chryssides has been working on for several decades now. He studied philosophy and theology at the University of Glasgow and received a doctorate in the philosophy of religion from Oriel College, Oxford University, in 1974. Since then, he has taught at several universities and presently holds the post of senior lecturer in religious studies at the University of Wolverhampton. But knowledge is not enough—it must be presented in a manner accessible to the general public as well as specialists, an ability Dr. Chryssides has gained through writing dozens of articles and chapters, as well as several books, including *The Advent of Sun Myung Moon* and *Exploring New Religions.* Particularly relevant here is Dr. Chryssides' experience with various working parties and groups, such as the Centre for the Study of New Religious Movements in Selly Oak Colleges, Birmingham, England, and the Council for Religious Freedom. Nor should we neglect the considerable effort of past years in writing a unique work which allows us, the readers, to have such a broad and deep view of a still poorly known field.

Jon Woronoff
Series Editor

Preface

Compiling a historical dictionary of new religious movements (NRMs) is a daunting task, not only on account of the prestigious nature of the historical dictionaries series but also because of the sheer extent of new movements. The term *historical* in the series title requires a diachronic as well as a synchronic approach, making the undertaking all the more demanding. How can one possibly do justice to the origins, ideas and developments of so many movements in so many diverse cultures?

When faced with a reference work, readers with a critical eye will no doubt scan it to see whether their favorite topic has been omitted, or question the inclusion of certain items. In such a controversial area as new religious movements I doubt whether any author can devise a range of entries that will satisfy every reader or interest group. The usual methodological problems abound: What is a religion? When is a movement "new"? Does an author include movements in the sense of nebulous currents of thought, or only identifiable organizations?

Several organizations have been at pains to emphasize their professed nonreligious nature, notably the Association for Research and Enlightenment (ARE), Emin, *est,* Transcendental Meditation, Elan Vital, and the Rosicrucians. Others, whose claim to be religious is sometimes questioned—for example, the Church of Scientology—have insisted that they are religions. Still other movements (notably the International Society for Krishna Consciousness, the Church of Jesus Christ of Latter-day Saints, and the Jehovah's Witnesses) claim that they are not new, but are rather reviving or restoring an ancient tradition. Despite academia's insistence that the term *new religious movements* is considerably preferable to "cults," "sects," or "fringe religions," numerous NRMs still dislike the term, fearing that it tars them with the same brush as the groups that have attracted notoriety through adverse media publicity.

To pursue theoretical and methodological issues concerning definitions could occupy a volume in itself, and I can do no more than be somewhat dogmatic here. I have defined a new religious movement as an organization or current of thought that has arisen within the past 150 or so years and which cannot be uncontentiously placed within a traditional world religion. Being thus classified carries no value judgment: a movement's inclusion does not make it a "destructive cult" or a "spiritual counterfeit." The principal criterion for inclusion is a pragmatic one: I have endeavored simply to create entries that the informed reader would expect to find. These include the names of new religious groups and their leaders, as well as key concepts used within NRMs and in the study of them, for example, Akashic Records, "brainwashing," and Jesus People Movement.

No single-volume reference work can hope to do justice to the vast range of the world's new religions. Despite the various public commentators who, after some "cult" incident, appear on television screens bearing the subtitle "cult expert," there can be no such being as a cult expert in general. In a number of cases these self-styled experts lack formal qualifications and have limited direct acquaintance with new religions—sometimes no more than brief former membership of a single NRM. Such presumed omnicompetence might be justifiable if all new religions were much the same—a claim frequently implied when these "experts" talk about a "typical cult." However, even a superficial acquaintance with NRMs makes their diversity obvious. The five "killer cults" that gained notoriety in the past 25 years have little in common: Jonestown was a liberal, socially involved Protestant group; Waco a fundamentalist millennialist Adventist sect; the Solar Temple a revival of Templarism; Heaven's Gate a UFO-religion drawing largely on its leader's homespun interpretations of Revelation; and the Movement for the Restoration of the Ten Commandments an indigenously African post-Catholic organization.

The last mentioned of these five highlights the point that NRMs are a global phenomenon, and by no means a purely Western one. J. Gordon Melton has documented more than 2,000 alternative and emergent religions in the United States alone; Great Britain is said to have 600, Africa 10,000, and Japan 220,000. In selecting which NRMs to include here, a number of considerations have been taken into account: their numerical strength, media and anticult publicity, their likely future significance, their impact on the West, whether they seem distinctively religious, and whether they still exist. Some of these criteria are nebulous—in particular, whether a group or movement is religious rather than a therapy group, a mutual interest society, or simply a "cult" in the sense of being loosely organized, or unorganized, interest group. In what follows I have tended to focus on what W. S. Bainbridge calls "client cults" rather than "audience cults": thus someone like T. Lobsang Rampa does not feature in this dictionary, being a popular author, rather than a religious leader. Techniques such as Reiki, although religious in origin, appear to be more forms of therapy than religions. Other groups have been included despite their denial of a religious status: Emin, Elan Vital, and TM have some religious characteristics, but—more importantly—they remain prominent in anticult literature, and I think readers would expect to find them here.

My selection has also been influenced by the fact that there already exist a *Historical Dictionary of the Bahá'í Faith,* a *Historical Dictionary of Mormonism,* and a *Historical Dictionary of Sikhism,* and at the time of writing the possibility of a forthcoming *Historical Dictionary of New Age Movements* is under consideration. I have therefore tried to avoid substantial overlap, and readers who are seeking information on schismatical Mormon groups, modern Sikh sects, or New Age ideas can be safely referred to these companion volumes.

One problem about new religions is that they frequently undergo name changes, or adopt a variety of names for different purposes. To avoid having multiple entries that simply cause the reader to embark on a paper chase around the book, the principal entry is listed under what I have judged to be either the best-known or the most current name. To avoid taking up undue space with entries that simply redirect the reader, this volume (unusually for the series) has an index to help readers who may have difficulty in locating an entry that deals with a particular topic under a different heading.

Brief mention should be made of methodology. I write as a scholar in the field of religious studies, rather than a sociologist, a counselor, or a Christian theologian attempting a "cult critique." These other perspectives have their place, but followers of new religions themselves normally claim that their teachings and practices are of supreme importance. In what follows I have therefore tried to focus, as far as possible, on origins, beliefs, and practices and to convey the impression that the ideas of most NRMs have a definite train of thought and internal coherence. All too frequently, writers in this area (even academics) have done little more than convey odd unrelated points about NRMs, often simply focusing on their misdemeanors. I have therefore tried to avoid short, staccato entries, making them fractionally longer than is usual for this series, in the hope that something of their internal logic will be apparent, even if the reader (and indeed the author) cannot in the long run accept their truth. I have avoided scurrilous scandalmongering, although at times it has been necessary to mention atrocity tales when these have affected an organization's development, for example, by causing schism, reappraisal of beliefs and practices, or dissolution.

In compiling any work of NRMs, it can at times be difficult to adjudicate on conflicting information. Media reports are frequently unreliable, and these are often the first source of information that the public (and sometimes academics) receive about a new religion. Once errors appear in print, they tend to become replicated in subsequent literature and difficult to identify and correct. Some NRMs keep meticulous records and make these readily available to researchers, but others do not: hence there are inevitably gaps in one's information about people, events, and past publications. Readers will notice in what follows that it has not always been possible to resolve conflicting evidence. While, for example, I have usually been able to provide dates of birth and death for key individuals, some details have been unavailable, and readers should not necessarily assume that an NRM leader is still alive where no date of death is provided. At times, too, extant information is simply unbelievable and can only be presented as a movement's hagiography, or as incorrect guesswork on some writer's part.

Wherever possible, I have given some indication of the numerical strength of specific NRMs. This can at best be a very rough guide: statistics come from different sources, some of which want to exaggerate, while others may want to minimize an NRM's impact. Some groups provide their own statistics, while others do not, and different groups measure their allegiance in different ways. Some count formal membership, others measure presumed adherents, while others again report attendees at key events or successful completion of seminars. It would be a mammoth task to disentangle the various meanings of all the available religious statistics, and while I have endeavored to present statistical information in as clear a way as possible, it could be misleading, for example, to make judgments about the relative allegiance to various groups simply by comparing the figures that are given here.

Finally, a word on "political correctness": I am aware that some academics, as well as some religious believers, take exception to terms like "Old Testament" and justifiably object to non-gender-inclusive language. When speaking in my own voice, I have tried to offend as few people's sensitivities as possible, but not all religions subscribe to present-day Western liberal expectations. It would be grossly misleading to suggest that the Unification Church, for example, talked about a "Hebrew Scriptural Era," and I have therefore resisted any attempts to change a religious group's official vocabulary. As I say when my students question such vocabulary, I do not invent religions, but simply expound them!

With all these caveats, I hope this volume will make a useful contribution to the understanding of religions and ideologies, and that it will help to advance a difficult, although fascinating, area of religious studies which its students are gradually piecing together.

Acknowledgments

Those who wrote a century ago about the world's religions were sometimes accused of being "armchair theorists" who wrote from no wider a boundary than their own writing desks. In the twenty-first century, of course, it is quite impossible for those who write on religion to do so with only the aid of other textbooks, particularly in the field of new religious movements (NRMs), where the subject matter is not always properly documented.

I am therefore grateful to numerous organizations and individuals who have helped to make the present volume possible. Among colleagues, thanks are due to Ron Geaves, Stephen Jacobs, and Martin Durham. The exponents of NRMs themselves are too many to name, but I should like to express special thanks to Jim Belither (NKT), Rosemary Goring (Brotherhood of the Cross and Star), Bill and June Thompstone (Jehovah's Witnesses), and Graeme Wilson (Church of Scientology) for commenting on entries relating to their organizations.

I am grateful to Paul Theodolous, editor of the journal *Global Dialogue,* for allowing me to use, in a somewhat adapted form, my article entitled "The New Age: A Survey and Critique," which constitutes a part of the introductory essay. My own students at the University of Wolverhampton have been invaluable for their lively interest in NRMs and for information and discussion that they have provided.

Two people deserve special thanks: Peter Clark for carefully reading the entire manuscript in draft form and suggesting improvements; and my wife Margaret Wilkins, who was always available and willing to discuss the subject matter, and who also commented on the material in its various stages of preparation.

Finally, my thanks go to the staff at the Scarecrow Press. I should like to thank the series editor, Jon Woronoff, for his help and patience: the compilation of the dictionary took much longer than I anticipated, and I very much appreciate his understanding of the pressures of academic life.

As author, of course, I take full responsibility for accepting or rejecting the suggestions that I have been given, and I should make the usual author's disclaimer, that none of the above are responsible for any deficiencies or errors that may have crept into the text.

Abbreviations and Acronyms

3HO	Healthy Happy Holy
ABMJ	American Board of Missions to the Jews
ACJC	Apostolic Church of Jesus Christ
ACM	anticult movement
AFF	American Family Foundation
AIC	African Initiated Churches
AMORC	Ancient Mystical Order of the Rosy Cross
ARE	Association for Research and Enlightenment
ATOM	Ancient Teachings of the Masters
BCC	Berkeley Christian Coalition
BK	Brahma Kumaris
BOTA	Builders of the Adytum
CAN	Cult Awareness Network
CARP	Collegiate Association for Research into Principle *(Unification Church)*
CAUSA	"Cause" *(Unification Church)* (previously Confederation of Associations for the Unity of the Societies of the Americas)
CC	Contentious Christians
CFF	Citizens' Freedom Foundation
COBU	Church of Bible Understanding
CoG	Children of God
CSA	The Covenant, the Sword and the Arm of the Lord
CUT	Church Universal and Triumphant
CUUPS	Covenant of Unitarian Universalist Pagans
CWLF	Christian World Liberation Front
DLM	Divine Light Mission
ECK	Eckankar *(abbr.)*
ESP	extrasensory perception
est	Erhard Seminar Training
FAIR	Family Action Information and Resource (formerly Family Action Information and Rescue)

FECRIS	European Federation of Centres for Research and Sectarianism
FF-ing	flirty fishing
FFWPU	Family Federation for World Peace and Unification *(Unification Church)*
FOI	Fellowship of Isis
FREECOG	Free the Children of God
FWBO	Friends of the Western Buddhist Order
GAAA	General Assembly of Apostolic Assemblies
GO	Gospel Outreach
G-O	Gurdjieff-Ouspensky
HOPE	Help Other People Everywhere
HPB	Helena Petrovna Blavatsky
HPM	Human Potential Movement
HSA-UWC	Holy Spirit Association for the Unification of World Christianity *(Unification Church)*
IBSA	International Bible Students Association
ICC	International Churches of Christ
ICF	International Cultural Foundation *(Unification Church)*
ICUS	International Conference for the Unity of the Sciences *(Unification Church)*
ILC	Inner Light Consciousness
INFORM	Information Network Focus on Religious Movements
INM	International Network of Ministers
IPM	Inner Peace Movement
IRF	International Religious Foundation *(Unification Church)*
ISKCON	International Society for Krishna Consciousness
IYI	Integral Yoga Institute
JFC	Jesus Fellowship Church
KJV	King James Version
KKK	Ku Klux Klan
LDS	(Church of Jesus Christ of) Latter-day Saints
LOTUS	Light of Truth Universal Shrine
LSD	League for Spiritual Discovery

MANS	Mysterion, Agape, Nous, Sophia (mystery, love, mind, wisdom)
MAPS	Ambassadry Movement of an Awakened Positive Society
MCC	Metropolitan Community Churches
MCWE	Morris Cerullo World Evangelism
MEST	matter, energy, space and time *(Scientology)*
MRA	Moral Re-Armament
MSIA	Movement of Spiritual Inner Awareness
NAM	New Age Movement
NKT	New Kadampa Tradition
NOI	Nation of Islam
NRM	New Religious Movement
NSAC	National Spiritualist Association of Churches
NSIM	Neo-Sannyasin International Movement
OGD	Order of the Golden Dawn
OICST	International Order of Chivalry Solar Tradition
ORT	Renewed Order of the Temple
OT	Operating Thetan *(Scientology)*
OTO	Ordo Templi Orientis
PAJC	Pentecostalist Association of Jesus Christ
PAW	Pentecostal Assemblies of the World
PK	Promise Keepers
PROUT	Progressive Utilization Theory
PSI	People Searching Inside
PWPA	Professors' World Peace Academy *(Unification Church)*
SDA	Seventh-day Adventists
SES	School of Economic Science
SGI	Soka Gakkai International
SKY	simplified kundalini yoga
SNU	Spiritualists National Union
SRF	Self-Realization Fellowship
SRM	Spiritual Regeneration Movement *(TM)*
TABOF	The Ancient Brotherhood of Fhasz
TM	Transcendental Meditation
UC	Unification Church

UFO	Unidentified Flying Object
UNADFI	National Association for the Defence of the Family and the Individual
UNARIUS	Universal Articulate Interdimensional Understanding of Science
UNISOC	Universe Society Church
UPC	United Pentecostal Church
UPCI	United Pentecostal Church International
UU	Unitarian Universalist
UUA	Unitarian Universalist Association
VPA	Volunteer Parents of America
WBO	Western Buddhist Order
WCG	Worldwide Church of God

Chronology

1744   Emanuel Swedenborg's first vision

1776   Illuminati founded

1787   Church of the New Jerusalem (Swedenborgian) founded

1830   Joseph Smith establishes his church in Palmyra, New York

Book of Mormon published

1831   William Miller begins to preach on the imminent end of the world

1834   Transcendentalist Club founded

1844   Joseph Smith murdered

The "Great Disappointment" (22 October)—William Miller's prophecies fail to materialize

Declaration of the Báb

1848   Madame Blavatsky's "veiled time" begins, lasting until 1858.

Fox sisters hear the Hydesville "rappings"

John Thomas's followers assume the name Christadelphians

1852   Date ascribed to the commencement of Bahá'ú'lláh's mission

1861   Ellen G. White establishes the Seventh-day Adventists

1875   Theosophical Society founded by Madame Blavatsky and Colonel Olcott

Publication of Mary Baker Eddy's Science and Health with Key to the Scriptures

Anglo-Israel Association founded in London

1877 Publication of Madame Blavatsky's *Isis Unveiled*

1879 Mary Baker Eddy establishes the Church of Christ, Scientist

First edition of the *Watchtower* published

1881 Zion's Watch Tower Tract Society established

Charles and Myrtle Fillmore found "Unity"

1888 Founding of the Order of the Golden Dawn

Publication of Madame Blavatsky's *The Secret Doctrine*

1893 World's Parliament of Religions, Chicago

National Spiritualist Association of Churches founded in Chicago

1894 Ibrahim Kheirella introduces the Bahá'í Faith to the U.S.

1895 Bible Conference of Conservative Protestants formulate "five points of fundamentalism" at Niagara

Ordo Templi Orientis (OTO) founded

1897 Ramakrishna Mission founded in India

1899 Vivekananda begins tour of U.S. and Europe

1901 Spiritualists' National Union founded

1904 Ancient Mystical Order of the Rosy Cross founded

1906 Azusa Street Revival (Pentecostalist)

1907 Rosicrucian Fellowship founded, along with the Societas Rosicruciana in the U.S.

1908 Annie Besant and Charles Leadbeater "discover" Krishnamurti

1910 Pir Hazrat Inayat Khan introduces Sufism to the U.S.

Sufi Order of the West established in England

1911 Order of the Star of the East founded to promote Krishnamurti

1912 Aleister Crowley joins OTO

1913 Rudolf Steiner founds the Anthroposophical Society

1914 International New Thought Alliance founded

Aurobindo establishes his first ashram

Ven Ledi Sayadaw rediscovers Vipassana

1916 Charles Taze Russell dies and is succeeded by Joseph Franklin ("Judge") Rutherford

1917 Charles Taze Russell's *The Finished Mystery* published posthumously

1919 British Israel World Federation founded

1920 Joseph Franklin Rutherford completes *Millions Now Living Will Never Die!*

1921 Frank Buchman founds the First Century Christian Fellowship (later Moral Re-Armament)

1922 George Ivanovitch Gurdjieff founds the Institute for the Harmonious Development of Man in France

Yogananda arrives in the U.S.

1923 Alice Bailey establishes the Arcane School

1926 Ramakrishna Vedanta Society of Boston founded

1927 Ernest Holmes establishes the Institute of Religious Science and School of Philosophy

1928 Opus Dei founded

1929 Krishnamurti breaks away from the Theosophical Society

Aleister Crowley publishes *Magick in Theory and Practice*

1955 Publication of *The Urantia Book*

George King founds the Aetherius Society

Maharishi Mahesh Yogi visits the U.S.

1956 The Mother proclaims herself an avatar, following Aurobindo

1957 Transcendental Meditation introduced to the West

1958 Mark L. Prophet founds Summit Lighthouse

First Rastafarian Universal Convention

1959 Chinese invasion of Tibet

Muhammad Subuh visits the U.S., and Gurdjieff becomes a follower

1962 Second Vatican Council begins, presiding through 1965

Neo-Catechumenate founded

Focolare receive papal approval

Beginnings of Findhorn community

1963 Jane Roberts begins to channel "Seth"

Bahá'í establish the Universal House of Justice in Haifa, Israel

1964 Sri Chinmoy arrives in the U.S.

Gerald Gardner dies, and Alexander Sanders assumes the title "king of the witches"

1965 Swami Prabhupada arrives in New York

Eckankar founded

Malcolm X assassinated

1966 LaVey establishes the Church of Satan

Swami Satchidananda established Integral Yoga Institute in the U.S.

Association of Unity Churches founded

1967   Inception of Children of God ("The Family") in California

Beginnings of the California "Jesus movement"

Indra Devi lectures on Satya Sai Baba in Santa Barbara, California

Friends of the Western Buddhist Order founded

Narayanananda Universal Yoga Trust established

1968   Beatles meet Maharishi Mahesh Yogi in India

David Berg (Moses David) begins his ministry

Yogi Bhajan comes to the U.S. and Canada

Worldwide Church of God assumes its present name

The Mother establishes new city of Auroville

1969   The Charles Manson murders

Yogi Bhajan founds 3HO (Healthy Happy Holy)

Paul Erdmann founds the Church of Armageddon (Love Israel)

Acharya Vimalananda brings Ananda Marga to the U.S.

1970   Franklin Jones founds Free Daist Communion

Muktananda (Siddha Yoga Dham) arrives in the U.S.

Rajneesh initiates first sannyasins

Sri Mataji begins teaching Sahaja Yoga

Sun Bear expands his teachings beyond American Indians

Gurudev Amrit Desai establishes community at Summit Station

1971   Himalayan Institute founded by Swami Rama

The Farm founded

Arica Institute founded

First Erhard Seminars Training (est) seminar held in San Francisco

Guru Maharaj Ji visits the U.S.

Zsuzsanna Budapest establishes a coven in the Dianic tradition

1972   Sun Myung Moon moves to the U.S.

Franklin Jones establishes Shree Hridayam Satsang (Company of the Heart) ashram and makes his teachings public

Beginnings of the anticult movement with FREECOG

1973   Raël's first contact with the Elohim

Beginnings of Spiritual Counterfeits Project in California

Dialog Center founded in Denmark

1974   Citizens' Freedom Foundation (later the Cult Awareness Network) established

Jach Pursel first channels Lazaris

1974   Rajneesh (Osho) establishes communities in Bombay and Poona

Chogyam Trungpa founds Naropa Institute in Boulder, Colorado

1975   Michael Aquino establishes Temple of Set

Helen Schucman publishes *A Course in Miracles*

Covenant of the Goddess founded in California

1976 Paul Rose founds FAIR (Family Action Information and Rescue) in Britain

Alamo Foundation establishes community at Arkansas

Kundalini Research Institute founded in California

1977 Death of Prabhupada

Brahma Kumaris establishes first center in the U.S.

Geshe Kelsang Gyatso arrives in England

Ramtha first appears to J. Z. Knight

1978 Jonestown suicide/massacre (919 die)

J. Z. Knight's first channeling session

Yahweh ben Yahweh founds Temple of Love

1979 Boston Church of Christ founded

American Family Foundation established

1981 Rajneesh moves to the U.S.

Unification Church loses its libel case against the British *Daily Mail*

1982 Beginnings of AIDS epidemic

1984 Citizens' Freedom Foundation becomes Cult Awareness Network (CAN)

Sun Myung Moon imprisoned for tax evasion until 1985

1985 Controversy and arrests regarding Rajneeshpuram, U.S.A.

Nityananda becomes a private meditation teacher in California

1986 Death of L. Ron Hubbard

INFORM established in Britain

1987 Rajneesh (Osho) returns to Poona

Shoko Asahara establishes Aum Shinrikyo

Shanti Mandir founded by Nityananda

1989 Berlin Wall demolished

Ulf Ekman (Word of Life Church) publishes *Financial Freedom*

1990 Death of Osho (Rajneesh)

1991 Kelsang Gyatso's followers assume the name "New Kadampa Tradition" (NKT)

Schism between Soka Gakkai and Nichiren Shoshu

1992 Falun Gong introduced by Master Li Hongzhi

1993 Waco siege (93 die)

1994 Solar Temple deaths (53 die)

FECRIS (European Federation of Centres for Research and Sectarianism) founded in France

Death of Moses David

Toronto Blessing

1995 Aum Shinrikyo attack on Tokyo underground

Joseph W. Tkach, Jr., assumes leadership of Worldwide Church of God

1996 NKT involved in Dorje Shugden controversy

CAN bankrupted and bought by Church of Scientology

1997 Heaven's Gate suicides (39 die)

1999 Chinese government bans Falun Gong

2000 Mass deaths in Movement for the Restoration of the Ten Commandments

360 million couples blessed by Sun Myung Moon

Introduction

All religions were once new; hence the phenomenon of new religious movements (NRMs) is nothing particularly new. Although it is popularly believed that the 20th century, and particularly the postwar era, saw a "mushrooming" of "cults," as they are popularly called, it is difficult to determine with any degree of precision how many NRMs exist and how many people are involved in them. Several factors make it seem likely, however, that the 20th century saw much more by way of religious diversity than previous periods in history: increased literacy, improved communication, and globalization, coupled with a decline in traditional organized religion in Europe, all suggest that the present era has seen more NRMs take their rise than before. It is also true, of course, that the 20th and 21st centuries have attached greater importance to keeping records and logging statistical information than previous generations, and it is no doubt the case that numerous new religions of the past have come and gone unnoticed.

Some records remain, of course, of religious "deviants": there were Europe's "witches," who were more probably wise women and healers, who were probably persecuted not because of their "spells," but because they presented competition to the authority of the Church and because they were perceived as a female challenge to a male-dominated religion. There were groups that were explicitly declared heretical, such as the Arians, the Nestorians and the Cathars, and breakaway groups like the Quakers, the Unitarians, the Shakers, and the Ranters. Some died out, such as the Muggletonians, while others—such as the Quakers, the Salvation Army, and some of the Seventh-day Adventists have come to be accepted by mainstream Christianity as legitimate expressions of the faith. Where the size of the movement increased, such as the followings of George Fox or John Wesley, it changed—in Max Weber's terminology—from *sect* to *church* or, as we would now say, to *denomination*.

Although the NRM phenomenon is not new, the academic study of it is. Until recent times, discussion of NRMs tended to be confined to evangelical Christian literature, while Western academics tended to focus almost exclusively on mainstream religious traditions, in particular Christianity. The study of world religions only began in the nineteenth century, becoming popular in university curricula as recently as the mid-1960s. New religious movements as a subject of serious academic study lagged behind, largely taking its rise in the late 1970s. This new interest can be attributed to two related factors. First, there was general public concern about the new wave of "cults" that had begun to sweep across the United States, Canada, and Europe. Second, the Unification Church (popularly known as the "Moonies" and now officially called the Family Federation for World Peace and Unification) started to make sustained attempts to win the confidence of academics and clergy by organizing numerous academic and interfaith conferences in various places throughout the globe. This was partly to persuade attendees that media coverage had been unduly negative, but it was also, in all probability, a sincere attempt to further their cause of "unification."

Initially, the studies of new religions that emerged were sociological, attempting to account for entry and exit to these movements, examining the composition of such groups and societal factors that might account for their rise. Only in later years did such movements begin to be taken seriously as religious phenomena in their own right, demanding serious attention to their origins, beliefs, and practices. The post-1970s interest in NRMs tended to leave the older new religions in their previous state of neglect, the one exception being the Latter-day Saints (Mormons), who had already gained for themselves some academic prowess through their own colleges in Utah. Jehovah's Witnesses, Christadelphians, Christian Scientists, and Spiritualists, have gained little attention in academic circles, although some interest in Theosophy is now beginning to emerge.

Many of today's new religions can trace a lineage to religious minorities of the past, and several dissenters from mainstream religions are particularly noteworthy. One such individual is Emanuel Swedenborg (1688-1772), whose importance far surpasses his strength of following today. Swedenborg was a brilliant mathematician and engineer, attaining important office in the Swedish Board of Mines, until in his mid-fifties he began to experience a series of visions, variously of Jesus, of angels, of heaven and hell, and on at least one occasion of God himself. One of Swedenborg's most powerful visions was of the New Jerusalem, described in the 21st chapter of Revelation, which Swedenborg saw descending from heaven to earth. Unlike the later and often more bizarre apocalypticists, Swedenborg regarded this as a symbolic reference to an event that had already taken place: Christ's second coming had actually occurred in the year 1757, and while his reign was invisible on a physical level, this invisible event marked a new dispensation, affording humankind new possibilities of evolution and spiritual development. Swedenborg sought to achieve a balance between the reason of the Enlightenment and the intuitive and imaginative spirituality that was evidenced by his visions: Swedenborg remained throughout his life a member of the Lutheran Church, even if he was not considered to be wholly orthodox. It was a number of later followers who, 15 years after Swedenborg's death, established the Church of the New Jerusalem—also known as the New Church—in 1787.

Swedenborg's true influence on the New Age was indirect, and comes through Ralph Waldo Emerson (1803-1882). Emerson was originally a Unitarian minister in Boston, Massachusetts, but despite the liberal nature of Unitarianism, he found problems with organized religion; in particular, he was unable to find meaning in the sacraments, which he was expected to celebrate. One Sunday, at the regular Communion service, he preached a sermon denouncing the sacrament and resigned his office. Emerson set out for England in 1834, where he met a number of prominent representatives of the Romantic movement, notably Samuel Taylor Coleridge, Thomas Carlyle, and William Wordsworth. When Emerson returned to America he published an important essay entitled "Nature," which urged that truth was not to be found in organized religion, in books such as the Bible, or even in learned institutions like universities: the true teacher was Nature itself. Together with a number of like-minded thinkers, he founded the Transcendental Club, and Emerson and his sympathizers came to be known as the Transcendentalists.

Emerson's Transcendentalism was a form of nature mysticism whereby the soul was one with God and God was one with nature—a notion which he partly derived from the Hindu Upanishads, where one finds the famous assertion "tat tvam asi" (literally, "you are that," i.e., the divine). Emerson was one of the first Westerners to own a copy of the Upanishads, and his synthesis of Western and Eastern ideas was one of the first attempts at such an innovation. Emerson's notion of the "Over-Soul"—an idea of which he and his followers made much use—was of an ultimate authority that transcended the intellect and served as the link between *atman* (the individual self) and *brahman* (the eternal, which is the ground of all existence).

Emerson's legacy lies in his dissemination of Eastern religious ideas, as well as emphasis on intuition rather than reason, and his rejection of formal institutionalized religion. His ideas are more readily accessible to today's public than those of Swedenborg. The latter's writings tend to be disseminated almost exclusively by the New Church, whereas Emerson's writings have become revitalized in New Age circles. His writings are not easy to read, however: his style is rather rambling and turgid, with long sentences and disconcerting punctuation. They have proved highly influential, however, and have drawn attention to the intellect's scope and limits in finding spirituality. Nonetheless, Emerson would not have endorsed everything that is now considered to be "New Age": in particular he was critical of spiritualism, as well as the beliefs and practices of an emergent school known as New Thought.

New Thought

The ideas of New Thought can be traced back to Anton Franz (Friedrich) Mesmer (1734-1815), the French hypnotist from whose name the word *mesmerism* is derived. Mesmer conducted a number of experiments involving the body's magnetic fields, as well as trance induction. His ideas were taken up by Charles Poyen, who lectured widely in America in 1836. One member of his audience was Phineas Parker Quimby (1802-1866), whose name is little known, but whose influence was nonetheless extensive. Quimby was one of the earliest advocates of "mind cure," the notion that one's mental disposition had a crucial role in achieving and maintaining health. The ensuing movement that emphasized the powers of mind over matter became known as New Thought.

Quimby had a number of pupils who gained recognition in their own right. Julius and Annetta Dresser and, to a greater degree, Warren Felt Evans gave initial momentum to the "positive thinking" and "self-help" schools of thought, made popular by writings such as Dale Carnegie's *How to Win Friends and Influence People* (1937) and, somewhat later, Norman Vincent Peale's *The Power of Positive Thinking* (1952).

Best known of Quimby's pupils was Mary Baker Eddy (1821-1910), the founder of Christian Science. Eddy had been an invalid in her childhood and youth and had first gone to Quimby for healing in 1862, whereupon she experienced an improvement in her condition. After Quimby's death, her health deteriorated, and she herself was near death. Determined to effect a cure, she read accounts of Jesus' healings in the Gospel according to St. Matthew and decided that she would cure herself by the powers of the mind.

Initially Eddy worked with Emma Curtis Hopkins, another of Quimby's followers, who edited the *Christian Science Journal*. Eddy and Hopkins had their disagreements, however, and eventually split. Hopkins set up the Hopkins Metaphysical Association in 1887, from which a number of groups emerged: these tended to be religious groups in their own right, rather than loosely organized currents that are characteristic of the New Age. Principally these included Divine Science, Homes of Truth, the Unity School of Christianity, and Religious Science. Eddy's followers, by contrast, did not set up their own organizations, but remained loyal to the Church of Christ, Scientist.

Most of the Hopkins-derived organizations, although still in existence, are small and receive little enthusiasm from New Agers, whose interests in healing are wider than any single set of techniques. Within the last two years or so, Christian Science has attempted to carve out a new market niche by promoting Mary Baker Eddy's *Science and Health* within New Age circles as a book dealing with alternative healing. As yet, there appears to be little enthusiasm amongst New Agers: Eddy's writing style is tortuous and lacking in clarity, and Christian Science itself is a tightly structured organization, not even permitting innovation in its Sunday worship, which consists largely of verbatim readings from Eddy.

The Legacy of the Theosophists

Most important in the development of new currents in religious thought is the Theosophical Society, founded in New York in 1875 by Helena Petrovna Blavatsky (1831-1891)—better known to her followers as Madame Blavatsky or simply HPB—and Col. Henry Steel Olcott (1832-1907). Whether Blavatsky really traveled around the world meeting Canadian Indians, Egyptian kabbalists, and voodoo magicians, finally reaching Tibet to study with Tibetan masters, is debatable. Whatever the truth about her "veiled time" between 1848 and 1858, her claims received enough credibility for her *Isis Unveiled* to circulate widely. Blavatsky was an occultist, claiming to be in touch with the Ascended Masters—a hierarchy of spiritual beings consisting of deceased philosophers and religious leaders, figures who belong to religious mythology (such as the Buddha Maitreya), and beings who had previously been unknown to humanity and are in all probability Blavatsky's own imaginative creations based on people she met in her travels (examples are Master Morya and Koot Hoomi).

Blavatsky's second journey in 1878 is much better documented. Traveling to India and Ceylon with Olcott, she undoubtedly made contact with Hindus and Buddhists, and Olcott was particularly instrumental in reviving Sinhalese Buddhism, which had lost ground as a consequence of Christian missionary activity. On her return, Blavatsky set to work on her second major piece of writing, *The Secret Doctrine,* which draws largely on Hindu and Buddhist ideas and affirms a common core of esoteric teaching underlying all the world's religions. The Theosophical Society provided a forum for exploring world religions in general and esotericism in particular. Although Theosophy is currently on the decline—and appears to attract an older rather than a younger generation of seekers—it served as the breeding ground for a large variety of spiritualities and minority religious organizations.

Among the most important early figures within the Theosophical Society was Jiddhu Krishnamurti (1895-1986), who was "discovered" in 1908 by Annie Besant (1847-1933) and Charles W. Leadbeater (1854-1934), the second generation of Theosophical Society leaders after the demise of Blavatsky and Olcott. Krishnamurti was at first proclaimed as Maitreya, the expected Buddha of the new eon, and Krishnamurti's early book *At the Feet of the Master* reflects early Theosophical thinking about his status. (It is frequently alleged that either Besant or Leadbeater was the real author.) In 1929, however, Krishnamurti reappraised his position within Theosophy and broke away, attracting his own following. Rudolf Steiner (1861-1925), the founder of Anthroposophy, was never able to accept the role given to Krishnamurti within the Theosophical Society, and left in 1912, forming his own organization. .

Among the second generation of Theosophists, Alice Bailey (1880-1949) ranks high in importance. In common with Blavatsky, Bailey maintained communication with the Masters, but professed a particular rapport with Ascended Master Djwahl Khul, an adept who did not have a place in Blavatsky's hierarchy. Bailey claimed that she was his amanuensis and that her books were channeled by him. This, together with her claim that Christ's reappearance on earth was imminent, proved unpalatable to the majority of Theosophists, and Alice Bailey, together with her husband Foster Bailey, were expelled in 1921. Bailey went on to form her own Arcane School, and her ideas influenced the recent interest in channeling, as well as subsequent generations of NRMs, notably the I AM movement of Guy Ballard (1878-1939) and Edna Ballard (1886-1971), from which the Church Universal and Triumphant took its rise. Also influenced by Bailey was Benajamin Creme, proponent of the Christ Maitreya movement in Great Britain.

Universal Sufism

J. I. Gurdjieff (c. 1874-1949) and P. D. Ouspensky (1878-1947) were not themselves associated with the Theosophical Society, but their ideas contain some affinities to it nonetheless. Both were esotericists, open to a variety of world religious traditions, and, like Blavatsky, Gurdjieff traveled widely, seeking an ancient brotherhood that could convey spiritual truth. Gurdjieff and Ouspensky taught a form of esoteric Christianity, but they are especially important in the development of Western Sufism.

Although Sufism is often regarded as the mystical tradition within Islam, Western Sufism—sometimes referred to as Universal Sufism—incorporates elements from several religious traditions, including Buddhism, Christianity, and Hinduism, and sometimes Jewish kabbalism. In common with Islamic Sufism, Universal Sufism offers a form of mysticism, employing *dhikr* (the recitation of God's name) and *sama* (meditation) as means of enabling the follower to attain a state of oneness with God. These techniques are generally accompanied by the use of music and dance, in common with the Islamic Sufi tradition of whirling dervishes.

Universal Sufism was initially introduced to the West by Hazrat Inayat Khan (1882-1927) and developed by Samuel L. ("Sam") Lewis (1896-1971), and Gurdjieff was profoundly influenced by them. Gurdjieff himself choreographed many Sufi dances, drawing on Eastern sources, which he called "sacred gymnastics" and later "movements." Gurdjieff's writings remain popular, but a number of more recent Sufi exponents have helped to disseminate Universal Sufism. The best known is Idries Shah (1924-1996), whose book *The Way of the Sufi* (1991) provides a historical account of Sufism, as well as presenting it as a spiritual path.

The World's Parliament of Religions

Just over 20 years after the Theosophical Society's formation, another supremely important event occurred, one which was to change the face of interreligious understanding. It was the World's Parliament of Religions, organized in Chicago in 1893, a gathering of some 7,000 representatives of the world's religious traditions. The event was masterminded by three people: Charles Caroll Bonney, a Swedenborgian; the Rev. Jenkin Lloyd Jones, a Unitarian; and the Rev J. H. Barrows, a Presbyterian.

The event, which lasted 21 days, was attended by a number of famous names, one of the most important of whom was Swami Vivekananda (1863-1902). Vivekananda was originally a follower of the Brahmo Samaj, an organization founded by Rammohun Roy (1772-1833), who promoted—unusually—a noniconic form of Hinduism, influenced by his encounters with Christians and Christian writings; Vivekananda was therefore familiar with interreligious encounters. He met Ramakrishna in 1891 and sometime later abandoned a potential career in law in favor of life as a sannyasin. At the parliament, his personal charisma, rather than any profundity in his address, won over the assembled gathering, and it caused one Christian later to comment, "Why send missionaries to a country which produces men like this?" The West was beginning to perceive that one-way traffic in missionary activity was a phenomenon that could be questioned.

Vivekananda was the first of a number of Indian gurus to disseminate Hindu teachings in the West. He was followed by Swami Yogananda in 1920, and thereafter by Meher Baba in 1931; Kirpal Singh (Ruhani Satsang) and the Maharishi Mahesh Yogi in 1955; Sri Chinmoy in 1964; Swami A. C. Bhaktivedanta Prabhupada in 1965; Swami Satchidananda in 1966; Indra Devi, who lectured in California and introduced Americans to Satya Sai Baba in 1967; Muktananda in 1970; the "boy guru" Maharaji (who led the Divine Light Mission) in 1971; and Bhagwan Shree Rajneesh, subsequently known as Osho, in 1981.

The World's Parliament of Religions also helped the dissemination of Buddhist teachings. Paul Carus (1852-1919), a publisher and speaker at the parliament, met Soen Shaku—a Rinzai Zen master—who impressed Carus greatly and prompted him to commission published material on Zen. Soen Shaku recommended his pupil D. T. Suzuki (1870-1966), now widely famous for making Zen accessible to the West. Other important influences included the translation of Buddhist scriptures by scholars such as T. W. Rhys Davids, E. B. Cowell, and Max Müller, among others, and also the work of the Theosophical Society, who established a Buddhist Lodge in Britain—subsequently renamed as the Buddhist Society of Britain and Ireland—under Christmas Humphreys' leadership. Improvements in global communication enabled Westerners to visit Buddhist countries, study under Buddhist teachers, and in some cases seek ordination into the Buddhist sangha. Reciprocally, Buddhist teachers were able to visit the West: the Chinese invasion of Tibet brought Buddhist teachers such as Chogyam Trungpa (1939-1987) and Geshe Kelsang Gyatso (b. 1932) to the West, and of course the Dalai Lama's displacement from Lhasa resulted in his numerous visits to America, Canada, and Europe, attracting large public interest and support.

The phenomenon of globalization did not merely result in the import of "non-Christian" religions. Christianity itself had expanded greatly in the nineteenth century, which was the heyday of world mission. Even though Christian missionaries have typically discouraged their converts from clinging to remnants of their former beliefs and practices, it is difficult in practice to distinguish between a foreign culture's distinctive expression of Christianity and unwelcome syncretism. As a religion spreads, too, its original propagators tend to lose ownership of its forms of expression, and thus new religious movements claiming a Christian identity can arise. This has happened on a large scale in Africa, and also in countries such as Korea, where the Unification Church is merely one example of a number of groups that combine Korean folk shamanism with Christianity. While most of these syncretistic groups largely remain in their country of origin, the Unification Church proved distinctive in its successful attempts to re-export its ideas worldwide. Young Oon Kim, one of its earliest propagators in the West, arrived in the United States in 1959, but met with very limited success until founder-leader Sun Myung Moon himself arrived in 1972 and attracted substantial crowds to his public rallies.

Spiritualism and Chaneling

One further strand in the development of NRMs, which resulted neither from Theosophy nor from the World's Parliament of Religions, deserves to be mentioned, namely, Spiritualism. Spiritualism occasionally intertwined with Theosophy: Blavatsky and Olcott had been associated with Spiritualism (they met at a séance), and their founding of their Theosophical Society may have reflected dissatisfaction with it, along with their perceived need for a wider, more eclectic and free thinking organization.

Although there was increasing interest in contacting the dead from around 1600 onward, Andrew Jackson Davies (1826-1910), known as the "Poughkeepsie Seer," is often referred to as the "father of Spiritualism." Influenced by lectures on mesmerism, he claimed contact through trance with Emanuel Swedenborg, and his trance communications are recorded in his book *The Principles of Nature, Her Divine Revelations, and a Voice to Mankind,* published in 1847. Notwithstanding Davies' undoubted influence, it is the Fox sisters who have gained primacy in the history of Spiritualism, on account of the mysterious "rappings" that were heard at Hydesville, New York, in 1848. The great showman Phineas Barnum, although himself a Universalist, promoted their activities, enabling them to perform séances on stage in various venues throughout the United States.

Spiritualism enjoyed its heyday in the 1850s, but then went into decline. There were occasional periods of revival after the American Civil War and after World War I, when numerous bereaved parties attempted to reestablish contact with those who had died in action. Out of the various Spiritualist churches that took their rise from the 1850s onward, various umbrella organizations were formed: principally, the National Spiritualist Association of Churches in 1893, the General Assembly of Spiritualists in 1897, and the International General Assembly of Spiritualists in 1936. In Britain, the Spiritualists National Union was founded in 1901, and the Marylebone Spiritualist Association—founded in 1892—was reorganized as the Spiritualist Association of Great Britain in 1960.

More recent times have witnessed an increase in interest in channeling, in contrast with older Spiritualism. Channeling is a phenomenon in which the "channel" (roughly equivalent to a medium) claims to be taken over by a spirit. Unlike the Spiritualist medium, however, who apparently mediates a variety of spirits of the departed, the channel is normally associated with a single spirit guide.

The context in which a channel is consulted also differs significantly from that for the Spiritualist medium, who typically works within the context of a Protestant-style church service. It is therefore understandable that the New Agers, who find much of organized religion too institutionalized and traditional, should prefer channeling to old-fashioned Spiritualism. Thus, Edgar Cayce (1877-1945) gained popularity to a large degree on account of his one-to-one consultations: individuals could bring their own problems and questions when the need arose, rather than wait amidst a Spiritualist congregation until he or she was fortunate enough to gain the medium's attention. The fact that much of Cayce's teachings are available in written form allows his message to be studied individually, rather than incorporated into formal worship. Cayce was innovative in introducing the concept of karma into his teachings, giving them an obvious rapport with the East, and hence further momentum.

Some channelers will mediate the spirit of an ordinary deceased person, while a small minority of others will claim to have a psychic link with some higher spiritual being, such as an Ascended Master. For example, Alice Bailey, one of the movement's precursors, claimed to channel Master Djwahl Khul. At a channeling session, the channel will induce a state of trance, which is often accompanied by a change in his or her voice, and the channeler's body acts the medium by which the spirit communicates with its audience. Members of the audience may be permitted to ask questions and seek guidance for life.

Channeled messages can be relayed through the written word as well as speech, and "automatic writing" is a phenomenon that is sometimes employed in channeling. At other times, spirits are believed to dictate their messages to their chosen channels. Channeling in written form, of course, enables these spirit messages to be more widely circulated, and entire books have been attributed to channeling. Davis' *The Principles of Nature* can be regarded as an early example of channeled writing, as can *Oahspe*, transcribed on a typewriter in 1882 by John Ballou Newbrough (1828-1891), a dentist and Spiritualist medium. Other more recent examples, more popular with New Agers, include Levi H. Dowling's *Aquarian Gospel of Jesus the Christ* (1964), *The Urantia Book* (1955), and—most recently—Helen Schucman's *A Course in Miracles* (1975). Other celebrated channels include Jane Roberts (channeler of Seth), J. Z. Knight (channeler of Ramtha), and Jach Pursel (Lazaris).

Templarism, Rosicrucianism, "Magick," and Witchcraft

Other forms of occultism made their mark on the 19th and 20th centuries, as Templarism—influenced by Freemasonry—and Magick intertwined. Templarism, originally a product of the Crusades, was formally disbanded by Pope Clement V in 1312. However, in the early part of the 19th century a Parisian physician, Bernard-Raymond Fabré-Palaprat (1773-1838) proclaimed himself as a surviving Grand Master, whose lineage could be traced back to medieval times, and founded the Johannite Church, consecrating his own bishops, in opposition to the Roman Catholic Church, which still proscribes Templarism. In 1895 in Germany, Karl Kellner established the Ordo Templis Orientis (OTO)—an occultist magical group which drew on Templarism and which was brought to the United States in 1909. Around 1945, L. Ron Hubbard, who was to become the Church of Scientology's founder-leader, had some contact with OTO, although the details are unclear: he was almost certainly not initiated, and there is no obvious influence of OTO on Scientology.

A pivotal figure in Templarist and magical circles was the notorious Aleister Crowley (1875-1947). Crowley joined OTO in 1912 and became head of its British branch in 1922. He had previously belonged to the Hermetic Order of the Golden Dawn, an organization which proved highly influential in the subsequent development of the New Age. The Order, founded in

1888, encouraged the practice of magic and the study of the kabbalah, Tarot, and astrology, as well as astral travel, scrying, alchemy, and geomancy.

Crowley's *Magick in Theory and Practice* (1929) remains an important work; it is still in print and readily available. He made two important innovations in the magical tradition: he developed "thelemic magick"—magic pertaining to the human will—and also "sex magick." Unsurprisingly, the latter proved much more controversial: his Sacred Abbey of the Thelemic Mysteries, located in Sicily, became a center for sex orgies as well as magical rites.

During the last two years of his life, Crowley made the acquaintance of Gerald Brosseau Gardner (1884-1964), who gained for himself the title "king of the witches." Gardner claimed to have met a number of witches within the Theosophical Society and to have been initiated in 1939 by their priestess, Dorothy Clutterbuck. This claim is highly suspect, as was Gardner's claim to have revived a tradition dating back to medieval times. Much less controversial is Gardner's connection with Margaret Murray, whose book *The Witch-Cult in Modern Europe* (1921) called into question the prevalent view that witches were devil worshippers, arguing instead that witchcraft was an important aspect of Europe's pre-Christian religious heritage. Although her ideas have been seriously challenged by subsequent scholars, her book remains an important milestone. Murray wrote the foreword to Gardner's *Witchcraft Today,* published in 1954.

After Gardner's death, Alexander Sanders (1926-1988), originally one of Gardner's students, assumed the title "king of the witches" and continued to develop modern witchcraft along lines similar to Gardner's, although with some differences in detail, principally in regard to ritual activities and initiation rites. Gardner tended to emphasize the celebration of rites and festivals, whereas Sanders focused more on ritual magic. In more recent times other wiccan traditions developed, mainly the Norse, Druidic, Egyptian, and Dianic.

Some comments are needed about the much-confused concepts of Satanism, witchcraft, wicca, paganism, and New Age. Although witchcraft—also known as wicca—elicits interest amongst New Agers, many wiccans, witches, and also pagans often take exception at being identified as New Agers, and all of them thoroughly dissociate themselves from Satanism. Paganism typically regards itself as a revival of pre-Christian religion, a form of earth-centered spirituality, acknowledging the various solar and lunar cycles of the year and endowing them with ritual significance. Witchcraft, as the name implies, is the craft of the witch, who devises and uses methods of controlling the world through the practice of magical rites for the benefit of the self and others. The magic used is typically "white" rather than "black," since witches typically believe in a law of "threefold return": the good or harm one does is believed to return to the doer threefold. Wicca combines the witch's craft with the pagan's religious ideas, and thus is the complete set of beliefs and practices. Many wiccans prefer that term, since it is more ancient than "witchcraft" and does not have the negative overtones that are popularly associated with the latter. Wiccans tend to deny having historical connections with Crowley, no doubt because of his unsavory reputation; however, it seems likely that many of his magical and initiation rites can be traced to this source. Paganism, witchcraft, and wicca must also be utterly dissociated from Satanism, which is the explicit veneration of Satan. The devil is not summoned during any rites practiced by witches.

Although the New Age Movement (NAM), which gained its momentum during the 1980s, includes interest in witchcraft and paganism, the NAM is a much wider and more eclectic alternative spirituality, emphasizing human potential, optimism, and experimentation with different expressions of truth, particularly Eastern spiritualities and the paranormal. Channeling, astrology, the power of crystals, "dream work," dowsing, visualization, and Tarot—to name but a few—are all part of the New Age, but certainly not part of wicca. The New Age, however, has done much to stimulate interest in wicca: the New Age which is said to be dawning is the Age of Aquarius, which supersedes the previous 2,000-year zodiacal Age of Pisces. Pisces, the fish, is the symbol of Christianity, which has lasted for a 2,000-year period that is now at an end. Consequently, the New Age can be viewed as a post-Christian movement, which challenges the authority of the Christian Church and its concept of the male warrior god whose will must be unquestioningly obeyed. Such thinking has led to a rejection of external authority in favor of the self and an emphasis on the feminine as well as the masculine. The goddess movement is promoted as a hitherto neglected form of spirituality, which the advent of Christianity nearly destroyed. The revival of Celtic religion can thus be viewed as something that is actively encouraged by New Age thinking.

Satanism occupies no more than a minuscule part of the NRM spectrum. Of the recent exponents of Satanism, the best known is Anton Szandor LaVey (1930-1997), author of *The Satanic Bible* (1968) and founder-leader of the Church of Satan. The belief, held in certain anticult circles, that Satanism is rife, stems partly from the "satanic ritual abuse" scares of the late 1980s and early 1990s in the United States and Britain, respectively, and partly from the tendency of some Christian evangelicals to use the term *satanic* either to describe the worship of "false gods" (those of other religions or of the material world) or to impose their evaluation on the many religions and ideologies which seem contrary to the Christian faith.

Conservative Christian Movements

If Theosophy and its successors explicitly sought to explore alternative expressions of religion to those of traditional Christianity, there were also professedly Christian movements which—at least initially—had no particular desire to depart from authentic Christianity. One of the most notable was the Adventist movement, pioneered by William Miller (1782-1849), who predicted that Christ's second advent would occur in 1843, then revised his calculation to 1844 when the expected event did not take place. Although many Millerites were disillusioned, one of Miller's followers—Hiram Edson—contended that Miller's calculations were correct, but that he predicted the wrong event: instead of a visible coming on the clouds of heaven, Christ had indeed established his presence in 1844, but invisibly.

The notion of Christ's invisible rule later found its way into the teachings of Charles Taze Russell, founder-leader of the

Watchtower organization (later known as the Jehovah's Witnesses). In his earlier years Russell attended an Adventist group, at first predicting that the world would end in 1878. Contrary to popular opinion, however, Russell's famous 1914 date was never used to designate a visible return of Christ, but of his *parousia* (presence), to be understood in the same manner as Edson had affirmed.

While the Jehovah's Witnesses maintained a separate identity, Edson's leadership of the Adventists passed to Ellen G. White (1827-1915). Under White's leadership, the movement took on its "seventh day" aspect, and White founded the Seventh-day Adventists in 1861. On her death, White's prophetic office passed to Victor R. Houteff (1885-1955), and this succession heralded a series of controversies amongst the Adventists. Houteff was ousted, and he then founded his own group, known as "The Rod" or "The Shepherd's Rod," based in Waco, Texas. A series of acrimonious disputes followed: Florence Houteff, who succeeded her husband, was rivaled by Ben L. Roden (d. 1978), who bought the Waco site and founded the Branch Davidian Seventh-day Adventists. The leadership of the community went to Lois Roden, Ben's wife, and subsequently to Vernon Howell (1959-1993), better known as David Koresh, who led the Waco community to its notorious disaster.

Whether Seventh-day Adventism should be classified as an NRM or not is debatable. Although it features largely in Protestant evangelical countercult literature, including Walter Martin's *Kingdom of the Cults,* many Adventists have become less sectarian, having successfully sought membership of national Councils of Churches. The same cannot be said of Pentecostalism, however, which has not sought any such alliances with other Christian denominations, although Pentecostalists are generally theologically orthodox, with a few exceptions, such as "Oneness" or "Jesus Only" Pentecostalism.

Pentecostalism is characterized by two main features: healing and "speaking in tongues" (glossolaliation), the latter being the utterance of sounds that are not characteristic of any human language but which are taken to be in some way spiritually efficacious. This phenomenon can be traced back as far as 1688, in Languedoc, France, where Isabella Vincent, who had witnessed a massacre of the Huguenots, spoke in tongues and prophesied against those who, under duress, had converted to Roman Catholicism. After Vincent's arrest, various other members of the community also made ecstatic utterances. During the 18th century, similar manifestations—as far as can be determined—took place among some English Quakers and American Methodists, and in the 1830s ecstatic utterance was particularly associated with the Catholic Apostolic Church in England and the Church of Jesus Christ of Latter-day Saints in America. After the American Civil War, the phenomenon became particularly associated with the Holiness Churches. These churches had taught that sanctity of life was the second blessing to be experienced after justification by faith, but those who experienced tongues saw the latter phenomenon as the guarantor of personal holiness. Of particular significance in the development of glossolalia were the meetings of R. G. Spurling and W. F. Bryant, who jointly established the Church of God in Cleveland, Tennessee—the first of many Pentecostalist churches bearing that name.

Up to this point, the phenomenon was not referred to as "speaking in tongues," nor identified with the Pentecost experience of the early disciples (Acts 2). The Rev. B. H. Irwin of the Holiness movement talked about "fire baptism," the allusion being to John the Baptist's prediction that Jesus would baptize "with fire" (Matthew 3:11). The issue of fire baptism proved contentious within the Holiness Churches, however, and consequently Irwin founded his own Fire-Baptized Holiness Association in 1895. It was the Rev. Charles Parham, who established the Bethel Bible College in Topeka, Kansas, who equated "fire baptism" with "speaking in tongues," an identification which is now taken for granted among Pentecostalists: in 1901, he and another leader—Agnes Ozman—experienced the phenomenon.

The event normally associated with Pentecostalism's inception is the Azusa Street "revival" of 1906. William J. Seymour, an African American Holiness pastor, having been rejected by a local Baptist Church, led his community in rented premises in Los Angeles, where they experienced what they regarded as an outpouring of the Holy Spirit. The phenomenon spread, and in 1914 a large convention of those who were sympathetic to Pentecostalism was convened in the Grand Opera House in Hot

Springs, Arkansas. This event helped to formalize the Pentecostalist movement, and one notable outcome was the formation of the Assemblies of God. Further impetus to the movement took place in 1947 when the World Conference of Pentecostals met in Zurich, Switzerland, one result of which was the Pentecostal Fellowship of North America, established the following year. The Latter-Rain movement, which also began in 1948, gave a further spur to Pentecostalism, as did the charismatic movement of the 1960s, and more recently the Toronto Blessing of 1994. These last two events bore an effect on mainstream Protestant churches, as well as Pentecostalism.

The 1960s Counterculture

In addition to Adventism and Pentecostalism, one further Christian movement had an impact on NRMs: Christian fundamentalism. The 19th century had presented Christianity with two major challenges from which it sought to recover: the scientific challenges of Charles Lyell's geology and Charles Darwin's evolutionary theory, which called into question the scriptural account of creation; and the rise of historical criticism, which challenged the Bible's inerrancy. A number of conservative Christian responses followed, one of the most significant of which was a Bible Conference of Conservative Protestants in Niagara, New York, in 1895. The conference affirmed the five principles which have come to be known as the "five points of fundamentalism": the verbal inerrancy of scripture, the divinity of Jesus Christ, the virgin birth, the substitutionary theory of atonement, and the physical resurrection and bodily return of Jesus Christ.

The rise of the older New Christian groups, such as the Watchtower organization, the Christadelphians, and the Brethren, predated the rise of fundamentalism. Belief in the Bible, however, was not necessarily congruent with acceptance of the principles of fundamentalism. The Christadelphians and the Jehovah's Witnesses, in common with earlier Unitarians, affirmed the inerrancy of scripture, but claimed that doctrines such as Christ's divinity were not to be found in scripture.

Belief in scriptural inerrancy presented the further problem of how to regard the Old Testament: was it inerrant, too, or had the New Testament superseded it? This question, which seems never to have received a clear answer from mainstream Christian fundamentalists, was approached in different ways by the New Christian organizations. The Jehovah's Witnesses pointed to the First Council of Jerusalem, described in Acts 15, where the early Church affirmed its stance on the Jewish food laws—hence the Jehovah's Witnesses' aversion to imbibing blood. The Worldwide Church of God (WCG), by contrast, affirmed the necessity of celebrating the Jewish pilgrim festivals, in accordance with scripture—although in very recent times it has reconsidered this position under its new leadership and now differs little in its beliefs and practices from mainstream Christianity.

It was the New Christian groups of the 1960s that received the main impact of fundamentalism, combined with Pentecostalism. In parallel with the charismatic movement that swept through Western Protestant denominations, the Jesus Movement was the expression of Christianity that manifested itself within the 1960s U.S. counterculture. The Vietnam War caused many of America's youth to consider whether to engage in combat or to protest. A protest therefore signified two important ideals: concern for peace and a questioning of the dominant culture. The hippies and the psychedelic revolution of the 1960s manifested both aspects: "peace" and "love" were hippiedom's bywords, and experiments with drugs, alcohol, and sex displayed a desire to flout the social mores enshrined in custom, conventional religion, and the law of the land. The best-known New Christian movements were Moses David's Children of God (now known as The Family) and Stephen Gaskin's The Farm.

The hippie counterculture by no means confined itself to Christian expressions. The popularity of Zen—usually in its "Beat" form—added legitimation to unconventionality, seemingly allowing that "anything goes" and providing permission for the seeker to discover his or her own inner nature as a potential buddha. When the hippie movement disintegrated, some of the ex-hippies remained within these alternative religious groups, while others continued their search for meaning in life outside any clearly defined movement.

Several other factors in the 1960s which reinforced the counterculture's radical questioning of authority are worth mentioning. In Western philosophy, relativism experienced something of a comeback, calling into question the absolute nature of values and of truth; and the increasing interest in anthropology, with its emphasis on fieldwork, gave greater legitimation to the worldviews of primal (no longer to be called "primitive") societies. Michael Harner's work began in 1959, but it was Carlos Castaneda who initially made a greater impact on the alternative spirituality of the 1960s.

Castaneda was an anthropologist, studying at the University of California, Los Angeles, and *Journey to Ixtlan* was the published version of his doctoral thesis. His first volume, *The Teachings of Don Juan,* is probably his best known, and it received popular acclaim. Castaneda claimed to have studied under a Yaqui sorcerer (a *brujo*) called Don Juan and to have learned shamanic practices, which included the use of hallucinogenic substances—principally peyote—to gain paranormal experiences and the ability to practice magic and healing.

Castaneda's work remains controversial, and there is no general consensus as to whether Don Juan was a genuine sorcerer or a creation of Castaneda's imagination. Castaneda found support in no less a figure than Harner, who had researched the Conibo Indians of the Peruvian Amazon, subsequently gained initiation as a shaman himself, and went on to teach shamanic techniques to Western audiences. Native American shamans who have taught the art to Western seekers include Black Elk (1863-1950), Rolling Thunder (b. 1915), Brooke Medicine Eagle, and Sun Bear (b. 1929).

Shamanism remains a popular New Age interest, partly because it presents an alternative spirituality, and also because the Native American is now viewed as the object of Western oppression. In many New Age journals it is very common to see advertisements for courses on shamanism or on "drumming"—a shamanic technique used to induce states of trance. The appropriation by Westerners of Native American rites remains controversial: while some American Indians are pleased to witness a revival of interest in their religion, others regard Westerners as unauthorized practitioners who are now stealing their religion, as they once appropriated their land.

New Religions and the Future

What of the future of new religious movements? Definitive answers are not possible, of course. Those who listened to Abraham, the Buddha, Jesus, Muhammad, or Guru Nanak in their time could not have predicted the paths that their spirituality would take. However, there are one or two indicators that may give us some clue. There has been a breakup of the youth counterculture which was so active in the 1960s, and this inevitably affects recruitment and evangelization tactics. Fewer young people seem to want to "opt out" of the dominant culture to engage in the communal living that was characteristic in the 1960s and 1970s of groups like the Unification Church, ISKCON, and the Children of God. The negative media publicity surrounding recruiting, fundraising, and lifestyle has tended to make NRMs more cautious about their methods. Those who still remain in NRMs after joining in the 1960s and 1970s are now 20 or 30 years older—in some cases more. Some have decided to return to secular work and serve the movement part-time; some have found that raising a family does not mix well with communal living; and many are concerned with instructing this second generation of members in their faith, rather than looking outside the organization for new converts.

The decline in organized religion in Europe has not been paralleled by a lack of interest in spirituality. On the contrary, the large sections on "Body, Mind, and Spirit" in most bookstores indicates an interest in new forms of spirituality rather than old ones. It is impossible to predict what novel religious groups may arise, if any, to satisfy this "spiritual hunger." One colleague believes that the West has not yet seen Sufism at its zenith—a judgment that is certainly not impossible. No doubt there will be some new groups, too, although it may well prove to be the case that the emergent spirituality that finds expression in "Body,

Mind, and Spirit" remains eclectic, individual, and noninstitutional.

It is sometimes suggested that the new millennium has given rise to a preoccupation with humanity's end-times, and that many NRMs will become suitably embarrassed as their prophecies fail to materialize. Although there will be some failed apocalyptists, the media have greatly exaggerated their number. In any case, religions are remarkably resilient to "failed prophecy," which can always be explained away by reinterpretation or new revelation. Mainstream Christianity, after all, has survived some 2,000 years after predicting Christ's imminent return. Already there are signs of apocalyptic pronouncements being reconsidered. For example, recent years have seen a shift in the Jehovah's Witnesses' understanding of Jesus' words, "This generation will not pass until all be fulfilled," which their second leader, Joseph Franklin Rutherford, applied to his own generation in 1920.

Finally, some comment is appropriate on the effect of the Internet in changing NRMs. Certainly, all the best-known NRMs have their own Web sites, and can disseminate information, sell literature, and hold e-mail discussion groups. Whether they are instrumental in securing converts is another matter, however: there is little, if any, evidence of significant conversion to new religions through the World Wide Web. Even less probable is the notion of a cyberchurch. The few groups claiming to be cyber-religions in their own right are mere parodies and unworthy of serious consideration. While some web sites offer ordination, divinity degrees, and even the opportunity to confess one's sins, it is difficult to see how one could engage in communal rites, for example. The whole concept of a religion is of a community that is bound together through simultaneous assembly and joint communal activity. The celebration of births, marriages, and deaths needs human contact, which technology cannot readily replace. While the Internet will continue to provide a mine of information on NRMs, invaluable for the researcher, one should not expect to see the NRMs of the future disappearing into cyberspace.

The Dictionary

-A-

AETHERIUS SOCIETY. Probably the first, and certainly the longest-lasting, UFO-religion (q.v.), founded in 1955 by Sir George King (q.v.) (1919-1997). King claims to have received visitations and communications from the "spiritual Hierarchy of Earth," otherwise known as the Great White Brotherhood (q.v.). His inaugural experience in May 1954 commissioned him to become "the voice of Interplanetary Parliament." The Aetherius Society holds that this Interplanetary Parliament operates from Saturn, and is in turn accountable to the Lords of the Sun. It aims to disseminate the teachings of the Cosmic Masters, to promote closer contact with extraterrestrials with a view to an eventual meeting with them, and to undertake "advanced metaphysical missions" in cooperation with the masters for the improvement of humanity and Mother Earth. The society also aims to prepare for a coming Master, who will arrive in a flying saucer and herald a millennium of peace on earth.

The great teachers of religions have arrived from other planets to show humanity the way: Confucius, Jesus, and the Buddha are said to have come from Venus, while Krishna was from Saturn. However, everyone has the opportunity to become a master, evolving toward perfection. King is Jesus' mouthpiece and has channeled his "Twelve Blessings," believed to be an expansion of the Sermon on the Mount. A second, equally important text is the "Nine Freedoms," divulged to King from Karmic Lord Mars Sector 6.

The activities of the society have included Operation Starlight (commenced in 1958), which established 19 designated mountains as receptacles of spiritual energy from the Cosmic Masters and as places of pilgrimage. Operation Prayer Power commenced in 1973, making "prayer energy" available for transmission to those parts of the earth in which it is most needed. Major cosmic events are celebrated, the most important being 8 July, the Day of Prayer for Mother Earth.

AFRICAN CHURCH INCORPORATED. One of the earliest African Independent Churches (q.v.), founded in Lagos, Nigeria in 1901. The church seeks a distinctively African expression of the Christian faith, in contrast to that of the white missionaries. Although it has made use of Anglican liturgy, services are in the Yoruba language. In common with several such churches, a policy on the issue of polygamy was needed: it was decided that clergy must be monogamous, but not necessarily the lay members.

AFRICAN INDEPENDENT CHURCHES. Various New Christian movements arose in Africa, largely through dissatisfaction with the activity of the white Western Christian missionaries, and sought to introduce traditional African elements into their character. Such elements include greater exuberance in worship, with greater spontaneity and the use of traditional African music, together with healing and prophecy, high regard for dreams and visions, and distinctively African interpretations of Scripture. Less emphasis is given to Christianity's credal affirmations, although in most cases these churches do not explicitly reject them. Most of the Independent Churches reject African fetish magic, but many (although not all) retain other traditional practices such as polygamy.

There are two distinctive types of African Independent Churches. The "Ethiopian" Churches (q.v.) are so called as a way of signifying that a form of Christianity exists which is older than that of the Western missionaries. The second type is the "prophet-healing" churches, principally the Aladura (q.v.) in West Africa and the Zionist (q.v.) churches of South Africa. African Independent Churches are now known as African Initiated Churches (q.v.). *See also* AFRICAN CHURCH INCORPORATED.

AFRICAN INITIATED CHURCHES (AIC). Formerly known as African Independent Churches (q.v.), this is the collective name for indigenous new religious groups in Africa, of which there are estimated to be between 5,000 and 10,000. The largest type of group is post-Catholic, often based on visions of the Virgin Mary, and sometimes with apocalyptic elements. *See also* MOVEMENT FOR THE RESTORATION OF THE TEN COMMANDMENTS OF GOD; WORLD MESSAGE LAST WARNING CHURCH.

AHMADIYYA. *A.k.a.: Ahmadis; Qadianis; Mirzais.* Originally a reform movement within Sunni Islam, founded in 1889 by Hazrat Mirza Ghulam Ahmad (1835-1908), a.k.a. el-Qadiani. Following a divine revelation, Ahmad taught that Islam was in decline and claimed to be the renewer of the faith *(mujaddid)* and the expected one of various world religions, including Buddhism, Christianity, and Hinduism. In 1901 the movement's journal *Review of Religions,* published in English, brought it greater prominence, but it was the work of Dr. Mufti Muhammad Sadiq in the United States from 1921 onward that attracted principally black converts in the West, many of whom had been followers of Marcus Garvey (q.v.). The first headquarters was established in Chicago, later moving to Washington, D.C., in 1950.

In common with orthodox Islam, the movement teaches strict monotheism and does not acknowledge Jesus' divinity: Jesus did not die on the cross, but died in Kashmir at the age of 120. His tomb—the Tomb of Isa—can be found in Srinagar. The movement is pacifist, but is frequently accused of being aggressive in its evangelization tactics.

After Ahmad's death, a dispute arose concerning his status. Ahmad's family insisted that he was a prophet, thus calling into question the traditional Islamic belief that Muhammad was the final prophet. Most of Ahmad's followers accepted the family's teaching, resulting in the majority of the movement falling outside traditional Islam as the Ahmadiyya Anjuman Isha'at Islam, claiming some 100,000 members worldwide. The minority—some 10,000, mainly in the United States and Canada—remain as a reform movement within Islam, viewing Ahmad principally as the "renewer."

AKASHIC RECORDS. Variously referred to as the Akashic Chronicle, Universal Memory of Nature, or the Book of Life, the Akashic Records constitute the totality of knowledge regarding human actions, thoughts, emotions, and history. *Akasha* is Sanskrit for either "ether"—the fifth element which forms the "world soul"—or "all-pervasive space." Those who believe in the existence of Akashic Records thus hold that every physical and mental event that occurs in the universe is recorded in a kind of metaphysical library that exists on an astral plane. Such information can be located by psychically "tuning in" to it—according to some, with the help of spirit guides. Since such records contain a comprehensive account of human history, they can also tell of lost civilizations, such as Lemuria and Atlantis. The notion of Akashic records was first introduced by Madame Blavatsky (q.v.) and appears in the writings of Edgar Cayce, Rudolf Steiner, and, most recently, Harold Klemp (qq.v.) of Eckankar (q.v.). *See also* ANTHROPOSOPHY; COOKE, GRACE; FELLOWSHIP OF THE INNER LIGHT.

ALADURA. An African Christian revivalist movement that arose shortly after World War I, and which led to the formation of various African Independent Churches (q.v.), many of which are known as Aladura churches. The movement began during the influenza epidemic of 1918, when Joshiah Olunowa Oshitelu (1902-1966) and others turned to prayer as a means of healing. The movement gained further impetus through the preaching of Joseph Babalola (1904-1960) during the 1930s. The name "Aladura" means "One who prays." In common with many other African Christian movements, the Aladura emerged largely as an attempt to inject distinctively African elements into the Christianity presented by white Western missionaries. Great emphasis is given to exuberance in worship, spontaneity in prayer, and visions and dreams. The Aladura churches thus retain indigenous African elements, which also include polygamy and the use of traditional African methods of divination.

Aladura churches include the Christ Apostolic Church (the largest, claiming several hundred thousand members), the Faith Tabernacle (2), the Church of the Lord (Aladura), and the Cherubim and Seraphim (qq.v.). Aladura churches are found throughout West Africa, as well as in Great Britain.

ALAMO CHRISTIAN MINISTRIES. *A.k.a.: Alamo Christian Foundation; Holy Alamo Christian Church, Consecrated; Music Square Church.* Founded by Susan Alamo (born Edith Opal Horn; 1928-1982) and Tony Alamo (born Bernard Lazar Hoffman), this organization originated as part of the Jesus People Movement of the late 1960s and early 1970s, commencing with a street ministry in Hollywood, California, and managing to convert and rehabilitate a number of drug addicts. In 1969 it was incorporated as the Christian Foundation. Moving to Dyer and then Alma in Arkansas in the mid-1970s, a community was established with a tabernacle, a school, and publishing facilities. A number of businesses associated with the community provided its income. The Alamo organization is fundamentalist by conviction (using principally the King James Version of the Bible) and Pentecostalist (similar to the Assemblies of God). It requires a strict moral code and is vehemently opposed to drugs, homosexuality, sexual misconduct, and abortion. The Alamo organization opposes Roman Catholicism. It was reincorporated as the Music Square Church in 1981.

The church proved controversial as a result of legal problems in the mid-1980s and lost its tax-exempt status in 1985. Tony Alamo was convicted of tax violations and imprisoned from 1994 until 1998. Alamo's ministries have also been accused of targeting Jews for evangelism: both Tony and Susan Alamo were Jewish by birth. Membership estimates vary, ranging from 200 to 750.

AMERICAN FAMILY FOUNDATION (AFF). One of the principal American anticult organizations, set up in 1987 by psychiatrist John Clarke. AFF became one of the first anticult groups to address itself to NRMs in general, unlike the previous cult-specific organizations. In contrast to the cult-specific groups' tendency to be parents' support groups, AFF enabled inquirers to have access to the opinions of professionals, although mainly to a minority of American psychiatrists who espoused a controversial "brainwashing" (q.v.) hypothesis. Unlike the Cult Awareness Network (q.v.), AFF is not an activist group, instead focusing on research and education. Its publications include *The Advisor* and *Cult Studies Journal*, and it hosts a large Internet site with information on all major NRMs.

AMWAY. An international business company, founded by Richard De Vos and Jay Van Andel. It is said to be the world's largest "multilevel marketing" organization. Amway uses a form of pyramid selling, albeit one that has been ruled legal in U.S. courts. Some critics have declared it to be a cult (q.v.), since it has some aspects that are characteristic of religion, such as virtues of faith, hope (positive thinking for success and for wealth), and loyalty. Some of its seminars have allegedly taken on religious aspects and have been compared with revivalist meetings, beginning with prayer and affirmations of commitment. There are some three million Amway distributors worldwide. *See also* SELF RELIGIONS.

ANANDA MARGA. Founded by Prabhat Ranjan Sarkar (1921-1990), known to his followers as Shrii Anandamurti, Ananda Marga (literally, "The Way of Bliss") combines a path toward individual salvation with a program of social reform. Inquirers receive personal instruction, followed by *yama* and *niyama* (the first two stages of Raja Yoga, q.v.), and then *dharmachakra* (its meditation technique). Teachings are based on Sarkar's *Ananda Sutra*. Anandamurti is acknowledged as a miracle worker and God incarnate. Ananda Marga is opposed to all distinctions based on caste, race, religion, and nationalism. It has a political program that seeks to achieve a world government, a universal language, and a world army. In 1958 Renaissance Universal was established as its wing for social improvement, and subsequently PROUT (Progressive Utilization Theory).

During the period 1967-1969 the organization was active in Indian elections, in the course of which various members were accused of conspiracy and murder. Sarkar himself was sentenced to life imprisonment in 1969, but he was released in 1978 after being declared not guilty. Indira Gandhi declared Ananda Marga an illegal organization from 1975 to 1977. The movement was brought to the United States in 1969 by Acharya Vimalananda, who subsequently left in order to establish the Yoga House Ashram. Membership was reported as 250,000 in 1999.

ANCIENT MYSTICAL ORDER OF THE ROSY CROSS (AMORC). A Rosicrucian (q.v.) organization, founded by Harvey Spencer Lewis (1883-1939), its first imperator. Originally founded in 1904 as the Rosicrucian Research Society, otherwise known as the New York Institution for Psychical Research, it was chartered as AMORC in 1915. In 1926 it became possible to receive instruction by correspondence for those who could not attend lodges. Correspondence members became part of the Sanctum, constituting a "Lodge at Home."

AMORC's symbol is a red rose on a gold cross. The rose symbolizes love and secrecy; the cross, death and resurrection. Together they represent reincarnation as the means of achieving further progress toward perfection. Lewis's son, Ralph M. Lewis, succeeded him as imperator. The organization reported 250,000 members in 1990, and there were 1,200 lodges in 86 countries in 1995. *See also* AQUARIAN GOSPEL OF JESUS THE CHRIST; HOLY ORDER OF MANS; NEO-TEMPLARISM.

ANGELS. Messengers of God who act as intermediaries between God and humanity, angels have been most evident within Judaism, Christianity, and Islam (qq.v.). Although they receive some limited mention in Hebrew Scripture, they appear to have entered Judaism during the intertestamental period, probably as a result of Zoroastrian influence. Islam perpetuates the tradition of belief in angels, regarding Jibreel (Gabriel) as the intermediary who delivered the Qur'an to Muhammad and affirming their existence as the servants of God who oppose evil. Within Hinduism (q.v.) can be found a common belief in *deva*—beings of light who act as elemental nature spirits and protectors of households. Belief in angels still prevails within traditional Christianity, with a belief in a "guardian angel" assigned to each individual, and the Roman Catholic Church continues officially to affirm the existence of angels. Belief was prevalent throughout Jewish and Christian history until the Enlightenment, when it tended to be regarded as contrary to reason. A few thinkers were against this trend, notably followers of Emanuel Swedenborg, who claimed to have communicated with angels and regarded them as beings who had once lived as humans.

Psychologically, angels can be regarded as archetypal images, projections of what is good and positive in human imagination. It is therefore understandable that angelology has seen a revival with the optimism that typically characterizes New Age (q.v.) thinking. An early precursor of the recent interest in angels was Geoffrey Hodson, a Theosophist (q.v.) who claimed to be in contact with an angel called Bethelda, about whom he wrote in *The Brotherhood of Angels and Men* (1927). Hodson defined seven areas in which angels offered help: power, healing, the home, building (i.e., creativity in general), nature, music, and finally beauty and art. Rudolf Steiner (q.v.) posited a hierarchy of spiritual beings: above humans—in ascending order—were angels, archangels, Archai (original forces), Exusiai (beings of power), Dynameis (mighty ones), Thrones, Cherubim, Seraphim, and the Godhead. Alice Bailey (q.v.) also maintained a belief in angels as well as Ascended Masters and expressed this aspect of her thought in *A Treatise on Cosmic Fire* (1925).

Within the New Age, angels have been particularly associated with gardening and with healing. Their role in the former was evident in the Findhorn (q.v.) Community, which originated as an experiment in horticulture. *The Findhorn Garden* (1975) recounts the roles of founders R. Ogilvy Crombie and Dorothy Maclean, in particular, and their communications with nature spirits and *devas*. The Findhorn Community, in common with many subsequent New Agers, regards angels as part of a hierarchy of spirits, gnomes being the grossest form of nature spirit, with fairies, angels, and archangels representing subtler levels of being. A similar hierarchy can be found in groups such as Solara. Another— autobiographical—account of the relationship between *devas* and plant life is found in Machaelle Small Wright's *Behaving as if the God in All Life Mattered: A New Age Ecology* (1987).

Other forms of alternative spirituality (q.v.) which have experienced a recent revival and which have accommodated angelology in their schemes are: Kabbalism (q.v.), where an angel is associated with each emanation on the Tree of Life; modern Gnosticism (q.v.), which often posits an angelic hierarchy; Native American religion (q.v.), where winged creatures such as birds or shining human figures occupy a similar role to angels; and UFO-religions (q.v.), of which it has sometimes been claimed that what purport to be UFOs are angelic beings. In some circles within the New Age, spirit guides (q.v.) occupy a role similar to guardian angels. *See also* STAR-BORNE UNLIMITED.

ANTHROPOSOPHY. A breakaway group from the Theosophical Society, founded in 1913 by Ruldolf Steiner (q.v.) (1861-1925) and described by Steiner as a form of "Christian occultism." Steiner could not agree with the status that the Theosophists accorded to Eastern philosophy and their affirmation of Jesus Christ as no more than another avatar. Anthroposophy, by contrast, affirms Jesus' life, death, and resurrection as the "central happening of all history," for which the ancient mystics paved the way.

The respective names "Theosophy" (q.v.) and "Anthroposophy" reflect a further contrast between the two movements. While Theosophy ("god wisdom") posits a divine nature toward which humanity can evolve, Anthroposophy ("human wisdom") teaches that humanity originally possessed divine powers, but lost them and hence needs to rediscover them. Jesus Christ is the means whereby humanity can re-ascend to discover and attain its lost divinity. Humanity is a microcosm of the wider universe, and thus the universe's secrets can be attained through developing the human mind. These secrets have been deposited in the Akashic Records (q.v.), which include teachings on the evolutionary history of the universe and can be accessed by following Steiner's teachings.

Anthroposophy began to spread outside Germany after the World War I, gaining a foothold in the United States from 1925 onward. Its headquarters are currently in Dornach, near Basel, Switzerland, and its worldwide membership was around 55,000 in 1998. *See also* CHRISTIAN COMMUNITY CHURCH.

ANTICULT MOVEMENT (ACM). A group of organizations, principally in the United States and Europe, who are actively opposed to the activities of NRMs. The term tends to be rejected by critics of NRMs, on the grounds that they claim not to be against cults indiscriminately but against unacceptable practices of which certain NRMs are guilty. Notwithstanding such disclaimers, however, the ACM's attitude appears consistently negative toward the vast majority of new religions. The ACM is sometimes distinguished from the "Countercult Movement," the latter being more concerned to provide written and verbal critiques of NRMs' teachings, often from a Christian perspective.

Opposition to NRMs can be traced back to the early parts of the 20th century: William C. Irvine's *Timely Warnings*, published in 1917, opposed emergent forms of alternative spirituality primarily on doctrinal grounds, arguing that they were incompatible with the Christian faith. Until the early 1970s, opposition to NRMs was conducted by evangelical

Christians, mainly by pamphlets, books, and sometimes preaching, rather by means of campaigning organizations. Christian opposition continues, both in literature and in organized groups. The most prominent Christian groups are the Spiritual Counterfeits Project in Berkeley, California, founded in 1973; the Dialog Center in Denmark, founded in the same year; and the Reachout Trust in England, established in 1981.

Increased global communication heralded the rise of a variety of NRMs, mainly of Hindu and Buddhist origin, which made no claim to be Christian: thus a Christian critique seemed less appropriate. Although many Christian critics remained concerned that such groups did not accept the gospel message, other grounds of concern began to emerge: the new postwar wave of NRMs seemed to target the youth culture to a greater degree than their predecessors; they often involved community living, concentrated teaching, and sometimes the sharing of resources. Such features gave rise to criticisms that NRMs split up families, exploited young members, and "brainwashed" (q.v.) them. A number of countercult groups therefore emerged in the early 1970s with a more secular agenda.

Ted Patrick established the Citizens' Freedom Foundation, which became the Cult Awareness Network (CAN) (q.v.) in 1974. Patrick and other CAN leaders advocated and undertook the "deprogramming" (q.v.) of members. The American Freedom Foundation (AFF) (q.v.), founded in 1979, has been more moderate, focusing on education and dissemination of information about cults. In Great Britain, FAIR (Family Action Information and Resource) (q.v.) was founded in 1976, initially with a view to counteracting the Unification Church's (q.v.) activities but whose aims have widened to incorporate all cultic groups. In France UNADFI (National Association for the Defense of the Family and the Individual) continues to counter NRMs, and FECRIS (European Federation of Centres for Research and Sectarianism) was founded in 1994, with representatives from 10 European countries.

Denmark's Dialog Center is also a prominent countercult organization under the leadership of Johannes Aagaard.

Although the ACM admits of a variety of viewpoints, its supporters tend to view "cults" as secretive, deceptive, and exploitative, with authoritarian leaders who amass wealth through large donations and long hours of work on the part of members. "Cults," they claim, are damaging to health, family life, and education and are guilty of "mind control" or "brainwashing." *See also* SINGER, MARGARET THALER; WEST, LOUIS JOLYON.

APPLEWHITE, MARSHALL (1931-1997). Leader of Heaven's Gate (q.v.), the UFO-religion (q.v) 39 members of which committed ritualized suicide in spring 1997. Applewhite had worked as a professor of music, and after meeting Bonnie Nettles (1927-1985), a former psychiatric nurse and astrologer, in 1974, traveled with her in the United States. They became convinced that they were the "two witnesses" mentioned in the Book of Revelation and that their bodies had been commandeered by "next level" minds for the purpose of assembling a "crew" to be transported to the Next Level Above Human (called the Kingdom of Heaven in the Christian Bible). In order to demonstrate that they were working as a pair, Applewhite and Nettles assumed complementary pseudonyms, calling themselves Ti and Do, and later Bo and Peep. Their mission began in late 1975 and 1976 with newspaper advertisements announcing their connection with UFOs, and this was followed up by 130 public meetings in the United States and Canada. The size of their following was small, never more than 200 at any one time, and members came to live in an isolated community near San Diego, California. After Nettles died of liver cancer in 1985, Applewhite continued to lead the group on his own, giving extended lectures to his community and ensuring that his teachings were placed on the Internet.

AQUARIAN FOUNDATION. Founded in 1955 in Seattle, Washington, by Keith Milton Rhinehart, a former Spiritualist

minister who gained prominence through well-publicized séances in the 1950s, this organization combines Spiritualism
with Theosophy (qq.v.), Eastern philosophy, and Transcendentalism (q.v.). It has no definitive statement of belief, encouraging diversity of thought among members, but attaches
importance to communication with the Masters of the Great
Brotherhood of Cosmic Light (Great White Brotherhood
[q.v.]), emphasizing karma, reincarnation (q.v.), and the
evolution of the spirit, finally leading to self-mastery. The
movement expanded from Seattle during the 1970s, establishing branches in Canada and South Africa.

AQUARIAN GOSPEL OF JESUS THE CHRIST, THE.
Written by Levi (Levi H. Dowling, q.v.), this work is one of
the earliest channeled pieces of writing, and it did much to influence both present-day channeling (q.v.) and a number of
other new spiritual movements. Levi claims that he channeled
the text from Jesus of Nazareth, Enoch, and Melchizedek and
that the book is derived from the Akashic Records (q.v.). He
explains that the earth is on the cusp between the Piscean and
Aquarian ages and that the *Aquarian Gospel* is the New Age,
providing details of Jesus' alleged travels to India, Nepal,
Persia, Assyria, Greece, and Egypt before returning to be
baptized by "John the Harbinger." Jesus' subsequent Judaean
ministry, as recounted by Levi, is a harmonization of the four
canonical gospels, in places retaining the original wording,
although with some additions. The *Aquarian Gospel* ends
with Jesus' death and subsequent resurrection, after which he
appears not only to his disciples, but also to sages in Greece
and India.

Apart from being one of the early precursors of present-
day channeling, Levi's gospel influenced the rise of a number
of religious organizations. In the United States, the Universal
Church of the Master (q.v.) (founded in 1908), the Light of
the Universe (established in the early 1960s), and the Renaissance Church of Beauty (founded in 1969) all based themselves explicitly on Levi's gospel. The founder of the Ancient
Mystical Order of the Rosy Cross (q.v.), H. Spencer Lewis,

plagiarized whole chapters in his *Mystic Life of Jesus.* Timothy Drew (a.k.a. Noble Drew Ali, 1886-1929) founded the Moorish Science Temple of America in 1926, and his work *The Holy Koran* (not to be confused with the Qur'an that is universally used by Muslims) made use of Levi. Estel Peg Merrill, who founded the Believers' Circle in the early 1980s, claimed to be in touch with and to be guided by Levi's spirit.

ARCANE SCHOOL. Founded by Alice Bailey (q.v.) (1880-1949) in 1923, the Arcane School disseminates her teachings, which are believed to have been channeled by Djwahl Khul ("the Tibetan"), a member of the brotherhood of Ascended Masters. Although the Arcane School came into being largely as a result of Bailey's expulsion from the Theosophical Society, many of its ideas are derived from Theosophy (q.v.), in particular the notions of Ascended Masters and an Ageless Wisdom that is transmitted to various generations in accordance with their understanding. While the Arcane School shares the Theosophists' notion of a common core underlying all world religions, the former is distinctive in advocating a "fusion" between the Buddha and Christ.

The Arcane School does not demand any credal affirmations from its members, but seeks to train them in esoteric meditation, enabling students to progress to discipleship. Discipleship involves service to humanity, cooperation with the "Plan of the Hierarchy" (the Great White Brotherhood, q.v.), and expanding one's consciousness, guided by one's higher self. The Arcane School now forms part of the Lucis Trust (q.v.).

ARICA. A Sufi (q.v.) group, founded in 1971 by Oscar Ichazo in New York City. Arica is the name of a North Chilean town in which 54 North Americans first received Ichazo's teachings. Heavily influenced by G. I. Gurdjieff (q.v.), Arica also draws on Tibetan Buddhism (q.v.), Zen (q.v.), and Indian yoga techniques, aiming at self-integration, health, and spiritual unification. Ichazo's teachings are expressed in several books, including *The Nine Ways of Zhikr Ritual* (1976), which sets out nine levels of spiritual attainment. These are designed for men and women who simultaneously pursue secular employment, and they take some three or four years to complete. In 1992 there were 300 teachers worldwide.

ARMSTRONG, HERBERT W. (1892-1986). Founder of the Worldwide Church of God (q.v.). After an unsuccessful early career as an advertising executive, Armstrong became convinced that the true Church was sabbatarian and bore the name "Church of God." Accordingly, he sought out the Oregon Conference of the Church of God (Seventh-day), becoming ordained as a minister in 1931. In 1933 Armstrong established the Radio Church of God in Eugene, Oregon, and he is particularly remembered for his weekly program "The World Tomorrow." The same year saw the launch of *The Plain Truth,* which continues to be available to the public free of charge. Armstrong described himself as "God's chosen apostle," teaching that the Worldwide Church of God was the true church of the last days. One significant aspect of Armstrong's theology was his British Israelism (q.v.): Armstrong held that the people of Europe were the ten lost tribes of Israel and that Ephraim and Manasseh were represented by Great Britain and the United States. His writings include *The United States and British Commonwealth in Prophecy* (1967), *The Wonderful World Tomorrow: What It Will Be Like* (1979), *The Incredible Human Potential* (1978) and *Mystery of the Ages* (1985), the last of which was completed while he was in his nineties.

In Armstrong's later years his son, Garner Ted Armstrong, was assigned much of the church's preaching, but a rift emerged between father and son during the 1970s, partly on account of doctrinal disagreements and partly due to the latter's sexual misdemeanors. Garner was expelled in 1978 and started his own rival organization. Herbert Armstrong was succeeded by Joseph W. Tkach (q.v.), who introduced radical changes in the organization, bringing it more into line with mainstream evangelical Christianity. *See also* CHURCH OF GOD, INTERNATIONAL; FUNDAMENTALISM.

ARTHURIAN MYTHS. One of the New Age (q.v.) interests, particularly in Great Britain. It is historically uncertain whether King Arthur actually existed: it has been suggested that Arthur was originally a fertility deity, a "wind spirit" or the god of the hunt. A further hypothesis is that the name Arthur derives from the Celtic *Arth Fawr,* meaning "Great Bear," and that the name has astrological connotations.

According to legend, King Arthur is famed for his Knights of the Round Table and his quest for the Holy Grail (the chalice allegedly used by Jesus at the Last Supper). His various exploits involve not only determining the grail's physical location but also proving himself worthy of finding it by virtue of loyalty, courage, and chivalry in fighting against evil. Some New Agers, such as Gareth Knight, associate King Arthur with a secret mystery tradition, revived by 12th-century Troubadours and Trouvères, which relates to stone circles and ley lines. Magic (q.v.), of course, is a further Arthurian theme, personified in the figure of Merlin, the legendary court magician.

King Arthur's life is described in Geoffrey of Monmouth's *History of the Kings of Britain* (c. 1135), and he is finally portrayed as crossing the River of Death, where a hand emerges bearing his sword Excalibur. The location of this incident is said to be near Glastonbury (q.v.) in England, famed for its New Age interests. There are rival sites for Arthur's activities, however, particularly in Cornwall, England.

ARYA SAMAJ. Literally, "Pure Society." A Hindu reform group founded in 1875 by Dayananda Sarasvati (1824-1883). Dayananda was brought up as a Saivite, but early in life renounced his religion and became a wandering sadhu. He advocated a return to the teachings of the ancient Vedas, which he interpreted monotheistically. His movement brought together Hindus and Sikhs and was opposed to caste, the use of images in worship, and child marriages. Arya Samaj was less sympathetic to Christianity and Islam, however. From 1863 to 1883 Dayananda undertook various preaching tours in India. In 1875 he was in correspondence with Henry Steel Olcott and H. P. Blavatsky (q.v.) and influenced their decision to visit India. *See also* THEOSOPHY.

ASAHARA, SHOKO (b. 1955). Founder-leader of Aum Shinrikyo (q.v.). Asahara was born Chizuo Matsumoto, into a poor family, one of seven children, and almost totally blind. At the age of six he was sent to a boarding school for the blind, and the resultant separation from his family caused him deep resentment, which he appears to have harbored throughout his life. His disability led to an interest in healing, which in turn prompted a study of various religions. He was principally influenced by Buddhism (q.v.), but also by Japanese folk religion and Hinduism (q.v.). In 1986 he visited India, where he claims to have become enlightened as a "liberated guru." From 1984 Asahara had run a meditation and book distribution organization, out of which, following his enlightenment, he founded Aum Shinrikyo in 1987. In 1990 he established a political party as a wing of Aum, but it proved extremely unsuccessful at elections. Having failed politically, Asahara increased his emphasis on physical conflict, stressing apocalyptic elements in his teaching, which he derived from the Book of Revelation and the prophecies of Nostradamus. From 1992 onward he appears to have become increasing deranged, expressing the view that, because the physical world was evil, this necessitated killing everyone on the planet. Following the notorious incident in which he instructed his followers to release poison gas in the Tokyo subway in 1995, killing 12 people, he was arrested, together with a hundred of his supporters. Some members received the death sentence, and others long prison sentences. At the time of writing, Asahara remains in custody.

ASSEMBLIES OF GOD. Founded in 1914 in Hot Springs, Arkansas, by E. N. Bell and J. Roswell Flowers as a somewhat loose association of Pentecostalist (q.v.) churches, this movement distanced itself from Oneness Pentecostalism, affirming the doctrine of the Trinity. Its doctrinal statement was formalized in 1916, including belief in the Bible as the infallible word of God, baptism by total immersion, baptism of the Holy Spirit, and spiritual healing. Its Division of Foreign Missions was set up in 1919, and its publications wing is the Gospel Publishing House. The Assemblies of God has an ordained ministry and 11 Bible colleges. Its headquarters are now in Springfield, Missouri. In 1998 the organization claimed 28,156,000 members worldwide.

ASSEMBLIES OF YAHWEH (1). Founded in 1969 in Pennsylvania by Jacob O. Meyer, the Assemblies of Yahweh is the largest organization within the Sacred Name movement (q.v.). Holding that the Old Testament is the key to interpreting the New, it insists on using the Hebrew names Yahweh and Yahshua to refer to God and Jesus, respectively, presuming these to be their authentic forms. It is non-Trinitarian and observes the ancient Jewish festivals (although without animal sacrifices), practices tithing and abides by the Jewish food laws. Admission is through baptism by total immersion. Additionally the Assemblies teach nonviolence and members refuse to participate in armed conflict. The Assemblies sprang from Meyer's radio ministry, which began in 1966, and the organization continues to broadcast in the United States and 75 other countries. There are estimated to be several thousand members in 115 countries, and the Assemblies have offices in England, the Philippines, and Trinidad.

ASSEMBLIES OF YAHWEH (2). Originally called the Assembly of YHWH, this organization was founded in 1939 in Holt, Michigan, by C. O. Dodd. It is one of the earliest examples of the Sacred Name movement (q.v.) and insists on referring to God by means of the presumedly authentic names of Yahweh and Elohim, and to Jesus by the Hebrew name Yahshua.

ASSOCIATION FOR RESEARCH AND ENLIGHTENMENT (ARE). Founded by Edgar Cayce (q.v.) in 1931, ARE aims to preserve and research Cayce's teachings and to encourage his supporters to act upon them. ARE promotes parapsychology (principally the reading of auras, astrology, and research into psychic phenomena) and spiritual healing, as well as encouraging spiritual growth through meditation. Like Cayce, the organization is Christian-oriented, although it insists that it is not a religion and that many of its members have their own independent religious affiliations. After Edgar Cayce's death, his son Hugh Lynn Cayce (1907-1982) led ARE, and he was succeeded by Edgar Cayce's grandson, Charles Thomas Cayce. ARE claims 42,000 members worldwide, 40,000 of whom are in the United States.

ASSOCIATION OF UNITY CHURCHES. Founded in 1966, this association is located in Unity Village, Missouri—the headquarters of the Unity School of Christianity (q.v.). The association differs from the school in that the latter aims merely to disseminate the ideas of Charles and Myrtle Fillmore (q.v.), who did not intend to establish a separate church, encouraging members not to abandon their existing faiths. A number of distinctive Unity churches arose, however, and felt the need for an umbrella organization to link them. Since 1923 the Unity School of Christianity has distanced itself from the International New Thought Alliance, although some individual Unity churches belong to it. The Association is the largest body linking "metaphysical" or New Thought (q.v.) churches, having 628 member congregations ("ministries") in 1995. The body oversees ordination and the establishment of new congregations and generally maintains standards. Like the Unity School, it requires no specific doctrines, being committed to "spiritual freedom."

ASTARA. An occultist organization, founded in 1951 in Los Angeles by Robert and Erlyne Chaney, who were formerly Spiritualists. After helping to found the Spiritualist Episcopal Church, Robert Chaney became influenced by Theosophy (q.v.), and Astara is an eclectic synthesis of Spiritualism, Theosophy, yoga, and Christianity (qq.v.), with elements of Freemasonry and Rosicrucianism (q.v.). Astara seeks to become the center of all religions and philosophies. The name Astara is said to derive from Astraea, a name for the Greek goddess of justice, and its principal teachings are contained in the *Book of Life,* which is disseminated through correspondence tuition. The organization claimed 15,000 members in 1995.

AUM SHINRIKYO. *A.k.a.:* Aleph. Literally, "Absolute Truth Movement." Founded in 1987 by Shoko Asahara (q.v.), this organization gained notoriety in 1995 when some members, on Asahara's instruction, released poison gas in the Tokyo subway, killing 12 people and injuring hundreds more.

The teachings and practices of the movement are eclectic, drawing principally from Buddhism (q.v.) in its Theravadin and Tibetan varieties, with elements of Japanese folk religion and Hinduism (q.v.) and apocalyptic elements that draw on the Book of Revelation and the prophecies of Nostradamus. Aum Shinrikyo views the world as inherently evil, as well as illusory, teaching that the human body mirrors the evil world. The movement's aim is therefore to eradicate the bad karma of the population, to enable them to achieve salvation. Asahara viewed the universe as a hierarchy, with the hells as the lowest level and the buddhas as the highest: particular emphasis was placed on saving souls from the hells. Since the laws of science relate to the evil material world, stress was also laid on transcending such laws, for example, in the paranormal: Aum therefore recommended psychic development, with practices such as levitation, as well as yoga and meditation (qq.v.).

The movement offered three levels of initiation: earthly, astral, and causal. Causal initiation involved complete allegiance to Asahara, and this was symbolized by drinking his bath water and blood. Such initiation entitled the initiate to enter the order, which lived in communes (known as "lotus villages"): hence the allegation that Aum Shinrikyo was disruptive of family life.

From around 1988 violent elements began to enter the movement. In 1990 Asahara organized a political party from within Aum; when this proved singularly unsuccessful, he began to emphasize physical combat, and from 1993 onward began to arm his "sacred warriors" or "bodhisattvas," as his order members were called. In 1995 Asahara had a series of apocalyptic visions, which caused him to predict an imminent war that would erupt by the end of the century. Tending to equate *samadhi* with both enlightenment and extinction (the Sanskrit word means both), Asahara came to believe that the populace's evil *karma* could only be eradicated through physical extinction.

In 1995 Aum Shinrikyo had a reported total worldwide membership of 50,000: 40,000 in Russia and 10,000 in Japan, with a few supporters in Sri Lanka, Germany, and New York. In 2001 between 1,000 and 1,600 members remain. In January 2000 the organization assumed the new name of Aleph.

AUROBINDO, SRI (1872-1950). Born Aurobindo Ghose in Calcutta, Aurobindo received a Western education, becoming a student at King's College, Cambridge. He returned to India in 1893 to become professor of English at Baroda College. An ardent nationalist, Aurobindo was imprisoned from 1908 to 1909 for his active opposition to British rule in India. While in prison he gained a spiritual experience, which profoundly influenced his development of "integral yoga." After moving to Pondicherry, then a French colony, in 1910, he met Mira Richard (née Alfassa, 1878-1973) in 1914, who was instrumental in the establishment of Aurobindo's ashram and who became subsequently known as "the Mother" to their disciples.

Integral yoga combines the three yogas (q.v.) prescribed in the Bhagavad Gita—*jnana, karma,* and *bhakti*—together with a fourth, the yoga of self-perfection. Aurobindo's teachings on jnana include the insight that there are lower and higher hemispheres of existence, which are integrated by the "supermind." The higher spheres are *sat, cit,* and *ananda* (being, consciousness, and bliss): these, however, do not have a static existence in their own right, but need fulfilling by transforming the lower elements of mind, life, and matter. These lower elements, in turn, require to be transformed into the higher. Thus Aurobindo's philosophy concerns the evolution of matter to spirit and supraconsciousness as the final goal. (Aurobindo's teachings have sometimes been compared with those of Pierre Teilhard de Chardin.) On bhakti, Aurobindo noted that Krishna did not require merely ritual devotion but also a life of self-abandonment, and thus bhakti related to karma yoga. On karma, Aurobindo taught—in contrast to conventional Hinduism (q.v.)—that one's dharma is not fixed for all time but changes in accordance with historical and societal change and with one's own self-development. For example, although ahimsa may be desirable in certain situations, there are others in which violence is necessary.

Aurobindo and the Mother are jointly regarded as avatars, complementary manifestations of the divine. After Aurobindo's death, the Mother continued to lead the movement, proclaiming herself as avatar in 1956. The Mother established the new city of Auroville in South India in 1968, a city with over 50,000 inhabitants who seek to spread the new spiritual consciousness that Aurobindo proclaimed, and which they believe supersedes all traditional religions. *See also* MOTHER MEERA.

AVATARA ADI DA. Born Franklin Jones in 1939 near New York, Adi Da has been known under various names, including Bubba Free John (1977), Da Free John (1979), Da Love-Ananda (1986), Jagad-Guru (1989), and Da Avabhasa (1991), as well as Da Kalki and Ruchira Buddha. His many names are said to reflect the many attributes of the divine. Since 1995 he has preferred to be called Avatara Adi Da, meaning "the descent or incarnation of deity, the primordial eternal lawgiver."

Adi Da claims to have been born enlightened and to have "incarnated" as Franklin Jones at the age of two. In childhood he had frequent fevers, which he regards as yogic signs of kundalini (q.v.) awakening, or experiences of "the Bright." These experiences waned—Adi Da refers to this as "divine amnesia"—and in 1957 he decided to study philosophy at

Columbia University in New York to regain this divine awareness. In 1964 he made the acquaintance of Rudi (Swami Rudrananda), who directed him to a Lutheran seminary, and in 1968 he took up residence at Muktananda's (q.v.) ashram. He also met Nityananda (q.v.). Muktananda gave Jones the spiritual names of Dhyanananda and Love-Ananda. He later became a Shakti devotee, moving to Los Angeles, where he attached himself to the Vedanta Temple, run by the Ramakrishna (q.v.) organization. On 10 September 1970 he experienced the appearance of Shakti, which he regarded as his re-awakening of "sahaj samadhi."

From this time onward Adi Da attracted a few followers and decided to make his teachings public in 1972, when he founded the Shree Hridayam Satsang ("Company of the Heart") ashram. He referred to his teachings as "radical understanding" or "the Way of the Heart." The following year he departed for India, where he assumed the name of Bubba Free John, which he claims was "spontaneously revealed" to him. ("Bubba" means "brother" or "friend" and was a childhood nickname: it is not a variant of "baba.") Returning to Los Angeles in 1973, Bubba Free John developed his "radical understanding" into "Crazy Wisdom": this combined spirituality with sexuality (including homosexuality), money and material wealth, and psychic phenomena.

Adi Da taught that the experience of separate existence, either from one another or from the divine, was an illusion: all are *sat, cit, ananda* (being, consciousness, and bliss): all are already enlightened, hence the need to realize their enlightenment rather than attain it. Life, he has taught, involves seven stages: birth and adaptation to the world; the integration of the emotional and the physical; the development of the mind, will, and emotions (including sexuality); spiritual awakening; inner search for samadhi; death of the ego, in which one transcends the notion that one is a distinct self; and recognition that everything is a manifestation of Radiant Transcendent Being.

As with Jones's various name changes, the movement has also assumed several names. Originally the Dawn Horse Fellowship in 1970, it has become variously the Free Primitive Church of Divine Communion, the Johannine Daist Community, the Free Daist Communion, and the Laughing Man Institute. The movement became controversial in 1985 as a result of a court case in which an ex-member sued the organization for physical and sexual abuse, fraud, and false imprisonment (the case was settled out of court, but fueled anticult stereotyping of NRMs). Notwithstanding such problems, Adi Da impressed Alan Watts (q.v.) and Ken Wilbur, and the movement might be said to be a kind of Hinduized equivalent of "Beat Zen" (q.v.).

-B-

BAHÁ'Í. Founded in Persia (now Iran) by Bahá'u'lláh (Mírzá Husayn Alí, 1817-1892), the Bahá'í faith developed from Bábism, a religious movement led by Siyyid 'Ali Muhammed (1819-1850), more usually known as the Báb, meaning "the Gate." In 1844 the Báb declared the presence of "God's manifestation," and after his martyrdom in 1850, Bahá'u'lláh claimed to occupy this role. In 1852, while serving a prison sentence for allegedly conspiring against the Shah, Bahá'u'lláh is believed to have received an inaugural vision, which he revealed 11 years later, after being forced to flee from Baghdad. This "Declaration of Bahá'u'lláh" in 1863 marks the transformation of Bábism to the Bahá'í faith. After Bahá'u'lláh's death in 1892, Abdu'l Baha (1844-1921) assumed the leadership: he traveled widely, bringing the faith to Europe and North America. His grandson, Shoghi Effendi (1897-1957), subsequently took over the leadership: he is known as the "Guardian of the Faith" and did much to establish Bahá'í institutions. The Universal House of Justice, situated in Haifa, was completed in 1963 and continues to be the Bahá'í seat of authority, consisting of elected leaders and operating through National Spiritual Assemblies and Local Spiritual Assemblies.

The Bahá'í faith teaches that God has communicated progressively with humanity through a series of messengers ("Manifestations of God"), pertaining to various world religions: Abraham, Krishna, Moses, Zoroaster, the Buddha, Jesus, Muhammad, and in more recent times the Báb and Bahá'u'lláh. Bahá'u'lláh is viewed as the culmination of God's revelation, although he is not expected to be the last. Since God is said to communicate in all the various world traditions, Bahá'ís teach the unity of God, endowing him with the attributes typically associated with theistic religions, especially Islam (q.v.). Bahá'ísm is thus seen as the culmination of all world faiths, uniting them all. The Bahá'í faith regards itself as a new world religion, not as a new religious movement, and certainly not as an Islamic sect.

Bahá'ís teach a number of principles that emanate from Bahá'u'lláh: the oneness of humanity; the equality of women and men; the elimination of prejudice; the elimination of extremes of wealth and poverty; the independent investigation of truth; universal education; religious tolerance; the harmony of science and religion; a world commonwealth of nation; and a universal auxiliary language.

The Bahá'í faith has defined its own calendar, beginning at the end of March and dating Bahá'í years from the Declaration of the Báb in 1844. Its months have 19 days, and the year includes some intercalary days, and 'Alá (in March) is observed as a month of fasting, culminating in the New Year festival of Naw-Rúz. Festivals in the Bahá'í calendar are associated with events in Bahá'í history.

Bahá'u'lláh forbade aggressive proselytizing, and hence Bahá'ís do not actively seek converts, preferring to "pioneer"—that is, to introduce and maintain a presence in areas where there are few or no Bahá'í members.

BAILEY, ALICE (1880-1949). British-born esotericist, former Theosophist, and founder of the Arcane School (q.v.). Originally a Christian who believed in biblical inerrancy, in 1895 she claimed to have received a visitation from a gentleman wearing a turban, whom she initially took to be Jesus, but, on subsequent acquaintance with Theosophy (q.v.), later identified as Koot Hoomi, one of the Ascended Masters, with whom H. P. Blavatsky (q.v.) had claimed a special relationship.

Bailey departed for California in 1915, and this is where she became acquainted with the teachings of Theosophy. In 1919 she made contact with the Ascended Master Djwahl Khul and claimed to be his amanuensis, channeling his teachings, which appeared in the form of her books. The first of these writings was entitled *Initiation: Human and Solar* (1922). Subsequent books combined Theosophical ideas with an expectation of a "reappearance of the Christ."

Bailey's claims to having spiritual relationships with a new Master, together with her eschatological ideas on Christ's reappearance, brought her into conflict with the main body of Theosophists, and in 1921 she was expelled. She went on to found her own school—the Arcane School, established in 1923.

Bailey's writings continue the theme of an "Ageless Wisdom," consisting of esoteric teachings that are believed to have been transmitted from ancient times to the present day, handed on in a form that is particularly suited to the age. The teachings from Djwahl Khul concern a Path of Spiritual Evolution, the hierarchy of spiritual teachers, a "new psychology of the soul," and the prospect of a new world religion, since there exists a "common thread of truth linking all the major world faiths." Bailey taught that there must be fusion of the works of Buddha and Christ: the Buddha elicited discipleship, while Christ offered initiation into the Ageless Wisdom. An important theme is service to humanity. In contrast with the Theosophists, Bailey laid less emphasis on individual seeking, teaching the importance of group, in which one can contribute toward "the enlightenment of planetary consciousness." *See also* LUCIS TRUST.

BAWA MUHAIYADDEEN FELLOWSHIP. A Western Sufi (q.v.) organization, with a mainly American following, founded by Bawa Muhaiyaddeen (d. 1986). Bawa Muhaiyaddeen was a Singhalese ascetic who gained prominence as a teacher during the 1940s, drawing from the Hindu Puranas, as well as from Islamic hadiths, and teaching the absence of distinction on the grounds of race, caste, creed, religion, or gender. Despite such apparent inclusivism, it has been argued that Bawa Muhaiyaddeen wished to direct his followers toward more mainstream "exoteric" Islam—a view that is evidenced by his encouragement of mosque building: there is a mosque on the site of the Fellowship's headquarters in Pennsylvania.

Bawa Muhaiyaddeen was invited to the United States and arrived in Philadelphia in 1971. His original following came from the hippie counterculture. Bawa Muhaiyaddeen taught the existence of nothing other than God, the importance of eradicating evil from one's life, and the need to appropriate within oneself the numerous qualities of God: this is achievable through silent *dhikr*, the repetition of God's names and attributes. When he died (allegedly at over 100 years of age), no one succeeded him as shaykh, since it is believed that his essence remains alive and guides the true seeker. Two imams were appointed to lead the organization, which has between 15 and 20 branches in the U.S.A. and Canada, as well as in London and Colombo.

BENNETT, JOHN G. (1897-1974). An interpreter in the British Army, Bennett spoke fluent Turkish and was able to study under G. I. Gurdjieff and P. D. Ouspensky (qq.v.). After 25 years with Ouspensky, a disagreement arose, and Ouspensky disowned him. Bennett became an independent teacher after Gurdjieff's death in 1949, but found difficulty in maintaining a rapport with Gudjieff's followers, whom he accused of "ossifying" his teachings. Bennett traveled to Turkey in 1953 and encountered Subud (q.v.) four years later. He was particularly instrumental in bringing Subud to a Western audience: his book *Concerning Subud* (1958) is one of the first detailed introductions to the movement. Bennett's association with Subud was short lived: on a visit to India in 1961 he met Shivapuri Baba, who advised that he would gain God-realization by joining the Roman Catholic Church. From 1971 onward, Bennett began to receive "auditions"—voices—which told him that he had previously incarnated as one of the Kwajagan (Sufi masters of wisdom, dating from the 15th century). In the same year, Bennett founded the International Academy for Continuous Education, in Sherborne, England, to promote his teachings. The academy closed in 1975, following Bennett's death, but some of his students established the Claymont Society for Continuous Education in West Virginia in the same year. The Claymont Society teaches the Gurdjieff 10-month program, which Bennett taught, and also promotes Sufi, Hasidic, and Eastern teachings. Bennett's *Long Pilgrimage* is autobiographical; *The Dramatic Universe* is his most widely read piece of writing.

BERG, DAVID BRANDT (1919-1994). Founder-leader of the Family (q.v.) (formerly known as the Children of God [CoG], and the Family of Love), known to his followers as Moses David or Father David. Berg became known initially through radio and television, presenting "Church in the Home" with Pentecostalist preacher Fred Jordan from 1964 to 1967.

Together with his wife, Jane Miller (known as "Mother Eve"), Berg moved to California, where his mother was attempting to evangelize members of the hippie movement. Berg adopted the names "Revolutionaries for Jesus" and "Teens for Christ" for their mission. He subsequently moved to Canada, leaving his wife and marrying Karen Zerby, who came to be known as "Maria," and jointly headed the Children of God. His adoption of the name Moses David at this point in his career emphasized his claim to have direct revelations from God, and his followers regarded him as a final-day prophet.

Berg firmly believed that humanity was living in the last days, and in the early 1970s his members organized vigils, in which they publicized CoG end-time doctrines. Despite the negative publicity that the vigils attracted, CoG had become an international organization by 1973, with branches in 50 countries.

Berg disseminated his teaching through *True Comix*, which presented the biblical teaching in comic strip form, and he circulated the New Testament under the title *The Jesus Book*. The movement gained particular notoriety on account of Berg's *MO Letters* (q.v.) to his supporters, which advocated extremely liberal attitudes to sex. Particularly controversial were his teachings that it was legitimate to have a variety of sexual partners simultaneously and that members should engage in "flirty fishing" (q.v.). After Berg died, Maria continued to lead the organization.

BESANT, ANNIE (1847-1933). Writer, lecturer, social reformer, and feminist activist, Besant first met Madame H. P. Blavatsky (q.v.) in 1889 and succeeded her as head of the Esoteric Section of the Theosophical Society after Blavatsky's death in 1891. Following a dispute in 1894 with co-leader William Q. Judge, whom she accused of turning Theosophy (q.v.) into a "Blavatsky cult," the American section of the Theosophical Society split off from the European and Indian branches, with Judge leading the former. Besant was keen to incorporate Hindu (q.v.) and esoteric Christian elements, in addition to Blavatsky's Buddhist (q.v.) ones, and supported Charles W. Leadbeater (q.v.) against his critics. Besant and Leadbeater promoted Krishnamurti (q.v.) as the new world avatar, eventually leading to a further split involving Krishnamurti, who later rejected this role. Besant helped to promote social reforms among Indians and Sinhalese and became the first woman to preside over the Indian National Congress. She founded several schools, including the University of Benares.

BESHARA. A Sufi organization founded in 1971 in Gloucestershire, England, by an unknown Turk. Claiming to be an authentic version of "real esoteric" Sufism (q.v.), its teachings are based on those of Jalal Al-Din Rumi (1207-1273) and Muhyiddin Ibn 'Arabi (1165-1240). Beshara claims to teach no specific dogmas, aiming instead to enable the follower to return to and to merge with the source (God). This is attainable through *dhikr* (remembrance of the names of God), study (particularly "29 pages" of teaching), meditation (no particular method is taught), and service, by means of which one's will becomes aligned to God's through sacrifice. Headquarters are based at Swyre Farm, Gloucestershire, with groups countrywide.

BLACK ELK (1863-1950). Oglala Sioux medicine man and second cousin of Crazy Horse, who led the Sioux against the U.S. government in 1876. From the age of five, Black Elk experienced visions of men from the clouds, whom he later identified with the Power of the Earth. His "great vision" occurred when he was nine, when, in the grip of shamanic possession sickness, he was taken to the earth's center and given the sacred hoop and sacred stick. He was instructed to place the stick inside the hoop, to blossom as a tree—thus symbolizing the flourishing of Indian spirituality in the wider world.

After Crazy Horse's death, Black Elk joined Sitting Bull in Canada, but soon returned to America, where he became part of Buffalo Bill's Wild West Show for over a decade. In 1889 he joined the Ghost Dance (q.v.) religion, which came to an end with the Wounded Knee Creek massacre in 1890; Black Elk was sent to Pine Ridge Reservation in South Dakota. In 1930 Black Elk recounted his reminiscences to John G. Neihardt, with his son Ben acting as translator. These were published in 1932 as *Black Elk Speaks,* now translated into several languages. Black Elk passed on the sacred pipe to Neihardt, who apparently did not understand the Sioux mysteries, which were later entrusted to Joseph Epes Brown. Wallace Black Elk (b. 1921), a medicine man who knew Black Elk during his lifetime, continued to teach about the sacred pipe and Indian medicine.

Black Elk is significant as the first Native American *wichasha wakon* (holy man) to make his ideas accessible to Westerners and to pass on to them the symbols and rituals of Native American religion (q.v.).

BLAVATSKY, HELEN PETROVNA (1831-1891). Occultist and cofounder of the Theosophical Society, frequently referred to as "Madame Blavatsky" or "HPB" by her followers. Born into a Russian aristocratic family, Blavatsky is said to have displayed paranormal powers at an early age, effecting "materializations" of flowers and other objects. She is said to have traveled the world between 1848 and 1858, reaching the Far East and most importantly Tibet, where she studied under "Secret Masters." This uncorroborated 10-year journey is referred to as the "veiled time." During this period Blavatsky claimed to have encountered Master Morya, one of a number of beings who comprise the brotherhood of Ascended Masters. She regarded Morya and another Master called Koot Hoomi as supernatural beings who exerted a particular influence upon her.

Blavatsky's subsequent travels are better attested. She came to America in 1873, where she met Colonel Henry Steel Olcott the following year. Together with Olcott and William Q. Judge (1851-1896) she founded the Theosophical Society, an organization with the express purpose of establishing a universal fraternity of inquirers who would study "unexplained laws of nature" and further their acquaintance with comparative religion, philosophy, and science.

In 1877 Blavatsky published *Isis Unveiled*, an occultist treatise derived largely from ancient Egyptian cosmology. This is one of two major pieces of writing by Blavatsky, the other being *The Secret Doctrine*, first published in 1888. This latter piece of writing drew its inspiration from an extended journey with Olcott to India and Ceylon. Unlike the "veiled time" journeys, this visit is well attested, and *The Secret Doctrine*, unlike *Isis Unveiled*, draws heavily on ideas derived from Hinduism and Buddhism (qq.v.), particularly the latter's Tibetan variety. *The Secret Doctrine* contends that underlying all the world's major traditions there is a hidden teaching, which Blavatsky purports to disclose. *See also* AKASHIC RECORDS; ARYA SAMAJ; BESANT, ANNIE; GNOSTICISM; THEOSOPHY.

BRAHMACHARI/BRAHMACHARINI. In Hinduism (q.v.), a brahmachari is a male unmarried student who follows a spiritual path under the supervision of a guru (q.v.) and is committed to celibacy. A brahmacharini is a female who assumes a similar role. The brahmachari(ni) can either be a lifelong celibate or at a stage before progressing to the *grihastha* (householder). He or she lives with the guru and other students, following the prescribed yoga or tantra. The term "brahmacharya" is also used in Buddhism to designate the (exclusively male) *bhikkhu* or monk.

In ISKCON (q.v.), the brahmachari(ni) constitutes the first stage of initiation *(diksha)* which the devotee may undergo. Brahamacharis are recognizable by their saffron robes, in contrast with the married male students, who wear white. Brahmacharinis may wear saris of any color and are not so visibly distinguishable from other devotees. The brahamachari(ni) is one of several types of membership: one may be a part-time supporter, a householder, or—more rarely—a sannyasin (world renouncer).

BRAHMA KUMARIS (BK). A Saivite religious organization founded by Dada Lekhraj (1876-1969) and sometimes known as the Brahma Kumaris World Spiritual University. Dada Lekhraj was a multimillionaire jeweler, who began to experience visions late in life and is believed to have become Shiva's medium. He is not himself regarded as divine, although he has sometimes been given the name "Prajapati Brahma," and he never claimed any *parampara* (lineage of initiation by gurus). Lekhraj's original organization was founded in 1936—the year in which he first experienced his visions—and was known as Om Mandali. The organization moved to Karachi in 1937, at which time Lekhraj assigned its management to a committee of eight women. The name "Brahma Kumaris" was adopted in 1938. In the 1950s its headquarters was established in Mount Abu, India, which remains its center. The movement did not extend outside India until after Lekhraj's death: centers in London and Hong Kong were set up in 1971, and the BKs continued to expand, establishing centers in over 40 countries by 1980.

Brahma Kumaris attaches great importance to the role of women, who continue to govern the organization's affairs. Lekhraj believed that women were to be valued for the distinctively feminine virtues of patience, tolerance, kindness, and self-sacrifice and that these virtues could encourage spiritual growth. When Dada Lekhraj died in 1969, the movement was entrusted to two senior women: Dadi Prakashmani and Dadi Janki. Women BKs are readily identifiable by their white dress.

BK's teachings are based on Lekhraj's revelations. They teach that humanity once inhabited a perfect paradise, but men and women soon gave in to attachments, wealth, possessions, power, and lust and hence will reap the effects of their karma. Celibacy is encouraged, and Lekhraj described sex as "poison," "criminal assault," and "the gateway to hell." BKs are also opposed to tobacco, alcohol, and recreational drugs. Members are encouraged to purify their minds by the practice of Raja Yoga (q.v.). This entails sitting tranquilly, in front of a screen on which Dada Lekhraj's picture is projected, then making a number of "affirmations," regarding the eternal nature of the soul, the original purity of one's nature, and the nature of God. The practice of Raja Yoga is believed to enable spiritual progress, but it also has pragmatic benefits, for example, business success. Not infrequently BKs organize seminars on business management and on developing personal life skills. BKs teach, too, that when sufficient numbers of people practice Raja Yoga, this will bring about the *sat yuga*—the golden age in which peace, prosperity, and justice will reign. World membership in 1999 was 450,000.

BRAINWASHING. A technique attributed to NRMs by the anticult movement (ACM) (q.v.). Originally the term was coined to describe the North Korean army's treatment of American prisoners during the 1950-1953 Korean War. Psychologist Robert Jay Lifton subsequently suggested that new religions practiced similar techniques of controlling the environment of new inquirers, and that such methods explained the sudden changes of behavior and worldview experienced by attendees. The brainwashing theory has tended to gain credence within the ACM with the support of a handful of American psychiatrists, notably Margaret Thaler Singer (q.v.).

Different explanations are given about the ways in which NRMs manipulate their environments. Some critics allege that inquirers are physically constrained, while others claim that sleep and food deprivation are used. Still others maintain that the pressures are psychological rather than physical, citing peer group pressure or the personal magnetism of a charismatic leader as irresistible factors in securing allegiance. Hypnosis has also been suggested as an explanation.

The common feature of such explanations is that they imply that joining an NRM is a passive rather than an active process, and hence the ACM tends to use terms such as "recruitment" and "mind control" rather than "conversion." Essentially, the brainwashing theory purports to explain radical changes that are evident when someone joins an NRM, and also how converts come to accept a worldview which at times has been described as "bizarre" or "irrational" by those who remain outside, sharing the worldview of the dominant culture.

A few sociologists, for example, Benjamin Zablocki, follow Lifton in supporting "mind control" theories. In her study of the Unification Church (UC) (q.v.), *The Making of a Moonie* (1984), Eileen Barker made detailed study of how UC seminar attendees progressed to subsequent levels of study. Barker noted that, on average, only 15 percent of attendees went on to the next level of seminar and that the average length of allegiance to the UC after joining was two years. Although the ACM has expressed doubts about Barker's research, no anticultist, nor any other academic known to the present author, has produced counterevidence to refute Barker's findings. *See also* SNAPPING.

BRANCH DAVIDIANS. A Seventh-day Adventist (q.v.) group, founded in Waco (q.v.), Texas, by Ben Roden (d. 1978). The Branch Davidians were the largest splinter group following the breakup of the Rod (q.v.) after Florence Houteff's failed prophecies. Roden claimed variously to be the returned Elijah (Malachi 4:5-6)—thus indicating a continuing belief that humanity was experiencing its last days—and "the man whose name is The BRANCH" (Zechariah 6:12).

Vernon Howell arrived during Roden's wife Lois's period of office, which lasted until 1983. Following subsequent disputes regarding the leadership, Howell assumed control in 1988, claiming to be the present-day messiah and insisting that all the women belonged to him and were excluded from any other sexual contact. In 1990 Howell became known as David Koresh (q.v.).

The final demise of the Waco community began when two ex-members alerted the authorities about the group's activities. In 1990 one of Koresh's "wives," Robyn Bunds, presented evidence to the Waco police that led them to charge Koresh with statutory rape. In response to outside opposition, the community began to accumulate arms, and Koresh's preaching gave even greater emphasis to apocalyptic themes. Following reports of child abuse, ATF (U.S. Bureau of Alcohol, Tobacco, and Firearms) agents obtained a search warrant to enter the premises, and the confrontation that followed led to 93 deaths. *See also* ROSS, RICK.

BRANHAM, WILLIAM MARRION (1909-1965). After receiving healing in a Pentecostalist (q.v.) church as a young man, Branham became a preacher, establishing a tabernacle at Jeffersonville, Indiana. He claimed to experience an angelic visitation in 1946 and, together with Gordon Lindsay, launched "The Voice of Healing," which led to a revival of interest in spiritual healing and inspired American evangelists such as Oral Roberts, Morris Cerullo, and A. A. Allen. During the 1960s Branham permitted unorthodox opinions to arise within his movement: he denied the Trinity and allowed some of his followers to espouse a "Jesus Only" (q.v.) theology (the belief that "Jesus" is the name of the Father, Son, and Holy Spirit). From 1963 onward, he laid great emphasis on Malachi's prophecy that God would send Elijah (Malachi 4: 5). Although he did not explicitly identify himself with Elijah, many of his followers made the equation. Branham is sometimes named as one of the precursors of the Word-Faith movement (q.v.).

Branham was killed in a car accident in 1965. After his death, his sermons were collected and disseminated by Spoken Word Publications and Voice of God Recordings, Inc. The organizations merged in 1986 under the name Voice of God, headed by Branham's son Joseph M. Branham. Another son, the Rev. Billy Paul Branham, established the William Branham Evangelistic Association to further his father's ministry. The association claimed some 700,000 members worldwide in 1995, with 75,000 in the United States and Canada; there are over 300 affiliated congregations in 29 countries.

BREATHARIANS. A New Age movement (q.v.), whose leader Jasmuheen (born Ellen Greve) claims to live entirely on "pranic nourishment," without the necessity of eating or drinking. Jasmuheen draws eclectically on a range of spiritualities, incorporating Yogananda's (q.v.) *kriya yoga,* Theosophy (q.v.), Alice Bailey (q.v.), Edgar Cayce (q.v.), Leonard Orr, Charles Fillmore (q.v.), and New Age writers such as James Redfield *(The Celestine Prophecy)* and Deepak Chopra. Jasmuheen claims to be in contact with "Ascended Ones," also called Arcturians, whose information she is apparently able to channel. Her teachings purport to bridge the etheric and physical realms of existence, recognizing the oneness and inter-connectedness of all existence. Jasmuheen's techniques involve breath control, visualization, and meditation (q.v.), including the use of crystals, mantras, and light, with a view to raising one's "vibration frequency." A vegetarian and alcohol-free diet are a prelude to a 21-day process leading to an ability to exist literally without physical food or drink, only being fed on "liquid light." A breatharian is one who has achieved this state.

In 1996 Jasmuheen founded the Ambassadry Movement of an Awakened Positive Society (MAPS), which seeks to achieve "balance," "integration," "empowerment," and "enlightenment" for its followers. Pranic nourishment, she believes, could also be a solution to world hunger. Jasmuheen has authored several books, including *Living on Light* (1997) and *In Resonance* (1999).

Her movement aroused particular controversy in 1999, when the media exposed cases of followers who had died, allegedly as a result of forgoing food and drink in an attempt to live exclusively on pranic nourishment.

BRETHREN. Sometimes known as "Plymouth Brethren" on account of their origins in Plymouth, England, under the leadership of B. W. Newton, this movement began with Edward Cronin in 1831 and was subsequently supported by A. N. Groves and J. N. Darby (1800-1882), the latter previously a curate in the Episcopal Church of Ireland. A lay movement, the Brethren endeavor to restore Christianity (q.v.) to its New Testament form. Its members are in the Protestant Calvinist tradition, believing in the inerrancy of Scripture and laying great emphasis on worship, especially the "breaking of bread"—their name for the communion service. There are two main types of Brethren: the Open Brethren (q.v.) or "Christian Brethren" and the Exclusive Brethren (q.v.). The latter broke away under the influence of Francis Newman and stressed the need to separate themselves from the world. There are 1,500,000 Brethren worldwide.

BRITISH ISRAEL. *A.k.a.: Anglo-Israelism.* A movement that affirmed white Britons and Americans as the lost tribes of Israel, and which was at its height in the 1930s. John Wilson (d. 1870) should probably be regarded as its founder, although precursors of the white supremacist thesis can be found as early as 1649, when John Sadler (b. 1615) wrote his *Rights to the Kingdom.* In 1840 Wilson gave a series of lectures entitled "Our Israelitish Origin," which were published under the same title a decade later. M. M. Eshelman published similar opinions in *The Gospel Messenger* in 1886, and his book *Two Sticks* (1887) was influential. In 1902 J. H. Allen published *Judah's Sceptre and Joseph's Birthright,* which gave added momentum to the theory. In Great Britain similar ideas were popularized in a pamphlet entitled "Britain's Place in Prophecy" and M. H. Gayer's *The Heritage of the Anglo-Saxon Race.* The Anglo-Israel Association was founded in London in 1875, and the British Israel World Federation in 1919.

Born from an Adventist background, British Israelite ideas are based on belief in the inerrancy of Scripture, often coupled with sabbatarianism, non-trinitarianism, dispensationalism, and "Sacred Name" (q.v) themes (the use of "Yahweh" and "Yahshua" for God and Jesus). Principally, however, the distinctive ideas of British Israelism are based on three tenets: that God's promise to Abraham that he would father a great nation (Genesis 17:3-8) has a literal and physical fulfillment; that the 10 lost tribes continued to exist unseparated as a nation under Davidic dynastic rule (2 Kings 17:6, 18:11); and that Britain and America are the great nations descended from the lost tribes and constitute the "New Israel." According to many British Israelites, they are the tribes of Ephraim and Manasseh (Joseph's two sons) and thus are especially blessed (Genesis 48). British Israel teaching contends that the lost tribes reemerged as the Scythians, the Cimerians, and the Goths and that the tribes invaded England as the Angles, Saxons, Jutes, and Normans. The British Israel movement has been much criticized for its racism being anti-Semitic and antiblack. Its ideas live on in the Identity Movement (q.v.). *See also* ARMSTRONG, HERBERT W.; CHURCH OF GOD INTERNATIONAL; NATIONAL ASSOCIATION OF KINGDOM EVANGELICALS.

BROTHERHOOD OF THE CROSS AND STAR. Founded in Nigeria in 1958 by Olumba Olumba Obu (q.v.) (b. 1918), Brotherhood of the Cross and Star is a predominantly black movement whose leader's teachings are held to be confirmed by the Christian Bible, which is its basic religious text. Brotherhood teaches that the Holy Spirit has now come and that humankind is in the Age of the Spirit. Principal themes are repentance, forgiveness, honest living, and healing: members are admitted by baptism after confession of sins. There are two types of members: "sitting members," who remain at home, and those who give "public witness," the three outward marks of which are wearing a white soutane (robe), walking barefoot, and praying on one's knees after knocking one's head three times. The white soutane alludes to Revelation 7:13: "these which are arrayed in white robes" (KJV); and the barefootedness recalls the incident when Moses was asked to take off his shoes at the burning bush (Exodus 3:5), adding the belief that all the earth is sacred.

Worship tends to be exuberant, with emphasis on singing, dancing and extempore prayer; choirs are an important feature of Brotherhood. Feasting and fasting also play an important role: Obu recommends a vegan diet, although this is not obligatory. Modern processed food is disapproved of, and meat is blamed for much of the illness and aggression within society. Weekly fasts are observed, on Thursdays from 6 a.m. until 6 p.m., as well as "Pentecostals," which involve a total of four weeks of "six to six" fasting. "Dry fasting" (abstinence from drink as well as food), lasting three consecutive days, is also practiced. Although "grounded in Christianity," the movement respects other religions and draws on them: Obu teaches reincarnation, although claiming that it is also implied in Christian Scripture. The movement has some two million members, who worship in "bethels" (meetinghouses).

BRUDERHOF. *A.k.a.: Hutterian Brethren; Hutterian Society of Brothers.* An Anabaptist movement in the Hutterite tradition, founded by Eberhard Arnold (1883-1935) and his wife Emmy. A theologian, writer, and lecturer, Arnold read about the Hutterites and discovered that they were still in existence. In 1931 he visited every Hutterite colony in the United States and Canada and returned to his native Germany to found his own community *(hof).*

The Bruderhof seeks to revive the community living of early Christianity, with possessions shared in common without private property, and aims at bringing about a new social order based on love, freedom, and truth. Although individuals can be welcomed into membership, emphasis is given to the family and to traditional family values. The Bruderhof members engage in community service and finance themselves through small businesses: Community Playthings, Rifton Equipment for the Handicapped, and a publications wing (Plough Publishing House), which disseminates their journal, *The Plough.* Worship is offered most evenings and is known as a *gemeindestunde* (brotherhood hour), consisting of a talk, silent prayer, and "waiting in the Spirit."

The movement suffered persecution from the Nazis from 1937, and the Bruderhof emigrated to Paraguay in 1940 and 1941. From there, some were able to travel north, establishing a U.S. *hof* in 1954. The community finally left Paraguay in 1961, emigrating to the United States. In the 1960s there was a drive to return to the Bruderhof's original German roots, and a significant number of members left. There are presently six communities in the United States and two in England, the first of which was set up in 1971. Current membership is 2,500.

BRUNTON, PAUL (1898-1981). Born as Raphael Hurst, Brunton was one of the Western pioneers who traveled in India, met numerous gurus (q.v.), and disseminated their teachings in the West. His *Search in Secret India* (1935) was the first of many writings, in which he tells of encounters with Meher Baba and Ramana (qq.v.), among others. Brunton became a Western teacher in his own right, combining Indian philosophy with Western esotericism. His book *The Secret Path: A Technique of Self-Discovery* contained a foreword by Alice Bailey (q.v.). Brunton's own teachings were written in note form as "seed thoughts" during his lifetime, and published posthumously as *The Notebooks of Paul Brunton* (16 volumes). The Paul Brunton Foundation continues to disseminate his teaching.

BUCHMAN, FRANK NATHAN DANIEL (1878-1961). Founder-leader of Moral Re-Armament (MRA) (q.v.). Of German-Swiss extraction, Buchman was born in Pennsburg, Pennsylvania, and trained for the ministry of the Lutheran Church. Following a dispute in his first congregation, he departed to England, where in 1908 he had a decisive spiritual experience in a Keswick chapel. In 1921 Buchman established the First Century Christian Fellowship, supported by Oxford and Cambridge students. This became known as the Oxford Group Movement—a name given by journalists when the group visited South Africa in 1929.

In 1938 Buchman issued his "moral rearmament" program, thus initiating the name by which the movement came to be known. Buchman's program emphasized the need for moral reform as a means of obtaining reconciliation with God. He traveled widely, visiting Europe, India, Ceylon, and Japan, disseminating his teachings. The movement has been accused of pro-Nazism, largely on account of a statement attributed to Buchman: "I thank God for a man like Hitler who has built a front-line defense against the anti-Christ of communism." Characterization of the movement as fascist, however, was largely the result of a smear campaign by journalist Tom Driberg, who was later discovered to be a KGB agent; but it is certainly true that MRA is fiercely anticommunist. In the postwar years, Buchman did much to achieve healing and reconciliation between Germans and British, bringing together those who had been on opposing sides during the conflict. The movement continued after Buchman's death, although without the formal appointment of a successor. Several MRA offices remain in the United States; it is not a membership organization.

BUDAPEST, ZSUZSANNA EMESE. Feminist wiccan leader. Budapest developed her coven in the Dianic wicca (q.v.) tradition in 1971 to provide a "matriarchal spiritual center." A lesbian separatist, Budapest is renowned for her use of the terms *womon* and *wimmin* in place of *woman* and *women*, the latter pair of words being allegedly derivative from *man* and *men*. Her coven was derived from the Susan B. Anthony Coven No. 1 in Venice, California. Budapest authored *The Holy Book of Women's Mysteries* (1990), which sets out the beliefs and rituals of her version of feminist wicca (q.v.).

BUDDHISM. Buddhism arose in North India in the sixth century B.C.E., as a result of the teaching of Siddhartha Gautama (also known as Shakyamuni). Of the two major traditions that arose—Theravada and Mahayana—it is principally the Mahayana schools that have given rise to new religious movements, although the modern revival of Vipassana (q.v.) is Theravadin. The Theravada tradition is the more conservative, claiming to be nearer to the teachings of the historical Buddha. By contrast, the Mahayana schools claim that the Buddha's teachings were provisional and that he used "skillful means" *(upaya),* imparting to human beings only the instruction for which they were ready at that time and place. This doctrine has facilitated the kinds of innovation that are characteristic of many Buddhist NRMs.

There are four main Mahayana schools: Pure Land, Tibetan, Nichiren (q.v.), and Zen (q.v.). The four schools are often categorized respectively as devotional, symbolic-ritual, pragmatic, and meditative. While all have existed for many centuries, a number of movements that have drawn on their teachings have caused questions to be raised about their authenticity. Although the New Kadampa Tradition (q.v.) is Tibetan in origin, its current dispute with the Dalai Lama, together with its deliberate Western adaptations, have caused many Buddhists to regard it as outside the mainstream. Modern Nichiren groups are pragmatic and appear to emphasize fulfilling one's desires rather than eliminating desire: they include the Soka Gakkai (q.v.), Nichiren Shu, and Reiyukai (q.v.). While many Zen groups in the West endeavor to follow the traditional meditative practices, Zen underwent a major transformation in the 1960s—principally in the United

States—when it was taken up by the beatniks and hippies in a form that came to be known as "Beat Zen."

Some groups, such as Osho (q.v.), draw liberally on the Buddhist tradition (Zen, in the case of Osho), while not overtly claiming a Buddhist identity. Other groups, such as the Western Buddhist Order (q.v.), wish to be regarded as Buddhist, but are attempting to develop a new kind of Buddhism specially aimed at Western seekers. *See also* ASAHARA, SHOKO; WON BUDDHISM.

BUGBROOKE JESUS FELLOWSHIP. The Jesus Fellowship Church (q.v.) was originally a Baptist congregation in Bugbrooke, near Northampton, England, founded in 1805. Following its serious decline during the 1950s, Noel Stanton was appointed as pastor in 1957. Influenced by the charismatic movement of the 1960s, some members received the "baptism of the Spirit" at a Saturday prayer meeting in 1968. In the early 1970s the congregation began to attract some of the youth counterculture: bikers, drug addicts, and early New Agers (q.v.). Following the resignation of about half of the older members, the youth culture came to predominate. The Jesus Army (q.v.), organized by Stanton in 1987, became the organization's campaigning wing. *See also* CHARISMATIC MOVEMENT; PENTECOSTALISM.

BUILDERS OF THE ADYTUM (BOTA). An occultist-magical organization, founded by Dr. Paul Foster Case (1884-1954). Case joined the Hermetic Order of the Golden Dawn (q.v.) in Chicago and founded his own school in the 1920s, based on spirit messages from "Master R," commonly identified with the Comte de Saint-Germain. Case was apparently entrusted with the task of reinterpreting the Ageless Wisdom for the West. He is regarded as a world authority on the Tarot and Kabbalah (q.v.), and BOTA specializes in Tarot, Kabbalah, and alchemy. Much of its work is done by correspondence, using the writings of Case, his successor Dr. Anne Davis (d. 1975), and also Dion Fortune's (q.v.) *The Mystical*

Qabala. The organization has an outer school and an inner mystery school for higher initiates.

BOTA aims at mastery of the self and its attainment of "awakening," "illumination," or recognition of the God within. Allied to this is the "promotion of the welfare of humanity," which has seven aspects: universal peace, political freedom, religious freedom, education, health, prosperity, and "spiritual unfoldment." BOTA has an international following, with branches in the United States, Canada, Central and South America, the Caribbean, New Zealand, and Europe.

-C-

CALVARY CHAPEL. Originally a congregation of around 25 members in Costa Mesa, California, the Calvary Chapel gained momentum after Chuck Smith assumed leadership in 1965. Smith coordinated an outreach to hippies, making the Chapel the hub of the Jesus Movement (q.v.) of the early 1970s. As the organization's fame spread, 600 other chapels were established, some with as many as 6,000 members. The Calvary Chapel seeks to be nondenominational, affirming *agape* (love) as its basis. Its teaching is Bible-based, importance being attached to verse-by-verse analysis. The gifts of the Holy Spirit are emphasized, particularly the fulfillment of prophecy in recent times; however, members do not regard speaking in tongues (q.v.) as a sign of baptism in the Spirit. The Calvary Chapel of Costa Mesa claims a membership in excess of 20,000, and around 35,000 people in the surrounding area claim it as their home church. The Word for Today is the movement's method of outreach through literature and tape distribution. (The Calvary Chapel is not to be identified with the Calvary Pentecostal Church, founded in 1931, and now defunct.) *See also* SHILOH.

CANDOMBLÉ. An African diaspora religion, practiced in Brazil, combining elements of Christianity and African—principally Yoruba—religion and gaining recognition in the 19th century. The first center was established in Salvador in 1830. Of all the African diaspora religions of Brazil, Candomblé retains the most African elements. It pervades Bahia state and is variously known as Shango (in Pernambuco), Macumba (q.v.) (in Rio de Janeiro), Tambor de Mina (in Maranhao), and Catimbó or Batuque (in central Brazil). Candomblé cosmology consists of a belief in *orishas* (gods) and especially spirits, who are capable of inflicting misfortune on their victims and hence must be placated. Mediums are predominantly female: originally mistresses of white Portuguese settlers, they became known as "Mothers of the Saints" *(Mãis de santo),* and their subsequent generation are called "Daughters of the Saints." They mediate between the earthly world and the world of spirits, by becoming possessed by one of the orishas, and are capable of offering spiritual healing. *See also* UMBANDA; WINTI.

CAO DAI. *A.k.a.: Dai Dao Tam Ky Pho Do ("The Third Great Universal Religious Amnesty").* A Vietnamese spiritist (q.v.) organization, founded in 1921 by Ngo Van Chieu. The founder claims to have received messages from Duc Cao Dai ("Venerable High Tower or Palace," synonymous with God), who subsequently identified himself to Caodaist mediums. Caodaism teaches that in the previous two "amnesties" or "alliances," God spoke through prophets, such as Confucius, the Buddha, the prophets of Judaism, Jesus, and Muhammad, but that God now speaks directly to humanity. Caodaists have séances in the Great Divine Temple (a place of pilgrimage some 90 kilometers north of Ho Chi Minh City) or use devices such as corbeille-à-bec or ouija boards to make contact with the world of spirits. Cao Dai draws on ideas from Taoism and Asian divination and shows signs of influence from H. P. Blavatsky (q.v.), Alan Kardec, Victor Hugo, and Ralph Waldo Emerson (q.v.).

Cao Dai's theology is expressed in its institutional structure, which acknowledges three "powers": Bat-Quai-Dai—the heavenly council—which is directed by Duc Cao Dai; Hiep-

Thieu-Dai—the medium's legislative branch—directed by Ho-Phap ("protector of the laws and of justice"); and Cuu-Trung-Dai—the executive body—headed by Gia-Tong (the Caodaist "pope"). Caodaists undertake to live by five "interdictions," similar to Buddhism's (q.v.) five lay precepts: to avoid killing; not to be dishonest; to avoid adultery; not to overindulge (especially regarding alcohol); and to abstain from falsehood. It is world-affirming, emphasizing duties to oneself, one's family, one's society, and humanity, although it teaches that attachment to the material world should be renounced. Membership estimates vary between six and eight million in Vietnam, where it is the third largest religion after Buddhism and Roman Catholicism. It is also represented in the United States, Europe, and Australia. In Salvador, Brazil, there are said to be 1,000 temples. There are also several Caodaist splinter groups. *See also* SHAMANISM.

CARGO CULTS. Syncretistic millenarian groups, primarily in Melanesia, spanning Fiji to Irian Jaya. They have arisen in the last hundred years in the wake of encounter between Pacific primal religions and European and American colonial culture. Having seen the material wealth brought by Westerners, which is seen as a sign of divine approval, cargo cults expect a future visitation, by air or sea, which will be accompanied by the provision of material goods and wealth. The belief in material cargo is only one aspect of cargo cults, however: expectations can include "spiritual cargo," and their millennialism (q.v.) includes a belief in the return of ancestors or of cultural heroes, and a new age in which equality with white people will be attained. Preparation for this final state includes moral renewal and the building of wharves, airstrips, and storehouses, as well as rituals.

Cargo cults include the Jon Frum movement (q.v.), Manseren cults, Vailala Madness (q.v.), Paliau, Yali, and the Peli and Pitenamu Societies. Their reported following is 72,000 in Papua New Guinea (1991), 15,730 in Vanunatu (1991), and 9,240 in the Solomon Islands (1998).

CARP (Collegiate Association for the Research of Principles). Founded in Korea by Sun Myung Moon (q.v.) in 1955, CARP is a Unification Church (q.v.) organization for younger members, principally those at university or college. CARP facilitates the study of *Divine Principle* (q.v.) and seeks to promote "spiritual renewal, new moral commitment, and positive solutions to global injustice." It has organized public rallies on matters such as drugs and pornography in the United States and in Europe.

CASTANEDA, CARLOS (b. 1931). A South American anthropologist, whose writings on Don Juan Mathus (b. 1891) became best-sellers in the 1970s and did much to arouse public interest in Native American religion (q.v.) and shamanism (q.v.). Born Carlos Aranha, he changed his name to Castaneda on obtaining U.S. citizenship in 1959.

Castaneda studied anthropology at the University of California, Los Angeles, obtaining a Ph.D. for what he subsequently published as *Journey to Ixtlan.* His first book, *The Teachings of Don Juan,* purported to be an account of his meeting Don Juan, a Yaqui sorcerer or *brujo* (one who heals by magical powers), and how he was taken on as Don Juan's student to learn shamanic practices. Castaneda describes his experiments with hallucinogenic substances, principally peyote *(mescalito),* datura, and psilocybe mushrooms and how in time he came to meet the god Mescalito himself. The popularity of Castaneda's work was assisted by the interest in hallucinogens that existed among a youth subculture.

According to Castaneda, the ordinary person and the sorcerer inhabit two different realities, the former being rational, based on sense perception and conventionally "real," while the latter transcends conventional reality, is nonrational and is "magically real." Although the authenticity of Castaneda's work has been questioned, Castaneda remains one of the pioneers of the renewed interest in shamanism and Native American spirituality.

CAUSA. A Unification Church (q.v.) organization, political in character, aimed at ideological opposition to communism. The acronym originally signified "Confederation of Associations for the Unity of the Societies of the Americas" when the organization operated primarily in Latin America in its early years. On becoming a worldwide organization, the name was explained as meaning simply "cause." Membership is open to all, not merely to Unificationists.

The *CAUSA Lecture Manual* (1985) proclaims "Godism" as an ideology superior to communism. This consists of selected ideas from *Divine Principle* (q.v.), principally those relating to God and the human predicament, but omitting the distinctively Unificationist soteriological elements.

In the 1980s CAUSA was accused of funding *contras* (right-wing guerrilla fighters) in Nicaragua, but CAUSA has consistently insisted that its anticommunist stance merely consists of propagating anticommunist ideas.

CAYCE, EDGAR (1877-1945). Psychic, healer, and author. Edgar Cayce was known as the "sleeping prophet" on account of his ability to make psychical pronouncements in a state of trance. Born in Hopkinsville, Kentucky, Cayce was brought up as a Christian and never abandoned his Christianity, which predominated his teachings and "readings." From an early age he experienced visions. As a young man in 1898 he lost his voice and tried various remedies unsuccessfully until he underwent hypnotism and apparently was able to prescribe his own cure. From 1901 onward he was able to give readings for consultees, many of which entailed remarkable medical diagnoses: the remedies he recommended were generally orthodox, although Cayce was one of the early proponents of holistic healing. By 1910 Cayce's fame had spread throughout the United States.

In 1911 Cayce began to speak of karma as a possible cause of illness, and from 1923 onward undertook "life readings" which enabled his clients to discover their past lives, a significant number of which related to Lemuria and Atlantis. Cayce is also known for his predictions for humankind. He is said to have predicted the 1929 Wall Street crash 10 months before it happened. Other predictions were of cataclysmic events destined to happen at the end of the 20th century: the earth's magnetic poles would become reversed in 1998, and New York and Japan would be submerged by tidal waves. Few would survive, but those who did could expect an improved quality of life. Christ would return in the year 2000 to herald in an era of peace. Cayce further predicted that Lemuria and Atlantis would rise from the ocean in 1968 or 1969. He also claimed to identify his own past lives, some of which extended back to the age of Lemuria and Atlantis, and he predicted his own rebirth in Nebraska in 2100.

Cayce gave over 30,000 readings during his lifetime, 70 percent of which were medical, the remaining 30 percent religious or metaphysical. Unusually, Cayce made recordings and transcriptions of many of these readings, and more than 14,000 stenographic records, for some 8,000 people, are owned by the Edgar C. Cayce Foundation, based at Virginia Beach, Virginia, where the headquarters of the Association for Research and Enlightenment (ARE) (q.v.), founded by Cayce in 1931, are located. *See also* AKASHIC RECORDS; BREATHARIANS.

CELESTIAL CHURCH OF CHRIST. An African Independent Church (q.v.), founded in Lagos, Nigeria, by Samuel Bilewu Oshoffa (b. 1906) in 1958. Oshoffa had a mystical experience during a solar eclipse in 1947, as a result of which he acquired miraculous healing powers, followed by a commission to preach. Prophecy and healing are dominant interests, but the church is not Pentecostal (q.v.) and members do not speak in tongues (q.v.). Alcohol and tobacco are prohibited, as is pork. In accordance with the laws of Leviticus, impurity rituals are also prescribed for women.

CENTERS NETWORK. Founded by Werner Erhard, the Centers Network coordinates and organizes Erhard's various interests. It is responsible for the activities of the Forum (formerly *est*), including the various Communication courses and other seminars available to those who have successfully completed the Forum. *See also* ERHARD SEMINAR TRAINING.

CERULLO, MORRIS (b. 1931). Evangelist and alleged healer. A Jew by birth, Cerullo converted to Christianity at the age of 14 and trained as a preacher at Metropolitan Bible Institute, New York. After a wheelchair user reported a miraculous cure at one of Cerullo's rallies, audiences escalated in size. Cerullo began his overseas missions in 1955, visiting more than 70 countries, particularly in the Third World. The year 1961 saw the founding of Morris Cerullo World Evangelism (MCWE), now a worldwide organization.

Cerullo has proved particularly controversial on a number of grounds. He has particularly targeted Israel for evangelism, setting up Operation Israel and mailing copies of MCWE materials to hundreds of thousands of Israeli households. In 1970 he set up an Israel Bible Correspondence Course and in 1971 began radio broadcasting to Israel from Cyprus. Cerullo's "miracles" have proved equally controversial: although MCWE publicity material has claimed that the blind have had their sight restored and that wheelchair users have been rendered able to walk again, no alleged cure has been medically substantiated. In Great Britain in 1992 the Advertising Standards Authority required such publicity to be withdrawn, and several Christian evangelical journals refused to accept MCWE advertising. Cerullo's aggressive and demanding fundraising tactics have also attracted criticism. In 1967 Cerullo was arrested and imprisoned in Argentina, accused of practicing medicine without a license, and in 1981 he and several MCWE leaders were refused entry to Nicaragua. Although theologically orthodox, the organization's activities have caused it to be marginalized even by many evangelical Christians. *See also* PROSPERITY THEOLOGY.

CHAITANYA (c. 1485-1533). Depicted in Hindu (q.v.) iconography as yellow (in contrast with Krishna, for example, who is typically blue), the Indian scholar-saint Chaitanya is known as "the golden avatar" and is particularly popular in Bengal. He is especially venerated within ISKCON (q.v.), since he is believed to be the avatar ("descent") jointly of Krishna and Radha. Chaitanya has been described as a "Krishna-intoxicated ecstatic," engaging in dancing and singing in honor of Krishna, whom he regarded as the supreme form of deity. In particular, Chaitanya is accredited with the propagation of the "maha mantra," central to ISKCON's devotional practice: "Hare Krishna; Hare Krishna; Krishna Krishna; Hare Hare; Hare Rama; Hare Rama; Rama Rama; Hare Hare."

Chaitanya taught vegetarianism and the renunciation of caste, both of which were later to become features of the Gaudiya Math (q.v.) movement that profoundly influenced Swami Prabhupada (q.v.) and hence ISKCON. Chaitanya visited the holy city of Vrindaban in 1515: his followers claim that he restored it as a place of pilgrimage, although many Western scholars believe that Vrindaban only became a pilgrimage city after Chaitanya's work there. Among Chaitanya's followers were six especially intimate disciples who became known as the "six goswamis," five of whom wrote commentaries on the Vedas and the Puranas.

CHAKRAS. An occult system of anatomy, originating in the East and popular especially in New Age (q.v.) thought. The chakras are points on the body, by means of which universal prajnic energy is believed to transfer itself to the physical body's energy system. The system is accepted within Hinduism and Buddhism (qq.v.) and is also traditionally associated with the Kabbalistic (q.v.) Tree of Life. There are variously said to be five, six, or seven chakras. Seven usually feature in the Hindu system; the Ayurveda identifies the following seven, together with 21 minor chakras: the base of the spine *(muladhara),* the sacral *(svadhishthana*—the genitals), the solar plexus *(manipurna*—associated with one's emotions), the heart or chest *(anahata)*, the throat *(visuddha)*, the forehead *(ajna*—the "third eye"), and the crown chakra *(sahasrara*—commonly identified with the pineal gland). The five chakras acknowledged in the Tree of Life are the soles of the feet *(malkuth)*, the genitals *(yesod)*, the heart *(tiphareth)*, the throat *(daath)*, and the crown *(kether)*.

It is claimed that the chakras can be used diagnostically: chakras can be overactive or insufficiently active, with corresponding consequences to one's health, and the chakras can be used in a preventative as well as a curative way, since imbalances can sometimes herald an illness years before its physical symptoms appear. Since chakras have their distinct associated colors, sounds, and vibrations, their state has traditionally been determined clairvoyantly, for example by recognizing the auras that they exude. Within New Age thinking, the state of one's chakras can supposedly be determined by New Age therapeutic aids, such as pendulum dowsing, color therapy, and crystal healing. Chakras can also be associated with spiritual development, not merely physical, mental, and emotional health: the practice of kundalini yoga (q.v.) offers one such method of using the chakras to progress toward enlightenment.

CHANNELING. A more recent version of Spiritualism (q.v.), in which contact is made with the dead or with higher spiritual beings. Channeling gained momentum in the 1970s and 1980s as part of the New Age Movement (q.v.), and it differs in several ways from older Spiritualism. While much Spiritualism is Christian, channeling tends to be independent of Christianity, drawing on ideas outside the Christian tradition. Unlike a Spiritualist Church, channeling sessions lack any formal order of worship. Reincarnation (q.v.) is a commonly held belief, supporters typically holding that the soul evolves through a metaphysical hierarchy of states of being. Not infrequently channeling draws ideas from a variety of religious traditions, including Kabbalism (q.v.), shamanism (q.v.), and neo-Gnosticism.

Unlike older Spiritualism, where the medium typically contacts a variety of spirits whose communication is unpredictable, channelers are inclined to have one-to-one relationships with particular spirits. Alice Bailey (q.v.) (1880-1949), for example, one of the precursors of the movement, claimed to channel Master Djwahl Khul.

Channeling occurs through altered states of consciousness: trance, deep meditative states, out-of-the-body experiences, or even sleep. Messages can be relayed through speech or through writing, and a number of books have supposedly been written either by automatic writing or through the dictation of spirits. One well-known example is *A Course in Miracles* (q.v.), transcribed by Helen Schucman, which became popular in the 1980s. Other celebrated channeled writings include Levi H. Dowling's (q.v.) *Aquarian Gospel of Jesus the Christ, Oahspe* (q.v.), and *The Urantia Book* (q.v.). Other channels who have secured international recognition are Edgar Cayce (1877-1945), Jane Roberts (channeler of Seth), J. Z. Knight (channeler of Ramtha), and Jach Pursel (Lazaris) (qq.v.). Advocates of channeling have pointed out that many classical religious figures have in effect been channels, mediating a message from the eternal world to humanity: these might include Moses, Zoroaster, and Muhammad, as well as shamans, medicine men, witches, soothsayers, and other seers. *See also* BREATHARIANS; HUMAN POTENTIAL MOVEMENT.

CHARISMATIC LEADERSHIP. NRMs are frequently characterized, particularly by the anticult movement (q.v.), as having charismatic leaders who exert authoritarian control over members' lives. A charismatic leader is one who appears to be set apart from others by his or her appearance, manner of speech, self-confidence, or even apparently superhuman qualities such as prescience or presumed knowledge of esoteric secrets. While it is true that NRMs frequently emanate from individuals who attract followers by virtue of their personality rather than any institutional authority, the immediate power of the leader tends to diminish as a movement grows in size: the Unification Church (q.v.), for example, now assumes such a large scale that the vast majority of its members have not personally met founder-leader Sun Myung Moon (q.v.). As Max Weber pointed out, charismatic leadership tends to become "routinized" and institutionalized through time, with authority coming to derive more from the formal organizational structure that has developed, rather than any personal magnetism accruing to the leader. Problems of succession, after a founder-leader's death, also raise issues about the true source of authority within an organization.

CHARISMATIC MOVEMENT. A movement which spread across Protestant and Roman Catholic churches in the 1960s. The charismatics laid great emphasis on the power of the Holy Spirit, which was manifested in greater exuberance in worship and freedom from the confines of prescribed liturgy. Considerable importance was attached to the gifts of the Spirit mentioned in 1 Corinthians 12:4-11, particularly their manifestations in healing and in glossolaliation. Although essentially a phenomenon within mainstream Christianity, the Charismatic Movement had considerable influence on the more fundamentalist (q.v.) -inclined NRMs, such as the Jesus Army (q.v.). The movement gained renewed momentum with the Toronto Blessing (q.v.) of 1994, although the latter proved to be more controversial within mainstream Christian circles.

CHEN TAO. *A.k.a.: God's Salvation Church; God Saves the Earth Flying Saucer Foundation.* Founded in 1997 by Hon-Ming Chen (b. 1958?), Chen Tao (literally "True Way") originated in Taiwan and is a synthesis of Buddhism, Christianity (qq.v.), and Taiwanese folk religion. Chen aims "to establish the U.S.A. as the Holy Medical Land of God's Super-Hi Technology," particularly focusing on cancer and AIDS. Claiming that illness is the result of past karma and that bacteria and viruses are souls within the cycle of samsara, Chen seeks to liberate them from their host bodies, thus effecting cures. This can supposedly happen through prayer and ritual. Chen also claims the ability to open the Book of Life and Death, which is a record of all karmic influences on living beings, as well as a variety of psychic services such as exorcism and geomancy.

Chen Tao gained media attention on account of Chen's apocalyptic prophecies: a series of calamities would occur in the East, with millions of refugees seeking asylum in the West, and God would personally appear on television on 25 March 1998, accompanied by miraculous signs. Other less falsifiable claims include the establishment of the Medical Research Center of God's Super Hi-Tech Salvation in Central Park, New York City—a center that is in the "fifth dimension" and only visible by the spiritually enlightened.

Chen has written two self-published books, *The Practical Evidence and Study of the World of God and Buddha* (1996) and *God's Descending in Clouds (Flying Saucers) on Earth to Save People* (1997).

CHERUBIM AND SERAPHIM (SACRED CHERUBIM AND SERAPHIM SOCIETY). Part of the Aladura (q.v.) movement, established in 1925 by the Yoruba prophet Moses Tunolashe (1885?-1933). Tunolashe received a vision to found a society called "seraf," to which a later vision added "Kerub." Together with Victoianah Abiodum Akinsowon ("Captain Abiodum"), who belonged to the Anglican Church but finally broke her connection in 1928, they founded the society. The organization is supported by Christians, Muslims, and followers of African primal religions, and it seeks to find an expression of Christianity (q.v.) that is amenable to black Africans. While retaining significant Anglican elements and accepting the authority of Scripture, the Cherubim and Seraphim believe in exuberant worship, including glossolaliation, prophecy, and prayer-healing, and pay high regard to visions and dreams. Alcohol and pork are disallowed. The organization is manifested by its white-robed processions to holy hills—a practice which originates from indigenous African geomancy. There are roughly 2,000 congregations in Africa.

CHINMOY, SRI (b. 1931). After various childhood religious experiences, Sri Chinmoy Kumar Ghose is said to have attained Nirvikalpa Samadhi—a profound state of enlightenment—at the age of 12 and entered the Aurobindo (q.v.) ashram. There he composed many poems, essays, and devotional songs and engaged in extensive meditation. In 1964 he obeyed an inner command to go to the West. He settled in the United States, where he conducted weekly meditations from 1970 onward at the United Nations Church Center in New York. He became the first director of the U.N. Meditation Group.

Sri Chinmoy's meditations are nonsectarian and open to anyone, irrespective of religious affiliation; Sri Chinmoy himself expresses a high regard equally for Krishna, the Buddha, and Jesus Christ. Followers are expected to commit themselves to daily meditation lasting 15 minutes every morning and evening. The final aim is union with God, which is achieved through the "path of the heart," involving "love, devotion, and surrender." In common with many Hindu teachers, Sri Chinmoy regards God as infinite consciousness, and the human soul as the spark of the eternal. Separation from the world is not encouraged, since God is said to work through the human body. Followers, however, are expected to be vegetarian and to avoid tobacco, alcohol, and recreational drugs; physical cleanliness is encouraged, and celibacy is recommended. Sri Chinmoy commends athletics as a means of perfecting one's body, and from 1987 onward the Sri Chinmoy Oneness-Home Peace Run has been held every two years.

Since 1970 Sri Chinmoy has held public meetings worldwide. A prolific writer, he has composed some 13,000 devotional songs, over 1,300 books of poetry, and four million "mystical paintings," in which the human soul is typically portrayed as a bird. In 1998 the movement reported 5,000 followers worldwide and 200 centers.

CH'ONDOGYO. A Korean religion, derived from the Tonghak political movement, founded by Ch'oe Che-u (1824-1864). An activist reformist movement, the Tonghak was founded in 1860 as a result of a vision Ch'oe Che-u received during a shamanic (q.v.) trance. *Tonghak* means "Eastern learning," and the movement harmonized ideas from Confucianism, Buddhism (q.v.), and Taoism, in contrast to the Western learning of Roman Catholic missionaries. The Tonghak made their mark on Korean history through the Tonghak Rebellion of 1892, which was quashed by government forces. In 1905 Song Pyong-hi (1860-1922), the third of three Tonghak leaders (the second was Chou Pong-jun), changed the organization's name to Ch'ondogyo, meaning "The Religion (or Society) of the Heavenly Way."

The Ch'ondogyo teaches the oneness of God and humanity, God being innate human potential or ultimate energy, rather than a personal being distinct from humankind. This teaching entails a divinization of human beings, thus demanding respect and equality. Although nationalist and empirically oriented, Ch'ondogyo incorporates ritual elements, including a regular Sunday service consisting of hymns, prayers, and a sermon. Five "rules of practice" are binding on members: prayer *(shimgo)*, which is internalized rather than spoken, since God is within oneself; pure water, to be present for family services and public worship; a day for a public service (Sunday); a 21-character incantation, invoking Heaven within the individual; and "sincerity rice": a spoonful of rice is put aside by each member and sold at religious gatherings to raise funds (bringing money is now an acceptable alternative).

Although relatively unknown in the West, Ch'ondogyo reported three million followers in North Korea (1999) and 50,000 in the South (1996). *See also* SHINCH'ON-GYO.

CHRISTADELPHIANS. Originally known as the Thomasites after their founder-leader John Thomas (q.v.) (1805-1871), the name—adopted in 1848—literally means "brothers of Christ" and is a term that they prefer to "Christian," since they hold that the Christian Church is apostate. Christadelphians claim to revive the beliefs and practices of the early Church, and they regard the Bible as the sole source of authority—not the classical creeds, which they view as unscriptural. Members use a *Bible Companion*, which is a reading plan, taking them through the Old Testament once a year and the New Testament twice. Non-Trinitarian, they find no basis in Scripture for the Trinity doctrine and view Jesus Christ as the Son of God, not God the Son; the Holy Spirit is equated with God's power and influence. They are also non-Unitarian, affirming Jesus as God's only begotten Son, who atoned for human sin, not merely as a great teacher and example. Christadelphians avoid participation in political activities, not seeking civic office and declining to vote; they do not participate in armed conflict. Traditional in their values, they extol marital fidelity and family life, disapproving of homosexuality. Satan is regarded as a personification of humanity's evil tendencies, rather than as a supernatural being.

The organization is millennialist (q.v.) and from its inception has expected Christ's imminent return, first predicting that it would happen in 1868, and subsequently 1910. Although they no longer set exact dates, they believe that Christ will return visibly, beginning in Jerusalem, and that his second advent will herald the final judgment. The unredeemed are expected to experience not punishment, but mere nonexistence.

The Christadelphians are a lay movement, congregational in government, and each *ecclesia* (congregation) is led by "presiding brethren" and "managing brethren." Admission is by baptism (total immersion), but this is only administered after the candidate has demonstrated understanding of the faith. Communion is celebrated, but is closed to nonmembers. The organization does not publish membership statistics, but there are possibly 50,000 members worldwide. *See also* UNAMENDED CHRISTADELPHIANS.

CHRIST APOSTOLIC CHURCH. One of the Aladura (q.v.) churches, emerging from the Faith Tabernacle (2, q.v.) movement at Ijebu-Ode in Nigeria in 1918, when the influenza epidemic there caused several African Christians to lay emphasis on prayer for healing. The founder, Joseph Shadare ("Daddy Ali"), experienced a dream, as a result of which he founded a prayer group, which subsequently expanded. The church gained further impetus in the 1930s as a result of the preaching of Joseph Babalola (1904-1960), assisted by Pentecostal (q.v.) churches in the United States. The Christ Apostolic Church lays emphasis on prayer-healing, prophecy, and enthusiastic congregational participation, with due credence given to dreams and visions, and it seeks to create an indigenous African expression of Christianity. The church is theologically orthodox, and, unlike some African Independent Churches (q.v.), does not permit polygamy.

CHRISTIAN COMMUNITY CHURCH (CHRISTENGE-MEINSCHAFT). An organization formed in Dornach, Germany, in 1922 by Rudolf Steiner (q.v.) (1861-1925) and Friedrich Rittelmeyer (1872-1938). The church was formed to give ritual expression to the teachings of the Anthroposophical Society, with a priesthood and sacraments. Christian Community Churches are congregational in organization. The church made its initial appearance in the United States in 1928, when Wilhelm Hochweber celebrated the "Act of Consecration of Man," but a more permanent presence was not established until 1948, by Verner Hegg and Alfred Heidenreich. *See also* ANTHROPOSOPHY.

CHRISTIAN CONSERVATIVE CHURCHES OF AMERICA. A white supremacist organization, with headquarters in Louisville, Illinois. Originally founded in 1959 by John R. Harrell, it did not become operational until 1975, as a consequence of law enforcement problems brought on by the disappearance, arrest, and subsequent conviction of its founder-leader. Its declared aim was the preservation of whites, for whom a "golden triangle" was designated in the center of the continent, which Harrell's followers could appropriate and defend upon the U.S. government's imminent collapse. In common with other Christian Identity groups, the Christian Conservative Churches have identified the nations of Western Europe as the descendants of ancient Israel. However—unusually—they allow the possibility of spiritual ingrafting of others, upon acceptance of Christ. They do not accept a continuity between Davidic and British dynasties. A set of "Articles of Religion" outlines its key beliefs, which are consistent with Christian fundamentalism (q.v.). *See also* IDENTITY MOVEMENT.

CHRISTIAN IDENTITY CHURCH. Part of the Identity Movement (q.v.), the Christian Identity Church was founded in 1982 by Pastor Charles Jennings, who was much influenced by Wesley Swift. Its current pastor is Fred Demoret. In addition to white supremacist teachings, the church lays emphasis on "Sacred Name themes," using the words "Yahweh" (YHWH) and "Yahshua" for "God" and "Jesus," respectively. The church holds an annual "Family of God" reunion at Pentecost, which is attended by Christian Identity supporters more widely. *See also* SACRED NAME MOVEMENT.

CHRISTIANITY. There are three major strands in the Christian faith: Eastern Orthodoxy and Roman Catholicism, which separated in the Great Schism of 1045, and Protestantism, which arose from the Reformation in Europe from the 16th century onward. Of the three traditions, Protestantism has generated the largest number of new religious movements, no doubt because of its rejection of centralized authority, its principle of the "priesthood of all believers," and its emphasis on Scripture as the sole source of authority *(sola scriptura).*

In the wake of the Protestant Reformation, the Quakers (a.k.a. Society of Friends) and Unitarians emerged as radical developments, the former dispensing with liturgy, and the latter with creed. The Age of Enlightenment (late 18th and 19th centuries) steered much of mainstream Christianity in a rationalist direction, accommodating scientific innovation and pioneering the critical study of Scripture. Emanuel Swedenborg's (1688-1772) writings provoked a reaction against the Enlightenment's rationalism, emphasizing visionary experiences, and Swedenborg's ideas had an important bearing on the quite diverse movements of Spiritualism and Transcendentalism (qq.v.).

The authority of Scripture was much emphasized by the Adventist movement, pioneered by William Miller (1782-1849) and Ellen G. White (1827-1915) (qq.v.). Miller's end-time predictions were much criticized by his contemporary John Thomas (q.v.) (1805-1871), who founded the Christadelphians (q.v.), and was largely discredited by the 1844 "Great Disappointment." Miller's ideas nonetheless proved highly influential in the subsequent development of the Jehovah's Witnesses (q.v.).

Three important factors in 19th and early 20th centuries affected the development of NRMs: the Christian missionary heyday, the rise of fundamentalism (q.v.), and Pentecostalism (q.v.). Missionary activity brought interactions between Christianity and indigenous cultures, giving rise to movements such as the Unification Church and numerous African Independent Churches (qq.v.). Although fundamentalism continues to thrive within conventional Protestantism, organizations such as the Brethren and, more recently, the Family, and the International Churches of Christ (qq.v.), although doctrinally orthodox, remain outside the mainstream Christian fold. The Family emerged from the Jesus movement (q.v.), and was marginalized as a result of its sexual practices. Other NRMs emerging from Protestantism perceived a conflict between Scripture and traditional creeds and came to question traditional Christian doctrine: examples have been the Christadelphians, Jehovah's Witnesses, the Way International (q.v.), and the Worldwide Church of God (q.v.). Pentecostalist Churches appear to have chosen to remain outside national Councils of Churches, although they have sought to affiliate to mainstream Protestant evangelical organizations, such as the Evangelical Alliance in Great Britain. They continued to influence evangelical Christianity through the 1960s charismatic movement and the 1994 Toronto Blessing (qq.v.).

Roman Catholic-derived NRMs are mainly of two kinds: reformist groups which remain controversial within Catholicism, such as the Focalare, the Neo-Catechumenate, and Opus Dei (qq.v.); or those which have found reason to question papal authority, as in the case of the Sedevacantists (q.v.).

Eastern Orthodoxy lacks central organization, consisting of numerous autocephalous Orthodox Churches, arranged by country, for example, Greek, Bulgarian, Serbian, and Russian Orthodoxy. Some innovators in non-Orthodox countries have attempted to establish new forms of Orthodoxy in new countries and ethnic groups, for example, the English and Celtic Orthodox Churches.

Recent years have seen an interest in Jesus outside the Christian Church, for example the New Age (q.v.) perception of Jesus as a sage who visited India. Modern-day Essenes (q.v.) view Jesus as part of the Essene community, thus regarding the Essenes as part of early Christianity.

CHRISTIAN REFORMED CHURCH IN NORTH AMERICA. An organization that originated in the Netherlands as a result of the 1834 "succession," whose leaders Hendrick De-Cock, Henrik Scholte, and Albertus C. van Raalte opposed moves to bring churches under state control. After persecution they moved in 1847 to western Michigan and in 1848 founded Classis Holland with help from the Reformed Church of America. A schism occurred in 1857, led by Gysbert Haan; some individual churches followed him to form the Christian Reformed Church. Others formed the Dutch Reformed Church in 1859. The name "Christian Reformed Church in North America" was adopted in 1904. The church's teachings are based on the Belgic Confession, the Heidelberg Catechism, and the Conclusions of Utrecht, and it emphasizes the importance of using the catechism in preaching. In 1995 the number of members was 295,307.

CHRISTIAN SCIENCE. The system of thought "discovered" by Mary Baker Eddy (q.v.) (1821-1910) and propagated by the Church of Christ, Scientist. Eddy's principal writing, *Science and Health, with Key to the Scriptures* (1875), teaches the unreality of evil and illness and how healing can be achieved through the powers of the mind. Eddy's system is based on Scripture, and Christian Science worship is addressed directly to the one God, whose son Jesus is the "Way-shower" and exemplar of how self-cure can be effected. Healing is to be understood in the broadest sense and not merely as the curing of specific maladies: it encompasses overcoming emotional and personal traumas, solving business problems, improving one's intellect, resolving moral uncertainty, and remedying social injustice. In addition to "mind cure" for existing ailments, Christian Science recommends healthy living as a preventative device: members do not smoke or drink alcohol.

Christian Scientists meet weekly for worship. There are 26 themes that Eddy prescribed, and each is used twice yearly. The service is led by two readers, who use prescribed passages from the Bible and Eddy's writings to develop the theme. There is no sermon. The Church is headed by five directors, but each congregation is autonomous, and men and women alike are eligible for office. The principles of Christian Science are propagated through a number of journals: the *Christian Science Monitor* (a daily newspaper established in 1908), *Christian Science Sentinel* (a weekly), and *Christian Science Quarterly:* all Christian Scientists are obliged to subscribe to these publications. A series of Reading Rooms in major cities enable the public to make inquiries about Christian Science.

Christian Science experienced a decline from the 1930s onward. At the time of writing it is seeking to revive itself by means of the renewed interest in spiritual healing within the New Age Movement (q.v.). It does not publish membership statistics, but is reckoned to have around 400,000 members worldwide, a quarter of whom are active. *See also* NEW THOUGHT; SPIRITUAL SCIENCE CHURCH.

CHRISTIAN WORLD LIBERATION FRONT (CWLF). Part of the 1960s Jesus Movement (q.v.), founded by Jack Sparks, who arrived at Berkeley, California, in 1969, where he spearheaded a campus crusade at the University of California. The movement's ideas were disseminated in the newspaper *Right On!* and Sparks's *Letters to Street Christians*. Sparks subsequently left to join the Antiochan Orthodox Church, and the CWLF reconstituted itself as the Berkeley Christian Coalition (BCC) with the journal *Radix* succeeding *Right On!* BCC was the precursor of the Spiritual Counterfeits Project. In 1976, the BCC, influenced by the House of Elijah, formed a commune known as the Bartimaeus Community; the commune broke away in 1985 and finally dissolved.

CHRIST THE SAVIOR BROTHERHOOD. Established by Andrew Rossi in 1988 as a continuation of the Holy Order of MANS (q.v.), the Brotherhood aims at conducting a mission to the United States, especially to the New Age Movement (q.v.), warning them to prepare for the coming Last Judgment. The organization espouses a form of Eastern Orthodox Christianity (q.v.) that is not wholly acceptable to the Orthodox Churches. In 1990, Rossi's leadership was challenged; he resigned and was succeeded by Metropolitan Pangratios and Father Podmoshensky, who began a move toward securing unification with Orthodoxy. This has not yet been achieved at the time of writing. The movement retains MANS's regard for monasticism, as well as its charitable work among the poor and the oppressed. It also emphasizes "light mysticism" as a means of theosis.

CHURCH OF ALL WORLDS. Founded by Tim Zell (q.v.), this was the first neo-Pagan organization to gain federal recognition in the United States. Its teachings were originally based on Robert Heinlein's science-fiction novel, *Stranger in a Strange Land* (1961). Founded as "Atl" in 1962, later the Atlan Foundation, the group appropriated the description "pagan" in 1967. The Church of All Worlds became legally incorporated in 1968, finally gaining tax-exempt status in 1971. The group's teachings expanded from the notion of reviving a form of ancient religious consciousness to pantheistic ideas concerning the interconnectedness of all reality and the living nature of the earth. The Church can thus be regarded as a precursor of the Gaia (q.v.) and Deep Ecology movements. Other teachings emphasized the divinity of all men and women, and the importance of sensual love, regarding sexuality as an experience of divine union. Rites included the observation of seasonal festivals, initiations, "vision quests," and hand-fastings.

The church is organized in a number of autonomous "nests," linked together by its periodicals *The Green Egg* and *The Pagan*. It was the largest pagan organization until 1976, when Zell moved to California, relinquishing his offices as leader and as editor of *The Green Egg*. For a period the church ceased to exist as a national organization, but it was revived in 1988. By 1992 there were six California nests, with a few others elsewhere in the United States; a membership of 2,000 was reported in 1998. *See also* PAGANISM.

CHURCH OF BIBLE UNDERSTANDING (COBU). *A.k.a.: Forever Family.* Founded in 1971 by Stewart Trill (b. 1936), it is a New Christian communal organization teaching a form of evangelical, although non-Trinitarian, Christianity. Once an atheist, Trill converted to the Christian faith in 1970, joining a Pentecostalist (q.v.) church in Allentown, Pennsylvania, from which he was later expelled. He then founded his own community, which bore similarities to those of the Jesus movement (q.v.), although Trill's followers did not establish links with them. Trill's interpretation of the Bible was distinctive for his "Colored Bible Method": the "light of understanding," he taught, had to be broken down into its constituent "colors" to be understood aright. Communities were headed by male leaders, known as "guardians," who were responsible for their "sheep" (more mature followers) and "lambs" (new converts). Detractors were referred to as "CCs"—"Contentious Christians."

The movement changed its name to COBU. in 1976. In the same year, Trill aroused controversy by divorcing his wife and marrying COBU's secretary, giving rise to accusations of adultery. The movement, which attracted some 10,000 followers at its peak, with 110 communes throughout the United States, had dwindled to 700 members by 1980.

CHURCH OF GOD INTERNATIONAL. A breakaway organization from the Worldwide Church of God (q.v.), founded in 1978 by Herbert W. Armstrong's (q.v.) son, Garner Ted Armstrong. From the early 1970s the Worldwide Church of God was dogged by controversy between Armstrong and his son, mainly on doctrinal matters, but also relating to the former's expensive lifestyle and the church's finances. After alleged sexual misconduct, Garner Ted Armstrong was expelled in 1978. In common with the Worldwide Church of God, the Church of God International has a radio and television ministry, but the church has no paid ministers. Garner Ted Armstrong's book *Europe and America in Prophecy* propounds British Israelite (q.v.) ideas that are associated with his father's teaching.

CHURCH OF JESUS CHRIST AT ARMAGEDDON (LOVE ISRAEL). Founded by Paul Erdmann (b. 1940) in 1969 in Seattle, Washington, this church arose from the 1960s Jesus movement (q.v.). Its alternative name came from the practice of members adopting spiritual names, the forename consisting of a virtue and "Israel" as the common surname of all members. "Love Israel" was Erdmann's name: he is believed to have received dreams and revelations regarding his church, the name of which derives from Revelation 16:16, where Armageddon is identified as the gathering place in the end times. Membership involved living in families (with the father regarded as the household's head) within a wide commune of members. This was an attempt to return to the early Church's practice of communal living and common ownership. Family relationships are regarded as eternal, and all are married to each other through the universal marriage of Christ to the Church. The church gained public notoriety in 1972 when two members died from sniffing toluene: the use of drugs, particularly cannabis, appears to have been prevalent in the community, and it has been alleged that Love Israel himself took cocaine.

The church had a total of 300 members in 1983; however, various internal power struggles and disruptions caused it to relocate to Arlington, Virginia, near Washington, D.C., in 1984, with dwindling numbers. Following a further, more recent split, there is evidence of reorganization and revival in Seattle.

CHURCH OF JESUS CHRIST CHRISTIAN, ARYAN NATIONS. A white supremacist group of congregations, developed from the Church of Jesus Christ Christian, which Wesley Swift (1913-1970) founded in the 1940s. After Swift's death, Richard Girnt Butler established the Church of Jesus Christ Christian, Aryan Nations. In common with the rest of the Christian Identity Movement (q.v.), the organization teaches that the white nations are the physical descendants of the ancient people of Israel. It is associated with the Ku Klux Klan (q.v.) and the American Nazi Party. Butler organized the Pacific States National Identity Conference in 1979 and the World Aryan Conference in 1982. Reported membership is 11,000 in the United States and Canada, and there are also branches in Australia, Denmark, France, Germany, and Italy.

CHURCH OF MERCAVAH. A New Age (q.v.) church, founded in 1982 by the Rev. James R. Montandou. Montandou trained at the International Spiritualist University, and his church emphasizes meditation and enabling seekers to find their own path to self-knowledge. Members cooperate with a variety of esoteric organizations. There is no official statement of doctrine. In 1992 there were 19 ministers and 612 members, with one branch in England and the remainder in the United States.

CHURCH OF SATAN. Founded by Anton Szandor LaVey (q.v.) in 1967, the Church of Satan was the first organized Satanic (q.v.) institution. Its beliefs and practices are based on LaVey's *The Satanic Bible,* which first appeared in 1969. The church's tenets are not so much based on any belief in or veneration of Satan as a person, but are rather based on viewing Satan as a symbol that embodies virtues that stand in contrast to those proclaimed by the Christian Church. The Church of Satan sees Christianity's virtues as hypocritical or unrealistic: teaching love, yet sanctioning wars; teaching abstinence and chastity, when sexual desires are perfectly natural. Accordingly, *The Satanic Bible* contains nine "Satanic statements": indulgence, not abstinence; vital existence, not "spiritual pipe dreams"; undefiled wisdom; kindness to the deserving, not the ungrateful; vengeance; responsibility (people should not be "psychic vampires"); humanity as essentially animal; all of the "so-called sins"; and Satan as the Church's best friend. The last Satanic statement means that the Christian faith has largely drawn on a need for its followers to repent and be absolved from "sins" for which they should really feel no guilt, being the enactment of natural and harmless human desires.

The Church of Satan is therefore characterized by physical and mental self-gratification, self-assertion, and antiestablishmentarianism. Sex is encouraged, but not drugs, which are "escapist" and illegal: those who defy the law of the land are liable to excommunication. While there is no compulsory set of rituals for members to enact, *The Satanic Bible* makes recommendations for sexual, compassionate, and destructive rituals. The Black Mass is little practiced, and LaVey viewed self-development as more important than overt rituals that set out to offend followers of the Christian faith. The Church of Satan declined to provide statistical information after declaring a following of 7,000 in 1972, but the best recent estimates suggest a following of between 2,000 and 5,000 (1993).

CHURCH OF THE LIVING WORD. *A.k.a.: The Walk.* An organization established in 1951 by John Robert Stevens (1919-1983), the son of a pastor, and formerly a pastor in the International Church of the Foursquare Gospel and subsequently the Assemblies of God (q.v.). Stevens was dismissed from both denominations, in 1949 and 1951, respectively, and founded his own independent congregation, which grew into a fellowship of 75 congregations by the mid-1970s. Part of the Latter-Rain Movement (q.v.), the Church of the Living Word is organized in accordance with the fivefold ministry described in Ephesians 4:11 (apostles, prophets, evangelists, pastors, teachers). Stevens is regarded as apostle and prophet, and the expression "Living Word" refers to the church's belief in present-day prophecy, principally through its leader. The organization emphasizes speaking in tongues (q.v.) and holds a firm belief that humanity is in its last days. It rejects mainstream Christianity, claiming to set up a New Divine Order. The Living Word churches have been accused of occultism, since Stevens is alleged to become Christ while prophesying and members are encouraged to "raise their vibrations" to merge with God's nature. Headquarters are in Kalona, Iowa, and membership reached 5,000 with 100 churches worldwide in 1982.

CHURCH OF THE LORD (ALADURA). Founded in 1930 by Josiah Olunowa Oshitelu (1902-1966), this church emerged as a synthesis of African Yoruba and Christian practice. Born a Yoruba, Oshitelu received a Church of England education and seemed destined for a church career. However, following a series of visions, he separated from mainstream Christianity. At the commencement of his mission in 1929 he made brief contact with the Cherubim and Seraphim (q.v.), but was not accepted by them. Influenced by the Faith Tabernacle (2, q.v.) movement, he finally broke with them in 1931, having first established his own congregation in his home town the previous year. Oshitelu's mission was further developed by E. A. Adejobi, who studied at the Bible Training Institute in Glasgow, Scotland, and took Aladura (q.v.) practices as far as Sierra Leone, Ghana, and Liberia. The Aladura emphasize exuberant worship, prayer, and especially healing, and make use of African culture in worship. The church allows polygamy, and Oshitelu himself had seven wives. Its reported membership was three million in 1996.

CHURCH OF WORLD MESSIANITY. *A.k.a.: Sekai Kyusei Kyo; World Messianity; Johrei Fellowship.* Founder-leader Mokichi Okada (1882-1955)—known to his followers as "Meishsama" ("enlightened spiritual leader") in Japan—was brought up in poverty and turned at first to the Omoto religion (a Japanese NRM). After experiencing various visions during the 1920s, he came to regard himself as the channel of God's light. A vision on 15 June 1931 at Mount Nokogiri proved particularly decisive: Okada saw a spiritual paradise descend to earth to become a paradise here. He abandoned Omoto in 1934, setting up the Dai Nihon Kannon Kai (Japanese Kannon Society). Seeing his mission as the transmission of Johrei (divine light) for the purification of the spirit and body, Okada founded the World Messianity and Johrei Fellowship in 1935. Johrei combines elements of Shinto, Buddhism (q.v.), and Christianity (q.v.), offering health, prosperity, peace, and—at a wider level—an ideal paradise on earth. Owing to suppression of religion during the war, Okada temporarily abandoned Johrei, but reestablished his organization in 1957 as Sekai Kyusei Kyo (Church of World Messianity). The church established a number of "sacred centers," the most prominent being at Hakone, Atami, and Kyoto, designed as prototypes of earth's imminent paradise. Practices include the veneration of a sole deity (Meishusama) and "giving Johrei"—emanating healing energy from the palms of one's hands. Outside Japan, the church has centers in 40 countries, including the United States (a Honolulu branch established in 1953, and a Los Angeles one in 1954), and Brazil, where it is said to be the second-largest religion.

After his death, Okada was succeeded by his wife Yoshi (d. 1962) and subsequently by his daughter Itsuki Fujieda, who remains the present leader.

CHURCH UNIVERSAL AND TRIUMPHANT (CUT). Founded in 1958 as Summit Lighthouse (q.v.) by Mark L. Prophet (1918-1973), this organization develops teachings derived from the I AM movement and from Theosophy (qq.v.). Prophet married Elizabeth Clare Wulf (b. 1939) in

1963, and they jointly led the organization until Mark Prophet's death, when Elizabeth Prophet assumed sole leadership.

CUT teaches a form of Gnostic (q.v.) Christianity, holding that there are lost years and lost teachings of Jesus that have now been rediscovered through communication with the Great White Brotherhood (q.v.) of Ascended Masters. Jesus is said to have studied in India and Tibet, where he taught—in common with Hindu (q.v.) philosophy—that there exists a divine spark ("God-identity") within each individual, and thus each human being has unlimited potential, including the ability to free oneself from the cycle of reincarnation (q.v.), achieving eventual reunion with the I AM presence. Jesus, it is taught, was a man who realized the Christ-consciousness within himself; he immediately ascended into heaven upon death, and he is an Ascended Master, together with Mary Magdalene, his "twin flame," whom he married during his lifetime, and who is now known as Master Magda.

CUT believes in progressive revelation and sees no problem in adding elements of Hindu and Buddhist (q.v.) teaching to its originally Christian message. CUT's most important practice is the invocation and visualization of the violet flame (representing the Holy Spirit), which enables the individual's manifestation of the God Flame, offering power, wisdom, and love. The organization's important texts include *Climb the Highest Mountain, The Lost Years of Jesus*, and *The Lost Teachings of Jesus.* Estimated membership for 1991 was 30,000.

COHEN, ANDREW (b. 1955). Founder of the Moksha Foundation. Following a religious experience at age 16 and a disappointing career as a musician, Cohen explored various forms of spirituality, including Sufism (q.v.), Zen (q.v.), kriya yoga (with Swami Hariharananda), Krishnamurti (q.v.), and vipassana (q.v.), and finally became a disciple of H. W. L. Poonja (Poonjaji) in Lucknow, India. Poonja was an exponent of *advaita vedanta* (nondualism), and Cohen claimed to have experienced enlightenment at a very early stage of discipleship. A rift became apparent between Cohen's teachings and those of Poonjaji, and the former founded his own organization in the United States in the late 1980s. Cohen taught "evolutionary enlightenment," claiming that enlightenment is only the beginning of the spiritual path and that his teachings went beyond those of Poonjaji. Cohen's books include *My Master Is My Self* (1989), *Enlightenment Is a Secret* (1991), *Autobiography of an Awakening* (1992), *An Unconditional Relationship to Life* (1995), and *Who am I? and How Shall I Live?* (1998).

CONCERNED CHRISTIANS. An apocalyptic Christian fundamentalist (q.v.) group, led by Monte Kim Miller (b. 1954). Formerly a businessman in Denver, Colorado, Miller received no formal training in religion. In 1985 in Denver he founded Concerned Christians, whose ministry consisted of preaching against "cults" (q.v.), New Age (q.v.) activities, and anti-Christian bias in the media. Miller taught that the world was under Satan's control and made various end-time prophecies, apparently claiming to be one of the "two witnesses" mentioned in Revelation 11 and advocating the need to prepare for Christ's imminent second coming. Viewing the world as the realm of Satan, and America as "Babylon the Great," Miller predicted America's destruction, to be heralded by a massive earthquake in Denver in 1998. Later that year, Miller and his followers disappeared, some of them resurfacing in Jerusalem. At the time of writing, it is rumored that Miller predicts a new Arab-Israeli conflict, which will be a prelude to the Battle of Armageddon and the rebuilding of the Jerusalem Temple on the Temple Mount, which will herald Christ's return. He reportedly predicted that he would die in Jerusalem in December 1999 and be resurrected three days later. Some anticultists have compared Miller's movement with Charles Manson's (q.v.) Family and with Waco (q.v.), fearing physical conflict and possibly multiple suicide by his 60—or possibly 80—members.

CONFRATERNITY OF DEISTS. Founded in St. Petersburg, Florida, by Paul Englert in 1967, this organization affirms the application of human intelligence to the glory of God, emphasizing the importance of scientific knowledge and the arts. It is opposed to organized churches and regards religious scriptures as human creations, with no religious, historical, or chronological reliability.

CONSERVATIVE JUDAISM. A progressive movement within Judaism (q.v.), influenced by the 18th-century Enlightenment, which its supporters believe necessitates changes in Jewish life. Conservative Judaism's innovations include the ordination of women and adaptations of divorce laws and rules regarding conversion. They have their own Jewish Theological Seminary, since they are not accepted by Orthodox Judaism. Roughly one-third of all Jews in the United States are Conservative Jews, belonging to the United Synagogues of America, which serves as its umbrella organization. Estimated U.S. membership is 1,600,000 (1995). *See also* LIBERAL JUDAISM; RECONSTRUCTIONISM; REFORM JUDAISM.

COOKE, GRACE (1892-1979). Founder of the White Eagle Lodge (q.v.). Cooke claimed to have experienced visions of White Eagle and other Native American spirits from her childhood onward. In 1913 she became a Spiritualist (q.v.) medium, but preferred to emphasize spiritual development and esoteric teaching (claiming to have access to the Akashic Records [q.v.]), rather than contact with the dead. In 1936 she claimed that White Eagle instructed her to establish an organization for "light bearers." Later in life Cooke claimed previous incarnations as Mayan and Egyptian priestesses, both of whom were guided by previous incarnations of White Eagle. Her experiences in these civilizations are recorded in her *The Illuminated Ones* (1966). Other writings include *Meditation* (1955), *The Jewel in the Lotus* (1973), and *Sun Men of the Americas* (1975), all published by the White Eagle

Publishing Trust. *See also* NATIVE AMERICAN RELIG-
ION.

COURSE IN MIRACLES. First published in 1975, *A Course
in Miracles* is a book channeled (q.v.) by Helen Schucman (d.
1981), purportedly from Jesus Christ. A Jewish agnostic by
origin, Schucman worked in the Department of Psychiatry at
Columbia University's College of Physicians and Surgeons.
Having witnessed the treatment given to patients, Schucman
felt the need for a "better way" and claims to have heard an
inner voice over a seven-year period, the messages of which
comprise this three-volume, 1,200-page book. The first volume is for self-study and the second for teachers, while the
third contains 365 spiritual exercises. The book emphasizes
the need to remove blocks to love's presence and to experience forgiveness, letting go of fear and guilt, as a means to
experiencing wholeness. In common with much New Age
(q.v.) philosophy, it extols oneness, peace, joy, and love as
being identical with "heaven." The book continues to be a
best-seller. Not only can the 365 "lessons" be followed on an
individual basis, but the course has generated many group
seminars, classes, and workshops in Europe and the United
States. In 1992 there were 1,000 groups worldwide studying
Schucman's book.

COVENANT OF THE GODDESS. Founded in California in
1975, the Covenant of the Goddess is an organization linking
wiccan (q.v.) covens and individual solitary witches whose
focus is on the goddess. It enables cooperation among feminist wiccans in particular and campaigns for member organizations to gain legal and tax-exempt status. Originally a
confederation of 10 covens, it is now a national organization,
linking some 65 covens by 1992. The Covenant respects diversity and confidentiality among wiccans, but emphasizes
the wiccan ethic: "An ye harm none, do as ye will." Prominent feminist wiccans who are active in the Covenant include
Szuszanna Budapest (q.v.), Margot Adler, Starhawk (q.v.),
Allison Harlow, and Deborah Bender.

COVENANT OF UNITARIAN UNIVERSALIST PAGANS (CUUPS). An organization within the Unitarian Universalist Association (UUA) that seeks to promote Paganism (q.v.) and earth-centered spirituality. Following a well-received summer solstice ritual enacted as part of the UUA's General Assembly in 1985, some attendees felt the need for a formal Pagan organization within the denomination. Margot Adler was invited to address a General Assembly seminar in 1987, after which CUUPS was founded. The organization provides a forum for Unitarian Universalists (UUs) (q.v.) who are interested in earth-centered spirituality to engage in dialogue. The formal recognition afforded to Pagans enables them to be included within an established denomination, and in some cases to gain formal credentials as UU ministers. The UUA's recognition of Pagans reflects the denomination's tradition of tolerance and liberal religion. However, not all UUs express approval of Paganism, some viewing it as contrary to the Unitarian principle of Reason in religion, and others believing that it detracts from its original Christian ethos. U.S. membership is around 700, with 60 chapters. In Great Britain, a sister body, known as the Unitarian Earth Spirit Network, with around 60 members—in reality a neo-Pagan organization—tends to be marginalized within British Unitarianism.

COVENANT, THE SWORD, AND THE ARM OF THE LORD, THE (CSA). An Identity Movement (q.v.) church centered on the border between Arkansas and Missouri, founded by James D. Ellison. Following a vision, Ellison established a community in the Ozark Mountains to survive God's imminent judgment. Armageddon would entail the demise of America and war involving whites against blacks, Jews, foreigners, homosexuals, witches, and Satanists. The community, founded in 1976, was known as Zarephath-Horeb, and within two years members had begun to stockpile food and weapons. One leader was involved in murder in 1983, and in 1985 Ellison received a 20-year prison sentence for murdering an Arkansas state trooper. There were 100 reported members in 1985.

CREME, BENJAMIN (b. 1922). Founder and proponent of Christ Maitreya. After studying Theosophy (q.v.), Creme came to accept Alice Bailey's (q.v.) teaching of the imminent coming of Maitreya. Creme equates Maitreya with the second coming of Christ, the coming Hindu avatar Kalki, the awaited Jewish messiah, and Imam Mahdi. Creme claims to have received messages from the Ascended Masters, commencing in 1959, concerning Maitreya's advent. In 1982 he asserted that Maitreya had returned and was living in London. Since then there have been various reports of alleged sightings: in 1988 in Nairobi, 6,000 people reportedly saw him at a healing convention; from 1992 onward he has supposedly appeared in various cities throughout the world, speaking in London in 1994 to more than 300 Christians.

CROSSROADS MOVEMENT. Influenced by the Churches of Christ at the Crossroads Movement in Gainesville, Florida, in the early 1970s, the Crossroads Movement began as a revivalist movement within a Churches of Christ (Noninstrumental) congregation in a Boston suburb. This group developed into the Boston Churches of Christ and subsequently the International Churches of Christ (ICC) (q.v.). The ICC's controversial methods of securing growth and commitment were derived from the earlier Churches of Christ at the Crossroads' evangelization tactics on the University of Florida campus, which leaders were forced to abandon. *See also* DISCIPLING.

CROWLEY, ALEISTER (1875-1947). Born Edward Alexander Crowley, of a family of Plymouth Brethren (q.v.) in Leamington Spa, England, Crowley is renowned as an occultist and magician and is particularly noted for his "sex magic." Having read the writings of A. E. Waite, he was drawn to the Hermetic Order of the Golden Dawn (OGD) (q.v.), where he quickly gained a high grade of initiation. Following an acrimonious series of quarrels with S. L. MacGregor Mathers—one of the principal OGD leaders, Crowley left, taking up the study of Eastern mysticism. In

1903 he married Rose Kelly, who claimed to receive communications from an astral plane. The following year she communicated with Aiwass, the mouthpiece of Horus, who apparently dictated *Liber Legis* (The Book of the Law), which Crowley transcribed. This event was crucial in Crowley's life and is referred to as the "Cairo revelation." The book teaches a system of Egyptian "magick" (q.v.) and provides an interpretation of human history, the last period of which is said to be the eon of Thelema, or Will, and is encapsulated in Crowley's much-used dictum (originally from Rabelais), "'Do what thou wilt' shall be the whole of the law."

Part of the Cairo revelation was that Crowley should establish a new order, and in 1907 he founded Astrum Argentinium (Silver Star). From 1915 to 1919 Crowley lived in the United States. Crowley also became involved in the Ordo Templi Orientis (OTO) (q.v.) in 1912, becoming the head of its British branch in 1922. In 1920 when traveling in Italy Crowley had a vision of a villa on a hillside, which he located in Sicily. There he established the Sacred Abbey of the Thelemic Mysteries, which became a center for sex orgies as well as magical rites (Crowley appears to have been bisexual). Mussolini expelled Crowley from Italy in 1923.

Although Gerald Gardner (q.v.) met Crowley during the last two years of the latter's life, Crowley is not highly regarded by witches and wiccans (q.v.). Some practitioners of magic, although not all, view his *Magick in Theory and Practice* (1929) as an important work. *See also* THELEMIC MAGICK.

CULT. The term *cult* is applied by the anticult movement (ACM) (q.v.) to new religious movements and psychology groups, especially those emerging after World War II. The ACM claims that there are several distinguishing "marks of a cult," including authoritarian leadership, secrecy, indoctrination techniques, total commitment, unacceptable moral codes, and community living. The term *cult*, understandably, is disliked by members of NRMs, who regard it as pejorative and deny possessing the features that the ACM attributes to them.

The term came into popular usage from the mid-1960s onward, largely through media coverage of NRMs, although it can be traced back to William C. Irvine, a Christian writer who wrote *Timely Warnings* in 1917, to highlight the perceived dangers of emergent spiritual groups.

The term "cult" was subsequently employed by a number of sociologists who drew on Max Weber's distinction between "church" and "sect," to which Weber's pupil Ernst Troeltsch added a third category—the "mystical." Howard Becker in 1932 designated this category as the "cult." J. M. Yinger contended that a cult was thus a loosely unstructured way of expressing religious devotion. Yinger further suggested that a cult was distinguished from mainstream religion by lying outside the dominant religion. As examples Yinger cited Spiritualism, Theosophy, Christian Science (qq.v.), and "pseudo-Hinduisms." Thus there are three different grounds for regarding a movement as cultic: intensity of religious experience, looseness of structure, and distance from the dominant culture and religion.

It should be evident that new religious movements satisfy these criteria in different degrees—and some not at all. The vast majority of the better-known NRMs have a highly defined organizational structure, and therefore cannot be regarded as "cultic" in the second of the above senses. In general, the term *cult* is not favored in the academic study of NRMs, since it lacks an agreed and unambiguous definition.

CULT AWARENESS NETWORK (CAN). Originally an American countercult organization, formerly known as the Citizens' Freedom Foundation (CFF). Deprogrammer Ted Patrick in 1974 cofounded the CFF, which became the Cult Awareness Network in 1984. Other leaders have included Galen Kelly, Cynthia Kisser (executive director, 1987-1996), Michael Rokos, and Rick Ross (q.v.). CAN has drawn on the work of others who are hostile to NRMs, particularly Margaret Thaler Singer (q.v.), Louis Jolyon West (q.v.), R. J. Lifton, and Steven Hassan. CAN characteristically subscribed to the "brainwashing" (q.v.) hypothesis; although it originally stated its opposition to deprogramming (q.v.), there can be little doubt that many of its leaders were actively involved in such activities. In 1995 CAN was prosecuted for the kidnapping of a Pentecostalist (q.v.) youth, who demanded compensation. This, together with deleterious effects of lawsuits brought by the Church of Scientology (q.v.), caused CAN to declare itself bankrupt. In June 1996 its assets, including CAN's files and hotline number, were bought up by the Church of Scientology, who had vigorously campaigned against CAN for many years. CAN is now run by a Board of Directors drawn from a variety of backgrounds, and not exclusively Scientologists.

CYBERCHURCHES. With the advent of the Internet, it has been speculated that a new kind of religious community might emerge, one whose members do not meet physically but who interact through cyberspace. The few cyberchurches that exist on the web are the Church of the Sub-Genius, the Church of the Bunny, and the Ice Cream Church, although it is doubtful whether the last two of these are intended to be serious. They appear to amount to little more than a web site with e-mail discussion groups. At least one group has used a regular printed liturgy, with hymns, prayers, and homilies, and another web site offers the facility for confession. Although rites such as ordination are possible (in the Universal Life Church [q.v.]) over the Internet, it is difficult to see how other life-cycle rites could be marked by purely electronic means.

-D-

DAMANHUR. A New Age (q.v.) magical federation of communities in the Valchiusella Valley, northern Italy, established in 1977 by Oberto Airaudi (b. 1950). In his youth Airaudi visited healers and "pranotherapists" (healers who purportedly mediate "prajnic energy" through physical movement) and became acquainted with Theosophy and

Spiritualism (qq.v.). In 1974 he established the Horus Center and the School of Pranotherapy. The following year negotiations commenced for the purchase of property in Valchiusella, and community living commenced in 1979. A constitution, initially drawn up in 1981, developed into the Constitution of the Nation of Damanhur in 1989, defining the community as an independent nation, with its own laws and currency. As it expanded further, it became a federation of communities within a 20-mile radius of the Valchiusella Valley. The federation now claims 800 "citizens," and it boasts 40 different business activities, including the marketing of health foods, china, jewelry, paintings, and computer software.

Damanhur is particularly renowned for its underground Temple of Man—a vast complex of sanctuaries within a mountainside, in which its principal ceremonies are enacted. Although construction work had been progressing since 1977, the existence of this temple was not publicly known until 1992, when an ex-member, Filippo Maria Cerutti, disclosed its whereabouts. Worship is directed to a single supreme God, who is approachable through a series of intermediaries, namely, "intermediate deities" and "entities," the latter comprising angels (q.v.), nature spirits, and demons.

DAVIS, ANDREW JACKSON (1826-1910). A shoemaker's apprentice from Poughkeepsie, New York, Davis is known as the "Poughkeepsie Seer," having claimed to have achieved contact with Emanuel Swedenborg in the spirit world. He is also sometimes referred to as the "father of Spiritualism," since his experiences predate those of the Fox sisters (q.v.). His book *The Principles of Nature, Her Divine Revelations, and a Voice to Mankind* was published in 1847—a year before the Foxes' "Hydesville rappings." Davis's experiences were attained in a state of mesmeric trance (he attended lectures on mesmerism), and his book is a record of trance communications. It has been observed that the text bears marked resemblances to Swedenborg's *Arcana Coelestia.*

From 1850 onward Davis was a prominent exponent of Spiritualism (q.v.), and also a healer.

DEPROGRAMMING. A technique by means of which members of religious communities are forcibly abducted and brought back to conventional society. Originally pioneered in the United States by Ted Patrick of the Cult Awareness Network (q.v.), his techniques and exploits are recounted in his book *Let Our Children Go!* (1972), co-authored by David Dulack. The justification for deprogramming rests on the anticultist assumption that those who join NRMs do not do so voluntarily, but have been "brainwashed" (q.v.) and hence are unamenable to rational persuasion to leave. The perceived remedy is therefore to force them back to "normality." The process usually begins with a forcible abduction, followed by isolation and faith-breaking tactics.

While some deprogrammers are ex-members of NRMs, the majority provide the service purely for commercial gain. Deprogammings are expensive, costing several thousand dollars in most cases. Where deprogrammers do not offer their services out of conviction, they have proved willing to deprogram members of traditional religions as well as NRMs, and there have been well-attested cases of their techniques being used on Baptists, members of the Orthodox Church, and Muslims. Deprogramming is illegal in most countries, and several deprogrammers have served prison sentences for their actions.

There is disagreement about whether deprogramming is successful. Predictably, deprogrammers themselves boast impressive success rates, while NRMs themselves allege that they are singularly unsuccessful. Academic researchers have tended to adopt a middle position: David Bromley, for example, estimated that some 64 percent of abductions out of 397 he studied resulted in the victims making a permanent break with the organization. Much depends on the criteria of success, and some NRM members have been known to feign successful deprogramming and subsequently rejoin. *See also* EXIT COUNSELING.

DIANETICS. The teaching about the nature of self expounded by L. Ron Hubbard (q.v.) (1911-1986) and expressed principally in his best-seller *Dianetics: The Modern Science of Mental Health,* first published in 1950. Dianetics is delivered by the Church of Scientology (q.v.) and is a prelude to the study of Scientology proper. According to Hubbard, the real self (the "thetan") consists of neither mind nor body, though it possesses both. The self finds itself trapped amid matter, energy, space, and time (MEST), which are entirely its own creation, and its quest is therefore to rid itself of the encumbrances that weigh it down. There are two parts of the mind: the analytical mind and the reactive mind. The former is responsible for rational activity, for making distinctions, and for the logging up and remembering of factual information on the thetan's "time track." The latter, by contrast, is illogical and reacts adversely toward painful past incidents. These adverse reactions, which can reactivate themselves at later stages of one's life, are caused by "engrams," which can give rise to pain, irrational fears, and mental blocks. In particular, engrams can be created in states of unconsciousness, for example when a person has become the victim of an accident.

Dianetics aims to rid the thetan of all engrams, thus eliminating the reactive mind. Until this has occurred, a person is classified as a "pre-clear." The thetan is "cleared" by means of a process of "auditing"—an activity in which the pre-clear recounts past incidents to an "auditor" (one who listens). A trained Dianetics auditor will often employ a device known as an "E-meter" (electopsychometer), which consists of two metal cylinders connected by wire to a dial that only the auditor can see. The E-meter registers when engrams have been activated, thus enabling the auditor to determine the aspects of one's past that need to be worked on. Hubbard dissociated his techniques from hypnosis, psychiatry, or psychoanalysis and was heavily critical of modern psychiatry, particularly its behaviorist schools.

Once one is declared to be "clear," one becomes an "Operating Thetan" and can undertake progressive levels of Scientology courses for the purpose of further spiritual development. *See also* HUMAN POTENTIAL MOVE-MENT; SELF RELIGIONS.

DIANIC WICCA. The Dianic strand of wicca (q.v.) began in the 1940s, expanding significantly in the United States from the 1970s onward. It claims to be a wiccan tradition independent of Gerald Gardner (q.v.), who revived witchcraft in Great Britain in the early 1950s. Dianic wicca focuses on the veneration of the goddess Diana, who is represented by a high priestess, and claims to have originated in Central Europe. Its supporters tend to be feminists (such as Margot Adler, Szuszanna Budapest [q.v.], Diana Paxton, Starhawk [q.v.], and Merlin Stone) and typically believe in an original state of peace on earth, which subsequently became disrupted through men's rise to power and the patriarchal system which they imposed. Such patriarchy is reflected in the worship of a male god, particularly in the Semitic traditions, and the emphasis on the goddess is regarded as an important counter to mainstream patriarchal religion. Some supporters view Diana as the mother goddess from whom both sexes originate, and are gender-inclusive. Other feminist covens admit women only, and some of these are lesbian-oriented.

DI MAMBRO, JOSEPH (1920-1994). Coleader of the Solar Temple (q.v.), 53 of whose members were found dead simultaneously in Canada and Switzerland in 1994. An occultist with particular interests in Egyptian mythology and sex magic (q.v.), Di Mambro became a grand master in the Ancient Mystical Order of the Rosy Cross (AMORC) (q.v.) and subsequently leader of La Pyramide (renamed the Golden Way in 1974).

Although he gained less publicity than Luc Jouret (q.v.), he was the more senior coleader of the Solar Temple. It is speculated that a power struggle between Di Mambro and Jouret was instrumental in the 1994 catastrophe.

DISCIPLING. A process of close spiritual supervision of members, principally associated with the International Churches of Christ (ICC) (q.v.). The practice derived from the Crossroads Church of Christ, in which members were encouraged to choose their own "prayer partner." The Boston Church of Christ, which emerged from the Crossroads movement (q.v.), felt that this was insufficiently directive and inaugurated a nonvoluntary system whereby leaders paired older, more mature members with younger, less experienced members. Pairing is invariably of the same gender, and "disciplers" are in daily contact with their "discipleship partners" and have a face-to-face meeting at least weekly. This system is intended to elicit true Christian disciples, in contrast with the world's view of a disciple. Disciples are also expected to make disciples, and the ICC is renowned for its "multiplying ministry."

While the term "discipling" is characteristic of the ICC, the word "shepherding" is preferred by the Christian Growth Ministries and Maranatha Christian Churches (q.v.) to describe a similar institution. *See also* HOUSE CHURCH MOVEMENT.

DIVINE LIGHT MISSION (DLM). *A.k.a.: Dirya Sandesh Parishad.* Founded in 1960 by Shri Has Ji Maharaji (d. 1965), also known as Pratap Singh Rawat-Balyogeshwar, this organization's leadership was assumed on his death by his son, Guru Maharaji (q.v.) (the preferred Western spelling of "Maharaj Ji"), then only eight years old. Guru Maharaji visited the United States in the early 1970s and began to attract a Western following. By the mid-1970s around 30 ashrams had been established in the United States, where "premies" (or "devotees"—the name given to Maharaji's followers) could receive "the Knowledge." Maharaji was regarded as the *satguru,* the Perfect Master who is self-realized, and he claimed to come from a lineage of satgurus, of which only one exists for each age.

Members were expected to give up their possessions and to lead a lifestyle free from alcohol, tobacco, recreational drugs, meat, and any food brought in from external sources. Members engaged in four meditation practices ("procedures"): Divine Light (contemplation of the eternal light within oneself); Divine Nectar (water of life that flows within); Divine Harmony (meditation on inner sound); and Divine Word or Name (the primordial vibration which serves as an object of meditation). Fundamental to the movement was *satsang* (literally "company of truth")—spiritual discourses which premies receive from the satguru or one of his mahatmas.

Guru Maharaji's marriage in 1974 to an American woman, without parental approval, caused controversy within his family. His mother, disapproving of Maharaji's apparent Westernizing tendencies, assumed control of the Indian branch of the organization. Maharaji dissolved the ashrams in the West and went on to deny both his divine status and status as a guru (q.v.). The Divine Light Mission continues as a movement in India, led by Maharaji's mother and elder brother, while Maharaji now leads Elan Vital (q.v.), which continues to be supported by his numerous Western followers and which is regarded more as an organization for disseminating "the Knowledge" than as a religious organization. In 1990 there were said to be 1.2 million followers of DLM worldwide, with 50,000 in the United States. *See also* ISHVARA.

DIVINE PRINCIPLE. The principal text of the Unification Church (q.v.). The text originated from penciled notes written in Korean by Sun Myung Moon (q.v.) in 1951, and the present form is a collation of two later works by Hyo Won Eu, *Wol-li Hae-sul* (Explanation of the Principle) and *Wol-li Kang-ron* (Discourse on the Principle), published in English in 1973 as *Divine Principle* When Unificationism was brought to the United States in the 1960s, two proto-versions, written by leaders Young Oon Kim and Bo Hi Pak, were circulated under the title *The Divine Principles*. The 1973 book was superseded in 1996 by a "re-translation" entitled *Exposition of Divine Principle*. *Divine Principle* consists of interpretation of Hebrew and Christian scriptures, supplemented by revelations that are believed to have been received by the Rev. Moon.

The text is arranged in three principal sections: The Principle of Creation; The Fall; and Principles of Restoration. The book contains a very detailed account of how God planned that Adam and Eve and their descendants should grow to physical and spiritual maturity, becoming "true individuals," establishing "true families," and creating an "ideal world." This divine plan was thwarted when Satan tempted Eve into an illicit sexual relationship, which placed their descendants—the entire human race—in Satan's lineage.

In order to restore the lineage, a messiah is needed. Jesus came as messiah, but his untimely death enabled humanity to receive only "spiritual salvation" and not "physical salvation." The human race must therefore await the arrival of a new messiah, who will complete Jesus' unfinished work.

The third section of *Divine Principle* provides a detailed analysis of human history, calculating that the new messiah should appear on earth in Korea between 1917 and 1930 (Sun Myung Moon was born in 1920). Vehemently anticommunist, *Divine Principle* extols democracy as the superior alternative political system and predicts its ultimate triumph over communism.

Divine Principle is taught systematically at Unificationist seminars, as a significant part of an inquirer's introduction to the church. Additionally, there exist teachings that are not contained in this basic text, but which are transmitted orally within the movement. These oral teachings include the explicit identification of Sun Myung Moon as the "Lord of the Second Coming," and his wife as the co-messiah of the present age. The new messiah will marry, establish a new lineage of sinless children, into which his followers will become engrafted, thus enabling the creation of the kingdom of heaven on earth and the opening up of the highest level of the spirit world, the Kingdom of Heaven, a realm which is reserved for couples who have had their marriages blessed by the Rev. and Mrs. Moon.

DORJE SHUGDEN. A Tibetan Buddhist (q.v.) practice, banned by the Dalai Lama, but currently advocated by a number of Tibetan Buddhist teachers and by the New Kadampa Tradition (NKT) (q.v.). Geshe Kelsang Gyatso (q.v.), the NKT's founder-leader, teaches that Dorje Shugden is a *dharmapala* (protector deity) who presides over their place of worship and who guards the Dharma (Buddhist teaching). By contrast, the Dalai Lama and his supporters contend that Dorje Shugden is a *dabla*—a ghost or malevolent spirit.

Belief in Dorje Shugden appears to emanate from an incident during the reign of the fifth Dalai Lama, who was defeated in debate by Drakpa Gyaltsen, an incarnate lama *(tulku)*. Drakpa Gyaltsen died in mysterious circumstances shortly after this incident, and some Tibetans attributed subsequent paranormal occurrences to the activity of his ghost and felt it necessary to placate him. Kelsang Gyatso and his supporters hold that Dorje Shugden is a bodhisattva who protects the Gelugpa Tibetan tradition (the most popular form of Tibetan Buddhism).

Dorje Shugden practice went into decline until the early parts of the 20th century, when a revival was initiated by Pabongka (1878-1941). Pabongka was the tutor of Trijang Rinpoche (1901-1981), who in turn taught Tenzin Gyatso—the present, 14th Dalai Lama—and Kelsang Gyatso. Dorje Shugden supporters therefore point out that the Dalai Lama himself practiced Dorje Shugden in an earlier stage of his life and accuse him of inconsistency when he formally banned the practice in 1996. NKT supporters took the unusual step of picketing when the Dalai Lama addressed the Buddhist Society in its London headquarters in the same year.

DOWLING, LEVI H. (1844-1911). More commonly known by his forename, Dowling is particularly known for *The Aquarian Gospel of Jesus the Christ* (q.v.), one of the first pieces of channeled (q.v.) writing. Born in Belleville, Ohio, Levi became a preacher in the Disciples of Christ and an army chaplain during the American Civil War, before enrolling as a medical student at Northwestern Christian University in Indianapolis. Later in life, Levi gave up medical work in order to devote himself to writing. *The Aquarian*

Gospel of Jesus the Christ, which proved highly influential and which continues to be published, was written as a consequence of a dream. Levi's manuscript *The Cusp of the Ages* testifies to his commissioning to write this new gospel for the dawning Age of Aquarius.

DRESSER, JULIUS (1838-1893). Early exponent of New Thought (q.v.). Julius and his wife Annetta Dresser were clients of Phineas Parker Quimby. Since Quimby had not published any of his teachings, the Dressers did much to popularize his work. After studying Christian Science (q.v.) under Edward J. Arens in 1882, Julius Dresser launched a fierce attack on Mary Baker Eddy (q.v.), accusing her of plagiarizing Quimby. This led to a legal battle, with Eddy suing Arens for allegedly plagiarizing *her* writings. Since Quimby's son refused to release his papers, Eddy won the case. Julius's son Horatio Dresser, in his *History of the New Thought Movement* (1919), eulogized Quimby and virtually ignored Eddy. Whatever the relationship between Quimby's ideas and those of Christian Science and New Thought, the Dressers had a major role in the inauguration of New Thought.

DRUIDISM. Possibly an ancient pre-Christian nature religion in Britain, known to have existed in the first century B.C.E. It has been suggested that it was associated with ancient stone circles at Stonehenge and Avebury in England, but this is unproven and the characteristics of ancient Druidism are uncertain. Even the meaning of the name is subject to a variety of interpretations, including "servant of truth," "all-knowing wise man," "equal in honor," and "oak." This last suggestion may be connected with ancient Celtic oak tree veneration, perhaps connected with the Green Man cult, now popular within New Age (q.v.) circles. The Druidic pantheon appears to have consisted of Taranis (the oak god and divine father), Belenos (the sun god), Cernunnos (the god of the hunt, sometimes identified with Pan), Lugh (the god of skills), and Esus (the pastoral god, who affords the power for magical practice). The Druids may have been the priests of the Celtic population; alternatively, they may have been philosopher-magicians who were able to practice the arts of astrology and healing. If astrology was indeed one of their arts, this may support the view that Druidism is connected with the celebration of the year's seasons. The Druids may also have taught that a similar eternal cycle worked within the human soul: life leads to death, which leads to a period in Summerland, where rebirth and evolutionary growth follow.

The 18th century saw a revival of Druidism in the form of Henry Hurle's Ancient Order of the Druids, and later the British Circle of Universal Bond and the Order of Bards, Ovates, and Druids. Some members of the Hermetic Order of the Golden Dawn (q.v.) had associations with Druidism, including Aleister Crowley (q.v.). Because of its falling into neglect for so many centuries, it cannot be established that present-day Druidism constitutes a revival of ancient Druid practices. In 1998 there were 35 Druid groups in Great Britain and 300 worldwide. The Order of Bards, Ovates, and Druids is reported to have 7,000 members (1998).

-E-

ECKANKAR. Founded in 1965 by Paul Twitchell (q.v.) (1908-1971), "Eckankar" (ECK) is translated as "Religion of the Light and Sound of God" or "Coworker with God." Twitchell is regarded as the 971st living ECK master of the Vairigi Order and is said to have received in 1944 the "Rod of Power" from Rebazar Tarzs, believed to be a 15th-century Tibetan who communicated with Twitchell on a spiritual plane. Eckankar teaches that there always exists one living ECK master: ECK masters are immortal, but drop their physical body when they experience physical death, going on to live at higher levels.

Emanating from the Radhosoami Satsang (q.v.) background, which is a synthesis of Hinduism and Sikhism (qq.v.), Eckankar teaches a form of surat shabda yoga—a method of experiencing the Supreme Being's energy as the light and sound of God. Followers, who are known as ECK-ists or "chelas," undertake spiritual exercises involving visualization, guided meditation, and "lucid dreaming" (a particularly vivid kind of dreaming in which the dreamer is able to take control of events within the dream). Twitchell introduced the chanting of the mantra "hu," which is regarded as particularly efficacious. Particularly important is the "science of soul travel": the soul's quest is for progression through a number of planes—each of which has a temple, a guardian, and a sound—until one finally reaches Sugmad (the "ocean of love and mercy").

Eckankar regards itself as the root of all other religions and philosophies, all of which teach fragments of the truth. Eckankar is thus not exclusive, but claims to teach the quickest way to attain Sugmad. Unlike the Sant Mat tradition to which Radhasoami belongs, chelas (followers) are regarded as coworkers with God, rather than sparks of the eternal who coalesce with the Ultimate. Eckankar emphasizes active spiritual exercises, rather than more passive meditation, and it rejects Eastern austerity, demanding no more than a moderate lifestyle from its followers.

After Twitchell's death, Eckankar was led by Darwin Gross (q.v.) until 1983. Harold Klemp, the present living ECK master, has introduced a number of specifically Western esoteric elements into its practices. Eckankar has a membership of 50,000 (1998). *See also* AKASHIC RECORDS; INSIGHT.

EDDY, MARY BAKER (1821-1910). Founder of Christian Science (q.v.), born in Bow, New Hampshire. Following an accident, Eddy turned to alternative healing, and for a time was a follower of Phineas Parker Quimby (1802-1866). After experiencing a relapse, she left Quimby and in 1866 received a revelation after reading the gospel account of Jesus healing palsy (Matthew 9). Eddy's "discovery" of Christian Science led her to view Jesus Christ as the "Way-shower" and to believe that healing was effected by self-cure through the powers of the mind. Her principal work, *Science and Health with*

Key to the Scriptures, was completed in 1875 and continues to be used (in its 1907 revised edition) by Christian Scientists. Much discussion has been generated concerning Eddy's degree of dependence on Quimby. She insisted that "no human pen nor tongue" had taught her, and her followers claim that Quimby's teachings derived from Franz Mesmer rather than the Bible.

Eddy established the first Church of Christ, Scientist, in Boston in 1879 and the Massachussets Metaphysical College—also in Boston—in 1881, where it attracted some 4,000 students in its first decade. The National Christian Science Association was founded in 1886. Initially, Eddy had a co-worker in Emma Curtis Hopkins, but the two parted company and Hopkins set up her own Hopkins Metaphysical Association in 1887.

ELAN VITAL. Following the dissolution of Guru Maharaji's Divine Light Mission (DLM) (qq.v.) in the West, Elan Vital was set up in the 1980s as a nonprofit organization aiming to promote Guru Maharaji and his teachings. Elan Vital insists that it is not a religion: Maharaji is not regarded as a god; DLM's ashrams no longer exist; members are no longer referred to as "premies" (devotees); and satsang (discourses given by a master or a follower) is no longer central, but is now generally maintained through listening to Maharaji rather than nightly talks by followers. Those who assist Maharaji in the process of giving "the Knowledge" are called "instructors" rather than "initiators." Elan Vital has a lower profile than DLM, attracting less media publicity. However, Maharaji still delivers the four meditative techniques known as the Knowledge which featured in DLM and which afford self-understanding and self-realization, but he insists that such Knowledge is independent of culture and is by no means bound to the religious traditions of India. As well as lectures given to his supporters, dissemination of Maharaji's teachings is mainly through videotapes of his discourses around the world. Elan Vital produces little written literature, apart from brochures and information on its web sites. Some

15,000 are estimated to practice the Knowledge in the United States and around 5,000 in Great Britain. Knowledge is practiced in over 80 countries.

EMERSON, RALPH WALDO (1803-1882). A Unitarian, "transcendentalist" (qq.v.), and early precursor of the New Age (q.v.). Following personal difficulties concerning the sacrament of communion, Emerson resigned as minister of the Second Unitarian Church in Boston in 1832. He departed for Europe, where he encountered a number of the Romantics, most notably Samuel Taylor Coleridge, William Wordsworth, and Thomas Carlyle. After returning to America in 1834, he formed the Transcendental Club, at which he and a number of like-minded people met to celebrate the ways in which the divine could be found in nature. Emerson had an important influence on Henry David Thoreau, Walt Whitman, Nathaniel Hawthorne, Emily Dickinson, and Herman Melville.

In his essay "Nature" (1834), Emerson contended that nature was the true teacher, rather than the Church, its sacraments, or its creeds. Drawing on the teaching of the Upanishads, he taught that the self was "part and particle of God," or—as he called it—the "Over Soul." Critical of academic knowledge, Emerson's essay "The American Scholar" (1837) accused Harvard University academics of pedantry, lack of originality, and irrelevance to everyday life. Elsewhere, Emerson criticized traditional Christianity (q.v.) for grossly exaggerating the person of Jesus and for treating revelation as a past rather than a present phenomenon that all can obtain. Despite Nature's omnipresence, Emerson allowed that there are special people ("representative men") whose insights surpass those of other human beings, for example, Plato, Montaigne, Shakespeare, Emanuel Swedenborg, Napoleon, and Goethe.

Emerson was one of the first Western thinkers to have appropriated Eastern ideas, particularly from the Upanishads and the Bhagavad Gita. However, Emerson did not totally share the optimism that characterizes the New Age: he acknowledged that Nature had its dark side as well as its attractive one. He was also somewhat scathing of certain elements in the emergent New Thought (q.v.) spirituality, explicitly mentioning "mind cure," "animal magnetism," omens, spiritism (q.v.), and mesmerism.

EMIN. An esoteric human potential group, founded in Great Britain in 1973, with branches in the U.S.A., Canada, Australia, and Israel. The organization's founder is Raymond Armin (b. 1924), born Raymond Schertenlieb and known to his followers as "Leo." National service took him to India and the Far East, where he became acquainted with Oriental philosophy and religion. In 1972 several others made the chance acquaintance of Armin and began to demand his writings and tapes; a number of seekers offered him consultancy fees to enable him to research on their behalf. The name "Emin" is said to derive from the Arabic *amin*, "faithful one," although various names have been used at different times and places, for example, the Faculty of Color (colors have a high significance for Armin's followers), the University of Life, and the Church of Emin Coils—the last of which denotes the branch founded in Florida in 1978.

Emin does not regard itself as a religion, describing its main functions as education and research. It has produced a set of "Philosophical Tenets of Emin," however, which emphasize the evolution of the world and the individual, one's duty to humanity and the universe, and the importance of the human race living in unison. Recommended practices include maintaining and improving one's standards, obedience to the law, and keeping oneself well informed. However, Emin emphasizes the importance of working out one's own answers to life's fundamental questions and defining one's own spiritual path.

Emin offers numerous lectures and classes on a wide variety of themes, spanning "Science and the Environment," "The Understanding of Human Society," "Civilizations," and "Theater and Arts," among others, and the use of color, music, and dance are highly regarded. Attention is also given to more "esoteric" subjects such as astrology, Tarot (Emin has designed its distinctive Gemrod Tarot deck), massage, herbalism, and "aura cleaning."

In the past, Emin members characteristically wore distinctive tunics for significant occasions. This has been discontinued, although members still characteristically assume a new name upon joining—typically a color, the name of a precious stone, or a virtue which one seeks to develop. There were 700 members in 1987.

EMISSARIES OF DIVINE LIGHT. Founded in 1932 by Lloyd Arthur Meeker (1907-1954), who wrote under the pseudonym of Uranda, the Emissaries originated as an esoteric Christian group and were variously known in their early years as the Divine Light Emissaries, the Ontological Society, the Universal Institute of Applied Ontology, the Foundation of Universal Unity, and the Integrity Society. Meeker established the first community at Sunrise Ranch, near Loveland, Colorado, and a second in 1951 in Mile House, British Columbia. Following Meeker's death in a plane crash in 1954, he was succeeded by Martin Cecil (1909-1988), who had worked with Meeker in formulating the organization's teachings, enshrined in a volume entitled *The Third Sacred School.*

The Emissaries teach that men and women were created in God's image, which becomes distorted through the mind's activities, such as feelings of fear, jealousy, hatred, and the like. Humans have free will and are able to accept divine control and to experience "re-emergence" as God-beings. Ontology, as understood by the Emissaries, is the technique by which one manifests one's reality as a God-being, making the invisible become visible. Community living is beneficial for this purpose, since a community makes available a larger area for divine energy to operate. Since God is the totality of God-beings, the ultimate aim is the experience of oneness. A meditative technique known as "attunement" aids this purpose.

Martin Cecil was succeeded by his son Michael Cecil (b. 1935), who made each community self-governing. The organization has moved into New Age (q.v.) activities, teaching Tai Chi, dowsing, eco-feminism, and sacred dance. The Emissary Foundation International cooperates with other sympathetic bodies and coordinates a variety of programs. Emissaries are active in the United States, Canada, Great Britain, and elsewhere. There are 12 communities worldwide and some 160 places for meeting. In 1988 there was a reported world membership of 3,000.

ENGAGED BUDDHISM. The term was first introduced in the 1950s by Vietnamese Zen (q.v.) monk Thich Nhat Hanh (b. 1926), who combined Buddhist (q.v.) meditative practice with social action, including nonviolent civil disobedience. Hanh studied at Princeton University, returned to the United States in 1966 on a humanitarian visit during the time of the Vietnam War, and sent a delegation of Buddhists to the ensuing Paris peace talks. Although Hanh did much for American-Vietnamese reconciliation, he remains exiled from Vietnam and currently resides in France, where he established a center known as Plum Village for monks, nuns, and lay people in 1985 (the name refers to some 1,250 plum trees, whose fruit is sold to provide medicine for the Vietnamese). Hanh's followers maintain an active interest in areas of social and political concern, including economics, animal welfare, peace, reform of the Indian caste system, ecology, and poverty. Supporters are organized though an International Network of Engaged Buddhists (INEB).

Thich Nhat Hanh has authored more than 70 publications, including *The Miracle of Mindfulness, Touching Peace; Living Buddha, Living Christ;* and *Peace Is Every Step.* His notion of "interbeing," originally devised during the Vietnam War, affirms the interdependence of all existence and contains his "Fourteen Precepts of the Order of Interbeing," or "Fourteen Guidelines for Engaged Buddhism."

More widely, the term "Engaged Buddhism" is applied to any socially involved form of Buddhism, whether or not inaugurated by Hahn, in contrast to more traditional Buddhism which seeks to develop one's individual consciousness.

ERHARD SEMINAR TRAINING *(est)*. A seminar program active between 1971 and 1984, offering "self-enlightenment" and "global transformation." *est*'s originator was John Paul (Jack) Rosenberg (b. 1935), who changed his name to Werner Hans Erhard. Erhard claims to have experienced being "transformed" one day as he drove over San Francisco's Golden Gate Bridge, and the seminars were devised to pass on this experience to others. Although lacking formal education, Erhard read widely, and his ideas were particularly influenced by Zen Buddhism (qq.v.) and also by Thomas Kuhn, Martin Heidegger, the transpersonal psychology of Abraham Maslow and Carl Rogers, Gestalt therapy, and Scientology (q.v.).

Erhard's seminars became particularly controversial on account of the conditions to which participants were subjected. Designed to demonstrate that attendees' lives "did not work," they aimed to provide a state which—like Zen *satori*—defies verbal encapsulation. The culmination point of *est* seminars was a presentation on "the Anatomy of the Mind," after which participants were asked to stand up if they had "got it": this indefinable "it" was not cognitive information but "empowerment," which differs from one's ordinary consciousness or "mind state," where imprints of past experiences are recorded, give rise to illogical associations, and when reactivated, are perceived as threatening.

In addition to the seminars, *est* instigated a number of projects ostensibly aimed at global transformation. These spanned a variety of social concerns, including education, youth, prisons, and world hunger. The Werner Erhard Foundation made funds available for research and aid in some of these areas, but others set out to raise public awareness and to influence attitudes rather than to offer direct assistance with the problems they address. This policy attracted much criticism, particularly in the case of the controversial Hunger Project of 1977, which elicited contributions from donors but gave out no money whatsoever for the direct relief of world hunger.

In 1984 Erhard sold his organization, which was subsequently renamed Landmark Education Corporation (q.v.). The seminars, which continued in a modified form, became known as the Forum. Although *est* and the Forum are frequently categorized as NRMs or "cults" (q.v.), leaders and participants have typically denied that undergoing the seminars involves following a religion. *See also* CENTERS NETWORK; HUMAN POTENTIAL MOVEMENT.

ESALEN INSTITUTE. Founded in 1962 by Michael Murphy, who studied Eastern spirituality at an Indian ashram, the Institute is part of the Human Potential Movement (q.v.). It teaches body work, visualization, Gestalt therapy, and the spiritualizing of the "enneagram." Its headquarters are in Big Sur, California, where around 1,500 visitors come each year.

ESSENE CHURCH OF CHRIST. An organization established in Oregon under the leadership of the Rev. Abba Nazariah, D.D. (born David Owen), who is its archbishop. Nazariah is accredited with a profound experience of oneness with Jesus at the age of eight, and he claims to have been subsequently trained by an elderly Essene master called Infinity, who initiated him into an ancient Egyptian Essene order and whom he helped to construct the Essene Garden of Peace, near San Diego. The Church's leaders claim to be reincarnated Essenes (q.v.), whose task is to restore the Church of the Essene Christ, whose teachings became altered by "men of perverse minds." However, Jesus prophesied that the true teachings would be restored at a definite "cusp" in history—our present time—which heralds a New Age of peace. Nonviolence entails vegetarianism, which is greatly emphasized and is said to have been practiced by Jesus.

The church uses the Gospel of the Holy Twelve (also known as the Essene New Testament), which Rev. Gideon Jasper Ouseley (1835-1905) is said to have rediscovered in 1888 and translated from the Aramaic. Much importance is also attached to Edmond Bordeaux Szekely's (q.v.) *The Essene Gospel of Peace* (1937) and his subsequent writings. Nazariah is also familiar with other world scriptures, and he draws on the Bhagavad Gita, the Tao Te Ching, the Srimad Bhagavatam, the Dhammapada, the Upanishads, and the Yoga Sutras of Patanjali. Nazariah possesses many other ancient scriptures, which he is currently preparing for publication, although this may take several years. Principal teachings include the sacredness and unity of all life, reincarnation (q.v.), vegetarianism, and the feminine aspect of deity. Jesus did not save by vicarious atonement, but salvation is gained by becoming attuned to his teachings. Followers are encouraged to attain a "sevenfold peace"—peace with one's body, mind, family, humanity, culture, the earth, and finally God.

ESSENE FELLOWSHIP OF PEACE. *A.k.a.: Spiritual Church of Ataraxia.* Founded in 1942, this group teaches that God is the source of light, law and love; that Jesus shows the way; and that spiritual progress is possible after death. Particular emphasis is give to esoteric meanings of color, as set out in *Creative Color* (1989) by George Weddell, Mary Weddell, and Miriam B. Willis.

ESSENES. Originally a Jewish messianic group of the Second Temple period, the Essenes lived in remote communes, pursuing a lifestyle of austerity and emphasizing ritual purity and cleanliness. There probably existed some 4,000 Essenes in the first century C.E., but they did not survive after 70 C.E. According to the renowned psychic Edgar Cayce (q.v.) (1877-1945), the Essenes were representatives of the Great White Brotherhood (q.v.).

A number of religious groups claim to have revived Essene practices in recent times, sometimes attributing a more ancient pedigree to the movement. Thus, the (now defunct) Essene Center founded by Walter Hagan in 1972 claimed that the Order of Essenes originated with Moses. Other Essene groups such as Reginald Therrien's Essenes of Arkashea (q.v.) gave the Essenes a pedigree dating back to

Pharaoh Akhenaten (1354 B.C.E.) Some have claimed that clandestine Essene communities survived and were only recently rediscovered, while other teachers have claimed to "channel" (q.v.) Essene teachings, thus giving them an appeal in certain New Age (q.v.) circles. Other New Age ideas have tended to be attributed to the Essenes, such as belief in reincarnation (q.v.), healing, psychic powers, and a concern for peace. It is commonly claimed that Jesus of Nazareth was an Essene. Recent concern for environmental conservation has sometimes been regarded as consonant with the simplicity and poverty of the Essenes. Modern Essene teachers have also attributed vegetarianism to this group, alleging that Jesus was a vegetarian. *See also* INTERNATIONAL COMMUNITY OF CHRIST; KABBALAH.

ESSENES OF ARKASHEA. Led by Reginald Therrien, this modern-day Essene (q.v.) group claims to trace its origins to Pharaoh Akhenaten (1354 B.C.E.). Although Akhenaten's monotheism allegedly survived to the first century C.E., the Jewish Essenes are believed to have departed from the practices of Akhenaten's ancient order. The rediscovery of this order is related in *The Discovery* (1993), which describes how a woman found surviving members in a monastery in Alabama during the 1980s. The group extols the virtues of poverty and celibacy, but has three orders of membership: the "cloister" for those who are committed to both; the "hamlet" for those who accept poverty but not celibacy; and the "hoblet" for new members who have not yet committed themselves to either.

ETERNAL FLAME FOUNDATION. *A.k.a. Arizona Immortalists.* An organization founded in Scottsdale, Arizona, by Charles Paul Brown (b. 1935), BernaDeane Brown (b. 1937), and James Russell Strole (b. 1949). Charles Brown claimed to have experienced a revelation of Jesus Christ in the 1960s, as a result of which his mission became that of creating a deathless world of physical immorality ("total physical aliveness"). The group believes that there exist immortal cells within the physical body and that these can be made to multiply, thus conquering death, "the last enemy to be destroyed." The movement attracted some 200 followers in Scottsdale in the late 1980s, when attempts were made to introduce immortalism to Europe and Israel.

ETHIOPIANS. Group of African Independent Churches (q.v.), laying stress on "Africa for Africans." The Ethiopian churches result from attempts to find expressions of Christianity (q.v.) that seem appropriate to black Africans, in contrast to the versions of the white Christian missionaries. The Ethiopians remain traditional in their theology, which is characteristically Protestant. Ethiopia serves as a symbol for black consciousness, being a predominantly Christian African country and being mentioned in Scripture.

EVANS, WARREN FELT (1817-1889). A pupil of Phineas Parker Quimby and a principal exponent of New Thought (q.v.). At one time a Methodist minister, Evans came to accept Emanuel Swedenborg's teaching, joining the Swedenborgian Church of the New Jerusalem. In 1863 he established himself as a healer, employing Quimby's techniques. From 1869 onward he wrote extensively on spiritual healing, combining ideas from German idealism, Ralph Waldo Emerson (q.v.), and Swedenborg with those of Quimby. Evans believed that illness was due to disturbances in the spiritual body and had physical repercussions. He recommended the use of "positive affirmations" and was an important precursor of "positive thinking," as advocated by writers such as Dale Carnegie (1888-1955) and Norman Vincent Peale (1898-1993). Evans did not found any church or spiritual movement, but his writings proved highly influential among "metaphysical" groups. His works include *Esoteric Christianity and Mental Therapeutics* (1866) and *Mental Medicine: A Treatise in Medical Psychology* (1873).

EXCLUSIVE BRETHREN. Originally part of the Brethren (q.v.), the Exclusive Brethren split away, following controversies between early leaders J. N. Darby and B. W. Newton. In contrast with the Open Brethren (q.v.) (the other type of Brethren), the Exclusive Brethren have regarded themselves as the only true Christian society and refuse to allow those outside the movement to share the sacrament ("the breaking of bread"). Unlike the Open Brethren, they permit child baptism, on the ground that the New Testament appears to allow the baptism of households (Acts 16:15). Firmly believing that the true Christian community should be separate from the world, Exclusive Brethren do not eat with unbelievers, do not watch television, do not attend meetings other than their own, and even refuse to be listed in telephone directories.

The Exclusive Brethren fragmented into a number of different groups: the Ames Brethren, the Booth Brethren, the Grant Brethren, and the Glanton Brethren, among others. A number of reunions took place variously in 1926, 1940, 1953, and 1974, as a result of which William Kelly's (1820-1906) group, which had moved away as a separatist "new lump," reunited with the continental Brethren, then the Tunbridge Wells Brethren, the Stuart Brethren, part of the Grant Brethren, and finally the Glanton Brethren. These mergers resulted in the Exclusive Reunited Brethren. The Tunbridge Wells Brethren in the United States continue to remain separate.

This wing of the Brethren is best known for the "Taylor Brethren," called after James Taylor, Jr. ("Big Jim Taylor"), the son of James Taylor, Sr., who assumed office after the death of F. E. Raven, their founder-leader, in 1906.

EXEGESIS. One of the "self religions" (q.v.), founded by Robert d'Aubigny in 1977; formerly Infinity Trainings (founded 1976). The name "Exegesis" was explained as "self-disclosure," and the "transformational seminars" aimed to enable participants to experience being "at source," increasing their awareness, self-confidence, and sensitivity. Much of the seminars' focus was on one's work, which participants were encouraged to regard as spiritual discipline, and for which one must assume personal responsibility. The seminars' techniques were applied to seemingly mundane activities, such as telephone selling. Following adverse media publicity, the Exegesis Standard Seminars were closed in 1984, but the organization continued under the name "Programmes Ltd." The seminars attracted around 6,000 participants between 1976 and 1984.

EXIT COUNSELING. This expression was formerly synonymous with "deprogramming" (q.v.), but now also straightforwardly refers to the voluntary process of counseling for those who have recently left an NRM or are considering doing so. Such counseling may be needed in order to enable the leaver to adjust to a more conventional lifestyle, to reestablish a circle of friends outside the former religious community, or to secure employment or new qualifications. Some Christian evangelical countercultists may discuss with the counselee whether his or her New Christian organization can credibly afford the means of salvation. *See also* ANTICULT MOVEMENT.

-F-

FAIR (Family Action Information and Resource). Founded by British Member of Parliament Paul Rose in 1976, FAIR was originally set up in response to parental concerns about the Unification Church (q.v.). Originally the acronym FAIR stood for "Family Action Information and Rescue," although this was changed in 1994, since FAIR does not offer to rescue individuals from NRMs by means of deprogramming (q.v.) techniques. FAIR seeks to raise public consciousness. It affirms a belief in human rights and claims to challenge unacceptable practices in NRMs rather than their beliefs.

Although FAIR has never advocated deprogramming in any of its literature, a breakaway group, which assumed the name of Cultists Anonymous (CA) in 1985, criticized FAIR for being unduly moderate; its members perceived deprogramming as a more effective means of countering NRMs. CA later rejoined FAIR in 1991. In the meantime, Cyril

Vosper, an officeholder in FAIR, had himself been convicted of deprogramming in Germany in 1987. Lord Rodney, who apparently was one of CA's leaders, became chairman of FAIR in 1988, when CA was still in full operation.

FAIR maintains links with a number of other anticult groups in Europe and the United States. In particular, it works with the Cult Information Centre (CIC) and Catalyst, the latter being a small organization headed by Graham Baldwin, a Pentecostalist (q.v.) lay pastor. International links have included the former Cult Awareness Network and the American Family Foundation (qq.v.). In Europe, FAIR is represented on FECRIS (the European Federation of Centers for Research and Sectarianism). *See also* ANTICULT MOVEMENT.

FAITH TABERNACLE (1). A Pentecostalist (q.v.) organization in the United States, active from the 1920s, emphasizing fervent prayer, divine healing, personal holiness, and an expectation of the imminent second coming of Christ. The church rejected infant baptism, favoring the baptism of adult believers.

FAITH TABERNACLE (2). A group of African New Christians, derived from the Precious Stone Society—a movement formed in 1920 within mainstream Christian churches, emphasizing prayer and healing. D. O. Odubanjo received literature from the U.S. Faith Tabernacle, which helped the African movement to gain momentum. The group of churches emanating from the Faith Tabernacle is known as the Christ Apostolic Churches (q.v.), with a membership of 3,000 in 1992.

FALUN GONG. *A.k.a.: Falun Dafa.* A Chinese system for effecting physical, emotional, and spiritual improvement, introduced by Master Li Hongzhi (b. 1951) in 1992. The essence of its teachings and practices is enshrined in his book *Zhuan Falun* (The Revolving Wheel of Dharma), which has now been translated into 10 languages. Falun Gong is said to come from an ancient oral tradition: one of Li's innovations is its written form.

From childhood, Li is said to have studied under teachers from various traditions—Buddhist, Confucian, Taoist and esoteric—and to have studied various forms of *qigong*, a system involving bodily and breathing exercises for therapy and self-improvement, that became popular in the 1980s. Falun Gong differs from qigong in at least two important respects. First, at an early stage the practitioner develops a "Falun," an intelligent entity located in the lower abdomen. The Falun rotates constantly, which entails that one receives the benefits of Falun Gong at all times of the day, unlike qigong, where benefit accrues from the hours at which it is practiced. Second, since the body is a mirror of the wider cosmos, the Falun's rotation and that of the universe are synchronized, enabling the Falun to absorb the universe's energy. It is believed that ill health is the result of past karma, accrued in previous lives, and the Falun's rotation progressively eliminates the effects of one's past deeds. It is thus to be equated with the Buddhist concept of the turning of the wheel of the Dharma ("law" or teaching) and the flow of the Tao, through which yin and yang interact. Falun Gong therefore offers a path to enlightenment or buddhahood, as well as physical and mental health.

Crucial to Falun Gong is the cultivation of *xinxing*—one's inner nature, or "heart or mind nature." Both the human individual and the universe are made up of three characteristics: *zhen, shan,* and *ren*—truthfulness, benevolence, and forbearance. These three are the basic constituents of matter, as well as the criteria for distinguishing good from evil.

In May 1999 the practice was banned by the Chinese government as an illicit form of religion, and its practitioners have been subjected to fines and even imprisonment. Estimates of the number of practitioners varies: Falun Gong itself claims 100 million, while government estimates place it as high as 200 million in the People's Republic of China alone.

FAMILY, THE. An organization founded by David Brandt Berg (q.v.) (1919-1994) as the Children of God (CoG) in 1968 and subsequently renamed the Family of Love in 1978, and the Family in 1991. CoG developed in California, where Berg propagated his distinctive and controversial version of evangelical Protestantism to the post-hippie, post-psychedelic youth culture, which had become part of the "Jesus Revolution." From a single small community, the Family expanded rapidly, establishing a presence in a total of 50 countries by 1973 and reaching a worldwide membership of around 13,000 in 1998.

A Christian fundamentalist (q.v.) organization, the Family attaches equal weight to the teachings of the Old and the New Testaments, together with a belief in the prophetic status of Berg, who was known to his followers as Moses David or Father David. Berg's teachings were disseminated by means of *True Comix,* which presented the Christian message in comic strip form, and by the *MO Letters* (q.v.), which were circulated among members. These letters gained the movement negative publicity because of their explicit sexual nature: they advocated "flirty fishing" (q.v.) and the enjoyment of sex in general, in which members were encouraged not to confine their sexual activity to one sole partner.

The Family's attitudes toward sex have taken public attention away from their other major teachings. Being fundamentalist, they firmly deny Charles Darwin's evolutionary theory. They interpret Old Testament prophecies to refer to Christ's advent and accept his role as the redeemer of the world, who was crucified, rose from the dead, and ascended into heaven. Members have a firm belief in Christ's imminent second coming, declaring that many biblical prophecies also have their fulfillment in present-day events, particularly regarding the nation of Israel. Believing that the days of the present age are numbered, they see no point in attachments to worldly possessions, preferring to rent rather than buy property. In common with the early Christian Church, Family members typically live in communities, although there is provision for "fellow members" to live outside, sharing in the activities of the "charter members."

Although the Family claims to be theologically orthodox, it does not practice "water baptism," holding that salvation is obtained through faith rather than any external rite. Berg and his followers have also maintained a firm belief in a spirit world, from which angels (q.v.), departed spirits, and demons can communicate with humanity. In 1999 there were 10,183 "charter members" (members in communities) worldwide, with 2,871 fellow members. *See also* JESUS MOVEMENT.

FAMILY FEDERATION FOR WORLD PEACE AND UNIFICATION. The name adopted by the Unification Church (q.v.) in 1997, and which is now its most widely used, in preference to the previous names Holy Spirit Association for the Unification of World Christianity (HSA-UWC—its original name) and Unification Church (UC). The proffered reason for the name change was the opening out of the Blessing (the so-called "mass marriage") to couples who are not UC members. According to current UC teaching, marriage, stable family life, and receiving the Rev. and Mrs. Moon's Blessing on one's marriage are more important than membership, since it is the Blessing that grants access to the Kingdom of Heaven after death. To receive the Blessing it is no longer necessary to attend one of the large ceremonies over which the True Parents preside, but merely to sign a short declaration committing oneself to a stable marriage and to conservative family values such as teaching one's children the value of chastity outside the marriage bond.

FARM, THE. Originally an ex-hippie community, originating from a series of classes on spiritual philosophy given by Stephen Gaskin (b. 1936). Gaskin, a professor at San Francisco State College known simply as "Stephen" to his followers, began a series of classes on "cultural ferment" in 1966. By 1969 they attracted audiences of 2,000, and the following year Stephen was persuaded to travel countrywide to reach an even wider public. Supporters traveled with Stephen in a caravan of school buses, and they eventually settled in a 1,000-acre site in Summertown in southern Tennessee, where they set up a commune. The community had no common philosophy or creed, since members regarded themselves as "free-thinkers," bound together by a number of "agreements," the most important of which was the affirmation "We are all one." The Farm was pacifist, with a deep respect for life, and most members have been vegetarian. Natural healing and natural childbirth were championed.

In its early days the Farm's lifestyle entailed communal living, common ownership of property, free love, and the imbibing of "sacred drugs." Such "sacraments" involved marijuana, peyote, and psilocybin mushrooms. This caused the community to fall foul of the law, for which Stephen and others served prison sentences in the early 1970s. The policy on drugs has now been revised, the majority of members expressing a commitment to abstinence from all drugs, including alcohol, tobacco, and caffeine. Free love has given way to more-traditional family values. Serious financial problems in the early 1980s had a number of effects: communal living gave way to the reinstatement of private ownership, and the need for greater austerity led to a drop in membership. At present there are only some 50 or 60 households in the community, with a total of just over 200 residents.

The Farm has initiated a number of outreach projects. PLENTY is a Third World charity, recognized by the United Nations as a nongovernmental organization. The community has also set up a Natural Rights Center and a New York Bronx voluntary ambulance service. Businesses which finance the organization include various publishing ventures (mainly books on vegetarianism, environmental issues, and Native American culture), a building company, and video production. Stephen Gaskin has written a number of books, including *The Caravan* (1972) and *Monday Night Class* (1974). In 1991 there were 300 members.

FATHER DIVINE'S PEACE MISSION. Born George Baker in Rockville, Maryland, Father Divine (1879-1965) came from an impoverished black Baptist family. Strongly influenced by the 1906 Azusa Street Revival in Los Angeles, Baker's mission combined Pentecostalist (q.v.) spirituality—particularly glossolaliation—with a social gospel that proclaimed the inner divinity of all and particularly entailed the elimination of race and color prejudice. The mission reached its pinnacle from 1929 onward, in the years of the Great Depression. It provided meals for 15 cents and accommodation for one dollar a week, thus enabling the needy to maintain self-respect since they paid for these benefits. The mission's headquarters were established in Harlem in 1933, but were moved in 1953 to Woodmont, Philadelphia, which currently remains its center. Father Divine's supporters were arranged into uniformed organizations: Rosebuds (young women), Lilybuds (older women), and Crusaders (men). They were committed to celibacy and to abstinence from tobacco, alcohol, and drugs. The sole sacrament that was celebrated was the "communion" or common meal, which was a free banquet, open to everyone each Sunday. This is still celebrated at Woodmont, with a place left vacant for Father Divine. In 1942 Father Divine married "Sweet Angel," or "Mother Divine" (as she is now known), a white woman whose marriage to Father Divine is regarded as a "spiritual marriage," being unconsummated, enacted to signify the union of races.

Father Divine's followers regard him as the Second Coming of Christ and hence do not accept that he was born in 1879, as outsiders claim, or that he died in 1965. Although the Woodmont headquarters contain his monument, his followers state that this only houses his body and that he remains alive. Father Divine taught that there is an important link between faith and health and that there is no death. As a consequence of celibacy and a progressively aging following, the movement has diminished in size. Those who have not died regard themselves as the "remnant" of which the Hebrew prophets spoke, and they await the bodily return of Father Divine. In the meantime, Mother Divine continues to head the movement. The Rev. Jim Jones (q.v.) of the Peoples Temple (q.v.) visited Father Divine's mission in the late

1950s and drew on some of his ideas. Membership in 1930 stood at 20 million, but has dwindled to a mere 300 (1994). *See also* GARVEY, MARCUS MOZIAH.

FELLOWSHIP OF ISIS (FOI). Founded in 1976, FOI is an association of various wiccan and Pagan (qq.v.) groups. It lays emphasis on the worship of feminine forms of deity, especially Isis and other Egyptian goddesses. FOI was founded by Olivia Durdin-Robertson, together with her husband Lawrence—who has authored several books on goddess worship—and his sister Pamela. In 1994 membership was around 12,000 in 65 countries.

FELLOWSHIP OF THE INNER LIGHT. *A.k.a.: Inner Light Consciousness (ILC).* A psychical group, founded in 1972 by Paul Solomon, a former Baptist minister who is frequently compared with Edgar Cayce (q.v.) by his followers. Solomon provides "readings" that are purported to come from the Universal Mind or Akashic Records (q.v.). These readings cover a considerable range of topics, including health, past lives, Atlantis and Lemuria, and the destiny of the universe. In particular, he encourages followers to develop the "light within," which is equated with the Holy Spirit. There are fellowships in the United States, England, and the Netherlands.

FILLMORE, CHARLES (1854-1948), and **MYRTLE** (1845-1931). Founders of the Unity School of Christianity (q.v.). After the collapse of their business in real estate, Myrtle Fillmore (née Mary Caroline Page) contracted tuberculosis. After listening to a lecture on New Thought (q.v.) in Kansas in 1886 by Eugene B. Weeks, she was prompted to use the affirmation, "I am a child of God and therefore I do not inherit sickness." She noticed a significant improvement in her condition, although a full recovery took two years. Charles, who had explored Eastern religious ideas as well as occultism, was finally drawn to the principles of New Thought. In 1889 he published *Modern Thought,* a magazine devoted to emergent religions in the United States and which included New

Thought ideas. This attracted a number of students, causing Charles to start a lending library of metaphysical books. In 1890 they began an association with Emma Curtis Hopkins, sponsoring some lectures and subsequently studying under her, becoming ordained as ministers of Christian Science (New Thought) in 1891. Unity was established in the same year, and the journal *Modern Thought* was replaced by *Unity*. In 1903 the organization was incorporated as the Unity School of Practical Christianity, subsequently renamed the Unity School of Christianity in 1914. A prolific writer, Charles Fillmore authored or coauthored 13 books, including *Christian Healing* (1909).

FINDHORN. A New Age center near Forres in Invernesshire, Scotland, established in 1962 by Eileen and Peter Caddy. The community began with some unorthodox horticultural experiments by the Caddys, who were forced to grow their own vegetables as a result of Peter's unemployment. Although the soil was extremely poor on the banks of the Moray Firth, the Caddys managed to grow outsize crops, and Findhorn became famed for cabbages that weighed as much as 40 pounds. The Findhorn community attributed this success to "devas"—spirits that they believed inhabited the plants and with whom the third founder-member Dorothy Maclean claimed successful communication. A fourth early leader, Robert Ogilvie Crombie, claimed to communicate with the god Pan and expounded a worldview incorporating a large variety of "para-physicals," ranging from gnomes (the "grossest" type) to angels (q.v.) (the highest).

In 1970 David Spangler (q.v.) joined the community and inaugurated the seminar program, which still continues (although Spangler himself has now left). At the time of writing, the Findhorn community no longer attempts to grow giant vegetables, but continues to promote its seminar program, including workshops on handicrafts, creative writing, yoga, personal development, and business skills. Although Findhorn's inception preceded the rise of the New Age Movement (q.v.), it shares many of the New Age's values: personal exploration, a positive view of the self, oneness with nature, and eclecticism. The community has organized New Age pilgrimages in Russia, as well as courses in spiritual development in Great Britain. There are 250 members, mainly at Findhorn itself. *See also* TREVELYAN, SIR GEORGE.

FIRE BAPTISM. Emanating from the Holiness movement, fire baptism was an antecedent of "speaking in tongues" (q.v.), which became characteristic of Pentecostalism (q.v.). The expression alludes to Matthew 3:11, wherein John the Baptist predicts that Jesus will offer baptism by fire. The Rev. B. H. Irwin of the Holiness movement taught that this did not merely mean "sanctification" through the Holy Spirit, but a more striking phenomenon in which believers became filled and empowered by the Holy Spirit. In 1895 he led the first "fire baptized congregation" in Olmitz, Ohio, and in 1898 founded the Fire-Baptized Holiness Association in Anderson, South Carolina. Initially the phenomenon was not associated with the Pentecost experience described in Acts 2:1-3—a connection that became characteristic of the Pentecostalist movement.

FLIRTY FISHING (FF-ing). A practice of the Children of God (CoG), now the Family (q.v.), in the 1970s and early 1980s. In 1973 founder-leader Moses David's (David Berg's [q.v.]) wife Maria began to have sexual relationships with male seekers as a means of gaining opportunities to preach the gospel to them. Other CoG members—mainly, although not exclusively, female—adopted the practice, at first in the Canary Islands from 1974 to 1976, and then more widely from 1978 onward. The reference to fishing was an allusion to Jesus' instruction that his disciples should become "fishers of men" (Matthew 4:19), while the reference to flirting was David's own invention. The practice was officially advocated in David's *MO Letters* during that period.

Members of the Family now claim that FF-ing was neither an opportunity to have free sex nor an attempt to entice new members into the community by seduction. Rather, they maintain the importance of satisfying people's physical as well as spiritual needs, contending that seekers were in a better position to hear the gospel once their physical needs had been satisfied.

The practice led to a variety of problems, principally unwanted pregnancies (CoG did not permit contraception) and sexually transmitted diseases. Finally the AIDS epidemic caused David to review CoG's policy on sex. A *MO Letter* in 1983 advocated the use of condoms for those who were already having sexual relationships with new seekers and directed that no further FF-ing initiatives were to be made. For those who lived in CoG communities, a six-month period had to elapse before any sexual relationships were permitted. FF-ing finally died out in 1987. In its place, members practiced "ES-ing"—offering their services as "escorts" to members of the opposite sex.

The Family's attitudes to sex still remain liberal, although sex with outsiders is disallowed. Members can engage in "sharing"—the practice of borrowing another member's marriage partner, with consent, for sex or companionship. The Family justifies its "revolutionary" attitudes to sex on the ground that the Christian is no longer "under law" but "under grace" (Romans 6:14) and hence not rigidly bound by the constraints of the Jewish law.

FLOATING. A term sometimes applied to the experience of someone who leaves an NRM. After giving up a way of life and a set of convictions, one is rarely ready to embrace an alternative lifestyle immediately or to embrace some other religious option. Hence there is often a period of uncertainty and noncommitment, during which time the leaver adjusts to life without belonging. This may involve a reappraisal of life's meaning and purpose, or more mundane practicalities such as finding employment (if commitment to the NRM has been full-time) or making new friends. Although the anticult movement (q.v.) typically portrays disengagement as problematic or even traumatic, there is undoubtedly a significant number of leavers who go through such transitions without difficulties.

FOCOLARE. A conservative Roman Catholic reformist movement, founded by Chiara Lubich (q.v.) (b. 1920). The Focolare originated in 1944, following the bombing of Trento, Lubich's home city, in which Lubich elected to stay in order to help war victims. Cofounders of the movement were Igino Giordani—an Italian member of parliament whom Lubich met in 1948—and Pasquale Foresi, who became a Roman Catholic priest in 1954. Starting in Italy, the movement spread to other European countries by 1952 and to other continents by 1959. Small communities ("little towns") were established from 1965 onward, although community living is not a requirement.

The Focolare emphasize the importance of human unity, social action, world peace, and interreligious dialogue. Membership is open to Catholics and non-Catholics alike. Some critics have accused Lubich of being more interested in converting members of other faiths than in dialogue. The movement secured papal approval in 1962. *See also* NEO-CATECHUMENATE; OPUS DEI.

FORTUNE, DION (1890-1946). Esotericist and founder of the Fraternity of the Inner Light. Born Violet Mary Firth, she changed her name to Dion Fortune on account of her family motto *Deo, non fortuna* ("By God, not by chance"). Her family were Christian Scientists (q.v.), but Fortune joined the Theosophical Society and became familiar with the notion of the Great White Brotherhood (q.v.). Fortune claimed to have visions of some of the Ascended Masters, including Jesus and the Comte de Saint-Germain. In 1919 she joined Stella Matutina, a breakaway group from the Hermetic Order of the Golden Dawn (q.v.), and in 1922 founded the Christian Mystic Lodge of the Theosophical Society at Glastonbury (q.v.). This became the Fraternity of the Inner Light in 1924, and subsequently the Society of the Inner Light (q.v.).

From 1927 to 1939 Fortune was married to Thomas Penry Evans, an occultist, with whom she studied magic (q.v.), combining esoteric Christianity with Tarot, Kabbalism (q.v.), and neo-Paganism. Fortune is particularly important in the recent revival of magic in the West. Her principal writings include *The Mystical Qabalah* (1935) and *Cosmic Doctrine*. Having studied psychology, especially the works of Freud and Jung, Fortune is also noted for her *Psychic Self-Defence* (1931)—a treatise on how to protect oneself from the psychic power exerted by others.

FOUNDATION FAITH OF GOD. Reconstituted from the Process Church of the Final Judgment (q.v.) in 1974, this movement was originally called the Foundation Church of the Millennium, becoming the Foundation Faith of the Millennium in 1977 and assuming its present name in 1980. Originally an attempt to reform the quasi-Satanist elements of the Process, the organization underwent numerous doctrinal progressions. It currently teaches mainstream Christian doctrines such as the Trinity, the Incarnation, and salvation through rebirth, but combines these with several occultist practices such as Tarot, astrology, and psychic healing. Believing that each individual has his or her own guardian angel (q.v.), clergy undertake "angel listenings" on behalf of members. The organization is headed by a nine-member Council of Luminaries, who oversee the Office of the Faithful. There are four categories of minister: luminaries, celebrants, mentors, and covenanters. Among the movement's projects is the Crusade of Innocence: a ministry to families with seriously sick children. During the 1980s leaders claimed a membership of 20,000, with 500,000 affiliates, but these figures are probably grossly exaggerated.

FOUNDATION OF HUMAN UNDERSTANDING. Founded in 1961 by Roy Masters (born Reuben Obermeister in England in 1928), this group gained formal recognition in the United States as a religious organization in 1987. Masters studied hypnosis and, having moved to South Africa in his early years, became acquainted with the methods of native African healers (sometimes pejoratively called "witch doctors"). In 1949 he moved to the United States, becoming a diamond cutter in Houston, Texas. Following the Bridey Murphy case in the 1950s, Masters's opinions were sought, and he founded the Institute of Hypnosis, which was a precursor of the Foundation of Human Understanding. Masters devised a series of radio talks entitled "Your Mind Can Keep You Well," which was published in book form in 1968. Masters's main technique was psychocatalysis—his specific brand of meditation, which purportedly cured illness and provided a religious, mystical quality of life. He taught that people were already hypnotized—by the media, preachers, politicians, and educators—and needed to awake from this condition. Membership figures are unreported, although the Foundation's mailing list was 150,000 in 1989.

FOX, MARGARETTA (Maggie, d. 1893), and **CATHERINE** (Katie, d. 1892). Commonly referred to as "the Fox sisters," they were precursors of modern Spiritualism (q.v.). On 31 March 1848, they heard inexplicable "rappings" at their home in Hydesville, New York. Concluding that the noises were those of a spirit, they established a code to enable mutual contact. The spirit, initially referred to as "Mr. Splitfoot" (a name for the devil), identified himself as a peddler by the name of Charles Rosa, alleging that he had been murdered near the house and buried under the cellar. Excavation of the site yielded some human remains. The Fox sisters traveled in the United States demonstrating their powers, at one point under the direction of showman Phineas T. Barnum. In the late 1850s Maggie lost interest in psychic phenomena, but Katie continued, adding "mirror writing" (a form of automatic writing) and materializations to her repertoire. In the wake of much criticism of fraudulent mediums, Maggie confessed in 1888 that the Hydesville rappings had also been a fraud, but—curiously—retracted this confession the following year. Although by no means the first to have claimed to contact the dead, the Fox sisters were significant in arousing public interest in mediumship, and it has been estimated that by 1855 some two million Americans were actively involved in Spiritualism.

FREECOG. The first organized anticult group, founded by William Ramur and Ted Patrick in 1972. When Ramur's daughter joined the Children of God (CoG, now the Family [q.v.]), he initiated a personal anti-CoG campaign after seeing CoG's living conditions at Thurber, Texas. Patrick's son and nephew had also become involved in CoG, and when Ramur and Patrick met, they established the Parents' Committee to Free Our Children from the Children of God. The name became abbreviated to Free the Children of God, and subsequently to FREECOG. Initially a cult-specific group, its base widened, resulting in the Volunteer Parents of America (VPA) and expanding further into a national organization, the Citizens' Freedom Foundation (CFF), in 1974. By 1975 it had a membership of 1,500. CFF was the precursor of the Cult Awareness Network (q.v.), one of America's principal anticult organizations. *See also* ANTICULT MOVEMENT.

FUNDAMENTALISM. While this term is popularly applied to Muslims and, less frequently, to Hindus, Sikhs, and Buddhists, it is only properly applied within the context of Christianity (q.v.). Although used by the media to designate forms of religion that are held to be extreme, overliteral, or reactionary, the fundamentalist movement in Christianity emerged as a response to two perceived threats to the Christian faith: Darwinism and the rise of liberal scholarship. At the Bible Conference of Conservative Protestants in Niagara, New York, in 1895, a number of conservative Protestants formulated five principles of fundamentalism: the literal inerrancy of the Bible; the divinity of Jesus Christ; the virgin birth; a substitutionary theory of atonement; and the physical resurrection and bodily return of Christ. A series of 12 tracts, entitled "The Fundamentals," was distributed worldwide between 1909 and 1914, and the term *fundamentalism* is derived from these. In 1919 the World's Christian Fundamentalist Association was founded. The fundamentalist controversy divided Protestants, who were classified either as "fundamentalist" or "modernist" according to their stance. In the period between the two World Wars, American fundamentalists attempted to ban the teaching of evolutionism in schools. Their efforts received a serious setback in 1925, when Charles Scopes was convicted of teaching evolutionary theory but had his appeal upheld by the state supreme court.

The term *fundamentalist* cannot appropriately be applied to many New Christian NRMs. In a number of cases (for example, the Christadelphians and the Jehovah's Witnesses [qq.v.]) their inception predates the fundamentalist controversy, and hence it is anachronistic to apply the term. In other cases, New Christian groups have perceived a conflict between the verbal inerrancy of Scripture and some of the other four principles. Thus the Jehovah's Witnesses contend that Jesus' resurrection was spiritual and not physical. Organizations such as the Church of Jesus Christ of Latter-day Saints (LDS) (q.v.) acknowledge the authority of Scripture, but add additional scriptures of their own. Both the LDS and Unification Church (q.v.) claim to interpret Scripture by means of additional revelations afforded to their founder-leaders and others who are held to be recipients of supernatural revelation. Examples of contemporary New Christian groups who would accept Fundamentalism's five principles are the Family, the International Churches of Christ, the Jesus Army, Adventist groups such as the Branch Davidians, and most (but not all) Pentecostalists (qq.v.).

In Islam (q.v.) *fundamentalism* is used to translate the terms *salafiyya* and *usuliyya*. In common with Christian fundamentalism, such positions attempt to reaffirm traditional Islam against intellectual and societal changes in modern culture, claiming that there is a clear interpretation of *shari'ah* law, which must be enforced.

The New Kadampa Tradition (NKT) within Buddhism (qq.v.) is sometimes accused of fundamentalism, despite its endeavours toward Western adaptation. This is largely due to its insistence on the practice of Dorje Shugden (q.v.), which the present Dalai Lama has banned. *See also* ALAMO CHRISTIAN MINISTRIES; BRITISH ISRAEL; CALVARY CHAPEL; CHRISTIAN CONSERVATIVE CHURCHES OF AMERICA; CHRISTIAN MINISTRIES; CONCERNED CHRISTIANS; LOCAL CHURCH OF WITNESS LEE; NEW WORLD ORDER.

-G-

GAIA HYPOTHESIS. The Gaia Hypothesis is a dominant New Age (q.v.) theme, originating from James E. Lovelock (b. 1919), whose celebrated book *Gaia* (1979) made the claim that the earth is a living, conscious organism that intelligently organizes and regulates the processes that go on within her, achieving a finely tuned balance in nature to provide the optimal conditions for the continued survival of life as we know it. Examples of this self-regulation include the relatively constant temperature of the earth's surface, despite the fact that the sun radiates 25 percent more heat than when life began three million years ago. The concentration of ocean salt remains constant at 3.4 percent despite the fact that salt is continuously poured into it: the earth organizes the disposal of salt, for example, into lagoons, where it becomes buried. Oxygen and methane maintain constant proportions within the earth's atmosphere, and the ozone layer protects the earth from harmful ultraviolet rays.

New Agers often perceive similarities between the Gaia Hypothesis and other religious ideas, pointing out, for example, that several primal religions—notably Native American religions and that of Australian Aboriginals—regard the universe as inherently alive. Comparisons have also been drawn with Teilhard de Chardin's notion that an evolutionary process unfolds as humanity progresses toward "Omega Point," after which a "planetarization of the mind" ("noosphere") will be created. Marshall McLuhan's notion of the "global village" also perceives the world as an interdependent whole. Aurobindo postulated the "supermind" as the next evolutionary stage, at which there would be consciousness at a collective level. Peter Russell, a physicist and exponent of Transcendental Meditation (TM) (q.v.), talks of a "Gaiafield," drawing comparisons with TM's notion of synchronization of brain activity, whereby TM practitioners can collectively influence their societal and even global environment.

The earth's ability to regulate itself successfully is, of course, undermined by planetary pollution, which acts as a kind of cancer in its organism. Lovelock maintains that three outcomes are possible: Gaia might die from the cancer of pollution; Gaia might maintain its self-regulation by eliminating humanity from its system; or a harmonious coexistence can be devised between humanity and the living earth, whereby human beings act as Gaia's brain and nervous system, anticipating environmental change and implementing appropriate corrective action. Lovelock has proposed a new science—geophysiology—which will bring together all sciences within a Gaian perspective. Lovelock's writings include: *Gaia: A New Look at Life on Earth* (1979), *The Ages of Gaia: A Biography of Our Living Earth* (1988), and *Gaia: The Practical Science of Planetary Medicine* (1991). James Campbell and Thomas Berry have suggested the need for a new planetary mythology in which to express the Gaia hypothesis. "Gaia" designates the mother-goddess Earth, who, bonded with Ouranos (the sky), results in life.

GARDNER, GERALD BROSSEAU (1884-1964). The first major figure to herald the revival of witchcraft in modern times, Gardner spent much of his life in Asia, where he encountered many Asian magicians. His book *Kris and Other Malay Weapons,* published in 1936, concerns the *kris,* a magical knife used by Malays, which may be the precursor of the wiccan (q.v.) ceremonial knife known as the "athame."

Such experiences prompted him to study the occult, and on return to England in the 1930s he made contacts with the Theosophical Society and Freemasonry. Gardner claimed to have encountered several witches at a Theosophical Society gathering and to have been initiated in 1939 by their priestess, Dorothy Clutterbuck. This claim has been questioned, and it seems unlikely that an unbroken lineage of witches can be traced from Gardner to medieval times. Gardner described himself as the "king of the witches," and his writings did much to spread the craft. Most important was his *Witchcraft Today*, published in 1954. Gardner organized his supporters into covens, whose devotional focus was the goddess and the horned god; they also observed lunar quarter days. In the Gardnerian tradition, ceremonies are practiced naked, or "sky clad." *See also* MAGIC; THEOSOPHY.

GARVEY, MARCUS MOZIAH (1887-1940). An early leader of the "Back to Africa" movement in Jamaica and precursor of the Rastafarians (q.v.). Garvey founded the United Negro Improvement Association in 1914 and in 1916 took up residence in the United States. His study of the Bible led him to believe that the black Caribbeans were to be identified with the 10 lost tribes of Israel, and that a king would arise in Ethiopia, who would enable them to return to Africa, having been crowned as their messiah. Garvey's notions of deliverance from white oppression gained him the nickname "Black Moses." After being imprisoned for his activism, Garvey was deported to Jamaica in 1927 and continued his work there. Interest in his movement began to decline in the late 1920s, and Garvey left for London in 1930. That year saw the crowning of Haile Selassie as emperor of Ethiopia, which revitalized the Jamaican "Back to Africa" movement. It was Leonard Howell (d. 1981) who developed the distinctively religious aspects of Garvey's teachings and organized an early Rastafarian community in Jamaica. Garvey's work proved instrumental in bringing into being Father Divine's Peace Mission (q.v), along with a number of black Muslim and black Jewish movements. *See also* AHMADIYYA; NATION OF ISLAM (1).

GAUDIYA MATH. A Hindu (q.v.) organization in the Vaishnavite tradition, founded by Bhaktisiddanta Saraswati in 1918. A. C. Bhaktivedanta Swami Prabhupada (q.v.), founder-leader of ISKCON (q.v.), claimed Bhaktisiddanta as his initiating guru (q.v.). Based in Vrindaban, Gaudiya Math attempted to revive veneration of the scholar-saint Chaitanya (q.v.) (c. 1485-1533), and the sacred sites associated with him in the Vrindaban area, as well as those pertaining to Krishna and Radha. The focus of the movement is on Krishna and Chaitanya, and it teaches the primordial nature of Krishna: Vishnu is thus regarded as an emanation of Krishna, rather than (as the Hindu religions more usually teach) Krishna as an avatar of Vishnu. Gaudiya Math organized itself as a monastic institution, with lay supporters. It rejected the caste system, claiming that the status of brahmin could be gained through spiritual knowledge and attainment, together with appropriate initiation.

Prabhupada resided in the Gaudiya Math temple during the final years of Bhaktisiddanta's life. When the latter died, Prabhupada continued to further many of the movement's aims, although he did not attempt to succeed Bhaktisiddanta as leader or to acquire ownership of Gaudiya Math property. In recent years, a number of ISKCON devotees who have broken away from Prabhupada's movement have reverted to using the name of Gaudiya Math.

GHOST DANCE. Euro-American name of a sacred dance developed by American Indians in the second half of the 19th century. Originating in the Paiute tribe of northern Nevada and derived from the Paiute Round Dance, the Ghost Dance was a slow trance-inducing dance that afforded visions of the dead and the final paradise. Its purpose was to assist the return of one's Native American ancestors and the final end to white civilization. The practice can be traced back to around 1850, although the first wave of the Ghost Dance movement, spreading to western California and Oregon gained momentum in the 1870s. Particularly influential in its development were Wodzuwob and his son Wovoka (1858-1932; also known as Jack Wilson), who experienced visions and composed songs to accompany the dance. Wovoka urged his peers to avoid "white ways," especially materialism and alcohol consumption; however, his opposition to the white settlers did not entail violence. The second wave of Ghost Dance began in 1890, moving West, southwest, and to the Plains. White settlers regarded it as threatening and banned it. When the practice continued, the whites attacked Sioux Ghost Dancers at the Wounded Knee Massacre in South Dakota on 29 December 1890. Although it is sometimes claimed that the massacre effectively ended the Ghost Dance religions, some scholars maintain that it was still practiced authentically in the 1950s by the Shoshoni, and in an adapted form by the Pawnee. In the 1970s the Oglala Sioux revived the dance, following a dispute over Wounded Knee territory. Leonard Crow Dog and Wallace Black Elk (q.v.) have been numbered with those who have revived the dance. *See also* NATIVE AMERICAN RELIGION; SHAMANISM.

GLASTONBURY. A town in Somerset, England, which has become a renowned New Age (q.v.) center. Glastonbury has a long Christian history, being the center of myths relating to Joseph of Arimathea, who was supposedly sent by St. Philip to England, bringing with him the Holy Grail—the chalice used at the Last Supper. It is believed that he buried the grail at the foot of Glastonbury Tor, out of which the Chalice Well flows. This well produces a constant supply of water with a brown ocher residue that is held to signify Christ's blood.

King Arthur, a legendary or mythical English king, embarked on a quest to find the lost grail; hence Glastonbury is one of a number of British places associated with Arthurian myths (q.v.). Such legends appear to originate from medieval times, but literary works such as Tennyson's *Morte d'Arthur,* which makes explicit mention of Glastonbury, have helped such myths to gain momentum. The Glastonbury Festival, first organized in 1971, combines performances of pop music with opportunities for promoters of new spirituality to disseminate teachings and materials.

It is claimed that Glastonbury was once a center of pre-Christian Celtic religion; hence there is a preoccupation with goddess and earth spirituality. The "Glastonbury zodiac" can reportedly be seen in the expanse of land surrounding the famous tor and is said to bear the features of the zodiacal signs. The area has also been the scene of several UFO sightings and crop circles, which some have associated with extraterrestrial visitation.

In the town of Glastonbury numerous shops promote New Age books, artifacts and other spiritual services and events, spanning the usual range of New Age interests, as well as several innovatory forms of spirituality.

GLOBAL CHURCH OF GOD. Founded in 1992 by Roderick C. Meredith, who was expelled from the Worldwide Church of God (q.v.). The church aims to revive the teachings of Herbert W. Armstrong (q.v.) in the wake of the major doctrinal changes initiated by his successor. There are currently some 7,500 members.

GNOSTICISM. A term that refers to a set of loosely defined movements, originating around the second century B.C.E., whose ideas are sometimes held to find expression in certain NRMs. Gnosticism has characteristically taught salvation through esoteric knowledge *(gnosis),* which enables the soul to rise from the world of physical matter, generally regarded as evil, through a succession of spiritual realms until the soul recognizes its oneness with God. Some have contended that Gnosticism's origins lie in Simon Magus, who sought to buy supernatural knowledge from Jesus' disciples. The main early proponents of Gnosticism were Basilides, Valentinus, and Marcion. A number of original Gnostic texts became lost until 1945, when they were discovered at Nag Hammadi in Egypt. They include secret teachings attributed to Jesus, the best known of which are contained in the Gospel of Thomas. The Christian Church has been consistently opposed to Gnosticism, defining it as a heresy, although it has reappeared at various points in its history.

It is often hard to determine whether certain NRMs have been historically influenced by Gnostic ideas, or whether their teachings and practices bear no more than superficial similarities. The UFO-religion Heaven's Gate (qq.v.) has been described as Gnostic, although it merely proclaimed that there was a "Next Level Above Human" and did not apply the term "Gnostic" as a self-description. H. P. Blavatsky (q.v.) certainly knew and used C. W. King's *The Gnostics and Their Remains,* and Gnosticism was undoubtedly an ingredient of early Theosophy (q.v.). The notion of a Great White Brotherhood (q.v.) bears affinities with Gnostic notions of the soul's evolutionary development, and the Ascended Masters feature in a number of Theosophically derived groups, such as the Church Universal and Triumphant (q.v.). Other religious movements that are said to bear affinities with Gnosticism are Sufis, Kabbalists, and Rosicrucians (qq.v.), and—less frequently—wiccans and Druids (qq.v.).

Recent times have seen some limited revival of Gnosticism, and explicitly Gnostic groups have included the Gnostic Society in Los Angeles, founded in 1928 by James Morgan Price, which has now become Ecclesia Gnostica of Los Angeles; the Gnostic Society, also in Los Angeles; and the Gnostic Association of Anthropology and Science, founded and led by Stephan Hoeller, who became active in the Gnostic movement in 1959.

GREAT WHITE BROTHERHOOD. *A.k.a.: Ascended Masters; Brotherhood of Ascended Masters; Himalayan Masters; Illuminati.* This concept appears to have originated in the writings of Helena P. Blavatsky (q.v.), who wrote of "mahatmas" or "adepts"—supernatural beings with whom she claimed contact. They are held to be enlightened beings who have become freed from the cycle of constant reincarnation and who communicate from their transcendent realm in order to guide humanity. This brotherhood is headed by the Lord of the World and includes figures from the Jewish-Christian tradition, such as Abraham, Moses, Solomon, Jesus, the Virgin Mary, and Jesus' disciples (sometimes said to be "officers"), and masters from other religions, such as Confucius, Lao Tzu, and Gautama the Buddha. Other masters are said to include Plato, Jakob Böhme, Roger Bacon, Francis Bacon, Alessandro Cagliostro, and Franz Mesmer, as well as beings who have no accredited historical pedigree: Blavatsky attached particular significance to Master Morya (El Morya) and Koot Hoomi (Kuthumi), with whom she is said to have communicated extensively. According to Blavatsky, the brotherhood forms part of a celestial hierarchy, beneath which are *arhats* (enlightened humans) and *chelas* (initiated seers, of whom Blavatsky was deemed to be one).

Their authority became widely accepted among Theosophists (q.v.) and other occultists and psychics such as Edgar Cayce (q.v.) (1877-1945), as well as subsequent religious groups such as the Ancient Mystical Order of the Rosy Cross, the I AM Movement, the Church Universal and Triumphant (CUT) and the Holy Order of MANS (qq.v.). After his death, CUT's founder-leader Mark L. Prophet became regarded as an Ascended Master by the name of Lanello and continued to send messages to his widow, especially from the Comte de Saint-Germain. The adjective "white" refers to the white auras of these Ascended Masters and has no connotations of race. The notion of a hierarchy of celestial beings has obvious affinities with Gnosticism, and the concept of the brotherhood has influenced the development of recent versions of Gnostic Christianity. Expression of interest can also be found amid some in the New Age Movement (q.v.), especially in channeling (q.v.). *See also* AQUARIAN FOUNDATION; ARCANE SCHOOL; HERMETIC ORDER OF THE GOLDEN DAWN; JOURET, LUC; LEADBEATER, CHARLES W.; SOLAR LIGHT RETREAT; SOLAR TEMPLE; TEMPLE OF UNIVERSAL LAW; UNIVERSE SOCIETY CHURCH.

GROSS, DARWIN. The 972nd ECK master and successor to Paul Twitchell (q.v.), Eckankar's founder-leader, who died in 1971. Gross's leadership was not universally accepted within Eckankar, and a power struggle ensued between Gross and Harold Klemp (q.v.), aided by Peter Skelskey. In 1983 Gross handed the "Rod of Power" (the metaphysical symbol of

Mastery) to Klemp. Klemp banned Gross's writings, denying the latter's claim to have been an ECK master. Gross severed all connections with Eckankar in 1984 and founded his own organization, Sounds of Soul, later renamed the Ancient Teachings of the Masters (ATOM).

GURDJIEFF, GEORGE IVANOVITCH (c. 1874-1949). Born in Alexandropol, Armenia, of Russian-Greek parents, Gurdjieff acquired an interest in ancient esoteric knowledge at an early age and traveled widely in search of an ancient brotherhood. The exact details of his travels are uncertain, but he undoubtedly encountered several spiritual and occult groups, including Sufis. Gurdjieff's travels are described in his *Meetings with Remarkable Men* (published posthumously in 1963). He returned to Moscow in 1911, where he gathered together a Community of Truth Seekers from the Russian aristocracy. He composed a "Hindoo ballet," *The Struggle of the Magicians,* which captured the interest of P. D. Ouspensky (q.v.) and began a lifelong relationship between the two men. World War I prevented him from leaving Russia, but the Russian Revolution caused him to flee to Istanbul and then France. In 1922 Gurdjieff founded the Institute for the Harmonious Development of Man at Chateau du Prieuré of Avon. Followers received Gurdjieff's teachings and were introduced to his "sacred gymnastics," later called "movements": these were dances derived from Eastern sources and choreographed by Gurdjieff.

Central to Gurdjieff's teaching is the System, or the Work. This entailed a transition from "sleep"—the state in which most humans characteristically find themselves—to ordinary waking, self-remembrance, and,—very rarely—to "objective consciousness." This is achievable through Gurdjieff's "Fourth Way," the other three being the ways of the fakir (physical discipline), the monk (who tames the emotions), and the yogi (who develops inner knowledge or awareness). The Fourth Way included silent meditation, breathing control, and rhythmic exercises and often subjected his followers to austere and demanding conditions, including fasting and sleep deprivation. Physical, often menial, work was also an important aspect of training.

Gurdjieff's teachings can be found in his three-volume *All and Everything* published posthumously. Gurdjieff did much to herald the subsequent rise of Western Sufism (q.v.); his disciples include J. G. Bennett (q.v.), A. R. Orage (q.v.), Dr. Maurice Nicoll, Thomas de Hartman, and Jane Heap. The Gurdjieff Society—later known as the Society for Research into the Development of Man—was founded in 1955. Gurdjieff's followers number 10,000 worldwide (1992), with 5,000 in the United States (1996). *See also* ARICA; STUDY SOCIETY.

GURU. This term admits of a variety of meanings, the most basic of which is "teacher," either of technical skills or of spiritual truth (*acharya* in the Hindu and Jain traditions). The concept goes back to ancient times: it is alluded to in the Vedas, and the word "Upanishad" (one of a number of classical Hindu scriptures) literally means "to sit at the feet of," implying a relationship between disciple and teacher. It has been suggested that the term is a compound of "gu" and "ru" in Sanskrit, meaning "darkness" and "light," thus signifying that a spiritual master—the "guru"—brings the disciple from darkness into enlightenment. The more plausible etymology of the word is that it means "heavy," signifying that the spiritual teacher is laden with transcendental knowledge which can be imparted to the pupil. "Guru" can sometimes be identified with God himself, particularly when the expression "sat guru" is employed within the Hindu tradition: the "sat guru" is liberated and at one with God.

In the *bhakti* (devotional) traditions, where an ultimate distinction between God and humanity is recognized, the guru is not God himself. In Sikhism (q.v.) the term designated the line of 10 human gurus, from Nanak (1469-1539) to Gobind Singh (1666-1708), and subsequently to the Sikh holy book (the *Guru Granth Sahib*) and the Sikh community (the *guru panth*). It has been defined as the aspect of divinity that reaches out to humanity, and it can also mean God.

Hinduism (q.v.) has no centralized authority that can authenticate Indian gurus. Nevertheless, it is normally held that a guru should not be self-appointed, but should be able to claim a lineage, or *parampara.* Some NRMs attach greater importance to parampara than others. The International Society for Krishna Consciousness (ISKCON) (q.v.), for example, is at pains to claim that its founder-leader A. C. Bhaktivedanta Swami Prabhupada (q.v.) is in a well-accredited lineage. Other Indian teachers, such as Osho (q.v.), have never claimed a parampara, perceiving no problem about being a self-appointed teacher.

In Tibetan Buddhist tradition, the notion of the guru is acknowledged. "Guru Rimpoche" (literally "Precious Teacher") designates Padmasambhava (8th century C.E.), who is credited with establishing Buddhism (q.v.) in Tibet. The tantric tradition accredits gurus with spiritual power *(siddhi),* which can be conveyed to disciples, bestowing liberation from *samsara.* Tibetan gurus are typically arranged in lineages, often pictorially represented as "dharma trees." Thus Tilopa (989-1069) heads a lineage of gurus, through Marpa (1012-1098) and Milarepa (1043-1123). This lineage of gurus is acknowledged not only by Buddhists who follow ancient Tibetan traditions but also by certain other new Buddhist groups, such as the Western Buddhist Order and the New Kadampa Tradition (qq.v.).

In much of the literature on NRMs, the term (q.v.) is used in the general sense of "teacher," encompassing classical founder-leaders such as the Buddha, Jesus, and Muhammad, as well as leaders of more recent spiritual groups in both Eastern and Western traditions.

-H-

HARNER, MICHAEL (b. 1929). An American anthropologist, often regarded as the world's leading authority on the Human Potential Movement (q.v.) and particularly on present-day shamanism (q.v.). Invited by the American Museum of Natural History in 1959 to conduct research into the Conibo Indians of the Peruvian Amazon, Harner received shamanic initiation as well as undertaking scholarly research.

On return, Harner taught shamanic techniques to Western seekers at the International Transpersonal Association, the Esalen Institute (q.v.), various spiritual "growth" centers in the United States and Europe, and at the Academy of Sciences in the former Soviet Union in 1984. Harner simultaneously continued his academic career and was variously visiting professor at Columbia and Yale Universities and at the University of California, Berkeley. Most recently he was associate professor at the New School for Social Research in New York. He studied shamans from the Pomo, Coast Salish, Lakota Sioux, and Jivaro, as well as the Conibo. He gave shamanic instruction to members of primal societies—particularly the Sami (Lapps) and the Inuit (Eskimos)—in an attempt to ensure that their cultural heritage did not become extinct, having been eroded by Christian missionary activity.

Harner has argued that, despite the cultural diversity of the various forms of shamanism, shamanic ecstatic techniques bear important similarities across all shamanic cultures. He has coined the term *core shamanism* to refer to these universal aspects of shamanism, which he believes are able to be transmitted outside the indigenous cultures in which shamanism is practiced. Harner has a particular interest in the healing aspects of shamanism, which he teaches in his workshops.

HEALTHY HAPPY HOLY (3HO FOUNDATION). *A.k.a.: Sikh Dharma.* An organization of white Sikhs, established by Harbhajan Singh Khalsa Yogiji (b. 1929), known to his followers as Yogi Bhajan. Yogi Bhajan came from India to Toronto and then Los Angeles in 1968, and in 1969 founded an ashram in which he taught kundalini yoga and meditation (qq.v.). His principal following was originally from ex-hippies. In 1971 he visited the Golden Temple in Amritsar, together with a number of his supporters, and was given authority to initiate others into the khalsa (Sikh "brotherhood"). During the 1980s the headquarters of 3HO moved to Santa Cruz, New Mexico. 3HO's following is principally in the United States and Canada.

3HO members are readily identifiable by their exclusively white attire; women wear white veils and—in common with the men—a white Sikh turban. Members follow the teachings of traditional Sikhism (q.v.), as propounded by the 10 gurus from Nanak (1469-1539) to Gobind Singh (1666-1708) who founded the khalsa in 1699. All adopt the five "Ks" of Sikhism: uncut hair *(kes)* tethered with a comb *(kangha)*, a bracelet *(kara)*, a small dagger *(kirpan)*, and a specific type of undergarment *(kachcha)*. Those who are baptized into the khalsa are known as Amritdhari Sikhs, while others are Sahajdhari. The importance of uncut hair is explained in terms of electro-magnetic fields operating in the body, which in turn is associated with the practice of kundalini yoga, which is characteristic of the movement. Additionally, laya yoga is taught—a method of altering one's state of consciousness through sounds and rhythms: in particular the use of the Sikh mantra (q.v.) "sat nam" ("true name," i.e., the name of God) is advocated. Tantric yoga is also a part of the practice, but this can only be taught personally by Yogi Bhajan himself when he visits a congregation. Care of the body is emphasized: members do not smoke, drink alcohol, or use recreational drugs; they are vegetarian and favor methods of natural healing.

Under Yogi Bhajan is a Khalsa Council, to whom regional ministers known as Mukhia Singh Sahibs (if male) or Mukhia Sardarni Sahibas (if female) are accountable. The regional ministers oversee local centers and their ministers. There exists a women's auxiliary known as GGMWW (Grace of God Movement of the Women of the World): women are regarded as "shakti" (the female aspect of divinity) and are equally eligible for all offices within the organization. Allied to 3HO is the Kundalini Research Foundation, established in 1973, dedicated to the scientific study of the effects of kundalini yoga.

HEAVENLY DECEPTION. A practice often attributed by the anticult movement (q.v.) to some religions, particularly the Unification Church (UC) (q.v.). The term is taken to mean perpetrating deceit at a human level for some higher divine purpose, for example, collecting monies by giving false information about their destination. While it is undoubtedly true that certain NRMs have employed dubious tactics, it is doubtful that the UC ever employed the term "heavenly deception" in this context. The term is used, albeit infrequently, by the UC in a theological context: many Unificationists hold that Zacharias, not Joseph, was Jesus' father and that Zacharias permitted the circulation of the falsehood that Joseph fathered Jesus, since this served God's purposes better at that time.

HEAVEN'S GATE. A UFO-religion (q.v.), 39 members of which collectively committed suicide in 1997 near San Diego, California. The group originated in the mid-1970s, led by Marshall Applewhite (q.v.) (1931-1997) and Bonnie Nettles (1927-1985).

The group was taught a blend of UFOlogy and Christianity, and Applewhite's lectures, which were placed on the Internet and survive on video, offer his somewhat idiosyncratic interpretations of the gospels and the Book of Revelation. Heaven's Gate members were taught that there existed a race of beings who lived at a higher level—the "Next Evolutionary Kingdom Level Above Human"—and who had interacted on various occasions with human beings on earth. The members of this higher level sent Jesus (the "Captain") as a representative to earth; "adversarial space races," called the Luciferians, exterminated the Captain and the members of his "crew" and ensured that his message became corrupted by the emergent Church. Traditional Christianity, and indeed all traditional forms of religions, were regarded as Lucifer's work, since they erroneously elevated space aliens to the status of gods.

The members of this Next Level, however, have not abandoned their attempts to elevate human beings. Applewhite and Nettles claimed to be representatives from the Next Level, who had incarnated on earth to assemble their crew, to bring them to this higher plane. Such an escape was particularly important at the cusp of the millennium, since Applewhite taught that the earth, being exactly 6,000 years old in 1997, had become dilapidated and was about to be "spaded over" by the Next Level inhabitants.

The "crew" lived a simple, communal life, having renounced their earthly possessions, and spent much of their time listening to Applewhite's teachings and putting Heaven's Gate's teaching on to the Internet. The group became convinced that the Next Level beings were arriving when the Hale-Bopp comet was sighted, believing that there was a spaceship behind it. The collective suicide was believed to be necessary because one had to leave one's physical body behind in order to gain access to the Next Level. At the higher level, a new body—genderless and without human attachments—would be provided for the incoming soul.

HERMETIC ORDER OF THE GOLDEN DAWN (OGD). Occultist magical group, derived from Masonic Rosicrucianism (q.v.) and founded in 1888 by W. R. Woodman, W. W. Westcott, and S. L. MacGregor Mathers (d. 1891). In 1884 Woodman discovered a manuscript dealing with Kabbalah (q.v.) and Tarot. It gave a contact address in Germany of Anna Sprengel, who sent a charter for the establishment of the Isis-Urania Temple. Accordingly, the Isis-Urania Temple of the Hermetic Order of the Golden Dawn was established on 1 March 1888.

The aims of the order were to further the "great work," directed by "secret Chiefs" (the Order's equivalent of Theosophy's [q.v.] Ascended Masters), to exercise control over nature and to develop the power within one's own being. The order's interests included ritual magic, study of the Kabbalah, Tarot, and astrology, as well as astral travel, scrying, alchemy, and geomancy. There were three orders and 11 degrees of initiation, 10 corresponding to the Kabbalah's *sephiroth,* plus one neophyte degree. The OGD gained the support of poet W. B. Yeats, A. E. Waite (occultist and re-designer of the Tarot), and Aleister Crowley (q.v.) (1875-1947), who was expelled in 1898.

Owing to internal strife among the leadership, the OGD fragmented, giving rise to several occultist groups. Mathers split away, founding the Alpha et Omega Temple, and Waite founded the Golden Dawn in 1903, whose main interest was mysticism rather than magic (q.v.). In 1905 Stella Matutina (Order of the Companions of the Rising Light in the Morning) was established, attracting the support of Dion Fortune (q.v.). In 1917 the Isis-Urania Temple was formed, giving rise to the Merlin Temple of the Stella Matutina.

HIMALAYAN INTERNATIONAL INSTITUTE OF YOGA SCIENCE AND PHILOSOPHY. Swami Rama, the organization's founder, was born in 1925 in Uttar Pradesh, India, and brought up by Sri Madhavananda Bharti, also known as "the Bengali Baba." Prominent Hindu thinkers whom he met included Neem Karoli Baba, Ramana (q.v.), Aurobindo (q.v.), Rabindranath Tagore, and Harikhan Baba. At the age of 24 he was initiated into the Shankaracharya monastic order, and from 1949 to 1952 he was a spiritual teacher at Karvirpithan in southern India. After almost a year of solitary meditation, he came to the West, studying psychology and philosophy at the universities of Hamburg, Utrecht, and Oxford. He moved to the United States in 1969, where a year later he became involved with Elmer and Alyce Green's Voluntary Controls Project at the Menninger Foundation. Rama demonstrated his proficiency at yogic control over involuntary bodily movements, such as heartbeat, pulse rate, and body temperature.

In 1971 Rama founded his own organization at Glenview, Illinois, the Himalayan International Institute of Yoga Science and Philosophy, which undertook advanced study of yoga, principally for health purposes. In 1978 the organization moved to the Poconos Mountains, near Honesdale, Pennsylvania. There are currently over 20 branches worldwide. The Himalayan Institute organizes conferences, training programs, meditation retreats, and hatha yoga courses. Central to its mission is holistic health, which is achieved through meditation, nutrition, and techniques such as biofeedback.

Rama's religious thought comes from Smarta Sampradaya, a Hindu nonsectarian tradition derived from Shankara's *advaita* (nondualist) philosophy. He affirms that all religions derive from an identical single truth, which is encounterable only through personal experience; love, he teaches, is the universal religion. Swami Rama's writings include *Living with the Himalayan Masters, The Art of Joyful Living, Perennial Psychology of the Bhagavad Gita,* and *Exercise without Movement.* The magazine *Yoga International* is produced by the Institute.

HINDUISM. This term encompasses a variety of Indian traditions, which are followed by some 800 million inhabitants of India and a further 30 million worldwide. It is not a unified system, but derives from ancient Aryan invasions, as a result of which Vedic religion became established. Hinduism's ancient texts consist of the Vedas (1500-1000 B.C.E.) and the Upanishads (c. 800 B.C.E.), and the two great epics, the Ramayana and the Mahabharata, have had a profound influence on Hindu mythology and spirituality. The Mahabharata includes the Bhagavad Gita, which is undoubtedly the best known of Hindu texts and is highly important within the cults of Vishnu/Krishna.

The term *Vedanta* is commonly used to describe the philosophical Hinduism of Shankara (trad. 788-820), Ramanuja (11th/12th c.), and Madhva (13th/14th c.) and also Pantanjali's Yoga Sutras. New Hindu-derived religions are much more inclined to emphasize philosophical ideas than village practice, which generally involves practices that are difficult to transpose culturally, such as exorcism or obligations that relate to caste, which, of course, white Westerners do not possess.

Fundamental to the work of Shankara, Ramanuja, and Madhva is their respective interpretations of the Chandogya Upanishad's identification of *atman* (the soul) and *brahman* (the eternal), encapsulated in the saying *tat tvam asi* ("You are it"). The interpretation of the text has given rise to two main schools: *advaita vedanta* (nondualism, espoused by Shankara) and *dvaita vedanta* (dualism, expounded in somewhat different ways by both Ramanuja and Madhva). Important in the debate between nondualists and dualists is the role of *bhakti* (devotion), which seems inappropriate if the devotee and the eternal are one and the same. Some monists claimed that bhakti was a provisional step in the path toward acknowledging literal oneness with brahman, and hence teachers such as Yogananda (q.v.) have been able to espouse monism, while finding room for bhakti. Ramana (q.v.), Swami Rama (of the Himalayan International Institute [q.v.]), and the somewhat idiosyncratic Western guru Andrew Cohen (q.v.) are all in the advaita tradition.

Bhakti, more obviously entailed by dvaita vedanta, is typically addressed to three forms of deity: Vishnu, Shiva, and Shakti. Vishnu is normally associated with a number of avatars ("descents"), of which Krishna and Rama are the most popular. NRMs focusing on Vishnu/Krishna include Aurobindo, the Vedanta Society, and the Gaudiya Math movement (qq.v.), including the International Society for Krishna Consciousness (q.v.). Saivite NRMs include Shirdi Sai Baba and Satya Sai Baba (qq.v.), both of whom are said to be embodiments of Shiva; Shivabalayogi's (q.v.) followers; and Brahma Kumaris (q.v.). Shakti is the female aspect of divinity, of whom Shri Mataji (Sahaja Yoga) and Mother Meera (qq.v.) are reckoned to be avatars. Shakti serves as the spiritual energy in Siddha Yoga Dham (q.v.).

HOLMES, ERNEST S. (1887-1960). Founder of Religious Science (q.v.), a New Thought (q.v.) metaphysical school. Born in Maine, Holmes was brought up in a Congregationalist background. At an early age he read Mary Baker Eddy and Ralph Waldo Emerson (qq.v.) and, after moving to California in 1912, became deeply influenced by the writings of New Thought protagonist Thomas Troward. From 1916 onward Holmes lectured on New Thought themes, founding the

Metaphysical Institute for this purpose and receiving ordination from the Divine Science Church of Denver, Colorado. He was instrumental in organizing the Truth Association, a body whose purpose was to build bridges between Divine Science and the Church of Truth, neither of whom felt able to affiliate with the International New Thought Alliance at the time. The alliance soon changed its policies, however, and was able to accommodate the two organizations as well as the Metaphysical Institute. Holmes studied briefly under Emma Curtis Hopkins in 1924 while in New York, but moved to Los Angeles the following year. Holmes's writings include *Creative Mind* (1919) and *The Science of Mind* (1926), the latter being undoubtedly his most important work. In 1927 he established the Institute of Religious Science and School of Philosophy, the first of a number of inter-related Religious Science organizations.

HOLY ORDER OF MANS. Founded in California in the mid-1960s by Paul W. Blighton (d. 1974), this organization originally attracted ex-hippies. It was a form of esoteric Christianity: Blighton had been acquainted with Freemasonry, Spiritualism (q.v.), the Ancient Order of the Mystical Rosy Cross (q.v.), the Subramuniya Yoga Order, and Theosophy (q.v.). MANS is an acronym for *Mysterion* (mystery), *Agape* (love), *Nous* (mind), *Sophia* (wisdom). The group held that the earth was about to enter a golden age and that the Holy Order of MANS had come into being to prepare its followers and to transmit esoteric doctrines. MANS had leanings toward Eastern Orthodoxy and was traditionalist, even to the extent of using the old Julian calendar in preference to the Gregorian. Its ideas were expressed in *The Golden Force,* authored by Blighton and his wife Ruth. Importance was attached to monasticism, and there were two suborders: the Immaculate Heart Sisters of Mary and the Brown Brothers of the Holy Light. They engaged in social action, working in hospitals and offering active help to victims of domestic violence.

After Paul Blighton's unexpected death in 1974, Andrew Rossi took over as leader. At that time the movement was growing, and it peaked at 3,000 members in 1977. Following the Jonestown massacre in 1978, the Holy Order of MANS found itself included in anticult lists and the object of apprehension. Rossi was conversant with Christian history and sought to emphasize the order's traditionally Christian elements. He converted to Eastern Orthodoxy in the 1980s, and in May 1988 all his members were baptized into a form of Orthodoxy. The organization subsequently became known as Christ the Savior Brotherhood (q.v.).

HONMICHI. Originally established in 1925 by Ajijiro Onishi (1881-1958) as the Tenri Kenkyukai (Tenri Study Association), Honmichi ("original way") is a breakaway group from the Tenrikyo (q.v.). Onishi claimed a separate revelation, independent of Nakayama, the Tenrikyo founder-leader. The Honmichi opposed the system of emperor rule and was therefore disbanded by the government; Onishi was imprisoned. The movement was reconstituted, however, after World War II. Current membership in Japan is around 900,000.

HO NO HANA SAMPOGYO ("Flower of Buddhist Teaching"). An organization founded in Japan in 1980 by Hogen Fukunaga (b. 1945) and officially recognized for preferential tax eligibility in 1987. Fukunaga is said to have founded Ho no Hana as a result of a vision, in which he was declared the envoy of heaven, in succession to the Buddha and Jesus Christ. Fukunaga uses his *tengyo-riki* (heavenly powers) for medical diagnosis, predicting imminent illnesses and offering personality assessment: this involves a technique of examining the soles of consultees' feet. Five-day seminars, in which attendees "listen to the voice of heaven," are offered as means of addressing problems. Fukunaga also claims powers to "deliver souls" in the afterlife. Members of the group use a training manual, which allegedly instructs them to target surgeries and hospitals for recruiting purposes. Ho no Hana has recently been the subject of substantial litigation, principally for exploiting numerous housewives during 1994 and 1995. The estimated following in Japan is around 2,000.

HOUSE CHURCH MOVEMENT. *A.k.a.: Restorationism.* An umbrella term for a number of independent Christian groups espousing Protestant charismatic evangelicalism. The name relates to the early Christian practice of meeting in people's homes for celebration of the Lord's Supper (communion) (Acts 2:46), although, owing to increased numbers, house churches now more typically meet in larger rented premises. The movement's initial growth was in the 1960s and 1970s, in the wake of the Charismatic Movement, with individual groups coming substantially from the Brethren (q.v.), but also from the Church of England, the Baptist Church, and other Protestant denominations. House churches are evangelical, charismatic, and fundamentalist (q.v.) and emphasize the "spiritual gifts" enumerated by St. Paul (1 Corinthians 12:4-11), particularly speaking in tongues (q.v.), prophecy, and healing. Importance is also attached to "deliverance" ministry, in which demons are cast out. Congregations are typically millennialist (q.v.), expecting an imminent and literal return of Jesus Christ on the clouds. Although house churches are independent and autonomous, they tend to be networked into groups of congregations, with a predominantly, although not exclusively, male leadership. Congregations are divided into units, members of which are "shepherded" by a more senior member, who exercises spiritual oversight and often counsels them on matters of everyday life, such as their marriages and careers.

Groups of house churches and their leaders include the Association of Vineyard Churches, Community Resources (John Singleton), Cornerstone (Tony Morton), Covenant (formerly Harvestime) Ministries (Bryn Jones), Ground Level (Dave Kitchen), Ichthus Team Ministries (Roger Forster), New Frontiers (Terry Virgo), Outpouring Ministries (Alan Vincent), Pioneer (Gerald Coates), Plumbline (Simon Matthews), and Salt and Light (Barney Coombes). Antioch Ministries (Derek Brown), Network (Peter Fenwick), Team Spirit

(John Noble), and Team Work (Dave Tomlinson) are now defunct. Estimated combined membership in 1990 was 190,000.

HUBBARD, L. RON (1911-1986). Founder of Dianetics and Scientology (qq.v.). Scientologists claim that Lafayette Ron Hubbard was a precocious child who went on to gain mastery of 29 subjects, including philosophy, literature, anthropology, and psychology. He claimed to have studied mathematics and engineering at George Washington University. As a youth he is said to have traveled widely with his father, visiting the Far East, where he gained some of his ideas.

Since there are no biographies of Hubbard written outside the Church of Scientology, it is impossible to be certain of what is myth and what is fact. It is certainly true that from 1933 Hubbard achieved success as a science-fiction and short-story writer. Public attention was aroused by the publication in 1950 of *Dianetics: The Modern Science of Mental Health,* in which Hubbard explained his views on the nature of mind and how it is possible to "clear" it of the effects of past incidents that retain their hold on the individual. The practice of Dianetics is said to address the present life of the practitioner, while Scientology takes the inquirer to further stages, which address past lives and the nature of the universe itself. The Church of Scientology was founded in 1954. Hubbard continued to act as executive director until 1967, when he resigned in order to set up the Sea Org for the training of younger Scientologists. In 1980 Hubbard ceased making public appearances, and the management of the Church of Scientology was effectively taken over by David Miscavige. *See also* ORDO TEMPLI ORIENTIS.

HUMAN POTENTIAL MOVEMENT (HPM). A term devised by Steven M. Tipton to encapsulate a number of strands of thought in psychiatry, spirituality, and business. It can be traced back to the 1940s where an interest arose in sensitivity training and group dynamics. The 1950s saw a move away from psychoanalysis to therapeutic methods that involved personal development and an emphasis on wholeness. Such ideas were further developed by Abraham Maslow, particularly in his notion of the "hierarchy of needs," culminating in self-actualization—a dominant theme in HPM—and the rise of Gestalt psychology was a further contributory factor. Thomas Kuhn's *The Structure of Scientific Revolutions* (1962) developed the notion of "paradigm shifts"—radical changes in fundamental presuppositions and methods brought to bear on scientific and other issues. In the case of the human self, HPM suggests a paradigm shift away from the presuppositions of traditional Christianity (q.v.), particularly in its Calvinist Protestant variety where humanity is viewed as "totally depraved," unable to save itself by its own efforts. By contrast, the very term "human potential" indicates a positive evaluation of humankind, which views it as having the potential to realize the divine nature that is latent within the self.

HPM techniques include bio-energetics, transactional analysis, psychosynthesis, biofeedback, meditation (q.v.), channeling, and shamanism (qq.v.). In the world of business, Neuro-Linguistic Programming has been regarded as an aspect of HPM. During the 1950s and 1960s a number of religious and quasi-religious groups grew up, emphasizing techniques of self-development. These include the School of Economic Science (SES), the Church of Scientology, Transcendental Meditation (TM), Erhard Seminar Training (*est*—subsequently the Forum and Landmark), and Exegesis (qq.v.) (subsequently Programmes Ltd). Some regard Sri Chinmoy and Osho (qq.v.), and indeed the whole "guru (q.v.) phenomenon," as falling within HPM. It is unclear where the boundaries of religion and self-improvement movements lie, and it is possible to regard HPM as part of the New Age (q.v.), which has promoted many of its ideas. *See also* AMWAY; ESALEN INSTITUTE; I AM MOVEMENT; SILVA METHOD.

HUNA. An ancient Hawaiian religion which has experienced a revival in recent times after being suppressed by Christian missionaries from around 1820 onward. Its mythology concerns an ancient people of Mu (sometimes equated with Atlantis) which was subdivided into three: the intuitives (the Order of Kane), the intellectuals (Order of Lono), and the emotionals (Order of Ku). This tripartite division is paralleled in the self's levels of consciousness: *unihipili* (the inner, emotional, intuitive); *uhane* (conscious, rational); and *aumakua* (the Higher Self, which connects with the Divine). Understanding how these levels work enables the adept to possess healing powers, psychic abilities, and the skill to work magic (q.v.). Magical powers are for benevolent rather than malevolent purposes and include countersorcery. Practitioners of these arts are the priests *(kahuna).*

Traditionally, Huna teachings are not divulged to those outside the tradition, and hence its revival proved problematic. Recent teachers of Huna have included David "Daddy" Bray (1889-1968), a *kahuna* who taught Huna practices near Kona and whose son David continues to propagate them. The best-known reviver is Max Freedom Long (1898-1971), who left Hawaii in 1931, having failed to learn Huna secrets, but in 1935 concluded that they were embedded in a secret code within the Hawaiian language. In 1945 Long founded the Huna Research Associates. Long's writings included *The Secret Science at Work* (1954) and *The Huna Code in Religions* (1965). Long believed that Huna could also be found implicitly within world religions, notably Christianity and Buddhism (qq.v.). Long was succeeded by Dr. E. Otha Wingo. Long's student William R. Glover is noted for his work *Huna: The Ancient Religion of Positive Thinking,* which is probably the most popular and accessible introduction to Huna for Westerners. Other Huna organizations include the Order of Huna International, founded in 1973 by Serge King, a non-Polynesian *kahuna.*

-I-

I AM MOVEMENT. An esoteric group founded in 1934 by Guy Ballard (1878-1939) and Edna Ballard (1886-1971). Guy Ballard had read various Theosophical (q.v.) writings and was influenced by their idea of the Great White Brotherhood (q.v.). On Mount Shasta in California, he is said to have encountered the Comte de Saint-Germain, a 19th-century alchemist, who divulged the "Great Laws of Life." Ballard subsequently claimed to have made contact with other Ascended Masters.

The Ballards taught the existence of an eternal spark, or Divine Flame, within each individual and the concept that one could experience the "Christ self" through contemplation, affirmations, and "decrees." The I AM movement thus has certain features in common with the Human Potential Movement (q.v.), as well as with earlier notions of positive thinking. The Ballards founded the Saint Germain Press, publishing *Unveiled Mysteries* (1934), *The Magic Presence* (1935), and *I AM Adorations and Affirmations* (1936).

When Guy Ballard suddenly died as a result of a stroke in 1939, many members were disillusioned, since his teachings had included mastery over death. The movement received a further setback in 1942, when ex-members challenged the legality of their use of U.S. postal services, claiming that they were being fraudulently used for propagating false religion. After having to distribute its publications by rail, the I AM movement finally achieved tax-exempt status in 1957 and regarded this as a victory for religious freedom.

At its height the movement probably had about a million members. Although now in decline, its influence continues in the Church Universal and Triumphant (q.v.) and certain other expressions of Gnostic (q.v.) Christianity, as well as in the New Age movement (q.v.).

IDENTITY MOVEMENT. *A.k.a.: Christian Identity.* A white supremacist Christian movement in the United States, belonging to the political far right. The Identity Movement teaches that the Anglo-Saxons are the true Children of Israel, being descendants of the 10 lost tribes of Israel, and the Aryan nation of racial purity. Many of its supporters regard Jews as the children of Satan, the offspring from Eve's illicit relationship with the serpent in the Garden of Eden. Africans are regarded as pre-Adamic in origin and hence outside any divine covenant relationship. "Israel" consists of the white Christian nations, and Jesus Christ came to redeem "white, Anglo-Saxon, Germanic and Kindred people." The movement is vehemently opposed to racial integration and to interracial marriages and is fiercely anti-Jewish. Viewing "racial survival" as paramount in the face of immigration and integration, the Identity Movement sees the end-time battle as being one between whites and Jews.

The movement's ideas are developed from those of British Israel (q.v.). However, unlike British Israel, the Identity Movement is activist. It rejects the authority of all civil government, claiming that the law of the land originates from Jews and is for their benefit. Consequently, a significant proportion sees no problem with physical violence. Many Identity supporters have condemned the taxation system, and William Potter Gale was convicted in 1987 for conspiring to send threats to the Internal Revenue Service. Posse Comitatus, a tax protest group, has attracted support from Identity protagonists, including Gale.

Principal Christian Identity exponents have included Wesley Swift (1913-1970), a defrocked Methodist minister who founded the Church of Jesus Christ Christian, and who influenced both Gale and Richard Butler, who were associated with the Ku Klux Klan (q.v.). Other Identity churches include the Christian Identity Church (q.v.) (founded in 1982 by Charles Jennings and currently led by Fred Demoret); the Ministry of Christ Church; the Christian Conservative Churches of America (q.v.); the Covenant, the Sword, and the Arm of the Lord (q.v.); and the New Christian Crusade Church—now the Christian Defense League. The movement has exerted important influence on the American Nazi Party. There are estimated to be 50,000 followers of the Identity

Movement in the United States. (1998). *See also* ORDER, THE.

ILLUMINATI. Literally, "enlightened ones." A secret society originally founded in 1776 by Bavarian scholar Adam Weishaupt (b. 1747/8), who sought to express ideas of the Enlightenment through esoteric practices and who claimed to receive light from some higher source. Members included Goethe, Franz Mesmer, and Alessandro Cagliostro. The society had associations with Rosicrucianism (q.v.) and Freemasonry, but was refused official recognition by the Masons in 1782. The Illuminati influenced the foundation of the Hell-Fire Club in England, with whom some of America's founders were associated (the Club's Masonic connections may explain the inclusion of the Illuminati pyramid and the Eye of Horus on the U.S. seal).

Being antimonarchical, the Illuminati were suppressed by the Bavarian government, to be revived later by Leopold Engel in 1880. When Karl Kellner (d. 1947) assumed control, he renamed the organization the Ordo Templi Orientis (OTO) (q.v.). In the 1970s Robert Anton Wilson attempted to revive the Illuminati in the United States and France. Wilson's Bavarian Illuminati did not survive his departure from America, however, and his ideas only continue by means of his books on magick (q.v.), which draw on Aleister Crowley (q.v.) and recent psychical studies.

The term "Illuminati" is also used by practitioners of magick to refer to secret masters upon whom they can call for assistance. These can be historical figures, such as Jesus, or mythical characters like Merlin.

INNER LIGHT FOUNDATION. A Christian occultist organization, founded in 1969 by Betty Bethards, a psychic and mystic. Followers seek conscious awareness of their unity with God, the Universal Consciousness. Methods include the use of dreams, affirmations, and meditation (q.v.), particularly visualization and "quieting," the latter being a process of calming the mind, enabling the development of mystical and psychic powers. Development of one's inner awareness is also held to be conducive to the "brotherhood of man." Bethards lectures, leads worship, and gives private readings to seekers. There were approximately 10,000 followers in 1995, mainly in the United States.

INNER PEACE MOVEMENT (IPM). Founded in 1964 in Washington, D.C., by Francisco Coll, influenced by medium Arthur A. Ford, whom he met in the 1960s at the Spiritual Frontiers Fellowship. The movement's teachings are expressed in Coll's two books, *Man and the Universe* and *Discovering Your True Identity.* Coll's teachings center on the nature of the soul, which is "spiritual electromagnetic energy" and the totality of thought and experience. Experience consists of feeling and interpretation, both of which need to balance, complementing each other. "Spiritual counselings" enable the individual to awaken his or her own inner potential. Coll founded two related organizations: the Peace Community Church and the Americana Leadership College. The latter trains IPM leaders. There are 90,000 adherents in the United States and 35,000 trained leaders elsewhere in the world (1996).

INSIGHT. Founded by John-Roger Hinkins (b. 1934), a former Eckankar (q.v.) student, who went on to found the Movement of Spiritual Inner Awareness (MSIA) (q.v.). Insight offers self improvement, mainly through a series of seminars usually organized on weekends, with a facilitator and around 20 volunteer assistants. Claimed results are greater confidence, better communication skills, and greater fulfillment. The seminars became popular starting in 1979.

INSIGHT MEDITATION SOCIETY. Founded in 1976 by Jack Kornfield, Sharon Salzberg, and Joseph Goldstein, this society teaches Vipassana meditation (q.v.) in the Theravada Buddhist (q.v.) tradition. Kornfield, Salzberg, and Goldstein studied under meditation teachers Ajahn Cha, Asabha Thera, Anagarika Munindra, S. N. Goenka and U Pandita Sayadaw.

Headquartered in Barre, Massachusetts, the society claims 13,000 followers in the United States (it is not a membership organization) and a total of 15,000 worldwide.

INTERNATIONAL CHURCHES OF CHRIST (ICC). A worldwide conservative evangelical Christian organization, which began in 1979 when Kip McKean became minister of the Church of Christ (Non-instrumental) in Lexicon, Massachusetts. McKean made his appointment conditional on its 30 members accepting a statement of "First Principles" and expressing their total commitment as disciples. The church moved to Boston and became known as the Boston Church of Christ. As McKean's church grew, disciples were sent to other cities to plant churches there, and in 1982 Churches of Christ were established in Chicago and in London. This method of "planting" churches from existing congregations has become typical of the organization's method of growth, and by 1997 some 300 churches had been planted worldwide.

The International Churches of Christ seek to reestablish New Testament Christianity. Followers believe the Bible's teachings literally, accepting Jesus Christ as the sole means of salvation. Baptism is necessary for salvation, which can be lost through backsliding and apostasy. The churches have reestablished the New Testament offices of elder, deacon, and evangelist, which—in accordance with New Testament practice—are reserved for men only. Although there is nothing in the Churches of Christ's teachings that differentiates them from other forms of Christian evangelical fundamentalism (q.v.), the organization has aroused comment largely on account of the demands made on its members, who are required to tithe, to study the Bible intently, to attend meetings during the week as well as on Sundays, and to evangelize. Each member is assigned a "discipler," who supervises one's spiritual practice. In addition to spreading the gospel message, the Churches of Christ have set up various social programs for the homeless and for alcoholics under the name of "Hope Worldwide" (HOPE is an acronym for "Help Other People Everywhere"). Membership was 100,000 worldwide in 1995, with 150,000 attendees each Sunday in 1997. *See also* CROSSROADS MOVEMENT; DISCIPLING.

INTERNATIONAL CHURCH OF AGELESS WISDOM. An organization founded in 1927 by Beth R. Hand (1903-1977) as the Church of Ageless Wisdom. Hand was a Spiritualist minister who was influenced by Yogananda (q.v.) and came to believe in reincarnation (q.v.). Forced to resign, she moved to Philadelphia, where she met the Rev. George Haas, leader of the Universal Spiritual Church, a Spiritualist organization which shared a belief in karma and rebirth. Haas became a Liberal Catholic (q.v.) bishop in 1956 and ordained Hand two years later. Failing to receive a charter from Haas, she set up her own organization. The church's teachings are eclectic—predominantly Christian, but with elements of Spiritualism, Hinduism, Buddhism (qq.v.), and ancient wisdom. It worships God as creator and affirms the brotherhood of humanity, Jesus as a teacher and example, and the laws of karma and reincarnation as an explanation for human beings' lot on earth. Hand consecrated a number of bishops, including her successor Muriel E. Matalucci, who became archbishop primate in 1977 and changed the church's name to its present one. The church is associated with the Michigan Metaphysical Society (led by Sol Lewis) and has the well-known psychic Col. Arthur Banks as one of its members.

INTERNATIONAL COMMUNITY OF CHRIST. *A.k.a.: Jamilians.* Founded in 1972 by Eugene Douglas Savoy (b. 1927), who studied the teachings of the Essenes (q.v.). The group's teachings are based on *The Decoded New Testament,* a work outlining teachings of Jesus that were not included in the Christian New Testament. Emphasis is given to light, with humans being regarded as "light beings," who gain benefit from contemplating the sun. Jesus is not regarded as divine but as a "man of God" who returned briefly as a new "spiritual Sun" in the form of Savoy's child Jamil Sean Savoy (1959-1962), who died in Peru at age three. The group's practices include studying color, light, and auras, as well as the interpretation of dreams, pyramidology, and biorhythms. A community lives near Reno, Nevada, and 500 members were reported in 1982.

INTERNATIONAL SOCIETY FOR KRISHNA CON-SCIOUSNESS (ISKCON). An organization in the Hindu (q.v.) bhakti tradition, which recognizes Krishna as the supreme personality of godhead. The movement was founded by A. C. Bhaktivedanta Swami Prabhupada (q.v.) in 1965, when he came from Vrindaban to New York to teach "Krisha Consciousness" to the West. ISKCON devotees became particularly well known for chanting the "Maha Mantra," said to have been taught by Chaitanya (q.v.) (c. 1485-1533): "Hare Krishna; Hare Krishna; Krishna Krishna; Hare Hare; Hare Rama; Hare Rama; Rama Rama; Hare Hare." Prabhupada's teaching, together with the now-famous chant, originally appealed to some among the American youth counterculture. The movement gained momentum by the involvement of former Beatle George Harrison, and the mantra became widely known as a result of his song "My Sweet Lord" (1968). ISKCON's first large temple was opened in San Francisco, and by 1973 a total of 21 temples had been opened worldwide.

ISKCON is particularly renowned as a means of making Hindu teachings and practice accessible to Westerners. There are two forms of initiation *(diksha)* within the movement: as a householder, or as a sannyasin (q.v.). All devotees are obliged to keep four vows: avoidance of meat, fish, and eggs; no intoxicants or stimulants; no illicit sex; and no gambling. Additionally, devotees are required to chant 16 "rounds" of the mantra daily, a round being 108 single recitations, measured with a rosary of 108 japa beads. Illicit sex for the sannyasin entails the total avoidance of sex, whereas the householder is permitted to have sexual intercourse, but only for the explicit purpose of procreation.

Krishna is regarded as the primordial form of God, with Vishnu and other forms of deity (both personal and impersonal) as emanations. Emphasizing the importance of bhakti (devotion), ISKCON follows the *dvaita* (personalist) philosophy of Ramanuja (11th/12th c. C.E.), rather than *advaita* (impersonalist) views of deity propagated by Shankara. Particular emphasis in given to the Bhagavad Gita and the Srimad Bhagavatam, both of which focus on Krishna and are studied in Prabhupada's own translation.

Following Prabhupada's death in 1977, the ISKCON movement was run by a governing council, headed by 12 swamis—mainly Westerners—whom Prabhupada initiated. Worldwide membership is 1,000,000, with 8,000 full-time devotees (1998). *See also* BRAHMACHARI; GAUDIYA MATH; GURU.

ISHVARA (LIFEWAVE). A British group in the Eastern tradition, founded by John Herbert Yarr (b. 1947). Yarr encountered the Divine Light Mission (q.v.) in 1974 and claimed enlightenment soon after. When this claim was rejected, he founded his own organization, which attained a following of 500 by 1984, 46 of whom also claimed enlightenment and were authorized to initiate others. The name "Lifewave" connotes the practice of meditation on one's inner light and sound. Yarr claimed to be the Supreme Being, the Messiah, the Saviour, and the Hindu avatar Kalki, claiming the title "Divine Master Ishvara." Following a scandal in which Yarr was involved in sexual misconduct with numerous female adepts, the organization was disbanded in 1987, leaving a number of rival factions who tried unsuccessfully to continue the movement.

ISLAM. Originating in Mecca, Saudi Arabia, Islam follows the teaching of the prophet Muhammad (570-632 C.E.). Two major schools exist, following a dispute regarding the leadership after Muhammad's death. The Sunni school followed Abu Bakr, while the Shi'ites followed 'Ali, Muhammad's son-in-law. Transcending these schools, however, is Sufism (q.v.), the mystical tradition that seeks oneness with God, and which also incorporates popular devotion such as the veneration of shrines of Muslim saints. Arguably, there has existed a "Universal Sufism" (q.v.) which transcends Islamic Sufism, incorporating elements from a variety of world religions. Hazrat Inayat Khan (q.v.) (1882-1927), Hidayat Inayat Khan, his second son, and Vilayat Khan (q.v.) (b. 1916) were responsible for introducing their respective forms of Sufism in Great Britain and the United States. Sufism was popularized by the writings of G. I. Gurdjieff (c. 1874-1949), P. D. Ouspensky (1878-1947), and more recently Idries Shah (1924-1996) (qq.v.).

Apart from Western Sufi organizations, there are relatively few new religious movements derived from Islam. Movements claiming a new prophet superseding Muhammad have proved decidedly unpopular in Muslim circles; most notable among them was the Ahmadiyya, whose founder Hazarat Mirza Ghulam Ahmad (1835-1908) was accorded prophetic status after his death.

Bábism, originating from Siyyid 'Ali Muahammed ("the Báb") (1819-1850), heralded Bahá'u'lláh (Mírzá Husayn Alí, 1817-1892), the founder of the Bahá'í, who is now claimed as God's messenger for the present age. This claim has given rise to the recent persecution of the Bahá'ís in Iran, and neither Muslims nor Bahá'ís now regard Bahá'ísm as an expression of Islam, the latter seeing it as an emergent new global religion.

In the United States, various Black Muslim groups have emerged, a number of which have assumed the title "Nation of Islam" (q.v.). *See also* SUBUD.

IYENGAR, B. K. S. (b. 1918). Founder of the Iyengar Yoga Institute. Born in Karnataka, India, Iyengar studied under Krishnamacharya in Mysore during the 1930s. He was invited to Europe in 1954 and then came to the United States in 1956. The Iyengar Yoga Institute, based in San Francisco, is one of the most prominent U.S. yoga organizations. Aimed at the householder rather than the sannyasin (q.v.), it seeks to enable the follower to maintain physical and mental well-being, based on a combination of hatha and raja yoga (q.v.). It draws on the Yoga Sutras and the Bhagavad Gita, and, in common with traditional Hindu (q.v.) teaching, aims at the union of the *jivatma* (the soul) and the *paramatma* (the ultimate). The organization has 150 centers worldwide and some 500 teachers. Iyengar's writings include *Light on Yoga* (1976) and *The Art of Yoga* (1985).

-J-

JEHOVAH'S WITNESSES. An organization formerly known as the International Bible Students Association (IBSA) or simply "Bible students," organized by Charles Taze Russell (q.v.) (1852-1916). Russell concluded that the Bible did not support doctrines of predestination, eternal punishment, or the Trinity, which had become embedded in mainstream Christianity (q.v.). Influenced by Adventists, Russell expected an imminent end to human affairs, heralded by the beginning of Christ's invisible presence *(parousia)*, which he believed to have begun in 1914. In 1884 Russell established the Watchtower Bible and Tract Society (q.v.), which continues to be the name of the organization's publishing house. After his death in 1916, Joseph Franklin Rutherford (q.v.) (1869-1941) assumed leadership of the movement, and in 1931 chaired the convention that formally established the name "Jehovah's Witnesses."

During Rutherford's period of office the Bible Students progressively assumed an antiwar stance and purged their faith of "pagan" elements, including the celebration of Christmas and Easter. Since Rutherford's death the Jehovah's Witnesses have been led by Nathan H. Knorr (1905-1977), F. W. Franz (1899-1992), and most recently Milton G. Henschel (b. 1920). Knorr developed the international missionary work, and Franz was particularly noted for his knowledge of Greek, assisting in the development of the *New World Translation* (1961), the Witnesses' own rendering of the Bible into English.

Witnesses accept the Bible as inerrant, regarding it as the final touchstone of doctrine. They have never published any separate creed, holding that the Bible alone is the arbiter in matters of religious truth. They hold that the First Council of Jerusalem (Acts 15) defined which dietary and ritual laws are binding. Among these is a prohibition on blood, which Witnesses believe entails a refusal to accept blood transfusions.

Witnesses hold that biblical prophecy is being fulfilled in the present day, the nations of America and the United Kingdom being the seventh king, represented by the seventh head of the beast in Revelation 17. Their domination of world affairs will herald the final battle of Armageddon, which will end worldly affairs in their present form. In the meantime, 144,000 of the faithful (Revelation 14:1) are being selected to reign with Christ in heaven. After Armageddon, the rest of the faithful will become citizens of a renewed and everlasting earth.

Witnesses regard baptism as an authentic Christian rite, insisting that it must be administered to adults and by total immersion. A second institution is the annual Memorial, celebrated on the 14th of the Jewish month Nisan, the night in which they believe Jesus instituted the Last Supper. *See also* MILLENNIALISM.

JESUS ARMY. Founded in 1987 by Noel Stanton, the Jesus Army is the campaigning wing of the Jesus Fellowship Church (JFC) (q.v.). It is not a legal entity or organization in its own right, but is simply a name used for the JFC's evangelizing wing. Its members are recognizable by their military-style jackets, originally purchased as a cheap form of clothing for those who were living in JFC communities. Uniforms are worn for their numerous rallies, the first of which was in Northampton, England, in 1987.

The Jesus Army is a fundamentalist (q.v.) Christian movement, originating from the Bugbrooke Jesus Fellowship (q.v.), a Baptist Church in Northampton, England, and sharing a theology and style of worship that is common to other mainstream evangelical groups. Originally a youth movement, a significant proportion of its "covenant members" (baptized members) engage in community living, where a celibate lifestyle is expected. The movement upholds traditional values, particularly in matters of sexual morality. Women must dress modestly and in characteristically feminine style (for example, skirts not trousers), and men and women are assigned distinctive roles in accordance with traditional gender-role expectations. In the communities, liaisons may not take place between members of different sexes without an elder's permission. Community members lead a simple lifestyle that extols the virtue of poverty: alcohol is prohibited, and even television sets and radios are not found on their premises.

The Jesus Army is a distinctively British movement, and—apart from members whose work occasionally takes them overseas—has made no attempts to establish branches beyond Great Britain. The Jesus Army has grown into a nationwide organization, with 2,600 members in 1999.

JESUS FELLOWSHIP CHURCH (JFC). Also known as the Bugbrooke Jesus Fellowship (q.v.), the JFC started life as a conventional village Baptist church in Bugbrooke, near Northampton, England. After a period of decline in the 1950s, Noel Stanton was appointed as pastor. At first there was little change, but it became influenced by Christianity's Charismatic Movement (q.v.) during the 1960s, and in the early 1970s began to attract members of the youth counterculture. The JFC began a mission to the poor and the marginalized of society, focusing on the homeless, prostitutes, and drug addicts. Under Stanton's leadership, community living became an option, and community life was financed by a number of business companies ranging from health foods to building services, which were run by members.

The success of the JFC gave rise to a "divide, grow, and plant" policy, and satellite communities were set up, at first in the surrounding neighborhood and subsequently nationwide. By 1987 the JFC had a presence in 20 British towns and cities. Within the communities, celibacy is encouraged. Men and women have separate and distinctive roles and practice traditional biblical virtues. While the movement allows different types of membership, particular importance is attached to "covenant membership," in which the convert undergoes baptism and is committed to active involvement. (Being a Baptist organization, baptism is for adults only, and by total immersion.) The Jesus Army (q.v.) is the JFC's campaigning wing, set up in 1987.

The JFC is fundamentalist (q.v.), laying great emphasis on the study and observance of Scriptures. It is thoroughly orthodox theologically, believing in the full incarnation of Jesus Christ, his atoning death and resurrection, and the doctrine of the Trinity. However, this has not prevented the JFC from having problems with mainstream Christianity.

The Baptist Union has barred it from membership, the main reason being that its members are individual congregations, not a nationwide network of communities. The Evangelical Alliance in Great Britain has also been concerned about some negative publicity attracted by the movement, which has aroused some public hostility on account of its keen evangelizing and the distinctive military-style uniforms of the Jesus Army.

JESUS MOVEMENT. *A.k.a.: Jesus People Movement; Jesus People Revival.* The collective name given to various Christian fundamentalist (q.v.) youth groups that were founded in the late 1960s and early 1970s, largely consisting of ex-hippies, who became known as "Jesus Children," "Jesus People," or "Jesus Freaks." They were conservative evangelical Protestants, basing their theology on the Bible, but sometimes propagating its message in unconventional ways, such as comic magazines, of which David Berg's *MO Letters* (qq.v.) is an example. Speaking in tongues (q.v.) was not normally a feature of the movement, and, unlike the wider hippie culture, drugs tended to be avoided. Communal living was also a typical feature.

One important pioneer was Duane Pederson (formerly of the Assemblies of God [q.v.]) who founded Jesus People International in 1969. In 1972 Jim Palosaari founded the Jesus People U.S.A. from the Milwaukee Jesus People, and in the same year Gene and Marsha Spriggs founded the Messianic Communities of New England. Other such communities were the Children of God (now the Family, q.v.), the Jesus People Army (which subsequently joined the Children of God), Shiloh Youth Revival Centers, and the Christian World Liberation Front (q.v.), which were among the largest. Other similar although smaller organizations included the Bible Way (founded by Billy Shoots), Gospel Outreach ("GO," a.k.a. Lighthouse Ranch), Highway Missionary Society (1976-1988), House of Elijah (c. 1968-1979), Order of the Lamb, and Voice of Elijah (founded in Spokane, Washington, by Carl Parks and dissolved in 1979). Many of the Jesus groups found their way back into mainstream churches, but it is estimated that over 100 "intentional communes" still survive. *See also* SHILOH.

"JESUS ONLY" PENTECOSTALISM *A.k.a.: Oneness Pentecostalism.* A Pentecostalist (q.v.) movement, originating from the Assemblies of God (q.v.), whose distinctive teaching is the identity of Jesus Christ with God the Father and the Holy Spirit. This doctrine is professedly based on Scriptural evidence: for example, Paul writes, "In him dwelleth all the fullness of the Godhead bodily" (Colossians 2:9).

The first Pentecostalist group to propound a "Jesus Only" theology was the Pentecostal Assemblies of the World (PAW), founded in 1906 and largely consisting of black Pentecostalists. From 1913 onward, pastors R. E. McAlister, Frank J. Ewart, Glenn A. Cook, and Garfield Thomas Haywood (1880-1931) used the baptismal formula "In the name of the Lord Church Christ" in place of the Trinitarian one. This practice was condemned in 1915 by the third General Council of the Assemblies of God, which formulated a statement of Fundamental Truths the following year. A number of pastors, including Howard A. Goss, H. G. Rodgers, and D. C. O. Opperman, dissented and founded the General Assembly of Apostolic Assemblies (GAAA). GAAA merged with PAW in 1918, and a further merger with the Apostolic Church of Jesus Christ (ACJC) in 1931 resulted in the Pentecostalist

Association of Jesus Christ (PAJC). Owing to racial problems, PAW withdrew as a separate organization, the remainder forming the United Pentecostal Church (UPC) in 1945; in 1972 the UPC was renamed the United Pentecostal Church International (UPCI).

Oneness Pentecostalism typically teaches justification by repentance and faith, baptism by water (total immersion), and baptism of the Spirit, which leads to speaking in tongues (q.v.) and healing. Respect for civil government is advocated, but not participation in armed conflict. Emphasis is given to holiness, and members are expected to observe modesty in dress and abstinence from worldly amusements. In 1992 the UPCI required all its pastors to refrain from watching television and from "worldly sports and amusements." This led to some 200 pastors seceding and forming the International Network of Ministers (INM).

Other Oneness Pentecostalist churches include the Apostolic Overcoming Holy Church of God (founded 1917), Assemblies of the Lord Jesus Christ (1952), Bible Way Churches of Our Lord Jesus Christ Worldwide (1957), Church of the Lord Jesus Christ of the Apostolic Faith (1919/1935), Pentecostal Churches of the Apostolic Faith Association (1957), and Global Christian Ministries, formed in 1986 by Pastor L. H. Hardwick, who split from the UPCI. *See also* BRANHAM, WILLIAM MARRION.

JEWS FOR JESUS (JFJ). A Hebrew-Christian organization, but without separate congregations, founded in 1973 by Moishe Rosen with the aim of converting Jews to fundamentalist Christianity (qq.v.). Rosen previously belonged to the American Board of Missions to the Jews (ABMJ) and served on the U.S. West Coast, where he founded JFJ. In 1973 the ABMJ dismissed him. There are 50,000 adherents in the U.S. (1996). *See also* MESSIANIC JEWS.

JONES, JAMES WARREN (1931-1978). Better known as Jim Jones, the leader of the Peoples Temple (q.v.) in which 919 people lost their lives, mostly by taking part in a mass suicide. Jones was born in Indiana, and after working as a hospital porter, went to college. In 1952 he became student pastor at Sommerset Southside Methodist Church, although he continued to seek spiritual solace among Seventh Day Baptists and Pentecostalists (q.v.). In a Pentecostalist congregation one of the women leaders declared that Jones was a healer, and healing played a dominant role in his subsequent ministry. There is serious reason to doubt, however, whether the healings were genuine: many were faked.

Jones had a deep interest in human fraternity, and racial integration in particular. He and his wife were sympathetic to communism and saw the Christian Church as a vehicle for propagating communist ideas. In 1954 Jones founded Community Unity, which was renamed Wings of Deliverance in 1955 and became the Peoples Temple in the same year. In 1959 the Peoples Temple became affiliated to the Disciples of Christ, a mainstream Christian denomination, and Jones was ordained as a full minister in 1964. In the late 1950s Jones visited Father Divine's Peace Mission (q.v.) near Philadelphia and was influenced by many of the latter's ideas.

Jones's theology contained apocalyptic interests. Convinced that there was a strong possibility of the world ending by nuclear annihilation, he considered several places in the world where there was a greater chance of escaping such a holocaust. Jones began to plan a move to Guyana in 1973, sending an advance party the following year. The reasons for the mass deaths in 1978 are unclear. Some doubt Jones's sanity, while others have suggested that Jones and other leaders preferred death to an impending U.S. investigation. A further theory alleges that Jones was a CIA agent who was commissioned to conduct a large-scale experiment in thought control.

JON FRUM MOVEMENT. A cargo cult (q.v.) that developed in the 1930s on Tanna Island, Vanuatu. Jon Frum's identity is uncertain: there have been various human claimants, but he has also been identified with an ancestral spirit, the mountain god Karaperamun, America's Uncle Sam, and Santa Claus. Whatever his identity, Jon Frum was an expected figure who would herald a cataclysm, followed by a plentiful world which was capable of being enjoyed without human effort. The Jon Frum movement surfaced intermittently in Vanuatu, attempting to reestablish traditional customs and to persuade the indigeneous population to leave the Presbyterian churches that had arisen through missionary activity.

JOURET, LUC (1947-1994). Coleader of the Order of the Solar Temple (q.v.). Born in the Republic of Congo, Jouret qualified as a medical doctor in 1974, but subsequently joined the Belgian army as a paratrooper. He had an interest in alternative medicine and claimed to have visited China, Peru, and India to study alternative medical techniques there; although there is some uncertainty about this, he undoubtedly went to the Philippines in 1977 where he met numerous healers. In 1980 he set up a homeopathic practice in Annemasse, France, and undertook various speaking engagements at New Age (q.v.) bookstores and esoteric groups. He also offered management training courses in human potential and sought recruits for the Solar Temple among the business executives who attended.

Jouret was possibly ordained as a Liberal Catholic (q.v.) irregular priest; in the Solar Temple he carried out an "Essene (q.v.) ritual," which bore similarities to a Roman Catholic Mass. His interest in Templarism (q.v.) led him to found the International Order of Chivalry Solar Tradition (OICST) in 1984. He met Joseph Di Mambro (q.v.) (1924-1994) at the Golden Way Foundation, an esoteric spiritual group, and between them they founded the Solar Temple, an organization in the Templar tradition, with branches in Montreal and Geneva.

Jouret perished with 52 other members who lost their lives in the mass deaths of 1994. The surrounding circumstances are unclear. It is rumored that there was rivalry between the coleaders and that there were difficulties in maintaining discipline within the organization. Members may have been taught that they could survive a coming apocalypse by securing transit to the planet Sirius, and that this entailed leaving one's body. One writer has speculated that Di Mambro advocated a multiple suicide for this purpose and that Jouret took the initiative in killing Solar Temple members when they proved unwilling to act on Di Mambro's instructions.

JUDAISM. Regarding themselves as God's "chosen people," Jews have assumed special obligations to God, deriving from various "covenants" made between God and successive patriarchs, particularly Abraham; Jacob, whose twelve sons are held to have given rise to the "twelve tribes"; and Moses, who is said to have received the Torah on Mount Sinai during the exodus from Egypt. Messianic expectations, typically associated with Judaism, probably only came into prominence around the first century B.C.E.

While Jews have traditionally believed in the absolute authority of the Torah, a number of Jewish scholars, in the wake of the Enlightenment, sought to subject Jewish scriptures to methods of Western scholarship, seeking interpretations that appeared more relevant to more modern times. Such movements include Conservative Judaism, Liberal Judaism, Reform Judaism, and Reconstructionism (qq.v.).

Jewish mystical tradition has held that, as well as the Torah, God orally transmitted to Adam the Kabbalah (q.v.), an occultist system of understanding the nature and origins of the universe. While Kabbalism continues to exist within Judaism, its ideas have been used in certain Christian circles, as well as Theosophy and the New Age Movement (qq.v.).

Jewish messianism has given rise to several movements. Lubavitch (q.v.) Jews have come to hold that the messiah has come in the form of their founder-leader Rabbi Menahem Mendel Schneerson (1902-1994), while Messianic Jews (q.v.) acknowledge Jesus as messiah while seeking to retain their Jewish identity. By contrast, the Jews for Jesus (q.v.) organization seeks to persuade other Jews to convert to Christianity.

After emerging as a separate religion from Judaism, Christianity (q.v.) continued to accept Jewish Scripture as part of its canon. Some NRMs have arisen from within Christianity through emphasizing Jewish Scripture. British Israel (q.v.) identified the "lost tribes" with Britain and America. The Worldwide Church of God (until recently) and the Sacred Name movement (qq.v.) advocated the importance of observing Jewish festivals. Additionally, the latter stressed the need to use the supposedly authentic Hebrew name for God.

The question of how much of Jewish Scripture is to be observed by Christians has never received a definitive answer from mainstream Christianity. The Jehovah's Witnesses (q.v.) have attempted to resolve the problem by pointing to the First Council of Jerusalem (Acts 15), where early Christian leaders defined those laws which remained binding on the emergent religion. *See also* CERULLO, MORRIS.

-K-

KABBALAH *(or CABALA; KABALA; QABALAH).* An occultist mystical portrayal of cosmology and cosmogeny, of Jewish origin, symbolically represented in the Tree of Life. *Kabbalah* means "that which has been handed down": according to Kabbalist mythology, God taught the Kabbalah to the angels (q.v.), who taught it to Adam as a way back to God after the Fall. Adam then transmitted it in an oral lineage going through Noah, Moses, and then 70 elders, down to Kings David and Solomon. Ideas of esoteric meanings within divine revelation probably commenced shortly after the Babylonian Exile and were developed in the third century B.C.E. by the Hasidim and numerous esoteric groups. The Sefer Yetzira (Book of Creation) is attributed to Rabbi Akiba (c. 50-132 C.E.), but was more probably compiled in the ninth century C.E. The Sefer ha-Zohar (Book of Splendor), attributed to Rabbi Simeon bar Yohai, was probably written by Moses de Leo (d. 1435); it enumerates 32 secret paths of wisdom, represented by 10 *sephiroth* and the 22 letters of the Hebrew alphabet, which are given esoteric meanings. Isaac Lucia

Ashkenazi (1534-1572) developed new terminology and symbolism and made the Kabbalah more widely accessible.

The Tree of Life is a symbolic diagram which sets out the relationships between the sephiroth and depicts humanity's relationship with God and the rest of creation. According to the Kabbalah there are four worlds: the world of archetypes or emanations *(atziluth)*, in which souls preexist; the world of creation *(birah)*; the world of formation *(yetzirah,* which includes angels); and the world of action and matter *(assiah),* which contains evil spirits, the 10 hells, and Samael (the devil). There are said to be seven lower *sephiroth* (sovereignty, foundation, endurance, majesty, beauty, loving-kindness, and judgment), and these have often been compared with the seven chakras (q.v.) in Hinduism.

The Tree of Life can be used for meditation (q.v.) and contemplation: one is meant to visualize the symbols vibrating with color and with the letters of the tetragrammaton (YHWH). It is also said to yield esoteric meanings in Hebrew Scripture.

The Kabbalah became harmonized with Christianity in certain circles and was said to portray the divinity of Christ. Hence the Kabbalah and the Tree of Life aroused interest among certain non-Jewish occultists in the 19th century, most notably Francis Barrett, Eliphas Levi, and Papus. Kabbalistic ideas exerted an influence on Freemasonry, the Rosicrucians (q.v.), and the Hermetic Order of the Golden Dawn (q.v.), and the magical school of NRMs drew to a large degree on the Kabbalah. Dion Fortune (q.v.) described the Kabbalah as "the yoga of the West." Some occultists claimed that Tarot and astrology were influenced by Kabbalistic thought. While it is unlikely that Kabbalism explains their rise, Kabbalism influenced certain versions of the Tarot, such as that of A. E. Waite. The more recent New Age Movement (q.v.) has shown some limited interest in the Kabbalah, at times finding parallels to the Tree of Life in Eastern thought, for example, in Taoism. Recent revivals of Gnosticism and Essene (qq.v.) religion, with which Kabbalism has been historically associated, draw on Kabbalistic ideas. *See also* BUILDERS OF

THE ADYTUM; MAGIC; REINCARNATION; SOCIETY OF THE INNER LIGHT.

KARDEC, ALLAN (1804-1869). Pseudonym of Hippolyte Leo Denizard Rivail, founder of Spiritism (q.v.), or Kardecism. First a schoolteacher and then an accountant, in 1855 Rivail attended a séance, which convinced him that illnesses, particularly epilepsy, schizophrenia, and multiple personality, had spiritual causes. One of the first Spiritualists (q.v.) to combine ideas of reincarnation (q.v.) with communication with the dead, Kardec taught a threefold division of the self, consisting of soul, body, and "peri-spirit," which bound soul and body together. On death this bond between soul and body is normally broken, and the soul can proceed to choose its next existence. Sometimes, however, the peri-spirit does not properly leave the body—particularly in cases of sudden or violent death—and this can give rise to spirit possession or obsession. In such circumstances "spirit vampirism" can occur. Possession cannot be dealt with through exorcism, however, but only through prayer and the powers of the mind.

Kardec is particularly noted for his *Le Livre des Esprits* (1857), written as a result of sittings with the medium Japhet, and the *Medium's Book* (1861), which was placed on the Vatican's index of forbidden books. Kardec's movement was founded in 1857, and his ideas continue to be particularly popular in Brazil and the Philippines. In Brazil Kardecism is taken extremely seriously as a form of therapy: the first "spirit hospital" was established in 1934 in Porto Alegre, followed by several others. Healing is mediated through prayer, counseling, the exploration of past lives, and techniques of "psychic surgery." Kardec's ideas have exerted a significant influence on Umbanda (q.v.), Martinism, and psychic surgery, which is particularly prevalent in the Philippines.

KELSANG GYATSO (b. 1932). A geshe in the Tibetan Buddhist tradition, Kelsang Gyatso is the founder of the New Kadampa Tradition (NKT) (q.v.), a form of Tibetan Buddhism (q.v.) in the Gelugpa tradition, designed for uptake by Western seekers. Born in Tibet, Gyatso studied under Pabongka (1878-1943), who was also the tutor to the present Dalai Lama, Tenzin Gyatso. Kelsang Gyatso was forced to flee from the invading communists, and he eventually arrived in England in 1977. There he set up the Manjushri Institute, a community in which Westerners could study Buddhism. Gyatso made himself controversial by maintaining the practice of Dorje Shugden (q.v.)—the veneration of a protector deity, whom other Buddhists regarded as a mere spirit— which had been forbidden by the Dalai Lama. A prolific writer, Gyatso has written 16 books to date on aspects of Buddhist teaching and practice.

KHAN, HAZRAT INAYAT (1882-1927). Often referred to as Pir-O-Murshid (Master, Shaykh and Guide) Hazrat Inayat Khan, he was born of a Muslim family of musicians in Baroda, India. He was initiated into four schools of Sufism (q.v.), including the Nizami branch of the Chisti Order. Having completed his studies in 1910, he was instructed by an Islamic seer to take Sufism to the West. He arrived in England the same year and eventually established the Sufi Movement (q.v.) in 1927, now known as the Sufi Order International (q.v.). Khan promptly took his teachings to continental Europe and the United States, settling in London from 1914 until 1920 and establishing various Sufi centers. Khan proclaimed a form of Universal Sufism (q.v.), which transcends Islam (q.v.): he preached world unity and the spiritual freedom of each individual.

Khan initiated his eldest son Vilayat Inayat Khan (q.v.), who became his successor at the age of 10, but did not take up his father's work until the late 1960s. Dissent after Khan's death caused the organization to split into the Sufi Order of the West (q.v.), founded by Vilayat Khan, and the Sufi Movement under the leadership of Khan's younger son, Hidayat Khan. Another initiate of Hazrat Khan was Rabia Martin, who established a Sufi center in San Francisco before World War I, of which Samuel L. Lewis (q.v.) (1896-1971) was a member. Martin's group, Sufism Reoriented (q.v.), accepted the teachings of Meher Baba (q.v.) and transferred its assets to their organization.

KHAN, VILAYAT INAYAT (b. 1916). Eldest son of and successor to Hazrat Ilayat Khan (q.v.) (1882-1927). Vilayat Inayat Khan was appointed by his father to become leader of the Sufi Order in the West (q.v.) at the age of 10. He studied psychology, philosophy, and music at the University of Paris and undertook postgraduate work at the University of Oxford. He showed little interest in his father's work, however, until the late 1960s, when he assumed control of the Sufi Order International (q.v.). He is believed to have inherited his father's spiritual qualities and continues to promote a form of Universal Sufism (q.v.) that transcends Islam. Vilayat Khan's teachings are enshrined in his "Ten Sufi Thoughts": these include the oneness of God, the one true Master and Brotherhood, and the one holy book (nature). The oneness of God entails that there should be no barriers between the different world religions, and Khan has done much to promote interfaith worship that transcends religious differences, having established the Universal Worship of the Church of All, Universel (a temple for all religions), and the Abode of the Message on a 430-acre center in Berkshire Hills, near Lebanon Springs, New York. Khan's forms of meditation draw on Hazrat Khan, Rumi, and Kahlil Gibran, thus incorporating a variety of spiritual traditions. Much use is also made of dance, and most sessions begin with the Dance of Universal Peace, created by Samuel L. Lewis (q.v.). Holistic health is a further interest, and the Sufi Order is also a healing order.

KING, SIR GEORGE (1919-1997). Founder-president of the Aetherius Society (q.v.). Born in Shropshire, England, King was brought up in a Christian family, but from an early age studied psychic phenomena. In May 1954 he claims to have heard a voice from one of the "Cosmic Masters," commanding him to prepare to become the "voice of Interplanetary Parliament." This was followed by a number of contacts by

Cosmic Masters: King claims a telepathic rapport with Aetherius—a pseudonym of a Venusian master. Having commenced the practice of yoga (q.v.) in 1944, King continued to practice various Indian yogas, mastering Raja (q.v.), Gnani (jnana), and Kundalini (q.v.) yogas and finally attaining the state of *samadhi,* thus enabling the Cosmic Masters to use him as a "primary terrestrial mental channel."

King's knighthood was not awarded by the Queen, but from the Byzantine Royal House in exile, and is not recognized by the College of Arms. It is one of a large number of honors apparently bestowed on King, including initiation from the Buddha as Grand Knight Templar of the Inner Sanctum of the Holy Order of the Spiritual Hierarchy of Earth (after he psychically projected himself to Shambhala) and appointment as bishop and subsequently archbishop in the Liberal Catholic Church (q.v.), enabling him to claim the title of metropolitan archbishop of the Aetherius Churches. King also claims to have received various Orders of Chivalry from nobility in Europe.

King founded the Aetherius Society in 1955, with the aim of disseminating the teachings of the Cosmic Masters and developing contact with extraterrestrials. Claiming to have received over 600 "cosmic transmissions," King did much writing and lecturing.

KIRPAL RUHANI SATSANG. *A.k.a.: Kirpal Light Satsang, Inc.* Following the death of Kirpal Singh (1896-1974), differences arose concerning the leadership of Ruhani Satsang (q.v.). Madam Hardevi was appointed as temporal leader and gave support to Thakar Singh (b. 1929), who was coming to believe that he was the guru (q.v.) who should succeed Kirpal. Following Hardevi's death in 1979, Thakar took control of the ashram, but this usurpation of authority was not accepted by the U.S. board of directors of Ruhani Satsang—Divine Science of the Soul. Some members who did not agree with the board's decision formed their own group, the Kirpal Light Ashram, with headquarters in the Bay Area of California.

Thakar Singh first met Kirpal Singh in 1965 and was initiated into Surat Shabd Yoga (literally, "practice of light and sound"). The movement encourages awareness of one's "inner music" enabling inner God-realization. Thakar teaches from a variety of scriptures, selecting those that are most familiar to his listeners. The Satsang offers free *langar* (communal food) and care for the disabled. Members are vegetarian and may not engage in political activity. In 1994 there were 45 satsang meditation groups. *See also* RADHASOAMI SATSANG; SANT BANI ASHRAM; SAWAN KIRPAL RUHANI MISSION.

KLEMP, HAROLD (b. 1942). Current leader of Eckankar (q.v.) and the 973d ECK master. Klemp assumed the leadership following a power struggle with Darwin Gross (q.v.), the second leader. From his youth Klemp had mystical experiences, which caused him to study the paranormal: he was particularly interested in Edgar Cayce and the Rosicrucians (qq.v.). His interest in Western esotericism heralded a shift within Eckankar, which originally emanated from Radhasoami (q.v.) roots. Klemp is known to his followers as the "oracle of God" and as "Wah Z," which is the name given to him when he communicates supernaturally to his followers ("chelas"), principally in dreams. Chelas frequently write petitions to him, seeking guidance: these are not posted or physically sent to Wah Z, since he is judged to be omniscient and omnipresent.

Klemp's period of office has been marked by the movement of Eckankar's headquarters from California to Minnesota and especially the completion of the Temple of ECK at a cost of $8.2 million. A prolific author, Klemp has written more than 30 books: *The Wind of Change* (1980) and *Child in the Wilderness* (1989) are among the best known and are autobiographical. *See also* AKASHIC RECORDS.

KNIGHT, J. Z. (b. 1946). Born Judith Darleen Hampton in Dexter, New Mexico, Knight is one of America's best known channelers (q.v.), renowned for her communication with

Ramtha. Ramtha first appeared to Knight in her kitchen in 1977, although previously she had no indication of any paranormal powers. Knight quickly engaged in reading about the occult and provided her first channeling session at Tacoma, Washington, in 1978. From 1979 onward, Ramtha spoke regularly through her, while she remained in a state of full trance. Demand for Knight's sessions grew rapidly, and she founded Ramtha's School of Enlightenment in 1988.

Unlike several other channeled spirits who make modest claims about themselves, Ramtha claims to be a "sovereign entity," appearing in royal regalia as "the Great Ram." He claims to have lived on earth over 35,000 years ago and to have been a leader of numerous Lemurian survivors at Atlantis. Knight claims to have been Ramtha's foster child, and actress Shirley MacLaine—a follower of Ramtha—claims to have been his brother in a previous existence in Atlantis.

According to Ramtha, the universe originated from the Void, in which a "Point Zero" appeared. The interaction between Point Zero and the Void caused vibrations of high frequency, generating space and time and the original particles of energy. As these moved away from Point Zero, further levels of existence were generated, at slower frequencies. The grossest of these are humans, who are at such a far remove from their origins that they have forgotten their true nature, which is divine and immortal. God is in us, and his love provides the freedom to live without judgment or limitation.

Ramtha's School of Enlightenment teaches not only these ideas but also the means by which the seeker can "turn philosophy into truth." The school offers a highly structured curriculum which students are required to follow. Knight's autobiography, *A State of Mind* (1987), describes her spiritual path, and MacLaine's *Dancing in the Light* (1985) details her relationship with Ramtha.

KONKOKYO ("Golden Light Teaching"). A movement founded by Bunjiro Kawate (1814-1883), who had a religious experience in 1859 in which he claimed to have encountered the fierce Shinto deity Konjin. Kawate came to recognize

Konjin's identity with Tenchi Kane-no-Kami (God the parent), claiming that God had possessed his body. He assumed the title of Konkyo Daijin, offering mediation *(toritsugi)* between humanity and God. The movement gained recognition as a Shinto sect in 1900 and was introduced to the United States in 1919. Practices are essentially Shinto, but are "demythologized"; the movement is monotheistic and rejects magical (q.v.) practices. Emphasis is given to the spiritual life, to preaching, and to social concerns, which have included the provision of a hospital, a museum, a library, and a mission to lepers. *See also* TENRIKYO.

KORESH, DAVID (1959-1993). Born Vernon Howell, Koresh became the messianic leader of the Branch Davidians at Waco (qq.v.) and perished with 92 other members in the inferno of 1993, which ended the community's existence.

Howell joined the Southern Baptists in 1979, but his copious references to sex caused widespread offense and his eventual disfellowshipping in 1981. The same year, Howell went to the Mount Carmel Center, the Branch Davidians' community (a Seventh-day Adventist [q.v.] group) headed by Lois Roden. Howell staked a claim for the contested leadership, but was evicted after the discovery of a sexual relationship with Roden.

In 1986 Howell visited Israel, where he claimed to have had a vision of himself as the new messiah, the present-day David and Cyrus, but this claim was rejected by the Seventh-day Adventists' General Conference. Howell had somewhat more success in gaining support in Australia when he visited former Branch Davidians later in 1986. In 1988, Koresh came to Great Britain, where he was supported by Steve Schneider, an expelled former student of Newbold College in Bracknell, Berkshire.

When Howell returned to the United States to lead the Waco community, members not only acknowledged him as leader but as the new messiah. Howell changed his name to David Koresh in 1990: "Koresh" was a variant of "Cyrus," and thus Howell was staking a claim to be the new king of

Jews and Gentiles (Cyrus, a Gentile king, is described as God's anointed one in Isaiah 45:1).

Following police investigations of sexual malpractices, the community began to arm itself. This led to the ATF and FBI raids, culminating in the siege that ended in 93 deaths in April 1993.

KRIPALU YOGA. Established by Gurudev Amrit Desai (b. 1932), this form of yoga is a blend of hatha yoga and kundalini yoga (q.v.) and originates from the Pasupata Siva sect of Hinduism (q.v.). In his youth, Gurudev became interested in self-improvement, having read Dale Carnegie and taken up hatha yoga, aided by Kripalvananda (1912-1981), who visited the town of Halol in Gujarat, India, where he lived. Gurudev went to the United States to study at Philadelphia College of Art, where he also taught yoga. His popularity grew, and on return to India in 1966 he was initiated by Kripalvananda. The Yoga Society of Pennsylvania, which he subsequently founded, proved immensely successful. In 1971 Gurudev received shaktipat initiation, which involves the awakening of kundalini energy.

Kripalu yoga entails "meditation in motion," in which the use of *prana* ("body wisdom") enables the practitioner to experience accelerated and automatic purification and self-evolution: this is achieved through a combination of physical exercises *(asanas),* meditation, bhakti, and service to others *(karma yoga).* Gurudev's teachings are set out in his two-volume *Kripalu Yoga: Meditation-in-Motion* (1985).

In 1970 Gurudev found a site at Sumneytown, Pennsylvania, and in 1975 a Kripalu Yoga Retreat Center was purchased at Summit Station, Pennsylvania. In 1983, some 700 acres of land was purchased for the organization at Lenox, Massachusetts—the largest yoga ashram in the United States. Kripalvananda gave Gurudev the title of "yogacharya" in 1980, and in 1982 Swami Gangeshwarananda honored him with the title Maharishi. However, in 1994, Gurudev was forced to resign as leader following accusations of sexual misconduct, and the movement is now controlled by a board of directors.

KRISHNAMURTI, JIDDHU (1895-1986). At age 13, Krishnamurti was discovered by Annie Besant and Charles W. Leadbeater (qq.v.), who brought him and his brother from India to England to be educated. Initially, he was associated with British Theosophists (q.v.), and he was said to have met the Great White Brotherhood (q.v.) and been initiated by Koot Hoomi. Besant proclaimed him as the "Vehicle of the next World Teacher," Maitreya and an avatar, although such claims proved divisive among Theosophists. In 1911 the Order of the Star in the East was founded to promote him. Krishnamurti's first book, *At the Feet of the Master,* tells of his encounter with the Brotherhood. In 1929 Krishnamurti denied the extravagant claims made on his behalf, declaring himself to be an ordinary human being. He resigned from the Order of the Star, which consequently was dissolved.

Having abandoned the Theosophists, Krishnamurti proclaimed his own teachings. These were eclectic, since he proclaimed that Truth was limitless and therefore could not be apprehended by any single spiritual path. Enlightenment was rather to be gained from individual experience, free from past conditioning, memories, and preconceived opinions, resulting in a "thought-free mind," which is awareness or "being," having no motives and no choices. Thoughts, Krishnamurti taught, are divisive and capable of leading to conflict: accordingly, Krishnamurti's supporters reject all forms of violence.

Krishnamurti declared that he wanted no followers, but his teachings proved popular and led to the establishment of the Krishnamurti Foundation in 1969. Its headquarters are in Ojai, California, on land purchased on Krishnamurti's behalf by Besant in 1922 and later augmented.

Krishnamurti's books include *The Future Is Now: Last Talks in India* (1989); *Commentaries on Living* (three volumes); *Freedom from the Known* (1963); *Think on These Things* (1964); and *The Awakening of Intelligence* (1973). *At the Feet of the Master* continues to circulate among Theosophists, but is not used by the Krishnamurti Foundation. *See also* STEINER, RUDOLF.

KU KLUX KLAN (KKK). A white, Anglo-Saxon Protestant secret brotherhood, originally founded by Gen. Nathan Bedford Forrest after the end of the American Civil War in 1865. As an ex-Confederate, Bedford was alarmed at the new freedom of the black slaves; hence the original targets of the KKK were blacks, Northerners, and Republicans. The KKK drew on Freemasonry for its rites and initiations, adapting them for its purposes.

Concerned at its amount of violence, Forrest ordered the disbanding of klansmen in 1869, and the Masons vehemently condemned the organization. By 1875 the Civil Rights Act ensured the presence of blacks on juries, and the successful conviction of KKK members. The KKK fell into decline until 1915, when the film *Birth of a Nation* was released, romanticizing the Klan. William Joseph Simmons of Alabama revived the organization as a secret brotherhood, becoming its "grand wizard," and initiating members as knights. In 1920 Edward Young Clarke and Elizabeth Tyler effectively controlled the KKK, later giving way to Hiram Wesley Evans. At its peak in 1925, the KKK had six million supporters. However, when David C. Stephenson, the "grand dragon" of Indiana, was convicted of rape and murder and divulged names of members, the movement once again experienced serious decline.

After a short period of inactivity during the World War II, momentum revived during the 1950s. Gerald L. K. Smith's serial *The Cross and the Flag* (first issue 1942) proved influential, as did the work of Wesley Swift and William Potter Gale, whose ideas have penetrated the Christian Identity churches (q.v.). After experiencing factions and splits during the 1960s, the KKK went underground during the following decade, emerging with only 10,000 members by 1984.

Officially the KKK exists to protect the white race and to ensure the "voluntary" separation of races. In practice the

KKK has targeted not only blacks but Catholics, Jews, and homosexuals, using terrorist tactics that have included lynching, murder, and bombing. The name "Ku Klux Klan" derives from the Greek word *kuklos,* meaning "circle," and klansmen are widely known for their white robes and hoods and for burning crosses, which they regard as a ceremonial act and not an act of desecration. *See also* IDENTITY MOVEMENT.

KUNDALINI YOGA. *A.k.a.: Laya yoga.* A form of Indian yoga, kundalini is a kind of psychospiritual energy, also referred to as *prana* or *shakti.* The word *kundalini* means "serpent," and the technique is so called because the kundalini power is believed to be coiled like a snake in the base chakra (q.v.) *(muladhara)* where it resides. Adepts report a feeling of heat in the base of the spine at the onset of arousal of kundalini energy, which rises up through the chakra system to the crown chakra on the head. As it does so, the practitioner experiences cold in the areas the kundalini has left. Signs of kundalini awakening include pain, itching, involuntary movements, irregular breathing, extremes of emotion, and hypersensitivity to one's environment. The aim is to enable the kundalini to rest permanently in the crown chakra, as a result of which enlightenment is experienced. In tantra yoga, kundalini is the aspect of shakti, the feminine form of divinity, often identified as the consort of Shiva. Experiencing kundalini in the crown charkra is thus identified with joining Shiva, recognizing one's oneness with divinity.

Kundalini yoga has been practiced in the West from the 1970s onward. Gopi Krishna (1903-1984) wrote a detailed account of his own experience of kundalini yoga, and his disciple F. Dippong founded the Kundalini Research Institute in California in 1976. Kundalini yoga has also been practiced by certain NRMs, notably Healthy Happy Holy and Osho (qq.v.). *See also* KRIPALU YOGA; SAHAJA YOGA; WORLD COMMUNITY SERVICE.

KUNDIONA, CLEOPUS. Leader of a schismatical group of the Unification Church (UC) (q.v.) in Zimbabwe. Kundiona claimed to be the "returning resurrection" of Sun Myung Moon's (q.v.) son Heung Jin, who was killed in an automobile accident in 1984. Unificationism's main text, *Divine Principle* (q.v.), defines "returning resurrection" as a departed spirit who makes particular contact with a human being who is alive on earth—akin to possession.

In the early years of this phenomenon, Kundiona's identity was kept secret from all but a small circle of members, and he was simply referred to as "the Zimbabwean." At first he merely channeled messages from Heung Jin, but around 1986, he began, in Heung Jin's name, to impose strict discipline not only on rank-and-file members but also on senior Korean UC leaders, allegedly subjecting them to beatings when he believed their lives or spiritual practice to be lax. Kundiona's authority began to rival that of Moon himself when he denied the latter's messianic status, claiming that his role was merely that of John the Baptist, who proclaimed that another figure was to come and fulfill the messianic role. Such a statement bore more than a hint that he regarded himself rather than Moon as the Lord of the Second Advent. Such a pronouncement was, of course, judged to be intolerable in the Unification Church, and Kundiona and his supporters were forced to split away from the main movement.

The Zimbabwean phenomenon may have been one of several factors that caused Moon to proclaim explicitly in 1992 that he and his wife were jointly the present-day messiahs. Until then, it had been widely assumed that the Rev. and Mrs. Moon had this role, but it had not been explicitly stated.

-L-

LANDMARK EDUCATION CORPORATION. *A.k.a.: Landmark Forum.* The organization that continues to offer *est* seminars, in a modified form, as Landmark Forum, or simply the Forum. Instead of offering the goal of "personal enlightenment" the Forum prefers to use the terms "personal growth" or "transformation." Much of the Forum's work involves training in interpersonal skills and personal efficiency, with seminars being offered on themes such as time management, human relationships, and parenting. In the wake of the criticism that *est* seminars attracted, Landmark Forum seminars are less demanding: hours are not so lengthy, seminar leaders are less abusive to participants, and more breaks in the schedule are permitted. Like *est,* Forum seminars are not regarded as religious, although some participants regard their experiences as spiritual and use them to bring out the god who resides within the self. *See also* ERHARD SEMINAR TRAINING; HUMAN POTENTIAL MOVEMENT; SELF RELIGIONS.

LATIHAN. *A.k.a.: Latihan Kejiwaan.* Literally, "spiritual exercise," the principal practice of Subud (q.v.), initially taught by Pak Subuh (q.v.) (Muhammad Sukarno Sumohadiwidjojo, 1901-1987) in Indonesia. Subuh received an inaugural experience in 1924, in which his body and chest pulsated violently and which came to be regarded as the first latihan. Subuh made the latihan available to his acquaintances in 1932 and to the wider public in the following year.

The practice, which is performed by men and women separately, consists simply of standing, in which followers "wait to receive," their minds empty in a state of surrender to God. No special instructions are given, and during the latihan practitioners may sway, sing, dance, jump, skip, or do whatever they feel spontaneously inspired to do. Latihan does not induce a state of trance or any other form of altered consciousness. New inquirers are assigned a "helper" of the same gender who acts as a mentor for an initial three-month period, supervising the practice and addressing any questions. During one's initial latihan session, one is given "opening." Subud members practice latihan two or three times each week, the latihan being considered too powerful to be undertaken more often. Its benefits are said to consist of the awakening of the soul, direct recognition of the Source of Life, and an increased sense of personal responsibility. Latihan is available free of charge to all who are over 18 years of age, and it has been described as the "path of the ordinary man."

From 1977 onward, Subuh developed the notion of "continuous latihan." The latihan, he declared, was more than two or three short periods in the week that were singled out for "receiving," but was the whole of one's life. It goes with the practitioner, exerting a powerful influence on his or her life at all times.

LATTER-RAIN. A Pentecostalist revivalist movement that sprang from the Assemblies of God (q.v.) and the Pentecostal Assemblies of Canada. The movement's inception in 1948 was spearheaded by George Hawtin and Percy G. Hunt (from the Assemblies of God) and Herrick Holt (of the Foursquare Gospel Church) at Sharon Bible College in North Battleford, Saskatchewan. The founders believed that Pentecostalism (q.v.) had lost its momentum and that there was a need to experience the "latter rain" referred to in Joel 2:3. The "former rain" was taken to refer to the original experience of Pentecost by the early Church, since Peter quoted this chapter in his Pentecost sermon (Acts 2:17-21).

The movement advocates a fivefold ministry, in accordance with Ephesians 4:11, consisting of apostles, prophets, evangelists (missionaries), pastors, and teachers. A further distinctive belief is in the fulfillment of the three major Jewish festivals: Passover is fulfilled in Christ's death and resurrection, and Pentecost (Weeks) is fulfilled in the coming of the Holy Spirit—thus leaving Tabernacles to await fulfillment, which will occur when the Church becomes one, without blemish. The movement perceives the Church as having deteriorated from the early Church of "former rain" times, particularly as a result of the rise of Roman Catholicism; while the Protestant Reformation and other revivalist movements (such as John Wesley's) effected improvements, the Latter-Rain movement looks unfavorably upon Christian denominations, preferring individual autonomous congregations and itinerant evangelists. Congregations tend to network through a literature ministry: the *Voice of the Overcomer* is a particularly popular periodical, produced by Graham Truscott at the Restoration Temple, San Diego.

In 1949 the Assemblies of God General Council formally denounced the Latter-Rain movement, thus initiating a split between Latter-Rain supporters and other Pentecostalists who believe the Latter-Rain interpretation of the Bible is overliteral, disapproving particularly of apostles and prophets being formally designated offices. The practice of mutual confession of sins also attracts criticism.

Early Latter-Rain congregations included the Glad Tidings Centers, the Bethesda Missionary Temple, the Latter Rain Evangel, the Faith Temple (Memphis, Tennessee, led by Paul N. Grubb), the Restoration Temple (San Diego, led by Graham Truscott), the House of Prayer Church (Springfield, Missouri), and the Praise Temple (Richlands, North Carolina). Among Latter-Rain literature, Grubb's *End-Time Revival* and *Manifested Sonship* have proved influential. Truscott's *The Power of His Presence* deals with the fulfillment of Tabernacles. Latter-Rain congregations exist in Canada, the United States, and Europe. *See also* FUNDAMENTALISM.

LAVEY, ANTON SZANDOR (1930-1997). Founder of the Church of Satan (q.v.) and author of *The Satanic Bible* (1968). At the age of 16, LaVey left home and joined the Clyde Beatty Circus, where he acted as a stage hypnotist and carnival organist. In 1948 he moved to California, where he had a brief affair with Norma Jean Baker (Marilyn Monroe). He married Carole Lansing in 1951 and studied criminology at San Francisco City College, becoming a police photographer for the San Francisco Police Department. He developed an interest in the occult, on which he read widely.

In 1966 LaVey founded the Church of Satan, shaving his head and donning a black robe in order to assume the part of the "Black Pope," as he came to be called. Defining the year 1966 as the Anno Satanas Year 1, LaVey proclaimed the Church of Satan's tenets in Witches' Sabbath, a topless club in San Francisco (this club was frequented by Susan Atkins/King, one of the members of Charles Manson's [q.v.] Family). The church's beliefs did not consist of a belief in a personal devil, but rather in the presumed virtues of self-assertion and hedonistic indulgence.

LaVey had a role in the film *Rosemary's Baby*. In 1967 the first Satanic wedding was conducted, between Judith Case and John Raymond, and this was followed later in the year by a Satanic baptism of their daughter Zeena. In December 1967 LaVey presided over the first Satanic funeral.

LEADBEATER, CHARLES W. (1854-1934). Early leader in the Theosophical Society (q.v.). In 1906 he was forced to resign following accusations of homosexuality, but he was reinstated in 1909, when Annie Besant (q.v.) assumed office as president. Besant and Leadbeater developed the Theosophical (q.v.) ideas of reincarnation (q.v.), human nature, the evolution of worlds, and Ascended Masters. In 1908 Leadbeater and Besant "discovered" Krishnamurti (q.v.) and inaugurated the Order of the Star in the East to promote him as the new avatar. In 1916 Leadbeater was consecrated as regional bishop of the Liberal Catholic Church (q.v.) in Australia and subsequently succeeded founder-leader James Ingall Wedgewood (1883-1951) in 1923.

LEARY, TIMOTHY (1920-1996). Proponent of the religious use of psychedelic drugs in the 1960s and founder of the League for Spiritual Discovery (LSD). In 1960 Leary was introduced to tioanactyle (psychedelic mushroom) by a Mexican anthropologist, and he described his first "trip" as his "most intense religious experience." Together with Richard Alpert, he conducted experiments at Harvard University into the effects of the drug LSD ("acid"), for which both Leary and Alpert were dismissed in 1963. Leary went on to campaign for the legalization of psychedelic drugs for religious purposes and to promote "psychedelic religion." The League for Spiritual Discovery was set up on the Ananda Ashram in Millbrook, New York, owned by William Hitchcock: a number of psychedelically inclined religious groups operated there, including Art Kleps's Original Kleptonian Neo-American Church (q.v.). Leary was arrested in 1966, during a police raid on the Ananda Ashram, and for much of the ensuing decade he served intermittent prison sentences. Leary's *The Psychedelic Experience* (1964) was coauthored with Richard Alpert and Ralph Metzner. Leary perceived connections between psychedelic experiences and Eastern religions: his *Psychedelic Prayers after the Tao Te Ching* (1966) describes both the Tibetan Book of the Dead and the Tao Te Ching as "psychedelic manuals." Although interest in psychedelic spirituality has now largely died out, Leary and Kleps may have been instrumental in prompting further research on the paranormal. *See also* RAM DASS, BABA.

LEWIS, SAMUEL L. (1896-1971). Also known as Ahmed Murad Chisti, Samuel (Sam) Lewis was a Western Sufi leader and creator of the "Dances of Universal Peace." He joined Rabia Martin's Sufi group in San Francisco, but when the group turned to Meher Baba for its inspiration, he could not accept his authority. When the Sufi Order became defunct at the end of World War II, Lewis traveled to Africa and Asia, where he received various initiations and became recognized as a Sufi murshid. Lewis also became acquainted with Hindu and Buddhist (qq.v.) teachings, which influenced his form of Universal Sufism (q.v.). In 1962 he returned to the United States and began to disseminate his teachings. In 1966 he founded a Sufi group in San Francisco, where his first disciples were principally drawn from the hippie counterculture. In 1968 he met Vilayat Inayat Khan (q.v.) (b. 1916), who initiated him, whereupon Lewis's group merged with Khan's.

The Dances of Universal Peace were Lewis's distinctive contribution to Western Sufism (q.v.), deriving from the whirling dervishes of the Middle East, but combining with elements of Zen (q.v.), Indian yoga, and Hasidic dance forms. They helped to induce a state of ecstatic devotion, with accompanying experience of loss of the self and union with the divine. The dances also involved breath control, mantras (q.v.) and rhythmic music. In addition to his dances, Lewis also produced a number of mystical writings in the Sufi tradition.

LIBERAL CATHOLIC CHURCH. An esoteric form of Christianity (q.v.), derived from the Dutch Old Catholic Church and from Theosophy (q.v.). The organization was founded in London in 1916 by James Ingall Wedgewood (1883-1951), who had been consecrated as a bishop by Frederick Samuel Willoughby. In 1915 Bishop Arnold Harris Matthew of the Dutch Old Catholic Church had declared his church's beliefs incompatible with Theosophy. This declaration precipitated the resignation of a number of priests, who regrouped, assuming the name "Liberal Catholic" in 1918. Wedgewood was succeeded by Charles W. Leadbeater (q.v.) in 1923, after the former had become involved in a homosexual scandal. In 1919 Wedgewood and Leadbeater jointly consecrated Irving Steiger Cooper as regionary bishop of the United States.

The Liberal Catholic Church gave liturgical expression to many Theosophical ideas and combined Catholicism's prayers, rituals, and sacraments with concepts of reincarnation (q.v.), the evolution of worlds, and belief in Ascended Masters. Leadbeater's *The Science of the Sacraments* (1920) expounded the church's ideas, while Cooper's *Ceremonies of the Liberal Catholic Rites* (1934) set out its liturgy. There were over 3,000 members in 1990. *See also* INTERNATIONAL CHURCH OF AGELESS WISDOM.

LIBERAL JUDAISM. A progressive Jewish movement established in 1901, to which a number of Jewish synagogues belong. The movement arose as a result of the perceived increasing tendency of Reform Judaism (q.v.) to backtrack on its theological innovations (for example, on its original challenge to the Talmud's authority) and to become more traditional. Liberal Judaism seeks to maintain a form of Judaism which adapts to the modern world intellectually, ritually, and ethically. *See also* CONSERVATIVE JUDAISM; JUDAISM; RECONSTRUCTIONISM.

LIFE SPACE. A Japanese human potential (q.v.) organization founded in 1983 by Koji Takahashi (b. 1938). The group organizes regular self-enlightenment seminars, which are reportedly highly expensive. The group became controversial when its leader was arrested in February 2000, having practiced "Shakty Pat" on a member, who was denied other forms of medical treatment and subsequently died. Shakty Pat involves tapping a patient's head repeatedly in an attempt to transfer the therapist's energy to the sick person. The group attracted some 10,000 seminar participants at its peak, but is now said to have only 150 members.

LOCAL CHURCH OF WITNESS LEE. *A.k.a.: Little Flock (Chu Hui So); Assembly Hall Movement.* A church founded in China in 1923 by Ni Shu-tsu (1903-1972), who assumed the name of "Watchman Nee." Nee was converted to Christianity (q.v.) by a Methodist missionary and was subsequently influenced by the writings of J. N. Darby. Nee proved to be unacceptable to the Exclusive Brethren (q.v.), however, by associating with those outside Darby's movement. Nee's version of evangelical Christianity entailed that in its origins there was only one true Church in each city; hence the Local Church movement seeks to establish one church of its own in each locality, refusing to recognize any other professedly Christian group as an authentic version of Christianity. After the Communist Party came to power and established the People's Republic of China in 1949, Nee was exiled from Shanghai and then imprisoned in 1952, spending the remainder of his life in prison.

In the 1930s Witness Lee (b. 1905) was converted by Nee and became one of his closest associates. After leading the Little Flock in Taiwan, he came to the United States in 1962, founding the Living Stream Ministry. The movement is made up of independent autonomous congregations, governed by a small number of elders, with no ordained clergy. Each congregation is known as "The Church in [City X]." Some Local Church workers travel to preach the gospel, and growth is effected by the "Jerusalem Principle"—a policy whereby some members move to a new area and plant a new congregation there.

The Local Church movement is fundamentalist (q.v.) and trinitarian, although critics have accused it of unorthodox interpretation of the Trinity. The movement adopts the distinctive practice of "pray reading"—the reading of biblical passages as a form of prayer. The reported membership in the United States and Canada was 15,000 in 1991, and 150,000 worldwide in 1998.

LONG, BARRY (b. 1926). Founder-leader of the Barry Long Foundation, established in 1982. Born in Australia, Long claims to have gained enlightenment in 1957, declaring himself to be the "Guru" (q.v.) and "Master of the West." He migrated to England in 1966, and in 1968 began to give public lectures. His book *Meditation: A Foundation Course* formed the basis of his teachings, which were given on a regular basis from 1977 onward. Long's followers are encouraged to recognize themselves as the Guru also. His teachings draw to some degree on Hinduism and Buddhism (qq.v.), although Long avoids the outer forms of all religions.

LOVE BOMBING. A term of somewhat nebulous meaning, principally used by the anticult movement (q.v.) to describe excessive displays of emotion, with ulterior motives, attributed to NRMs. At times it is used synonymously with "flirty fishing" (q.v.), a practice employed by the Family (q.v.) (formerly Children of God), whereby members sought to satisfy the seekers' sexual needs as well as their spiritual ones. Alternatively, the term has been used to describe the giving of undue care and attention, particularly to new members, allegedly in order to win them over to the movement. Love bombing in this latter sense has been attributed to the Unification Church (UC) (q.v.), and the instruction to "love bomb" new inquirers is found at one point in Ken Sudo's *120-Day*

Training Manual, a lengthy unpublished typescript that circulated within the UC from the mid-1970s onward, but which is no longer in use. Whether NRMs "love bomb" in the sense of showing an excess of love and warmth is, obviously, a matter of opinion. The Family, however, fully acknowledges that flirty fishing was a practice that prevailed until the AIDS scare of the 1980s. *See also* SNAPPING.

LUBAVITCH. The largest Jewish Hasidic group, which came into prominence in the 1990s when many of the followers of its leader, Rabbi Menahem Mendel Schneerson (1902-1994) proclaimed him as the messiah. The movement was originally founded in Lithuania in 1773 by Shne'ur Zalman Schneur (1745-1813), whose teachings were derived from the Kabbalah (q.v.) and from his own teacher Dov Baer (d. 1772), and became known as Chabad (Habad)—a Hebrew acronym for *hokmah* (wisdom), *binah* (discrimination), and *da'ath* (knowledge), the principal Jewish virtues and the three *sephiroth* on the Tree of Life. These three virtues are emanations of the divine mind, and humanity, being created in God's image, must allow its emotions to be controlled by these intellectual qualities. The priority given to reason, however, does not preclude celebration, and, in common with the rest of the Hasidic tradition, music and dancing play a prominent role, especially in Jewish festivals.

Schneur's son, also named Dov Baer (1773-1827), brought his father's teaching to Lubavitch in Belorussia, from which the movement's name originated and which was its main center until its headquarters were moved to the United States in 1940 by Rabbi Joseph Isaac Schneerson (1880-1950), following the establishment in the mid-1920s of the Agudas Chassidas Chabad of the United States of America and Canada.

The Lubavitch movement holds the rabbi in supreme authority, more so than in most other forms of Judaism (q.v.). The stress on hokmah, binah, and da'ath entails much educational work, and emphasis is also given to the necessity of converting non-Hasidic Jews to the practice of Torah observance, since it is believed that perfect observance is the key to heralding the messiah.

LUBICH, CHIARA (b. 1920). Founder-leader, together with Pasqale Foresi and Igino Giordani, of the Focolare (q.v.). The movement began with Lubich's rediscovery of the gospel as a young woman in 1943 and swiftly developed from a small women's group to a worldwide movement, emphasizing humanitarian concerns and the unity of humankind.

Following the Soviet invasion of Hungary in 1956, Lubich founded the New Humanity Movement, and in 1967 she established the New Families Movement to meet what she perceived as the crisis of Western family life. The year 1968 saw the inception of the Gen Movement, aimed at the new younger generation, and in 1970 Youth for Unity was founded. In 1991 she established the Economy of Communion in Liberty to assist those who lived in poverty in conurbations.

Lubich lays emphasis on interreligious dialogue, claiming the distinction of being the first woman to address substantial gatherings of Thai Buddhist monks and nuns, Black Muslims in Harlem, and Jews in Brazil. Her numerous honors include the Templeton Prize for Progress in Religion and Peace in 1977, the UNESCO Prize for Education for Peace in 1996, and the Council of Europe's Prize for Human Rights 1998.

LUCIS TRUST. Founded in 1922, the Lucis Trust is an umbrella organization which aims to disseminate the teachings of Alice Bailey (q.v.) (1880-1949). The Lucis Trust encompasses the Arcane School (q.v.) which Bailey founded in 1923, World Goodwill (founded 1932), and Triangles.

World Goodwill aims to identify the underlying causes of world problems and, by educating world opinion, to formulate solutions to them, in preparation for Christ's imminent reappearance on earth, which will herald a new civilization. It is supportive of the United Nations, believing it to be humanity's ground for hope in the future. It has no formal membership, but seeks to influence public opinion through pamphlets, discussion papers and periodicals.

Triangles aims to establish international goodwill through a "network of light." Supporters are grouped into threesomes, who undertake to establish mental links with each other at a predetermined time each day, "invoking the energies of light and goodwill," which they visualize circulating through each of the three points of their triangle. While doing this they recite the Great Invocation, which enables "the downpouring of light and love" from above.

-M-

MACLAREN, LEON (LEONARDO DA VINCI MACLAREN) (1910-1944). Son of British Member of Parliament Andrew MacLaren, Leon MacLaren succeeded his father as the leader of the School of Economic Science (SES) (q.v.). MacLaren shared his father's concern for social justice, but did not pursue a political career, believing that changing the laws governing human nature was an essential prerequisite of justice. Leon MacLaren joined the Study Society (q.v.) during the 1950s and resolved to find a guru (q.v.). When the Maharishi Mahesh Yogi (q.v.) visited Great Britain in 1960, members of the Study Society and SES attended his lectures and arranged a large public meeting in the Albert Hall in 1961. MacLaren subsequently visited India, where he met Sri Shantanand Saraswati—usually referred to as the Shankaracharya of the North—who, in common with the Maharishi, had been a disciple of Guru Dev (1869-1953). The Study Society and SES cooperated to form the School of Meditation, which drew on the teachings of the Maharishi and the Shankaracharya, and MacLaren did much to disseminate their teachings within SES.

MACUMBA. Originally brought to the New World by African slaves who entered Brazil in the mid-16th century, the movement combines African religious tradition, Roman Catholicism and the spirituality of the Native Brazilian Indians. *See also* CANDOMBLÉ.

MAGIC (MAGICK). The revival in the interest in magic has accompanied the increasingly popularity of the New Age (q.v.), wicca and Paganism (qq.v.). J. Gordon Melton's *Encyclopedic Handbook of Cults in America* (1992) distinguishes between "low magic," which has been part of folk culture, and "ceremonial magic," around which certain NRMs have been built. Folk magic was predominantly associated with the use of charms and spells for gaining pragmatic benefits, such as improved health or material abundance, and largely died out by the 18th century, being regarded as mere superstition. Magic was also part of the witches' craft throughout the centuries.

The recent revival of interest in "high" or ceremonial magic can be traced back to Eliphas Levi (1810-1875), whose *Dogme de la Haute Magie* (1855) and *Rituel de la Haute Magie* (1856) have been translated into English as *Transcendental Magic: Its Doctrine and Ritual* (1955). Levi and S.L. MacGregor Mathers (1854-1918) were important influences on Aleister Crowley (q.v.) (1875-1947), founder of the Hermetic Order of the Golden Dawn (OGD) (q.v.). Crowley devised the variant spelling *magick*, now in frequent use among wiccans and others, in order to distinguish high magic from the more trivial activities of the stage conjurer. Crowley's *Magick in Theory and Practice* (1929) remains an important work, making public a variety of esoteric rites. One of Crowley's distinctive ideas was "thelemic" magick (q.v.)—the magic pertaining to the will. His ideas on "sex magick" proved particularly controversial and offended many of his supporters. Levi and Crowley made significant use of the Kabbalah (q.v.), which remains a feature of some present-day magical practice.

Melton identifies three broad magical traditions. First, several magical groups draw their influence from Crowley and OGD, the best known being the Builders of the Adytum (q.v.) (in California) and the Fraternity of the Inner Light and the Servants of the Light (both in Great Britain). The Fraternity of the Inner Light was founded in 1928 by Dion Fortune (q.v.) (1890-1946). The prolific author Marian Green is noteworthy for her "gentle art of Aquarian magic." The second broad tradition is that of wicca/witchcraft, where it is part of the witch's craft to exert magical control over parts of nature. Third, there is Satanism (q.v.), in which the powers of Satan are invoked to effect changes in the physical world.

A distinction is commonly made between "black" and "white" magic. Apart from certain Satanists, the type of magic that is commonly practiced with the magical tradition is white magic, for benign purposes—particularly in the wiccan tradition, which has a prevalent belief in the "law of threefold returns": the results of any magical practice are believed to rebound on the perpetrator by a multiple of three. Practicing black magic therefore tends to be highly unpopular, and its practitioners have been known to be shunned by other wiccans.

As well as the rise of ceremonial magic within organized groups, the New Age has given momentum to an interest in individual magic working, using private rituals. *See also* ILLUMINATI; SOLAR TEMPLE; TEMPLE OV PSYCHICK YOUTH.

MAHARAJI. *A.k.a.: Guru Maharaj Ji* (b. 1957). Born Prem Pal Singh Rawat in Hardwar, India, Maharaji is the son of Shri Hans Ji Maharaji (d. 1965), founder-leader of the Divine Light Mission (q.v.) in India, and is regarded as a *satguru*—a fully enlightened teacher, of whom it is believed that only one exists at any one time. Following his father's death, Maharaji announced himself as the new guru (q.v.), although he was only eight years old at the time and the youngest of four sons, and he became known by the media as the "boy guru." Maharaji came into prominence in the early 1970s: in 1971 he embarked on a world tour, teaching in the United States, Great Britain, France, Germany, South Africa, and Australia, offering his followers—known as "premies" (devotees)—"the Knowledge." This Knowledge was self-understanding, yielding calmness, peace, and contentment, since the innermost self is identical with the divine. Knowledge is attained through initiation, which provides four techniques that allow the practitioner to go within. By the mid-1970s, Maharaji had established some 30 ashrams in the United States and 80 centers in Great Britain; around 50,000 people had received the Knowledge.

In 1973 Maharaji and his followers organized a large public rally in the Houston Astrodome; 144,000 attendees were expected, but only 20,000 came. This not only caused great disappointment, but left the Divine Light Mission in a grave financial crisis, since it had not covered its costs. Further problems occurred in 1974 when Maharaji married Marolyn Johnson—an American—without parental consent. This precipitated a split in the organization, his mother taking control of the Indian wing of the movement, with his brother Bal Bhagwanji as leader. Maharaji progressively dissolved the Divine Light Mission, closing the ashrams, affirming his own status as a master rather than a divine leader, and emphasizing that the Knowledge is universal, not Indian, in nature.

Maharaji continues to teach the Knowledge and its meditative techniques, but no longer as a religion. A new organization, Elan Vital (q.v.), was established in the 1980s, but does no more than arrange lectures by Maharaji and disseminate his teachings. Maharaji is now more a public speaker than a religious leader.

MAHARISHI MAHESH YOGI (b. 1917?). Founder-leader of the Transcendental Meditation (TM) (q.v.) organization. Little is known about the Maharishi's early life: even his year of birth is uncertain, as is his given name. Some state that it was Mahesh Prasad Varma, others J. N. Srivastava. The name "Maharishi" is an adopted title, signifying "great seer." The Maharishi was born at Jabalpur in central India. He attended Allahabad University, graduating in physics in 1940. Subsequently he studied techniques of Hindu mysticism under Guru Dev (Swami Brahmanada Saraswati) at Jyotir Math monastery. The Maharishi progressed from undertaking servile tasks to becoming a Shakaracharya and finally Guru Dev's secretary.

In 1956 the Maharishi published *The Beacon Light of the Himalayas,* his first book on TM, and in 1957 he founded the Spiritual Regeneration Movement (SRM), which was the vehicle for bringing TM to the West. In 1960 the Maharishi gave a lecture in London, which aroused considerable interest from the Study Society (q.v.). The TM movement gained further impetus when the Beatles visited him in India in 1968.

The Maharishi's most influential book is *Science of Being and Art of Living* (1963). This continues to be promoted and outlines the claimed benefits of practicing TM and the supportive evidence. The Maharishi's status as a Shankaracharya implies that his thought is the monistic tradition of the medieval Indian philosophy Shankara (trad. 788-820). Among the Maharishi's publications is a commentary on the Bhagavad Gita, which interprets this scripture (often regarded as a scripture advocating *bhakti*) along monistic lines. *See also* MACLAREN, LEON.

MAHIKARI. Literally "Divine True Light." This organization's founder, Kotama Okada (1901-1974), belonged to the Church of World Messianity (q.v.) when he received a revelation about how to use divine light. The light is the energy of Sushin (the creator), which can tune the soul and be used to promote healing, harmony, and well-being. In 1960 Okada established Sekai Mahikari Bunmei Kyodan (Church of the World True Light Children), in which he came to be regarded as *sukuinushisama* (savior). Central to Mahikari is the notion of Divine Plan: souls are sent to earth for the purpose of establishing an evolved civilization. Members learn to perform *Mahikari no Waza*—a method of radiating light from the palms of one's hands. At first this practice was reserved for a few spiritually advanced followers, but now Sushin has granted it to everyone, and it can be learned at a three-day seminar. On initiation, followers receive an *omitama* (a pendant). The Mahikari scriptures are known as *Goseigen* (Holy Words), available in English since 1982. Shortly before his death Okada appointed Seishu Okada, his daughter, as successor. This was challenged by Sekiguchi Sakal, a senior member, who took the dispute to court and won: Sakal presides over the movement's headquarters in Torrance, California, and is head of a second group in Japan.

MALCOLM X (1925-1965). Born Malcolm Little in Omaha, Nebraska, Malcolm X grew up in a poor family and embarked on a life of crime. He joined the Nation of Islam (NOI) (1, q.v.) while in prison, but later came to dissociate himself from its principles. In particular, he objected to the NOI's racism, being unable see whites as satanic, and he could not accept its claims that founder-leader Prophet Fard was a personification of Allah. There were also scandals, mainly sexual, concerning Fard. Malcolm X left the organization in 1964, establishing a rival mosque. The abandonment of his surname in favor of "X" reflected the belief that Western surnames were the product of slavery. Malcolm X was assassinated in 1965 by NOI rivals, and his death heralded a decade of violence between rival Black Muslim factions.

MANSON, CHARLES (b. 1934). Born in Cincinnati, Ohio, Manson became a young offender and served intermittent prison sentences until 1967. Released from jail, Manson went to San Francisco, where he attracted a number of followers from the hippie counterculture—16 women and four men. In 1969 the Manson "Family" moved to Spahn Movie Ranch. At its maximum, the Family consisted of 50 members. It was named "Helter Skelter" after the Beatles' song of the same name. Sex and psychedelic trips featured significantly in the group, and Manson's outlook was largely racist.

Manson's true notoriety accrues to a series of murders that he initiated. On 8 and 9 August 1969, at Manson's orders, some of his members carried out multiple killings in two homes, making them look like black racist attacks. Actress Sharon Tate was one of the victims. At his trial Manson alleged that the guilt lay with society, not with his Family, and thus Manson became a hippie icon of social protest. Manson and his followers received the death penalty, but this was later commuted to life imprisonment.

Although it is doubtful whether Manson's Family can be considered a religious movement, they were cited as indicative of the hold that authoritarian leaders could exert and as evidence of the "mind control" leaders could exert over their followers. The Manson murders served as a warning of the possible dangers of community living, until the mass suicide at Jonestown in 1978 confirmed the anticult movement's (q.v.) worst fears and eclipsed the Manson affair. *See also* BRAINWASHING; JONES, JAMES WARREN; PEOPLES TEMPLE.

MANTRA. A sacred word of power, used in a variety of Eastern religious traditions. The word *mantra* literally means "instrument of thought." Its earliest references are found in the ancient Vedas, particularly the Atharva Veda. The use of mantras spans a variety of religious traditions: Hindu (q.v.), Buddhist (q.v.), Jain, Muslim, and Sufi (q.v.). In Christianity (q.v.), formulae such as "Hail Mary" may effectively have the same function as mantras, although Christians do not generally use the term and do not particularly welcome such comparisons.

The mantra consists of a single sound or a series of sounds that are normally vocalized and repeated by the practitioner, often as part of a wider set of ritual activities, and they are believed to have important effects on one's state of consciousness. The term *japa,* meaning "repetition," is often used to refer to the activity of mantra recitation. They are to be distinguished from spells and from ritual magic (q.v.), both of which are believed to effect direct interventions in the physical world. Practitioners of kundalini yoga (q.v.) theorize that the mantra becomes effective by operating through the chakras (q.v.), affecting one's etheric body by raising the life force's energy up to the head.

Some mantras do not have cognitive meaning, for example "Aum," "Ah," and "Hum": these are sometimes referred to as "seed syllables" or "seed mantras." Others do have cognitive meaning: "Aum mani padme hum" can be translated as "Hail to the jewel in the lotus." However, the cognitive meaning is normally regarded as secondary to the power imbued in the mantra. A further class of mantra has esoteric meaning, known only to authorized gurus (q.v.) and their initiates. Mantras can be used straightforwardly as a means of paying homage to a deity, for instance the International Society of Krishna Consciousness's (ISKCON's) (q.v.) "Maha Mantra" ("Hare Krishna, Hare Krishna, Krishna Krishna, Hare Hare, Hare Rama, Hare Rama, Rama Rama, Hare Hare") is simultaneously an act of devotion to Krishna and Rama and also a means of expiating large amounts of karma.

Other mantras are used to further the devotee's spiritual attainment, while still others can be used for pragmatic purposes. Although some New Age (q.v.) books have propagated the idea of teaching oneself mantra chanting, traditionally a mantra may only legitimately be used if it has been imparted by one's guru through an initiation rite. Accordingly, Transcendental Meditation (TM) (q.v.) lays great emphasis on the need to receive one's personal mantra from one's teacher.

Mantras can allegedly yield pragmatic benefits. ISKCON devotees claim that the Maha Mantra, if practiced sufficiently widely, could be effective in solving the problems of society and indeed the world. TM mantras are said to promote personal effectiveness, better health, and greater relaxation; at a societal level, the movement claims that where there exists a sufficient concentration of TM practitioners in an area, one finds a significant reduction in accidents, hospitalizations, and crime. The Nichiren (q.v.) Buddhist traditions, particularly the Soka Gakkai (q.v.), emphasize the benefits of mantra chanting in terms of satisfying one's desires, although they also advocate the use of chanting "nam myoho renge kyo" for the furtherance of world peace. In Osho (q.v.), the Sufi mantra "Hoo" is employed as part of its "dynamic meditation" and is part of a wider set of techniques for attaining satori. Despite differences in aims and techniques, it is generally held that the important feature of the mantra is neither its meaning nor its pronunciation, but its power.

MARANATHA CHRISTIAN CHURCHES. *A.k.a.: Maranatha Campus Ministries.* Founded in 1972 by Bob Weiner, initially at Murray State University in Paducah, Kentucky, the Maranatha Campus Ministries are aimed principally at a student population. After dropping out of theological college, Weiner experienced the baptism of the Holy Spirit while serving in the U.S. Air Force. Together with Bob Cording, he established Sound Mind in 1971, which went on evangelical tours of American colleges. This gave birth to the Christian Life Center at Long Beach, California—another campus ministry. Coming from the Assemblies of God (q.v.), the Maranatha movement has an organization based on the various offices described in Ephesians 4:11. It lays particular emphasis on prophecy by members, who also speak in tongues (q.v.). By the end of the 1970s around 30 campus ministries were in existence. Reported membership in 1988 was 5,000 on college campuses and 7,000 worldwide.

MARTIN, WALTER (1928-1989). A popular writer, broadcaster, and critic of NRMs from an evangelical Christian perspective. Martin completed a Ph.D. in comparative religions at California Coast University, and devoted his career to writing on NRMs. He completed a total of 12 books, as well as booklets and articles, and is probably best known for *The Kingdom of the Cults,* first published in 1965, which spans a wide range of the new religions that had arisen by the mid-1960s. Martin founded the Christian Research Institute in Irvine, California, of which he was the first director. *See also* ANTICULT MOVEMENT.

MEDITATION. Practiced in a variety of traditional and new religions, meditation consists essentially of practices for training the mind. It differs from contemplation, which is discursive, and focuses instead on doctrines, scriptures, or events (such as the stations of the cross in Christianity [q.v.]). Meditation is most widespread in the Buddhist (q.v.) tradition, in which the last three points of the Buddha's Eightfold

Path (right effort, right mindfulness, right *samadhi*) refer to it. There are two main types of Buddhist meditation: *samatha*, breathing meditation aimed at calming the mind; and *vipassana* (q.v.), which aims at perceiving reality in its true nature. Other types of Buddhist meditation include visualization of buddha or bodhisattva images—particularly prevalent in the Tibetan tradition—and *metta bhavana* (development of lovingkindness), a traditional practice which is encouraged in the Western Buddhist Order (q.v.). Of all the Buddhist schools, Zen (q.v.) attaches particular importance to meditation, and Osho's (q.v.) idiosyncratic development of Zen involves a five-stage "dynamic meditation."

Within Hinduism (q.v.), Raja Yoga (q.v.) is based on Patanjali's Yoga Sutras. Initially taught by the Ramakrishna (q.v.) Vedanta Center, it has also been practiced with Brahma Kumaris (BK) (q.v.), although BK's current practice consists of using affirmations while sitting in front of their guru's (q.v.) picture. Meditation is a characteristic of jnana yoga, which is one of a number of yogas in which the practitioner seeks to realize oneness with the divine. This differs from bhakti yoga, which is practiced within devotional movements such as the International Society for Krishna Consciousness (ISKCON) (q.v.). Thus meditation differs from mantra (q.v.) chanting, although Transcendental Meditation (TM) (q.v.) centers on the use of a mantra.

Meditation is found more rarely in the Semitic traditions. Within Judaism (q.v.), it tends to be confined to Kabbalism (q.v.), which has influenced the Hasidim. Christianity has typically favored contemplation rather than meditation, and within Islam and Sufism (qq.v.), *dhikr* consists of the remembrance of God's name.

Within the New Age Movement (q.v.), meditation has flourished in various forms—some traditional, some eclectic, and some novel.

MEHER BABA (1894-1969). Born Merwan Sheriar Irani in Poona, India, Meher Baba came from a Parsee family. As a youth he became acquainted with Hazrat Babajan, a Muslim woman who was said to be one of the five "Perfect Masters," and she predicted that he would become a spiritual leader. Another Perfect Master, Upasui Maharaj, imparted Divine Knowledge to Irani. In 1921 Irani began to attract disciples, who gave him the name Meher Baba, meaning "loving father." Meher Baba's aims were to bring together all world religions and to show love for all, irrespective of creed or caste. He taught that he was God, the last avatar for the present cycle, previous avatars being Zoroaster, Krishna, Rama, the Buddha, Jesus, and Muhammad. All humanity, too, is divine, he taught, but should be involved in ordinary life and work. Meher Baba claimed to give them, and indeed all levels of the world, an "avataric push" to enable their evolution.

Meher Baba initially established an ashram near Bombay and subsequently founded a compound called Meherabad, near Ahmednagar, which contained a school, a hospital, and accommodation for the poor. He did much work for lepers, the poor, and the hungry, performing menial tasks and demonstrating his disregard for caste. Meher Baba was also concerned for more "advanced souls," or "masts"—those who had become "crazy for God"—and his ashram became known as the "Mad Ashram." The organization has no formal creed, but Meher Baba taught "seven realities": Real Existence (only God, who is identical with the self, is real); Real Love (becoming one with God); Real Sacrifice; Real Renunciation (of selfish desires, rather than worldly activities); Real Knowledge (of the God within all); Real Control (self-discipline); and Real Surrender (calmly submitting to God's will). Disciples *(mandali)* are not subjected to any distinctive lifestyle: meat is permitted, and only recreational drugs are disallowed; premarital sex is strongly disapproved of.

In 1925 Meher Baba ceased to give oral teachings, maintaining a silence that lasted for 44 years until his death and only communicating by means of an alphabet board. From 1956 onward he abandoned even this method of communication, favoring a complex system of hand gestures. Various explanations are offered for this practice: to show that humanity had been deaf to divine teachings, to raise the question of who was speaking, to emphasize that there had been enough words and that action was needed instead. Starting in 1931 Meher Baba made several visits to the West, contacting disciples in the United States, Europe, and Australia. *See also* BRUNTON, PAUL; SUFISM REORIENTED.

MESSIANIC JEWS. Influenced by Jews for Jesus (q.v.), Messianic Jews appeared in the 1960s, although a small group of Hebrew Christians in the 19th century was a precursor. The movement enables its followers to retain their Jewish identity while acknowledging faith in Jesus. It is both innovative and restorationist, contending that Yeshua's (Jesus') original message was for Jews rather than Gentiles, and that at a very early stage of development the Christian Church created a faith that was substantially different from Judaism (q.v.). Messianic Jews therefore see themselves as Jews whose faith is "completed" by the advent of Yeshua.

The movement acknowledges the full status of Yeshua, as affirmed by mainstream Christianity (q.v.). He is regarded as God incarnate, having been predicted by the ancient prophets; he underwent death on the cross in order to atone for the sins of world, rose again from the dead, and ascended into heaven. Gentiles are enabled to participate in the salvation Yeshua offers, without having to undergo the rites of passage, such as circumcision, that are the means of entry to the Jewish faith. The Gentiles are "spiritually circumcised."

Followers celebrate the Jewish festivals, rather than the traditional Christian ones such as Christmas and Easter, thus reflecting the practice of the early Jewish Christians. Since Yeshua is regarded as the fulfillment of the Torah, there are significant differences in the celebration of Jewish practices, and the prayer book has accordingly been rewritten. Many Messianic Jews do not observe the traditional dietary laws, for example, arguing that the Law cannot bring salvation and that the Abrahamic covenant contains the promise of the nations' blessing from his descendants (Genesis 12:3), and therefore has greater binding force than the Mosaic law.

Politically, Messianic Jews tend to support Zionism, and they regard the Six-Day War of 1967 as a turning point, since Jerusalem was then returned to the Jews: this is regarded as the fulfillment of the "times of the Gentiles" (Luke 21:24). Messianic Jews look forward to an imminent Second Coming of Yeshua, which they believe will happen in Israel and will be heralded by events prophesied in Scripture, probably involving a conflict between Israel and Syria.

Messianic Judaism is practiced in the movement's own distinctive synagogues, rather than in Reform Jewish synagogues or Christian churches. At the time of writing, there are some 125 messianic synagogues, most with small congregations of between 10 and 15 members. Estimates of adherents vary widely, ranging from 100,000 to 1,000,000 in 1998. *See also* JUDAISM; LUBAVITCH; REFORM JUDAISM.

METROPOLITAN COMMUNITY CHURCHES (MCC), UNIVERSAL FELLOWSHIP OF. Founded in 1968 in Los Angeles by Troy Perry, the Metropolitan Churches are an ecumenical Christian organization, seeking to meet the needs of homosexual Christians. Perry was formerly a pastor in the Church of God of Prophecy, but was dismissed after his homosexuality was discovered. In 1972 Perry published his autobiography, *The Lord Is My Shepherd and He Knows I'm Gay*. The movement grew rapidly in the 1980s and 1990s, reaching a worldwide total of 20,000 members and 200 churches spanning the United States, Canada, Europe, Australasia, Mexico, Costa Rica, and Nigeria. The MCC affirms the Apostles' and Nicene Creeds, but allows individual interpretation. Committed to the Reformation principle of the priesthood of all believers, it strongly encourages lay contribution to its life and worship. A General Conference elects a seven-person Board of Elders who head the organization. Following the AIDS crisis, the MCC did much to warn of the dangers and offer help to those affected, circulating its newsletter *Alert* starting in 1987. As well as ministering to homosexuals and blessing gay couples, the MCC supports the

Civil Rights movement more widely, championing world peace and justice.

MILLENNIALISM. Although the "millennium" is popularly associated with the 1,000-year period beginning with the year 1000 C.E., the term properly refers to the 1,000-year rule of Christ mentioned in Revelation 20:1-3, in which Satan is bound for 1,000 years before being freed for a brief period and finally defeated. Belief in this series of eschatological events is thus common to mainstream Christian fundamentalism (q.v.), and to certain New Christian NRMs, such as the Jehovah's Witnesses and the Family (qq.v.). The popular and religious senses of "millennium" are connected by the typical fundamentalist belief that the world's creation began around 4000 B.C.E.: this entails that the world has now been in existence for six millennia and is currently entering its seventh. Since various Christian and New Christian movements believe that a historical parallel exists between the days of creation and the universe's history, it therefore follows that the new millennium is God's sabbatical and therefore heralds the completion of affairs on earth. Owing to different calculations of the creation's date of completion, and also to some leeway in dating the birth of Jesus, few movements fix a precise date on the ending of human affairs, although several are convinced of an imminent final end.

Christian millennialists can be divided into three types: premillennialists, postmillennialists, and amillennialists. The first view is the most common, namely, that Christ's return is imminent and will be followed by the 1,000-year rule that Scripture predicts. According to the postmillennialist, the 1,000-year rule has already been completed, or at least is in the process of completion; hence the final defeat of Satan is imminent. This second view was prevalent in the ideas of the Great Awakening, in which it was believed that Christian missionary activity would ensure the vanquishing of "false religion" and the bringing of the entire world under Christ's rule. The amillennialist views all such descriptions of the endtimes as symbolic rather than as a literal calendar of apocalyptic occurrences. The Unification Church (q.v.), arguably, comes close to adopting an amillennialist position, since it views as purely symbolic the description of Christ returning on the clouds and prefers to talk of the "Completed Testament Era" rather than a literal millennium.

Millennialism, as defined above, draws exclusively on Christian ideas. Because other religions such as Buddhism, Judaism, Islam, and Bahá'í (qq.v.) use different calendars, any application of the term *millennialist* to movements related to these traditions entails an extended use of the term. In such use, the word comes to mean a religious group that affirms or expects the imminent realization of its eschaton. The New Age Movement (q.v.), believing that the new Age of Aquarius is dawning (or has dawned), can be said to espouse millennialist ideas, although the New Age worldview is based on astrological theories, rather than on biblical exegesis. *See also* CONCERNED CHRISTIANS; CREME, BENJAMIN; LUBAVITCH; MILLER, WILLIAM; SOLOMON'S TEMPLE.

MILLER, WILLIAM (1782-1849). Born in Pittsfield, Massachusetts, Miller joined the Baptist Church in 1816 and embarked on extensive personal study of the Bible. Having studied biblical prophecies in detail, he concluded in 1818 that the world would end with Christ's second coming "about 1843." Miller later became more specific, indicating that the world would end in the Jewish year that ran from 21 March 1843 to 21 March 1844. Interest grew in Miller's ideas, and he gained prominence as a preacher and writer from 1831 onward. His ideas on the Second Coming were first published in a series of articles in a weekly Baptist magazine, the *Vermont Telegraph*. Miller's end-time calculations were based on Scripture, which he regarded as inerrant, and particularly on dates and numbers in the Book of Daniel. Special significance was attached to a period of 70 weeks (Daniel 9:24-27) and 2,300 "evenings and mornings" (Daniel 8:14). One of Miller's principles of biblical exegesis was his "year-for-a-day rule," and the 2,300 days were therefore interpreted to signify 2,300 years after Artaxerxes' decree—assumed to have been given in 457 B.C.E.—permitting the return of the Jews from Babylon (Ezra 7:11-26). Miller also equated the "cleansing of the sanctuary" (Daniel 8:14) with Christ's second advent.

When the Second Coming failed to occur within the set period, Miller reconsidered his predictions. One notable problem was that he failed to take into account the fact that there was no year 0 separating "B.C." and "A.D.," thus creating a discrepancy of a year. One of his followers, Samuel S. Snow, therefore reexamined Miller's calculation and gave momentum to a "seventh month" movement, declaring 22 October 1844 as the expected date, being jointly the Jewish Day of Atonement and the presumed anniversary of the beginning of creation. (The expression "seventh month" relates to the occurrence of the Day of Atonement in the seventh Jewish month, Tishri.)

This second unfulfilled date became known as the "Great Disappointment." Erstwhile followers of Miller—notably Hiram Edson and Ellen G. White (q.v.)—developed rival interpretations of the "cleansing of the sanctuary," claiming that it designated events in heaven rather than on earth. Following the discrediting of Miller's predictions, the Millerites soon died out, and the interpretation offered by Edson and White has prevailed within subsequent Seventh-day Adventism (q.v.), as well as within the Jehovah's Witnesses (q.v.). John Thomas (q.v.), founder-leader of the Christadelphians (q.v.) and a contemporary of Miller's, challenged Miller's interpretation even before his predictions failed.

MO LETTERS. A series of publications by David Berg (q.v.) (1919-1994), otherwise known as Moses David or Father David, leader of the Children of God (now the Family [q.v.]). The *MO Letters* circulated in the 1970s and early 1980s and were addressed to "DOs" (meaning Doers Only—Berg's inner core of followers who lived in CoG communities). The letters were sexually explicit: Berg deliberately taught that the human body was nothing to be ashamed about, since the

Bible states that Adam and Eve were "naked and not ashamed" in the Garden of Eden. Accordingly the letters extolled the virtues of sexual pleasure. It is not true, as some critics have alleged, that the *MO Letters* had the status of Scripture; although Father David was regarded as a prophet, he plainly taught that the traditional Scriptures contained all that was necessary for salvation. The letters are no longer used by the Family, who have not systematically preserved them. The sexual permissiveness which they advocated was substantially reconsidered in the early 1980s, following the outbreak of the AIDS epidemic.

MOON, SUN MYUNG (b. 1920). Born in North Korea as Yong Myung Moon, Moon is the founder-leader of the Family Federation for World Peace and Unification, formerly the Unification Church (q.v.). Raised as a Presbyterian, Moon claims to have received a vision of Jesus Christ on Easter morning 1936, in which he was commissioned to complete Jesus' unfinished work. After being imprisoned in Hungnam from 1948 to 1950, Moon fled south to Pusan with two close followers, where he began to dictate the *Divine Principle* (q.v.). After becoming associated with a number of Korean NRMs, Moon established his own religious community in Seoul in 1954, called the Holy Spirit Association for the Unification of World Christianity.

As the movement grew, missionaries were sent to the United States, Europe, and Japan. Young Oon Kim, the first missionary to America, had limited success, but when Moon himself visited the United States in 1972 and addressed several public rallies, the movement gained momentum and attracted a larger following. In 1960 Sun Myung Moon married Hak Ja Han, and they raised a family of 13 children (two have since died). The couple are known as the "True Parents" and are jointly regarded as the messiahs of the Completed Testament Era. The Rev. and Mrs. Moon have gained particular attention from the media for the so-called "mass weddings" (more correctly known as the "Blessing" ceremonies), in which large numbers of couples undergo marriage at a ceremony over which the True Parents preside.

It was previously expected that Sun Myung Moon would be succeeded by his eldest son Hyung Jin Moon, but the latter has now been deprived of his future office, owing to sexual misconduct, alcoholism, and drug abuse. At least two of Moon's children have now questioned his messianic status. Predictably, this has caused problems at both a practical and a theological level. Although the longer-term issue of succession remains undetermined, Hak Ja Han Moon seems likely to lead the movement when Sun Myung Moon finally dies.

MORAL RE-ARMAMENT (MRA). Founded by Frank Buchman (q.v.) (1878-1961) in 1921 as the First Century Christian Fellowship, this group became known as the Oxford Group Movement in 1934. Buchman first used the expression "Moral Re-Armament" in 1938, and the name was adopted for the movement during World War II and the period thereafter. Buchman taught that religion was not a matter of intellect or emotion, but of will, and that alienation from God is caused by one's moral failings. MRA taught the importance of four "absolutes": absolute honesty, absolute purity, absolute unselfishness, and absolute love. Two important practices were employed: sharing and guidance. In the former, supporters were encouraged to confess their faults to each other at gatherings. A movement rather than a membership organization, it has spread worldwide, having currently offices in 28 countries.

Buchman used innovative methods of propagating his ideas. One popular event was a "house party," in which supporters met in the home of an affluent member or in a good hotel. Another method was the use of plays, often by Peter Howard, performed in the Westminster Theatre in London. Public testimony meetings also attracted attention. MRA has been criticized for pro-Nazi leanings. Such accusations are no doubt exaggerated, although the movement has been vehemently opposed to communism. After Buchman's death, the movement was led in a less structured way, with a much lower public profile.

MOTHER MEERA (b. 1960). Born Kamala Reedy in Andhra Pradesh, India, Mother Meera is regarded as an avatar of the Divine Mother. At the age of six she began to go into trances, and when she was 14 she went to the Sri Aurobindo (q.v.) Ashram at Pondicherry. Many of Aurobindo's followers did not accept Mother Meera, and she left, traveling all over India giving darshan. In 1979 she left India for Europe, finally settling in Germany in 1983. Meera offers "cosmic shakti" (shakti being the feminine form of divinity), bringing the Paramatman (cosmic soul) to the individual in order to gain spiritual transformation. Meera does not teach any specific doctrines, but preaches love and compassion. Many seekers claim to have experienced healing from her. Andrew Harvey's book *Hidden Journey* (1991) has done much to promote Mother Meera in the West.

MOVEMENT FOR THE RESTORATION OF THE TEN COMMANDMENTS OF GOD. A Ugandan neo-Catholic group, established in 1987, over 500 of whose members were burned alive on 17 March 2000. Other bodies were found buried nearby, bringing the total dead to over 1,000. Founded by Credonia Mwerinde (1960-2000) and Joseph Kibwetere (1931/2-2000), the movement's leaders claimed to have received visions of the Virgin Mary, who predicted an imminent end of the world due to humanity's widespread abandonment of the Ten Commandments. Members accordingly were expected to show enhanced observance of the commandments. Kibwetere informed members that the world would end on 31 December 1999, and it has been speculated that he planned the mass killings to silence mounting opposition, following the subsequent disillusionment. Other explanations are that the group expected the Virgin Mary to appear and take members to heaven on 17 March 2000 and were disappointed when this did not occur. Alternatively, the group's leaders may have organized the massacres for financial gain.

See also SEDEVACANTISTS; WORLD MESSAGE LAST WARNING CHURCH.

MOVEMENT OF SPIRITUAL INNER AWARENESS (MSIA, pronounced "Messiah"). A group founded by John-Roger Hinkins (born Roger Delano Hinkins in 1934), a former member of Eckankar (q.v.). After reportedly encountering Radhasoami (q.v.) leader Sawan Singh (1858-1945) on a spiritual plane, Hinkins claimed to have received final initiation as the Mystical Traveler in 1963. The Mystical Traveler is an office that has been held by various people throughout the ages—Lao Tzu, Jesus, and Shakespeare are particularly mentioned—guiding humankind as an embodiment of the Holy Spirit. After attracting a group of disciples, Hinkins established the Church of the Movement of Spiritual Inner Awareness in 1971, and subsequently the Peace Theological Seminary (1974), Baraha Holistic Center (1976), Insight Transformation Seminars (1978), and the John-Roger Foundation (1982). The last of these organizations coordinates MSIA's activities and celebrates Integrity Day (24 September), established by the U.S. Congress in 1988.

Hinkins's teachings bear striking similarities to those of Radhasoami Satsang and Ruhani Satsang (qq.v.), as well as Eckankar, to the extent that he has attracted accusations of plagiarism. Worldwide membership of the Church of MSIA was 4,500 in 1993. *See also* INSIGHT; HUMAN POTENTIAL MOVEMENT; SELF RELIGIONS.

MUKTANANDA, SWAMI PARAMAHANSA. (1908-1982). Founder of the Siddha Yoga Dham (q.v.) movement. Muktananda left home while still in his youth, leading the life of a wandering ascetic. In 1947 he was recommended to seek out Bhagwan Nityananda (1, q.v.) (d. 1961), who gave him shaktipat initiation (the awakening of kundalini energy). After nine years, Muktananda is said to have attained full self-realization. After Nityananda's death he established the Gurudev Siddha Peeth Ashram near Ganeshpuri, 50 miles from Bombay. Visitors to the ashram have included Werner Erhard, who invited Muktananda to the West. From the early 1960s American seekers came to Muktananda, and a decade later he visited Europe, the United States, and Australia, accompanied by Baba Ram Dass (q.v.). Following Nityananda's practice, Muktananda gave shaktipat diksha to his disciples; among his teachings, devotion to the guru (q.v.)—Muktananda—was important to the awakening of kundalini energy. On his death, Swami Chidvilasananda (b. 1955) and her brother Swami Nityananda (2, q.v.) (b. 1963) succeeded him, although the latter resigned his office, and established his own movement. Muktananada's autobiography is entitled *Play of Consciousness. See also* AVATARA ADI DA; ERHARD SEMINAR TRAINING; KUNDALINI YOGA.

-N-

NAMDHARI. *A.k.a.: Kuka.* A Sikh movement, founded in the 19th century by Ram Singh (1816-1885). The Namdharis claim to have establish a restored khalsa. They teach that Guru Gobind Singh (1666-1708)—the 10th and, according to traditional Sikhism (q.v.), the last of the line of human gurus (q.v.) —did not die at Nander, but passed on his guruship to Balak Singh (1797-1862). Founder-leader Ram Singh is believed to be a reincarnation of Gobind Singh and passed on the lineage to his successor Jagjit Singh, the present guru.

The alternative name "Kuka" derives from the sound of their ecstatic exclamations during worship. Importance is attached to *kirtan* (worship), especially music and the recitation of God's name, which is done with the aid of a 108-bead woolen rosary. The Namdhari *havan jag* (fire ceremony) also distinguishes Namdharis from other Sikhs. The movement is vegetarian and emphasizes cow protection. It seeks to advance the status of women and is also renowned for its multiple marriage ceremonies. The movement's headquarters are located at Bhaini, in the district of Ludhiana in India.

NARAYANANANDA, SWAMI (1902-1988). Born in Coorg, in southern India, Narayanananda began his spiritual life at the age of 27 when he assumed the life of a sannyasin (q.v.) and traveled to the Ramakrishna Math near Calcutta. There he was taught by Swami Shivananda (a disciple of Ramakrishna [q.v]), who in 1932 directed him to meditate in the Himalayas, where he attained the state of nirvikipa samadhi (recognition of oneness with the ultimate). Initially a recluse, he accepted no disciples but committed his spiritual experiences to writing. Following the partitioning of India and Pakistan in 1947 with the consequent human suffering, Narayanananda agreed to take disciples, including Europeans. After reading his notes, several of them demanded that they gain a wider readership and arranged for their publication. The Narayanananda Universal Yoga Trust was set up in 1967, and centers were established in India, Denmark, Germany, and Switzerland. In 1977 Swami Turiyananda was delegated the task of starting ashrams in Chicago and in Winter, Wisconsin.

Narayanananda taught "universal religion," contending that all the world's religions could be classified in terms of one or other of the Hindu (q.v.) yogas (karma yoga, bhakti yoga, jnana yoga, raja yoga [q.v.]), and that they shared a common ethic. Progress toward realizing Ultimate Truth involved meditation (q.v.), practicing a strict moral code, and "mind control," involving regulation of one's breathing and consciousness. Narayanananda spent most of his life in India, paying only one visit to the United States in 1980. He visited the Narayanananda Universal Yoga Ashram in Gylling, Denmark in 1971, which remains the international headquarters of the organization. In 1995 there were some 5,000 members worldwide.

NATIONAL ASSOCIATION OF KINGDOM EVANGELI-CALS. A loosely organized group of British Israelite (q.v.) churches, formed after World War II by C. O. Stadsklev. Unusually for British Israelites, the group is Trinitarian. It regards the former Soviet Union as the enemy and advocates radical reforms of the "Babylonian money system." Stadsklev made himself known through his radio broadcasts "America's Hope," and the Gospel Temple circulates his writings and tapes.

NATION OF ISLAM (NOI) (1). A Black Muslim movement, originally founded in the 1930s as the Lost-Found Nation of Islam by Wallace D. Fard ("Prophet Fard") (1891-1934). Fard's mission was taken over by Elijah Muhammad—born Elijah Poole (1897-1975)—whose followers regarded him as a prophet and messenger of God.

Elijah Muhammad's work *Message to the Blackman in America* taught that God was originally a black person (a physical being, no longer in existence), whose people's supremacy was challenged by white rivals. Muhammad taught black supremacy, advocating black rights and rejecting any political moves toward racial integration. His speeches and writings have also been accused of being anti-Semitic. Malcolm X (q.v.) belonged to the Nation of Islam during the 1960s, but seceded. His departure heralded a number of splits in the movement, whose fragmentation set in after Muhammad's death. In 1975 Elijah Muhammad was succeeded by his son Wallace D. Muhammad (Warith Deem Muhammad), who steered the movement in a much more moderate direction.

The organization has undergone various name changes: the Bilalian Community, the World Community of Al-Islam in the West, the American Muslim Mission, and finally the Muslim Mission. Wallace D. Muhammad even admitted whites, and he sought racial integration rather than black supremacy. A significant proportion of members wished to reaffirm Elijah Muhammad's teachings, and a number of dissident leaders formed their own breakaway groups which they called the Nation of Islam (2, 3, qq.v.). The largest of these was that of Abdul Haleem Farrakhan: other schismatical leaders whose groups were called NOI included Silis Muhammad, John Muhammad (Elijah Muhammad's brother), and Emmannuel Abdullah Muhammad. Estimates of worldwide allegiance vary from 10,000 to 100,000 (1998); the majority of supporters live in the United States. *See also* GARVEY, MARCUS MOZIAH.

NATION OF ISLAM (2). An offshoot of Elijah Muhammad's Nation of Islam (1, q.v.), led by Silis Muhammad. After Wallace Muhammad assumed leadership of the original Nation of Islam, transforming it into the World Community of Al-Islam in the West, a number of members disliked its more moderate policies. Wishing to reaffirm the original teaching of Elijah Muhammad (1897-1975), a number of groups broke away in 1977, reverting to the previous name, Nation of Islam. Silis Muhammad was a close ally of Elijah Muhammad and believed that God had personally appeared to him; hence Elijah Muhammad should be regarded as a present-day personification of Moses. The movement reaffirmed Elijah Muhammad's teachings of black supremacy and opposition to racial integration.

NATION OF ISLAM (3). A Black Muslim breakaway group under Abdul Haleem Farrakhan from the American Muslim Mission, which succeeded Elijah Muhammad's Nation of Islam (1, q.v.) when his son Wallace D. Muhammad assumed office after his death in 1975. Farrakhan was born Louis Eugene Wolcott in 1933 and is also known as Louis X. He could not accept the American Muslim Mission's more moderate policies, such as racial integration instead of black supremacy. Farrakhan and his supporters organized the well-publicized March of a Million Men in Washington on 16 October 1995.

Farrakhan's differences with Silis Muhammad's group of the same name (Nation of Islam 2, q.v.) related to the role of Jesus, whose prophecies the former declared to be fulfilled in the person of Elijah Muhammad. On 25 February 2000 Farrakhan met with Wallace Muhammad, arousing speculation that a reconciliation might be imminent. Farrakhan's group is the largest of the splinter groups and is reported as having between 5,000 and 10,000 members.

NATION OF YAHWEH. *A.k.a.: Hebrew Israelites; Temple of Love.* A black Jewish organization, founded by Hulon Mitchell, Jr. (b. 1935), the son of a Pentecostalist (q.v.) minister and at one time a professional football player. Mitchell joined the Nation of Islam (1, q.v.) for a period and was entrusted with the leadership of one of its congregations. He founded the Temple of Love in 1978, changing his name to Brother Moses the following year and subsequently to Yahweh ben Yahweh ("God, son of God"). The movement teaches that God is black (in accordance with Daniel 7:9), and that his son, Yahweh ben Yahweh, is the savior of the African Americans, who are the lost tribe of Judah. Believers are offered immortality, while those who oppose God are equated with Satan. On joining, members assume the surname "Israel," and many of them wear characteristic white robes as a visible sign of belonging. The movement is politically activist, campaigning for electoral reforms, improvements in education, better employment opportunities, and improved health and housing. Peace, love, harmony, and family values are proclaimed as ideals.

The Hebrew Israelites achieved notoriety when one of their members admitted to seven murders in 1988 and later implicated the leadership in the killings of 14 whites and seditious black disciples. Mitchell and other leaders were convicted of conspiracy to homicide in 1992.

NATIVE AMERICAN CHURCH. A synthesis of Christianity and Native American religion (qq.v.), principally attracting American Indians. Peyote is used in worship, having originally been introduced around 1870 to the Kiowa and Comanche tribes and promoted more widely by itinerant peyote teachers such as Quanah Parker of the Comanche. *See also* CASTANEDA, CARLOS; PEYOTE CULTS.

NATIVE AMERICAN RELIGION. A diversity of interrelated practices pertaining to the American Indian tradition before widescale Western settlement. Earth-centered spirituality is a salient feature, in which the earth is typically viewed as sacred and as animated with Spirit. Equally important is shamanism (q.v.), which incorporates contact with the spirit world, psychic and paranormal activity, the significance of visions and dreams, and healing, which is administered by medicine men and women. These ideas have become popular in Western alternative spirituality, principally through the New Age Movement (q.v.). More exclusively indigenous have been the Ghost Dance (q.v.) movement and the Indian Shakers. *See also* ANGELS; BLACK ELK; PEYOTE CULTS.

NEO-CATECHUMENATE. A renewal group within the Roman Catholic Church, founded in 1962 by Kiko Arguello in Madrid. Arguello was later joined by Carmen Hernandez and Fr. Mario Pezzi, and the three now lead the movement. Unlike Opus Dei (q.v.), the Neo-Catechumenate works within Roman Catholic dioceses and with the permission of their bishops. Emphasis is given to personal prayer and devotion, the study of the Bible and Catholic theology, and a Christ-centered life that takes precedence over career aspirations and material wealth. Through the renewal of their faith and understanding, the Neo-Catechumens seek to secure the renewal of the entire Church.

Itinerant Catechumens visit dioceses and give talks—usually at Mass—urging repentance and renewal. Those who respond positively are asked to meet weekly and to undertake weekly celebration of the Mass. After two years they become eligible for the Catechumenate. After a further three years members are permitted to "abandon themselves to the will of the Father" and go out as itinerants. A Neo-Catechumenate community was established in Rome in 1968, and there are now 80 countries in which the movement is represented.

NEO-TEMPLARISM. Founded by Bernard of Clairvaux (1090-1153), the Templars were a monastic order who engaged in military conflict during the Crusades (1118-1312). Although officially disbanded by Pope Clement V in 1312, a few of their number moved to Portugal, where they established the Order of Christ.

In more recent times there have been various attempts at reestablishing Templarism (q.v.). However, although many neo-Templars claim a lineage from St. Bernard's order, it is extremely doubtful whether such historical continuity can be established. One such claimant to be in a lineage of Templar grand masters was Bernard-Raymond Fabré-Palaprat (1773-1838), who is often regarded as the father of neo-Templarism. Because the Roman Catholic Church disbanded the Templars, it has remained officially opposed to attempts to revive Templarism. Fabré-Palaprat, however, declared that Roman Catholicism was a "fallen church" and founded a rival institution known as the Johannites. A number of bishops were consecrated within the Johannite Church, and thus neo-Templarism became associated with a number of Liberal Catholic (q.v.) organizations that are governed by "irregular bishops."

Among modern neo-Templar movements are the Renewed Order of the Temple (ORT), founded by Julien Origas (1920-1983), Ancient Mystical Order of the Rosy Cross (AMORC) (q.v.), and the Solar Temple (q.v.).

NEW AGE MOVEMENT (NAM). A popular form of alternative spirituality that gained momentum during the 1980s in the West. The term was probably first used by William Blake (1757-1827), who wrote, "Rouze up O Young Men of the New Age!" envisaging a new era of Christianity, characterized by Gnostic (q.v.) ideas and anticlericalism. The NAM is in part a reaction against institutional forms of religion, and the "new age" is identified with the zodiacal Age of Aquarius, which is held to supersede the previous 2,000-year period, the Age of Pisces, which is the period spanning the Christian era.

It is not possible to identify a definitive set of teachings or practices that feature in New Age thinking. Sociologist Marilyn Ferguson observes that the notion of "networking" is prominent, enabling various topics of interest and diverse interest groups to interact with each other. The title of her book—*The Aquarian Conspiracy* (1980)—highlights the fact that in New Age thought a cluster of diverse ideas "conspire": that is, breathe together symbiotically.

New Age interests include occultism—astrology, Tarot, crystals, various forms of divination, channeling (q.v.), and the use of spirit guides (q.v.)—and the paranormal more widely: ESP, telepathy, precognition, out-of-the-body experiences. Alternative forms of therapy, such as homeopathy, crystal therapy, and Tibetan and Ayurvedic medicine, as well as forms of spiritual healing, have aroused interest. Also encouraged is spiritual exploration into forms of meditation (q.v.), visualization, and Eastern religions—especially Buddhism, Hinduism, Sufism (qq.v.) and Taoism. New Agers tend to be eclectic and do not necessarily confine their interests to one single spiritual tradition. Traditional Christianity (q.v.) is less popular, although there exists a prevalent belief in angels (q.v.) in certain circles, and an interest in possible relationships between Jesus and the East—for example, theories that associate him with India.

The movement is characterized by an optimism, which expresses itself as a hope for a future of peace and concord. The New Age places a positive value on the earth, and an interest in ecology and conservation features prominently in the concerns of many supporters. New Agers tend to assign a positive value to the individual, who is seen as having potential—hence the interest in developing interpersonal and business skills: assertiveness, human psychology, neurolinguistic programming. Apart from specific interest groups and New Age periodicals, the nucleus of the New Age is sometimes identified as the new shops that can be found in most American and European cities, which indicate that, notwithstanding its spirituality, material and commercial interests are by no means disparaged. *See also* ARTHURIAN MYTHS; BREATHARIANS; CHAKRAS; CHURCH OF MERCAVAH; DAMANHUR; FINDHORN; GAIA HYPOTHESIS; GLASTONBURY; SPANGLER, DAVID; TREVELYAN, SIR GEORGE.

NEW APOSTOLIC CHURCH (NAC). Derived from the Catholic Apostolic Church (CAC), this church was founded under the influence of Edward Irving (1792-1834) and recognized the various ministries defined in Ephesians 4:11, particularly restoration of the office of apostle. The NAC arose around 1860, following a dispute as to whether restored apostles should be replaced after death. The NAC's practice is to replenish the apostolate, and the organization is led by a chief apostle, based in its headquarters in Zurich. Other branches throughout the world are led by district apostles, assisted by bishops, district elders, and district evangelists. All of these are lay offices, and their leaders receive no theological training.

The NAC celebrates three sacraments: baptism (normally of infants), communion (using unleavened bread with drops of wine sprinkled on it), and "sealing." The last of these is a rite by which the Holy Spirit is given, and which brings baptized adherents into full membership: this rite must be administered by an apostle. The NAC is conservative in its theology; it has its own creed, which is based on the Apostles' Creed but emphasizes the importance of the sacraments. Also included is an expanded section on Christ's imminent return and an affirmation of the importance of obedience to earthly authorities, except where obedience would conflict with divine law.

The NAC claimed nine million members worldwide in 2000, principally in Germany, Great Britain, India, Africa, Argentina, the United States, and Australia.

NEW KADAMPA TRADITION (NKT). An expression of Tibetan Buddhism (q.v.), founded by Geshe Kelsang Gyatso (q.v.) (b. 1932), who came to England in 1977 and settled within a Buddhist community at Ulverston in Cumbria. The movement has devolved into a number of small centers, mainly in England, but also in Europe, the United States, and Canada.

The Kadampa tradition goes back to the celebrated Buddhist teacher Tsongkhapa (1357-1419) and the Indian Buddhist master Atisha (982-1054), and the NKT aims to preserve the practices of this "Old Kadampa" tradition, but in a purified form that is more accessible to Westerners. One important Western adaptation is the translation of its ceremonies into English. Kelsang Gyatso teaches the fundamentals of Buddhism, such as the Four Noble Truths, the Eightfold Path, dependent origination, and the six realms of samsara in which rebirth is deemed to be possible. There are also distinctively Tibetan teachings and practices. NKT students study almost exclusively the writings of Kelsang Gyatso, which are read and elaborated on at meetings.

Its principal practices include meditation (q.v.) on Chenrezig (Avalokiteshvara), Manjushri, and Tara—all bodhisattvas who are revered in the Mahayana tradition. The practice of developing bodhicitta (striving for enlightenment on behalf of all living beings) is emphasized. Particular controversy has been aroused by the NKT's invocation of Dorje Shugden (q.v.), who is regarded as a protector deity, but whom other Buddhists, including the Dalai Lama, regard as a *dabla* (evil spirit). The Dalai Lama issued a ban on practicing Dorje Shugden, and NKT members took the unusual step of organizing a protest against him in 1996. There are some 5,000 supporters worldwide.

NEW THOUGHT. A cluster of religious and spiritual movements that gained prominence in the late 19th and early 20th centuries, originally influenced by Franz (Friedrich) Anton Mesmer (1734-1815) and emphasizing the power of mind over matter. Mesmer combined new discoveries in electricity and magnetism with advances in medicine and astrological and other occultist ideas. He developed a theory called "animal magnetism" (also known as "electro-biology"), which postulated the existence of a magnetic field or fluid that surrounded the body and could be obstructed, thus giving rise to illness. Mesmer devised ways of correcting such imbalances, sometimes inducing trancelike states in his patients, who would "prophesy" on occasion. Hence mesmerism came to be associated with clairvoyance.

The French hypnotist Charles Poyen disseminated Mesmer's ideas, first in France and then on a lecture tour in the United States from 1836 to 1839. Phineas Parker Quimby (1802-1866) was a member of one of his audiences, and it is Quimby who is often regarded as the father of New Thought. Quimby taught that the source of health was in the mind and thus was one of the early pioneers of "mind cure." Influenced by Quimby were Julius Dresser (q.v.) and his wife, Annetta, and Warren Felt Evans (q.v.), who promoted the practices of using "affirmations" to promote improvements in health and prosperity. Other writers produced a wave of books on "positive thinking" and "self-help"—dominant themes in New Thought.

Quimby's disciple Mary Baker Eddy (q.v.) (1821-1910) established Christian Science (q.v.), and her ideas are encapsulated in her much-used *Science and Health: A Key to the Scriptures*. In Christian Science's early years Eddy worked with Emma Curtis Hopkins, but Hopkins split away to found the Hopkins Metaphysical Association in 1887. Among those whom Hopkins taught were Melinda Cramer, Charles and Myrtle Fillmore (q.v.), and Frances Lord. Cramer founded Divine Science, the Fillmores established the Unity School of Christianity (q.v.), and Lord traveled to England, disseminating New Thought there. Other New Thought organizations included Homes of Truth and Religious Science (q.v.). The International New Thought Alliance was founded in 1914 as an umbrella organization for a variety of New Thought groups. *See also* ASSOCIATION OF UNITY CHURCHES; EMERSON, RALPH WALDO; HOLMES, ERNEST S.

NEW WORLD ORDER. An imminent state of affairs, in fulfillment of biblical prophecy, expected in certain Protestant fundamentalist (q.v.) circles, especially among some Adventists and Pentecostalists (q.v.), and traceable to Ellen G. White (q.v.) (1827-1915). It is expected to be a single world order, in which there will be one world government, allied to one religion; its advent is signaled by the inception of the United Nations and the ecumenical and interfaith movements.

Such organizations, together with general lawlessness, immorality, and the increase in occult practices such as Spiritualism and channeling (qq.v.), confirm that the present age is one of apostasy, led by a "man of sin . . . the son of perdition" (2 Thessalonians 2:3), often identified with the Pope, who is also equated with the Antichrist (2 John 7). The papacy is the "beast" of Revelation 13, and various proofs are adduced that the number 666 (the "number of the beast") applies to this institution.

Since the New World Order entails an alliance between state and religion, the beast can also be equated with America, and hence there is a tendency to see biblical prophecy as applying to present-day events. Supporters of this theory saw corroboration when in February 1991 U.S. President George Bush spoke of "a new world order, where diverse nations are drawn together in common cause," declaring that "only the United States has both the moral standing and the means to back it up." With the development of computer technology, some Protestant writers and preachers have connected the "mark of the beast" which is said to be found on his follower's wrists and forehead with barcodes and silicon chips, predicting that implants on one's body will come to replace credit cards. Others believe that the identity of the mark of the beast has still to be revealed.

NICHIREN (1222-1282). The historical founder of the Nichiren Schools of Buddhism (q.v.). Born in Kominato, Japan, Nichiren studied at a Tendai temple at Seichoji and traveled widely in an endeavor to study all the extant forms of Buddhism. Nichiren proclaimed the Mahayana scripture, the *Saddharma Pundarika Sutra* (the Lotus Sutra), to be the one true authentic version of Buddhism, encapsulating all its teachings. Nichiren's followers regard him as the one who speaks authoritatively to the present age and believe that the Lotus Sutra encapsulates all the authentic teachings of Buddhism.

After centuries of decline, Nichiren Buddhism experienced a revival beginning in the mid-19th century and is the second most popular version of Buddhism in Japan today. Among versions practiced in the West are Nichiren Shoshu, Soka Gakkai, Rissho Kosei Kai, Reiyukai, Nipponzan Myohoji (qq.v.), and Nichiren Shu. Nichiren Shoshu and Soka Gakkai Buddhists regard Nichiren as the *adi-buddha*—the primal Buddha, from which Gautama is merely an emanation—and criticize other schools for relegating his status to that of a bodhisattva.

It is believed that Nichiren left behind six chief disciples after his death. According to the Nichiren Shoshu and Soka Gakkai, his disciple Nikko was the only one to preserve his teachings in their pure form, taking the *dai-gohonzon* (a scroll inscribed by Nichiren) to Taiseki-ji, where he commenced the building of Nichiren Shoshu's principal temple. Other Nichiren schools claim that their founder-leader inscribed a number of gohonzons, and that the story of Nikko only underlines the sectarian nature of Nichiren Shoshu Buddhism.

Nichiren schools are renowned for their chanting of the mantra (q.v.) *Namu myoho renge kyo* (*Nam myoho renge kyo* in the case of Nichiren Shoshu and Soka Gakkai), literally, "Homage to the ineffable law of the lotus teaching." Key sections of the Lotus Sutra are particularly selected for ceremonial chanting, notably parts of chapters 2 and 16 (the "Hoben" and "Juryo" chapters). Chanting is believed to have pragmatic benefits as well as spiritual ones.

NICHIREN SHOSHU. A form of Japanese Buddhism (q.v.) that follows the teachings of Nichiren (q.v.) (1222-1282), who taught the supremacy of the Buddhist text the Lotus Sutra. The movement's headquarters are situated in the Taiseki-ji Temple at the foot of Mount Fuji, where its high priest presides. This is the resting place of the *dai-gohonzon,* a scroll believed to have been personally inscribed by Nichiren with the mantra (q.v.) *Nam myoho renge kyo.* The mantra is believed to have great material and spiritual efficacy, encapsulating the entire Lotus Sutra. The principal ceremony is the *gongyo,* in which brief sections of the Lotus Sutra are ritually chanted.

Formerly the Soka Gakkai (q.v.) was the lay movement associated with Nichiren Shoshu, whose priests took responsibility for rites of passage (mainly marriages and funerals) and without whose authority individual members' gohonzons could not be issued. In 1992 the lay and priestly organizations separated, following a series of disputes. One principal cause of acrimony was the use of Shinto symbols by the priesthood, in opposition to the lay movement, which wanted to maintain a form of Buddhism that was free from Shinto elements. A further source of controversy related to the dissemination of Nichiren Shoshu Buddhism. The Soka Gakkai, having become an international organization, taught that the practice of chanting was compatible with following one's previous religion, whereas the Nichiren Shoshu priesthood wanted to insist on the practice of *shakubuku* in evangelization. *Shakubuku* literally means "break and subdue," and the priesthood maintained the need to promulgate their own brand of Buddhism by forceful refutation of other Buddhist sects and of other religions.

Following the split, Soka Gakkai members are now barred from entering the Taiseki-ji Temple and are no longer issued with gohonzons. In 1998 there were 724 Nichiren Shoshu temples in Japan and 600,000 members outside the country.

NIPPONZAN MYOHOJI. *A.k.a.: Nichihonzon Myohoji.* A Buddhist (q.v.) organization in the Nichiren (q.v.) tradition, founded by Nichidatsu Fujii (1885-1985). After becoming ordained in 1903, Fujii founded his own Buddhist organization in 1924 and traveled widely to preach Nichiren doctrines. He met Mahatma Gandhi, with whom he had a close acquaintance, sharing a common quest for peace. After the bombing of Hiroshima and Nagasaki, Fujii renewed his efforts, traveling the world and establishing a number of peace pagodas in major cities. These pagodas form the center of small Nipponzan Myohoji communities and are the focus of interfaith pilgrimages, in which various world faiths affirm their common concern for peace.

NIRANKARI. A 19th-century Sikh renewal movement, founded by Dayal Das (1783-1855). The Nirankari seek to return to the Sikh faith as they believe it to have been taught by its founder Guru Nanak (1469-1539), in particular his teaching of *nam simaran*—remembrance or repetition of the name of God. Following the partitioning of India in 1947, the movement sought to rescue Sikhism (q.v.) from militarism, re-establishing devotion. The Nirankari disallow the use of images (including depictions of the gurus [q.v.]), seek to be casteless, and discontinue the practice of pilgrimage to Hardwar, since Nanak is held to have proscribed pilgrimage. Dayal Das is regarded as a guru, following on from Guru Gobind Singh, as are his successors Darbara Singh, Hara Singh, and Gurbakhsh Singh. There are two types of Nirankari: the Asali ("true") Nirankari and the Nakali Nirankari. *See also* SANT NIRANKARI MANDAL.

NITYANANDA (1). Bhagwan Nityananda (d. 1961), guru (q.v.) of Swami Muktananda Paramahansa (q.v.) (1908-1982), gave the latter shaktipat initiation.

NITYANANDA (2). Swami Nityananda (b. 1963) was appointed to assume leadership of the Siddha Yoga Dham Associates Foundation (q.v.), together with his sister, Swami Chidvilasananda, after the death of Swami Muktananda Paramahansa (q.v.) in 1982. He renounced his sannyasin (q.v.) vows and his office in 1985, becoming a private meditation (q.v.) teacher in California. In 1987 he established the Shanti Mandir (Temple of Peace), which taught meditation in the United States, Europe, Australia, and India. In 1989 Nityananda re-committed himself to being a sannyasin and to Muktananda's movement. In 1995 he was inducted by the Mahamandaleshwars in Hardwar, being, at age 32, the youngest person ever to be admitted to their number.

NORSE RELIGION. Although not particularly popular in the West, there have been a few attempts to revive ancient Nordic religion, as a specific form of Paganism (q.v.), sometimes overtly in opposition to Christianity (q.v.). The Runic Society, founded by N. J. Templin in 1974, viewed the Nordic race as the "chosen" one, and the various Norse gods as manifestations of nature. Stephen A. McNallen, once a student of Norse mythology and religion, founded the Viking Brotherhood, later renamed the Asatru Free Assembly in 1972. McNallen distinguished his group from other Odinist groups on the grounds that his followers did not exclusively venerate Odin, but all Norse deities, each of which represented a particular virtue (for example, Thor as courage, Odin as wisdom, Freya the eternal feminine). Both of these groups emphasized the individual's responsibility for salvation and encouraged freedom of religious expression. Religious observances tended to be in accordance with the seasonal cycles and phases of the moon. The Runic Society was dissolved in 1980 and Asatru in 1987.

-O-

OAHSPE. *A.k.a.: The Kosmon Bible.* A channeled scripture, transcribed by means of a typewriter in 1882 by Dr. John Ballou Newbrough (1828-1891), a dentist and Spiritualist (q.v.) medium. The book, which is written in the language of the King James Bible, tells of humanity's origins: how it evolved from a long-lost utopia of Pan and was guided by prophets from Zoroaster to Joshu (Jesus) and also by angels (q.v.). *Oahspe* describes life after death and the eternal progression of the soul, and gives advice on how to live and how to progress through a series of spiritual planes. The Kosmon era, which began in the 19th century, is a new age that will bring long-lasting joy and beauty. The Kosmon rites and ceremonies that Oahspe prescribes are enacted by a small number of Kosmon churches, which are loosely connected by the Universal Association of Faithists. These include the

Universal Faithists of Kosmos, centred in Riverton, Utah, and Eloists, Inc. The Cofraternity of Faithists was established in Great Britain in 1904 with a Kosmon Church in London, now defunct. Supporters keep in touch mainly by postal contact.

OBU, OLUMBA OLUMBA (b. 1918). Founder-leader of Brotherhood of the Cross and Star (q.v.). Born in Biakpan, Cross River State, Nigeria, Obu had striking religious experiences from an early age and asked to be called "Teacher" at the age of five. Without formal education, Obu worked in the Calabar market from the age of 18 and began his full-time ministry at the age of 26, achieving recognition as the coming Holy Spirit mentioned in John 14:16. Although his family was not affiliated to any Christian denomination, Obu was familiar with Christianity (q.v.) and its Scriptures, which feature predominantly in Brotherhood. However, Brotherhood sees Scripture as confirmatory of Obu's teachings rather than vice versa.

ONEIDA COMMUNITY OF PERFECTIONISTS. Originally founded in 1841 as the Putney Society by John Humphrey Noyes (1811-1886), the Oneida Community taught that Christians were expected to be perfect and sought to establish the kingdom of God on earth. Inherent in the notion of perfection was a new sexual order, practicing "male countenance" (i.e., coitus reservatus). Noyes taught that monogamy was not an aspect of perfection and that each male member was married to all the women. This resulted in a system whereby each male was assigned an exclusive female partner on a monthly basis. Under pressure from authorities in Putney, Vermont, the community moved to Oneida, New York, in 1841. A second community was established in Wallingford, Connecticut, in 1851. For reasons that are not fully understood, the Oneida communities were dissolved in 1881.

OPEN BRETHREN. One of two varieties of the Brethren (q.v.), established in 1831 in Plymouth and sometimes known as the Christian Brethren or the Plymouth Brethren. The movement gained its original impetus from Edward Cronin in Dublin in 1829, when a number of Christians of various denominations met together, believing that the communion service should be shared in common. Cronin's ideas were taken up by A. N. Groves and J. N. Darby (1800-1882). The latter served as a curate in the Episcopal Church of Ireland until 1827. Darby influenced Francis Newman—the brother of the famous Anglican clergyman John Henry Newman— and B. W. Newton, a friend of Newman's who lived in Plymouth and who established the Plymouth Brethren there in 1831.

The organization tends to be Calvinist in its theology, believing in the inerrancy of Scripture and viewing humanity as depraved and infected by original sin, necessitating the saving grace of Jesus Christ. The Brethren typically teach "dispensationalism," the belief that there are a number of periods (seven, according to the Brethren) of God's relationships with humankind: Innocence, Conscience, Government, Promise, Law, Grace, and finally the Personal Reign of Christ. The movement is lay-led, seeking to revive the Church of New Testament times and meeting in unpretentious buildings. It is evangelical and practices "believers' baptism."

The Open Brethren contrast with the Exclusive Brethren (q.v.). Unlike the latter, the former allow—and even encourage—relationships with other Christians and with the world and are willing to share the sacrament ("the breaking of bread") with those outside the movement. The Open Brethren have engaged in overseas missionary work, reaching Europe, Australasia, Iran, India, Africa, and America. They have also implemented new forms of social work, one of the best known of which is Dr. Barnardo's children's homes. World membership is estimated at 1,500,000.

OPUS DEI. A conservative renewal movement within the Roman Catholic Church, founded in 1928 by Josemaria Escrivá de Balaguer y Albas (1902-1975), who was beatified in 1992. Opus Dei is opposed to "modernism" within the Church and aims at the personal sanctification of members and promoting the Christian life of the Roman Catholic within the world. Members are assigned a spiritual director and undertake the daily performance of private prayer, devotion, study, and attendance at Mass. The organization, unusually, is set outside the Church's diocesan structure, with its own prelate, a role which has been occupied since 1982 by Monsignor Javier Echevarria (b. 1932). There are four categories of member. *Numeraries* are priests and celibate lay people who engage in sexually segregated communal living: the laity engage in paid employment, donating their salaries to the movement. *Associate members* adopt the same lifestyle as numeraries, but do not live in the communities. *Supernumeraries* are not necessarily celibate: they may have families, but otherwise support Opus Dei's objectives. *Cooperators* are "friends" who support the ideals of the movement, but do not necessarily commit themselves completely to its lifestyle.

The movement has attracted criticism on account of its ascetic practice: some members wear a "cilis" (a penitential spiked chain, worn around the wrist or thigh) for prescribed periods; others sprinkle holy water on the beds before retiring, as a reminder of their commitment to celibacy. Opus Dei, however, also undertakes social work among the poor, and many members work in "corporate apostolic undertakings"— business enterprises concerned mainly with education and youth work. In 1981 in England, Cardinal Hume issued guidelines regarding membership of Opus Dei, and an opposing organization—Our Lady and St. Joseph in Search of the Lost Child—published a critical *Parents' Guide to Opus Dei.* The movement has attracted around 80,000 members worldwide, including 1,800 priests and candidates for the priesthood and 8,000 numeraries.

ORAGE, A. R. (1873-1934). Orage joined the Theosophical Society in 1896, becoming one of its lecturers. He was acting secretary of the Society for Psychical Research for a time. Orage in 1909 established the journal *New Age*, which published literary reviews by well-known British writers, including George Bernard Shaw, H. G. Wells, Matthew Arnold, and G. K. Chesterton. In 1919 *New Age* published P. D. Ouspensky's (q.v.) *Letters from Russia*, which told of his experiences during the Russian Revolution. Orage subsequently met Ouspensky, and also G. I. Gurdjieff (q.v.), and went to France in 1922 to join Gurdjieff's Institute for the Harmonious Development of Man. The following year he was sent to New York as "Gurdjieff's representative," to pave the way for Gurdjieff's arrival there. Orage lost faith in Gurdjieff around 1930, claiming that he had nothing more to learn from him, and was subsequently disowned by his former teacher. He returned to England, leaving a group of followers in some disarray. The Gurdjieff Foundation of New York, and other Gurdjieff centers, reassembled the supporters of Gurdjieff, Ouspensky, and Orage in the mid-1950s.

ORDER, THE. A white supremacist group, with headquarters at Hayden Lake, Idaho, consisting in part of Christian Identity (q.v.) supporters. Its origins stem from the National Alliance and from former members of the Church of Jesus Christ Christian, Aryan Nations (q.v.). Following a massive hunt, leader Robert Jay Matthews was killed in a gun battle with the police. Other members have been convicted of murder and racketeering.

ORDO TEMPLI ORIENTIS (OTO). Founded in 1895 by Karl Kellner (d. 1905), OTO is an occultist magical group, influenced by Templarism (q.v.). It was introduced to the United States in 1909 by Charles Stanford Jones. The organization gained the support of Aleister Crowley (q.v.), who became leader of the British branch in 1912. Integral to the movement is the practice of sex or "thelemic" magic (q.v.), derived from the teachings of P. B. Randolph (1825-1875), although Crowley introduced his own innovations: in particular, he advocated that sex magic need not be confined to married couples. Linked to OTO is the Ecclesia Gnostica Catholica (the Gnostic Catholic Church), into which Crowley was ordained as a bishop. OTO lodges typically celebrate a Gnostic Mass.

Crowley was succeeded by Karl Johannes Germer, whose death in 1961 caused disruption within the movement, but in 1969 OTO experienced a revival under the leadership of Grady Louis McMurtry (d. 1985), who claimed that Crowley had established a continuing lineage of "caliphs," of which he was one. The current OTO leader is anonymous, and the movement has lodges in the United States, Canada, and Europe. Around 1945, L. Ron Hubbard (q.v.) had some contact with OTO, although the details are unclear: he was almost certainly not initiated, and there is no obvious influence of OTO on Scientology (q.v.). There were 3,000 OTO members in 1998. *See also* ILLUMINATI; STEINER, RUDOLF.

ORIGINAL KLEPTONIAN NEO-AMERICAN CHURCH. Founded by Art Kleps in 1964 and incorporated in 1967, the Neo-American Church championed the use of psychedelic drugs to induce religious experience. Its original directors ("Board of Toads") included Kleps, Timothy Leary (q.v.), William A. Hitchcock, Joseph Gross, and William Haines (Sri Sankara). Its twofold purpose was to campaign for the right to use drugs as an entailment of the right to freedom of religion; and to use psychedelic drugs as its sacraments. The Church taught that there was no objective reality and that life was a dream: it pointed to philosophers such as Heraclitus, Nagarjuna, Shankara, and David Hume, among others, as thinkers who championed subjectivity. Following opposition from legal authorities, the Neo-American Church was disbanded in 1968, but it was reconstituted in 1973. Kleps remains the leader, although interest in psychedelic religion has substantially declined. *See also* CASTANEDA, CARLOS.

OSHO. The name by which Bhagwan Shree Rajneesh (q.v.) preferred to be known after 1988, and the name of the movement after that date. According to Osho, this name was suggested by William James's term *oceanic*, connoting the drop dissolving in the ocean and signifying the Upanishadic teaching of the identity between *atman* (the self) and *brahman* (the eternal). Osho's teachings, however, are not Upanishadic, and

Osho firmly denied the existence of any god outside oneself. Laying more emphasis on finding one's individual way to enlightenment, Osho has much more affinity with Zen Buddhism (qq.v.), and its nontraditional character, combined with its original uptake by a largely youth culture and somewhat anarchic nature, plausibly make it a form of Beat Zen—with the difference that it is practiced within a clearly defined organization.

Osho was highly critical of religious institutions, warning of the dangers of spiritual leaders such as the Pope controlling the lives of millions of followers en masse. This militated against the spontaneous development of the individual, who possessed the buddha-nature within and who should be encouraged to develop it in his or her own way. Osho taught that attaining *satori* (enlightenment) was in no way incompatible with satisfying physical desires. He taught liberal attitudes to sex, although the AIDS epidemic which began around 1982 caused him to modify these. Material prosperity is encouraged, and Osho has been described as the "rich man's guru." His writings frequently speak of "Zorba the Buddha," indicating that enlightenment and material prosperity can go together.

Prominent among Osho's practices is "dynamic meditation." This consists of five stages, lasting 10 minutes each. The practice begins with "chaotic breathing," in which sannyasins (q.v.) breath in and out rapidly through the nose. This is followed by a "cathartic" stage, in which participants can scream, shout, jump, or do whatever releases their energies. At the next, "energetic," stage, sannyasins chant the Sufi mantra (q.v.) "Hoo." At the leader's signal, all become totally silent, falling to the ground and remaining motionless. In the final "celebration" stage, sannyasins express their thanks and dance to a background of relaxing music.

After Osho's death in 1990, the movement has survived and continued to introduce innovations. New Age (q.v.) elements have entered the movement, evidenced by the development of the Osho Zen Tarot in 1993 and the Osho Zen Runes in 1995.

OUSPENSKY, PYOTR DEMAINOVITCH (1878-1947). Esotericist, mathematician, and writer, P. D. Ouspensky was one of the principal exponents of G. I. Gurdjieff's (q.v.) teachings. He met Gurdjieff in Moscow during the years of the World War I, when Gurdjieff had staged his *Struggle of the Magicians*—described as a "Hindoo ballet," one of Gurdjieff's celebrated sacred dances. Ouspensky subjected Gurdjieff's teachings, which tended to be intuitive and from the emotions rather than the intellect, to more systematic treatment, and his writings are generally inseparable from Gurdjieff's. Their joint thought is often referred to as "G-O" (Gurdjieff-Ouspensky), since it is not possible to disentangle their distinctive inputs. G-O is variously known as "the System," "the Fourth Way," "the Gurdjieff Work," or simply "the Work." It is possible that Ouspensky, being a mathematician, contributed and developed the numerical-numerological components to Gurdjieff's teaching, which incorporates a "Law of Seven" relating to music and a "Law of Three" relating variously to the universe, to the human body, and to food. This Law of Three entails the notion that individuals are subject to three constituent elements: the physical, the emotional, and the intellectual—an idea that forms the basis of biorhythms. Ouspensky's interests encompassed the Kabbalah (q.v.) and the Tarot, on which he wrote a series of personal reflections on A. E. Waite's major arcana. Ouspensky's other writings include *In Search of the Miraculous* (an authorized account of his early years with Gurdjieff), *Fragments of Unknown Truth, Tertium Organum* (1920), *A New Model of the Universe,* and *The Fourth Way. See also* BENNETT, JOHN G.; ORAGE, A. R.

-P-

PAGANISM. The origins of Paganism are uncertain. The word *pagan* is probably to be understood as "country dweller" (Latin *paganus*), thus implying that Pagans were originally those who did not subscribe to Roman civic religions. With the advent of Christianity, *pagan*, by extension, came to mean "non-Christian." Being practiced by the country people, Paganism had the further dimension of relating to agrarian interests, such as fertility and the cycle of seasons.

Scholars often describe the present-day forms of Paganism as "neo-Paganism," since it is not possible to establish a continuity between modern and ancient practices. Neo-Paganism's origins lie in the revival of the occult, which gathered momentum from the 1950s onward. Present-day Paganism was heralded by Tim Zell (q.v.), who established the Church of All Worlds (q.v.) in 1961 and explicitly used the term *pagan* in 1967 to describe its character. In the 1960s and 1970s Isaac Bonewits was instrumental in the further development of Paganism, arousing interest in ritual and magic (q.v.).

It is difficult to disentangle Paganism from witchcraft or wicca (q.v.) and from the New Age Movement (q.v.), whose supporters, magazines, and shops have done much to promote Paganism. "Paganism" can be regarded as an umbrella term, spanning wicca, Druidism (q.v.), and ceremonial magic. Some Pagans are uncomfortable with the term "witchcraft" on account of its possible negative connotations, while others deny being "New Age" since their interests do not include the various forms of New Age psychotechnology.

Pagans frequently claim to be characterized by three important principles: love and kinship with nature, which includes the observance of the solstices and equinoxes associated with the agricultural year; the Pagan ethic "Do what thou wilt, but harm none"; and a polarity of deity, encompassing male and female ("goddess") attributes. Paganism has thus helped to develop the interests of some feminists, and Zsuzsanna Budapest and Starhawk (qq.v.) have attracted a significant following. *See also* FELLOWSHIP OF ISIS; FORTUNE, DION.

PENTECOSTALISM. A Christian revivalist movement which originated in the early 20th century, laying emphasis on receiving the gifts of the Holy Spirit and particularly on the experience of the early disciples on the Day of Pentecost, as described in Acts 2. Its origins can be traced to Charles Parham (1873-1929), who equated "baptism in the Spirit" (Acts 1:5) with the phenomenon of "speaking in tongues" (q.v.) or glossolaliation. This practice first gained public attention in 1906 at a revivalist meeting on Azusa Street in Los Angeles, where attendees were "baptized in the Holy Spirit." In less than a decade the movement began to become institutionalized, with specific Pentecostalist churches and denominations arising, the most significant of which are probably the Elim Foursquare Gospel Alliance in Ireland (1915), the Apostolic Church in Wales (1920), and the Assemblies of God (q.v.) in Great Britain and Ireland (1924). Black Pentecostalist Churches grew up in the United States and in Britain, sometimes as a result of the black population failing to secure acceptance within more traditional white-dominated churches.

Pentecostalist churches are characterized by informality in worship, rather than a fixed liturgy. Experience and spontaneity are judged to be more important than academic training, and hence leaders tend to be elected from each congregation rather than appointed from a trained ministry. Of the "gifts of the Spirit," particular emphasis is given to healing and prophecy.

Pentecostalism influenced mainstream churches and other NRMs, particularly with the Charismatic Movement (q.v.) of the 1960s and the Toronto Blessing (q.v.) of 1994. The Jesus Fellowship Church and the International Churches of Christ (qq.v.) have undoubtedly been considerably influenced by the Pentecostalist movement. The notion that the revival of the Spirit's power is associated with the last days finds support in the Latter-Rain (q.v.) ministries, among others. *See also* ALAMO CHRISTIAN MINISTRIES; BRANHAM, WILLIAM MARRION; FAITH TABERNACLE (1); "JESUS ONLY" PENTECOSTALISM; NEW WORLD ORDER; SNAKE HANDLING; VINEYARD MINISTRIES INTERNATIONAL; WAY INTERNATIONAL; WORD-FAITH MOVEMENT.

PEOPLES TEMPLE. Founded by Jim Jones (q.v.) (1931-1978), the Peoples Temple gained notoriety when 914 of its members, including its founder-leader, committed mass suicide in 1978. The Peoples Temple began as a religious organization in California with interests in racial integration. The name "Temple" derived from the Christian notion that one's body is a temple of the Holy Spirit (1 Corinthians 6:19). Originally founded under the name Community Unity in 1954 and later called Wings of Deliverance in 1955, the name was changed to Peoples Temple in the same year. In 1959 the Peoples Temple became affiliated to the Disciples of Christ (a mainstream Christian denomination), into which Jim Jones was ordained as a full minister in 1964.

The thousand-strong community in Guyana was set up as an attempt to establish an ideal society, free from the threat of (as Jones believed) an imminent nuclear holocaust. The community was predominantly black, although led by Jones and some 70 white members from the California church. Jones continued to preach a social gospel in Guyana and "suicide for socialism" is said to have been a recurring theme. On account of opposition from various sources, in particular from an organization known as Concerned Relatives, Jones prepared his followers for possible conflict.

The occasion for the mass suicide was the arrival of Congressman Leo Ryan, who had been commissioned to visit Jonestown to investigate alleged malpractices. After a day in the compound, 11 members accompanied him to the airstrip, wishing to return to America. One of Jones's followers pursued Ryan, shooting him, together with three reporters and one defector. Jones then ordered the community to commit suicide, with a total death toll of 919. Some 85 members managed to survive, either by hiding in the jungle or by being away from the compound on business at the time. *See also* BRANCH DAVIDIANS; HEAVEN'S GATE; MOVEMENT FOR THE RESTORATION OF THE TEN COMMANDMENTS OF GOD; SOLAR TEMPLE.

PEYOTE CULTS. Originally part of Native American religion (q.v.), these groups use peyote in worship, regarding it as "sacred medicine." Peyote contains mescaline, and its effects are comparable to those of psilocybin and the hallucinogen LSD. While Westerners have typically regarded their effects as hallucinogenic, practitioners have insisted that they yield access to a deeper level of spirituality than is afforded by unaltered states of consciousness. Western interest in the practice was aroused by the writings of Carlos Castaneda (q.v.) in the 1960s. *See also* NATIVE AMERICAN CHURCH.

POWER ANIMAL. Mainly a feature of shamanism (q.v.), the power animal bestows magical power on the shaman, taking him or her to the realms above or below the earth. It is the shaman's alter ego, realized in an altered state of consciousness: the shaman typically induces a state of ecstasy, often by "dancing" the animal. The power animal affords help, healing, paranormal knowledge, and special shamanic powers. In primal cultures a tribe frequently uses a power animal as a totem guardian, who represents collective power and protects the entire clan. In Siberia the totem is regarded as a tutelary spirit, and in Aboriginal culture it is called "spirit of the head."

The power animal is to be distinguished from the "familiar" (such as the witch's cat), which serves as a psychic force, effectively "running errands" for the sorcerer. An "animal guide" is a wider category of spirit, who offers help in life, but need not be associated with shamanic practice.

PRABHUPADA, A. C. BHAKTIVEDANTA SWAMI (1896-1977). Founder-leader of the International Society for Krishna Consciousness (ISKCON) (q.v.). Born Abhay Charan De in Calcutta, he grew up in the Vaishnavite tradition, initially pursuing a career in business. He met his initiating guru (q.v.), Bhaktisiddhanta (1873-1936), in 1922 and received *diksha* 10 years later. Abhay began his mission of literature distribution, publishing *Back to Godhead,* which continues to be one of ISKCON's principal journals. After the World War II, he began to experience business and marital problems and took this as a sign that he should pursue the spiritual life. He moved to Vrindaban in 1956, becoming part of the Gaudiya Math (q.v.) mission, which Bhaktisiddhanta had established. There is some uncertainty about how Abhay Charan De received his sannyasin (q.v.) initiation. ISKCON devotees insist that Bhaktisiddhanta was his initiating guru, but since his ordination took place long after the latter's death, it is generally held that the initiation was a "mystical" one, in which Bhaktisiddhanta appeared to him in a dream. His spiritual name became Abhay Caranaravinda Bhaktivedanta Swami, but he is more familiar to devotees as Srila Prabhupada. This name literally means "lotus feet" and may refer either to numerous disciples sitting at Prabhupada's feet, or else to Prabhupada himself sitting at the "lotus feet" of Krishna.

Prabhupada's greatest impact was bringing Krishna Consciousness to the West. He traveled by steamship in 1965, at the age of 70, and introduced his teachings to the hippie culture, which was then beginning to decline. Prabhupada wrote extensively, translating the Srimad Bhagavatam in its entirety into English, with his own commentary, and also the Bhagavad Gita in his distinctive version *Bhagavad Gita As It Is*. He also authored many other writings of his own, principally on themes related to Krishna.

Prabhupada made himself particularly controversial in Hindu (q.v.) circles by giving sannyasin initiation to young white Westerners: normally such initiation is reserved for elderly Hindus who have advanced well beyond the *grishastha* (householder) stage of life.

PRINERM. An abbreviation for "new religious movement in a primal society," designating religions that have arisen mainly within nonliterate cultures through interaction between primal religion and the missionary activity of traditional major religions, most notably Christianity (q.v.). The term is employed by Harold W. Turner and several other scholars.

PROCESS CHURCH OF THE FINAL JUDGMENT. *A.k.a.:* *The Process.* Founded as Compulsions Analysis in 1963 by Robert DeGrimstone Moore (b. 1935) and his wife Mary Ann (b. 1931), this group displayed affinities to Satanism (q.v.), although Anton LaVey (q.v.) refused to accept it as a Satanist organization. The Process Church taught the existence of four gods—Jehovah, Lucifer, Christ, and Satan—who would be reconciled in a final postapocalyptic judgment. Worship of Satan was justified on the grounds that Christ taught love of one's enemies and Christ's archenemy is Satan. For several months in 1966 the group lived as a 30-member commune in Xtul, Yucatan, Mexico. Organizationally the church was headed by a Council of Masters, "messengers" (i.e., ministers), and "disciples," all of whom constituted the "Inside Processeans," who dressed in black and wore a cross intertwined with a serpent. Other members were known as "Outside Processeans." In 1974 DeGrimstone Moore was expelled by other leaders, who accused him of placing too much emphasis on Satan and who wished to emphasize more-conventional Christian themes. The movement was renamed the Foundation Church of the Millennium. DeGrimstone Moore attempted to revive the Process, which maintained a small short-lived following. *See also* FOUNDATION FAITH OF GOD.

PROMISE KEEPERS (PK). A Christian men's movement, founded by Bill McCartney in 1990 and based on American Protestantism. PK believes that the churches have become "feminized" and seeks to restore traditional male leadership in homes, churches, and communities. It teaches three "nonnegotiables" of manhood—integrity, commitment, and action—and supporters undertake to keep seven promises: obedience to God; maintaining relationships with a few men for spiritual support; commitment to "spiritual, moral, ethical, and sexual purity"; building strong marriages based on love and "biblical values"; actively supporting one's pastor; demonstrating "biblical unity" by transcending barriers of race and denomination; and obedience to Christ's "Great Commission" (Matthew 28:18-20) to win the world for Christ. Its principal publications include Leighton Ford's *What Makes a Man?* Robert Hicks's *The Masculine Journey,* and the PK manual *Brothers! Calling Men into Vital Relationships* by Geoff Gorsuch and Dan Schaffer. PK's regular magazine is *New Man.* The organization has 437 staff members; there were 234,000 attendees at U.S. rallies in 1993 and 1994.

PROSPERITY THEOLOGY. The name sometimes given by academics to the theology of the Word-Faith movement (q.v.), in which it is alleged that followers can gain material and financial prosperity through prayer and naming one's desired boon. Many of its supporters claim that God is rich, owning the entirety of creation (Psalm 24:1), and that Jesus, contrary to popular conception, was not poor but enjoyed material prosperity. Evidence sometimes adduced for such claims is various: Jesus is described as a king; the Magi brought him gold, which must have made him materially wealthy; his clothes were of sufficient quality for the soldiers at the cross to consider it worthwhile to draw lots for them. E. W. Kenyon (1867-1948) and William Branham (q.v.) (1909-1965) are regarded as precursors of the movement, which has found more recent support in A. A. Allen, John Avanzini, Morris Cerullo (q.v.), Kenneth Copeland, Charles Capps, Ulf Ekman, Kenneth Hagin, Marilyn Hickey, Frederick F. C. Price, and Robert Tilton. The movement is prevalent in the United States, Great Britain, and Sweden.

PURSEL, JACH (b. 1947?). Channel (q.v.) of "Lazaris," who is believed to be a spirit who has never assumed physical form and who possesses "multileveled consciousness." Pursel's first contact was in 1974, when he entered a state of meditation (q.v.) in which a white-robed individual introduced himself as Lazaris. Encouraged by his (then) wife Peny, he received further trance messages from Lazaris and was prompted to make Lazaris more publicly available. Pursel channels Lazaris in seminars, which consist of lectures, guided meditations, and "blendings," in which Lazaris's energy comingles with that of the participants.

Lazaris explains that every living being can choose whether to exist in physical or nonphysical form, and that he has chosen the latter. He has a multifaceted existence and characteristically refers to himself as "we." Although typically referred to in the masculine gender, such beings have transcended gender. Lazaris does not "possess" the channel, but rather connects his energy to it; he is a friend, not a master or guru (q.v.), and "empowers" inquirers to solve their own problems and create their own reality. One learns by joy and love, not fear and pain, and it is possible for all to connect to the God or Goddess or "All That Is."

Lazaris books include *The Sacred Journey: You and Your Higher Self* (1987) and *Lazaris Interviews Books I and II* (1988). Friends of Lazaris is a supporters' organization, which includes Shirley MacLaine and Marilyn Ferguson.

-R-

RADHASOAMI. A movement originating in Agra, India, in the Sant tradition, founded by Param Sant Soami Ji Maharaj (1818-1878). Following a dispute about leadership after the death of the third leader, two groups emerged in Agra. Baba Jaimal Singh (known as Baba Ji, 1838-1903), a disciple of Soami Ji, brought the movement to the Punjab. This group, which settled in Beas, near Amritsar, became the largest of the Radhasoami groups, spreading throughout India and also to the United States and Canada, where it has attracted some Western followers. Julian Johnson, who was initiated in 1931, wrote *The Path of the Masters,* which sets out Radhasoami teachings for a Western readership.

The movement emphasizes *bhakti* (devotion), drawing on the teachings of Kabir, Nanak, Tulsi Singh, and Ravi Das. Central to its practice is surat shabd yoga, to which followers are encouraged to devote two and a half hours each morning. It consists of three parts: *simram,* the repetition of God's names; *dhyan*, contemplating the living master *(sant sat-guru)*; and *shabd*, word, or sound. The concept of sound is particularly important, since it is held that the world was created through the *shabd* of the Supreme Being (Radha Soami Dayal). The shabd of creation became imprisoned in the lower realms of matter, from which escape is only possible through the appearance on earth of the sant satgurus. The divine word is able to guide the soul back to its eternal abode. Radhasoami teachings are offered to all castes. External manifestations of devotion—such as pilgrimage, practicing austerity, and celibacy—are discouraged. Followers are vegetarian, avoid alcohol, and are committed to a life of moral integrity. *See also* ECKANKAR; RUHANI SAT-SANG.

RAËL. The assumed name of the French sports journalist Claude Vorilhon (b. 1946), the founder-leader of the Raëlian Church (q.v.), who is believed to have received communications from extraterrestrials known as the Elohim in 1973. Raël claims to have subsequently been taken to their planet some two years later and is the sole inhabitant of earth to have received their teachings and disseminated them to humanity. Raël's birth is believed to be the result of sexual union between Yahweh (the Elohim's leader) and Vorilhon's mother, making his birth comparable to that of Jesus. Raël is described as the "mashiach" (messiah), who has been entrusted with the task of arranging for an embassy to be built to receive the Elohim when they shortly return to earth. This embassy is ideally to be built in Israel, on land given to them by the government. However, if the Jews do not recognize Raël as the messiah and fail to cooperate with his mission, the Raëlians will seek to build their embassy in some neighboring country. *See also* UFO-RELIGIONS.

RAËLIAN CHURCH. Originally known as Madech, and subsequently the Raëlian movement, the Raëlian Church is based on messages delivered to their founder-leader Raël (q.v.) (Claude Vorilhon), who is said to have been visited in 1973 by extraterrestrials, known as the Elohim—also called the "creators"—who subsequently took him to their planet in 1975.

The teachings of Raël are enshrined in his key book *My Encounters with Extraterrestrials: They Took Me to Their Planet.* The book purports to set out the teachings given to Raël by the Elohim, along with an account of his visit to their planet. The first half of the book contains quite detailed biblical exegesis, telling how the Elohim arrived on earth several millennia previously and created life artificially on earth, and how one group of creators, the Nephilim, had sexual relationships with human beings, whose issue became the Jewish people. Jesus of Nazareth is held to have been born as a result of a sexual union between Mary and one of the Elohim.

The Elohim teach the virtues of scientific and technological advance, together with the virtues of peace, freedom, and fraternity. On their return the Elohim will establish a single world government with a universal world language, ruled by a "geniocracy" (political control by the intellectually most able). In addition to these earthly benefits, the Elohim offer the possibility of immortality to those who have earned it. Their advanced expertise in genetic engineering will enable them to construct replicas of the departed, which they will undertake if one's intelligence and deeds merit it.

Having an entirely physicalist cosmology, the movement is decidedly world-affirming, and one prominent practice is "sensual meditation," in which followers are encouraged to develop awareness of their contact with the physical world. *See also* UFO-RELIGIONS.

RAJA YOGA. One of the four types of yoga taught within Vedanta, the other three being *jnana yoga, bhakti yoga* and *karma yoga.* "Raja" literally means "royal," indicating that it is a superior form of yoga, being the yoga of the mind, in contrast with *hatha yoga,* which does no more than develop the body and control the breath. Raja yoga aims to concentrate the mind, enabling mental and psychic control. In its earlier days in the West, the Brahma Kumaris (q.v.) advertised their form of meditation (q.v.) as "Raja Yoga." It has also been taught by the Ramakrishna Vedanta Center and the Center for Human Communication. Satchakrananda, who equated raja yoga with *kriya yoga*, founded the Raja Yoga Math at the foot of Mount Baker in Washington—a somewhat eclectic organization combining Hindu and Christian teachings and practices. Vivekananda's (q.v.) rather idiosyncratic student Abhayananda (Marie Louise) incorporated some raja yoga into her teachings. *See also* ANANDA MARGA.

RAJNEESH, BHAGWAN SHREE. Born Rajneesh Chandra Mohan (1931-1990) and now known as Osho (q.v.) by his followers, he was variously dubbed the "sex guru" and the "rich man's guru" because of his controversial views on sex and wealth. Rajneesh was born in a Jain family, but his teachings were decidedly eclectic, drawing principally on Zen Buddhism (qq.v.), but also on Taoism, Christianity (q.v.), Hinduism (q.v.), Sufism (q.v.), and elements of Western philosophy. He claimed to have received a "first enlightenment" *(satori)* when he was 14 years old, and subsequently, in 1953, to have experienced a full enlightenment by sitting meditatively under a tree like Gautama, the historical Buddha.

After his school education, Rajneesh obtained a B.A. in philosophy in 1955, followed by a master's degree from Sangar University two years later. He became assistant professor of philosophy at the University of Jabalpur in 1960. Outside his university duties, Rajneesh led a "meditation camp" in 1964; he resigned his academic post in 1966, assuming the title of "Acharya," in order to lead his new spiritual movement. In 1971 he expressed a preference to be known as "Bhagwan"; although this literally means "the supreme Lord," Rajneesh consistently taught God's nonexistence, and was referring to the notion of the God or buddha-nature within oneself.

Rajneesh founded the "Neo-Sannyasin International Movement" (NSIM) in 1970, into which the first sannyasins (q.v.) were initiated, and from 1974 onward over 400 of his followers lived communally at Kailash, near Bombay, with a further 6,000 at his six-acre Shree Rajneesh Ashram at Poona. They adopted four "agreements," for which Rajneeshees were known in the 1970s: orange or red clothes; mala beads; a new spiritual name; and the practice of dynamic meditation (q.v.). The first of these "agreements" earned the sannyasins the nickname "the orange people," until this requirement was dropped in the early 1980s.

A sufferer from asthma among other ailments, he decided in 1981 to seek specialist medical treatment in the United States. Once there, Rajneesh and his sannyasins purchased 126 square miles of land in Oregon, creating Rajneeshpuram, which they described as "America's first enlightened city." It was here that Rajneesh kept his 93 Rolls-Royces to emphasize his teaching that enlightenment was perfectly compatible with material prosperity.

The Rajneeshpuram project was particularly controversial, leading to a police raid in 1985, followed by the arrest of Rajneesh and other leaders. Rajneesh's health deteriorated rapidly after 1985, and many of his followers allege that he was the victim of thallium poisoning while in prison. *See also* KUNDALINI YOGA.

RAMAKRISHNA (1836-1886). A leader of Hindu spiritual revival and teacher of Vedanta. Born Gadadhar Chattopadhyaha in Karmarpukar, Bengal, he became a Kali priest at age 19 at Dakshineshwar, near Calcutta. Ramakrishna obtained experiences of samadhi and received numerous religious visions, which included Muhammad and Jesus as well as Rama and Krishna. Ramakrishna taught that God had many forms (Christ, the Buddha, the Divine Mother Kali, divine energy) and that all spiritual paths led to the same goal. Vedanta teachings are based on the ancient Hindu scriptures, principally the Vedas and the Upanishads, and it is the principles enshrined therein that have precedence over the authority of the guru (q.v.) who teaches them. According to Vedanta, *brahman* is the absolute reality, beyond name and form; the physical universe is *maya* (illusion), distorted by being perceived through the categories of space, time, and causality. As the Upanishads teach, brahman is identical with *atman* (the soul or self), and one's aim is to recognize this identity. According to Ramakrishna's teachings, later codified by his principal disciple Vivekananda (q.v.), this is achieved through a system of spiritual practices, incorporating karma, jnana, raja and bhakti yoga (q.v.).

After Ramakrishna's death, a number of his disciples, led by Vivekananda, founded the Ramakrishna Mission in India in 1897. Western branches were formed in the 20th century: the Ramakrishna-Vedanta Society of Boston (1926), the Ramakrishna Vedanta Center in New York (1933), and the Ramakrishna Vedanta Centre in London (1948). There are also branches of the Ramakrishna Order in France, Switzerland, and Argentina. Much of the movement's work involves literature distribution: teaching the essential oneness of all religions, as it does, it is nonproselytizing. *The Gospel of Sri Ramakrishna,* by Mahendranath Gupta, is a record of conversations with Ramakrishna during the last four years of his life.

In 1998 there were 125 centers worldwide run by the Ramakrishna Order, and over 1,000 centers which incorporated the name "Ramakrishna" or "Vivekananda." *See also* AVATARA ADI DA; NARAYANANANDA; RAJA YOGA; SATCHIDANANDA; VEDANTA SOCIETY.

RAMANA. *A.k.a.: Sri Ramana Maharishi* (1878-1950). Ramana was born Venkataraman Ayyar in Madurai in southeastern India. He had an intense religious experience at the age of 17 and left home for the Arunchala Temple, Tiruvannamalai. From around 1900 he attracted followers from many parts of the world, and he established an ashram at Arunchala Hill in 1935.

Ramana was in the *advaita vedanta* (nondualist) Indian philosophical tradition. There is no ultimate difference between the individual soul and the Eternal: the self is *sat cit ananda* (being, consciousness, and bliss), and knowledge of reality is to be gained by introspection, in which the thought of "I" returns the individual to its source, achieving the goal of self-realization. Ramana's teaching develops the Upanishadic teaching of *tat tvam asi* ("you are that"), referring to the identity of *atman* (the soul) and *brahman* (the Eternal), and is in the tradition of the monist philosopher Shankara (eighth century C.E.).

The Sri Ramanashram in southern India and the Sri Ramana Maharishi Centre for Learning in Bangalore continue to propound Ramana's teachings. In the United States the Society of Abidance in Truth is led by Master Nome, a self-realized disciple of Ramana; based in Santa Cruz, California, it comprises a temple and an ashram, offering weekly satsangs, retreats, and the promotion of Indian culture and arts. *See also* BRUNTON, PAUL.

RAM DASS, BABA. *A.k.a.: Richard Alpert.* An erstwhile collaborator with Timothy Leary (q.v.), both were dismissed from their posts at Harvard University for their experiments with the hallucinogen LSD in 1963. Alpert departed for India in 1967, where he met Bhagwan Dass—a Westerner—who introduced him to his teacher Neem Karoli Baba (d. 1973). Neem Karoli Baba did not teach any distinctive philosophical ideas, but emphasized the principles of love and service *(sewa)*. He gave Alpert the spiritual name of Ram Dass (meaning "servant of God"), instructing him to return to the West.

In 1974 Alpert met Joya Santanya, who instructed him in tantric sex and informed him that he would become an international teacher. Joya emphasized the idea that one's teachings are "right here," meaning that one's spiritual path emanates from the conditions in which one currently finds oneself. Ram Dass's teachings, accordingly, are eclectic, encompassing the message of Jesus, vipassana (q.v.), the theory of the chakras (q.v.), Sufism (q.v.), and Buddhism (q.v.) in its Tibetan and Zen (q.v.) forms. He acknowledged the validity of different spiritual paths: yoga (q.v.), world renunciation, the use of mantras (q.v.), sex, and psychedelic experiences. One's answers to the question of life's meaning and purpose lie within oneself, and thus Ram Dass does not claim to be a guru (q.v.), or to be enlightened. Ram Dass's own path is karma yoga, manifested in service to others. Accordingly, Ram Dass established the Hanuman Foundation (incorporated in 1974): the deity Hanuman embodies the virtue of service, and the foundation offers programs for the dying and the bereaved, as well as a Prison-Ashram Project. Such projects rest on the premise that one should start with the conditions in which one finds oneself. The Neem Koroli Baba Hanuman Temple was built in Taos, New Mexico.

Ram Dass was associated with the Lama Foundation (established in 1967), whose first publication was Ram Dass's *Be Here Now* (1971). His other writings include *The Only Dance There Is* (1976), *Grist to the Mill* (1977)—both of which are reconstructions of Neem Kardi Baba's talks—and *Miracle of Love* (1979). Ram Dass has also given support to the Seva Foundation, an independent organization founded by Larry Brillant, which aims to end blindness.

RASTAFARIANISM. A politico-religious movement that developed from Black Power groups in Jamaica during the first half of the 20th century. Originating from the former slave population, it was inspired by political activists such as Marcus Moziah Garvey (q.v.) (1887-1940), who spearheaded a "Back to Africa" movement. Its focus was Ethiopia, and when Emperor Haile Selassie was crowned in 1930, this gave considerable impetus to the Rastafarian movement. Haile Selassie was typically hailed as the messiah, the "King of Kings and Lord of Lords" (Revelation 19:16).

Leonard Howell (d. 1981), one of the early black leaders, gave Garvey's ideas a more explicit religious dimension and organized a community of 500 people in the village of Pinnacle, Jamaica. Howell introduced the practice of smoking ganja (marijuana), and disseminated a "Black Man's Bible," which consisted of selections from Jewish and Christian Scriptures. While some Rastafarians reject Jewish-Christian Scripture totally, most accept the major Hebrew prophets and the apocalyptic literature, especially the Book of Revelation.

The Bible is said to relate a history of oppressed people, beginning with God's appearance in a physical form and subsequently incarnating as Moses, Elijah, and Jesus Christ. Haile Selassie is God's fourth and final "avatar" and the messianic redeemer.

The movement gained momentum in the 1950s, spreading to the United States and Great Britain and culminating in Selassie's state visit to Jamaica in 1956. However, Ethiopia's 1974 military coup, in which Selassie was overthrown, and his subsequent death in 1975, caused a substantial setback to the movement. During the 1970s the movement gained wider dissemination through its reggae music, particularly that of Bob Marley (1945-1981), which achieved wide popularity. There were estimated to be 700,000 Rastafarians worldwide in 1998.

RAVIDASI. Based on the teachings of Ravi Das (or Raidas, 15th-16th century), the modern Ravidasi movement can be attributed to Sant Hiran Das, who established the Ram Das Sabha in Punjab in 1907, the first of several such temples. As a result of emigration to Great Britain in the 1950s and 1960s, a number of Ravidasi temples were established in England.

Ravi Das, a teacher in the Sant tradition, belonged to the lowly *chamar* (leather worker) caste and taught in Benares. Many miracles are attributed to him. In common with Guru Nanak (1469-1539) and the subsequent Sikh (q.v.) tradition, Ravi Das taught that caste was irrelevant to obtaining salvation, which was gained through surrender to a God who is beyond attributes and whose grace is mediated through the guru (q.v.). The path of austerity is unnecessary for liberation, which can be won through devotion and the repetition of the divine name. Ravi Das composed many devotional songs, 40 of which are included in the Sikh Adi Granth.

The modern-day movement is followed by Punjabis, mainly from the chamar caste, and worship resembles the kirtan of the Sikh gurdwara. Ravi Das is regarded as a guru comparable to Nanak: his picture is prominently displayed in temples, and his birthday is celebrated. The movement is also called "Ad Dharm" (the primordial religion). *See also* NIRANKARI; RADHASOAMI.

REBIRTHING. More an alternative therapy than a religion, Rebirthing originated with Leonard Orr. The process is based on the notion that birth is traumatic and that therapeutic benefit derives from reenacting the experience of being born. This is done by employing *pranayama,* a yogic science of breathing, combined with a reenactment of birth, which can take the form of either "wet" or "dry" rebirthing. "Wet rebirthing" was the earlier form, in which the client entered naked into a tank of warm water, usually head down and breathing through a snorkel, assisted by a "rebirther," who eases one's passage back into the world. In "dry rebirthing" the client lies on a bed; music may accompany the process, and one employs "Grof breathing." A variation of the practice is "natal therapy," in which clients crawl under a 30-foot carpet. The aim of rebirthing is to release the hold exercised by the pain of birth, and—according to some Rebirthers—pain experienced in the embryo, where any bad experiences of the mother can be mediated through the umbilical cord and placenta, thus giving rise to phobias that arise after birth. Some Rebirthers use the process to afford memories of past lives to clients, enabling them to become aware of how their karma is acquired through previous rebirths and continues to influence one's body, mind, and emotions.

RECONSTRUCTIONISM. A progressive movement within Judaism (q.v.), established by Rabbi Mordecai M. Kaplan, a Conservative Jew (q.v.). The movement contends that Judaism continues to evolve and that it is a "religious civilization" rather than a fixed system of belief and practice. In 1922 Kaplan established the Society for the Advancement of Judaism in New York to promote Reconstructionist ideals, and in 1945 he brought out a Reconstructionist *Sabbath Prayer Book.* This prayer book was noteworthy for its omission of the notion of Jews as God's chosen people, God's revelation of the Torah to Moses on Mount Sinai, and the belief in the coming of a personal messiah. The movement's following is not large, but it is sufficient to sustain its own independent rabbinical college in Philadelphia, founded in 1968. *See also* LIBERAL JUDAISM; REFORM JUDAISM.

REFORM JUDAISM. Originating in Germany, Reform Jews seek to find an expression of Judaism (q.v.) that adapts to modern society. The movement was spearheaded by Isaac Harby, who established the Reform Society of Israelites in 1824. A number of rabbinical conferences in the 19th century advanced the movement's ideas, the most important of which was in 1855, when the Pittsburgh Declaration affirmed that only those laws that related to modern life were to be regarded as obligatory. In 1846 Rabbi Isaac M. Wise arrived in the United States from Bohemia. He published a prayer book in 1857 which contained alterations to the traditional Jewish liturgy. Wise also founded the Union of American Hebrew Congregations in 1875.

The main changes that Reform Judaism has brought include liturgical innovation, principally the use of the vernacular as well as Hebrew in worship; the ordination of women was a further significant feature. Originally much of the movement regarded the Tanakh (the Jewish Bible) as having authority and not the Talmud, and the earlier years of the movement promoted anti-Zionism. More recent times—principally since a conference in Columbus, Ohio, in 1937—have seen a tendency toward increasing conservatism: anti-Zionism has now been abandoned, and traditional Talmudic interpretations play an important role in preaching and in Jewish life.

Because of its innovations, the movement's claims to be authentically Jewish have been challenged by Orthodox Judaism, and Reform Judaism is not recognized in Israel. Reform congregations belong collectively to the World Union for Progressive Judaism and have their own training colleges: the Hebrew Union College in the United States, and Leo Baeck College in Great Britain. There are between 1.5 and 2 million Reform Jews worldwide. *See also* CONSERVATIVE JUDAISM; LIBERAL JUDAISM; RECONSTRUCTIONISM.

REINCARNATION. Belief in the recurrent return of individuals after death has been a typical belief within the Hindu (q.v.) religions. Buddhists (q.v.), who do not accept the existence of the soul, prefer to speak of "rebirth" or "rebecoming," but, in common with Hindus, typically affirm a belief in samsara (the cycle of birth and rebirth). Although officially rejected by Christianity (q.v.), having been declared heretical by the Council of Florence in 1439, the doctrine has gained momentum in recent times in Western culture, finding a foothold within the New Age Movement (q.v.). Some followers of Eastern philosophies (such as devotees of the International Society for Krishna Consciousness [q.v.]) have contended that reincarnation is to be found in Judeo-Christian Scripture, for example, in the claim that John the Baptist was the returned Elijah. The belief is not found within the Jewish Torah, although the concept of *gilgul* (rebirth) can be found in some Kabbalistic (q.v.) thinking. Islam (q.v.), too, has denied reincarnation, although it has occasionally appeared in some Ismaeli schools who have taught that Krishna reincarnated as the Buddha and was subsequently reborn as Muhammad.

Although at a popular level some Christians have been drawn to the idea of reincarnation, it has been more typically found in movements that have been on Christianity's fringes, such as Templarism (q.v.), Rosicrucianism (q.v.), and neo-Gnosticism. The belief has been held by many Theosophists (q.v.) (but not as a compulsory tenet), although Theosophists have tended to view reincarnation as a means of constant progress rather than—as in traditional Hinduism and Buddhism—a cycle in which there can also be "falling back." The Ascended Masters in the Theosophists' scheme are those who have achieved enlightenment and are free from the continual samsaric chain. Spiritualists (q.v.) have long been divided on the question of reincarnation.

Reincarnation has been an important theme in New Thought (q.v.), finding exponents in psychics such as Edgar Cayce (q.v.). Associated with the belief in karma, some psychics and New Agers believe that one's deeds in past lives can serve as the key to understanding one's present existence: hence the rise of interest in karmic counseling and past-life regression.

The final goal of rebirth is the experience of enlightenment (moksha, or nirvana), in which one is freed from the constant cycle. Some NRMs, however—such as the Soka Gakkai and Brahma Kumaris (qq.v.)—have contended that enlightenment is not a final state, but that humans will be drawn back once again into a long series of recurrent existences. *See also* BROTHERHOOD OF THE CROSS AND STAR; SOLAR LIGHT RETREAT.

REIYUKAI. A Japanese Buddhist organization in the Nichiren (q.v.) tradition. It was founded by a layperson, Kakutaro Kubo (1892-1944), who regarded the Japanese expressions of Buddhism (q.v.) in the 1920s as lifeless, and became inspired by the teachings of Mugaku Nishida (1850-1918). The first Reiyukai group was founded in 1924 and, despite some schism in the 1930s, expanded rapidly during the war years, reaching one million members in the 1950s. The movement came to Europe and the United States during the 1970s, claiming a total membership of 2.7 million by the mid-1980s, and three million by 1993. Kubo's son Dr. Tsugunari Kubo (b. 1936) now leads the organization, which is an entirely lay movement.

Reiyukai teachings and practices are based on the Lotus Sutra, attributed to the historical Buddha and made available in an abridged form, together with brief writings of its founders, as the "Blue Sutra" (so called on account of its blue pages). Members recite the Blue Sutra daily, together with the mantra *Namu myoho renge kyo,* in front of a *sokaimyo* (an inscription bearing the names of ancestors) and are committed to three practices: inward self-development; *michibiki* (literally, "encouragement"—encouraging others to accept the message of the Lotus Sutra); and ancestor remembrance. This last obligation emphasizes the interconnectedness of all living beings, which members regard as a central teaching of Buddhism. *See also* NICHIREN SHOSHU; RISSHO KOSEI KAI; SOKA GAKKAI.

RELIGIOUS SCIENCE. A New Thought (q.v.) school, based on the teachings of Ernest S. Holmes (q.v.) (1887-1960). Holmes had studied the writings of Ralph Waldo Emerson and Mary Baker Eddy (qq.v.) and was particularly influenced by New Thought writer Thomas Troward. For a brief period in 1924 he studied under Emma Curtis Hopkins. Holmes's main writing, *The Science of Mind,* forms the basis of Religious Science churches and promotes "spiritual mind treatment" for the purpose of healing. Holmes founded the Institute of Religious Science and School of Philosophy in 1927, incorporated as the Institute of Religious Science and Philosophy in 1935. The institute's graduates established "chapters," and in time some called themselves "ministers" and their centers "churches." These were linked by an Annual Conference of Religious Science Chapters and Churches until 1949 when the International Association of Religious Science Churches was formed. The renaming of the institute in 1953 as the Church of Religious Science accompanied a restructuring. When individual congregations were asked to resign from the International Association and affiliate with the Church of Religious Science, some complied, while others insisted on remaining under the aegis of the association; some churches preferred to continue unaffiliated. The International Association was later renamed Religious Science International, and in 1967 the Church of Religious Science became known as the United Church of Religious Science. In 1991 there were approximately 100 Religious Science churches worldwide.

RISSHO KOSEI KAI. A Japanese Buddhist (q.v.) organization in the Nichiren (q.v.) tradition. The name literally means "Society for Establishing Righteous and Friendly Relations."

A breakaway group from the Reiyukai (q.v.), it was founded in 1938 by Niwano Nikkyo (1906-1999) and Naganuma Myoko (1899-1957). The Rissho Kosei Kai emphasizes the Hokke Sutras (the Muryogi, Lotus, and Kaufugen Sutras), which are encapsulated in the mantra (q.v.) *(daimoku), "Namu myoho renge kyo."* In contrast with the Soka Gakkai (q.v.), who use the chant for its power, the daimoku expresses members' faith and gratitude. The movement's headquarters are at Tokyo and are visited by some 25,000 people each day, 10,000 of whom typically attend the daily service, which consists of chanting sections of the Lotus Sutra, repetition of the daimoku, and a sermon. This is followed by *hoza*—a counseling session which is carried out in smaller groups. Three festivals are celebrated annually: the Foundation Festival (5 March), the Flower Festival (8 April, commemorating the Buddha's birth), and the Grand Festival (13 October). Reported membership was five million in 1993.

ROBERTS, JANE (born Jane Butts, 1929-1984). Author, and channeler of "Seth" (q.v.), Roberts is generally regarded as the originator of present-day channeling (q.v.), revitalizing the Spiritualist (q.v.) movement. In 1963 she began to receive messages from a spirit called Seth. These were transcribed in numerous books, the first and most important of which was *How to Develop Your ESP* (1966), retitled *The Coming of Seth* (1976). Later in life, Roberts claimed to channel other spirit sources, including "Seth Two" (a group of spirits), Paul Cézanne, and William James.

ROD, THE. *A.k.a.: The Shepherd's Rod.* A Seventh-day Adventist (SDA) (q.v.) organization formerly headed by Victor T. Houteff (1885-1955). After the death of Ellen G. White (q.v.) in 1915, Houteff claimed her prophetic office within the SDA. Houteff, however, was deemed to be unfaithful to White's teachings and was disfellowshipped, together with his supporters. Houteff purchased land and property at Waco (q.v.), Texas, calling it the Mount Carmel Center. Houteff's teachings are enshrined in his best-known book *The Shep-*

herd's Rod. The title referred to the rod of Jesse, the father of King David, out of whose roots a branch will come, according to the prophet Isaiah (Isaiah 1:1). Using a typological interpretation of Scripture, Houteff maintained that many things and events mentioned in the Bible (the "types") foreshadowed subsequent occurrences (the "antitypes"), and that such anti-types could be seen in the happenings of his time. Following this line of reasoning, Houteff claimed that a latter-day King David would arise and lead Israel (meaning the Church) to the Kingdom of God. This particular branch of Adventism thus became known as the Branch Davidians (q.v.), subsequently to be led by David Koresh (q.v.).

Houteff was succeeded by his wife, Florence Houteff, who sold off the Mount Carmel site, purchasing New Mount Carmel, a 400-acre piece of land also situated in Waco. This site was subsequently sold off progressively, until only 77 acres remained, forming "the compound" which Koresh and his followers were later to occupy. In 1959 rival groups of Adventists assembled at Mount Carmel, expecting Christ's return. When this did not occur, Florence Houteff was discredited, and group fragmented.

ROSICRUCIAN FELLOWSHIP. A Rosicrucian organization founded in 1909 by Max Heindel (1865-1919). Born Carl Louis Von Grasshoff in Denmark, he moved to the United States in 1903, where he became a student of Theosophy (q.v.). When in Germany in 1907, he experienced the appearance of one of the Elder Brothers of the Rosicrucian Order, who gave him initiation. He was instructed to seek out the Temple of the Rosy Cross, near the Bavarian border, where he received material for his first book, *The Rosicrucian Cosmo-Conception.* On returning to the United States, he founded the Rosicrucian Fellowship, which aims to promote a form of esoteric Christianity (q.v.) and to carry out spiritual healing. Emphasis is given to "spiritual astrology," which is said to be effective in improving one's life toward the ideal exhibited by Jesus Christ. Professional astrologers, however, are barred from membership, as are professional mediums, hypnotists, and chiromancers. Members are vegetarian and abstain from tobacco, recreational drugs, and alcohol. In 1911 the Fellowship's headquarters moved to Mount Ecclesia, Oceanside, California, where it remains today. It claimed 8,000 members in 1995. Max Heindel was succeeded by his wife, Augusta Foss Heindel (d. 1949). *See also* ROSICRU-CIANISM.

ROSICRUCIANISM. An esoteric movement, named after Christian Rosenkreutz (trad. 1378-1484), who is said to have founded an organization called Spiritus Sanctum in 1409, dedicated to social reform, human betterment, and healing through esoteric and magical rites. The writings attributed to Rosenkreutz are more probably attributable to Lutheran pastor Johann Valentin Andreae (1586-1654), and it has even been suggested that he wrote about Rosenkreutz in jest. Andreae is possibly the author of two Rosicrucian "manifestos," dating from 1614 and 1615: *Fama Fraternitas* and *Confessio Fraternitas Rosae Crucis*. The latter work defines 37 aims, including the abolition of sickness, poverty, hunger, and old age, and is apocalyptic, expecting an imminent end to earthly affairs.

The movement has sometimes been described as a form of Gnostic Christianity (qq.v.), teaching a contrast between the divine nature-order (also called the Kingdom of Heaven) and the human nature-order, which inhabits the evil physical world. The human heart, however, contains a spark of divinity (the "Rose of the Heart") which requires transfiguration through self-mortification. The alchemical interests of the Rosicrucians symbolize the transformation of the human heart from evil to perfection, from human nature to spirit. The goal is often defined as admission to the Great White Lodge, and spiritual progress is accomplished through a number of "degrees" through successive incarnations.

Rosicrucianism experienced a revival in the second half of the 19th century. Fraternitas Rosae Crucis was the first, influenced by Eliphas Levi and founded in 1858 by Pascal Beverly Randolph (1825-1875). Other Rosicrucian organizations included the Rosicrucian Fellowship (q.v.) (1907), Societas Rosicruciana in America (1907), the Ancient and Mystical Order of the Rosy Cross (AMORC) (q.v.) (1915), and Lectorium Rosicrucianum (1928). The Rosicrucian Anthroposophical League was founded in the 1930s, and R. A. Straughn, one of its members, established the Ausar Auset Society, which gained Rosicrucianism considerable momentum in Africa. Similarities have been noted between Rosicrucianism, Freemasonry, and the Illuminati (q.v.); some Rosicrucian orders are open only to Freemasons, notably Societas Rosicruciana in Anglia (1865/6), whose members included S. L. MacGregor Mathers (1854-1918), and Societas Rosicruciana in Civitatibus Foederatis (originally Societas Rosicruciana Republicae Americae, founded 1878). Many Rosicrucians deny that Rosicrucianism is a religion. *See also* HERMETIC ORDER OF THE GOLDEN DAWN.

ROSS, RICK. An ardent campaigner against NRMs, Ross describes himself as a "private consultant, lecturer, and intervention specialist concerning destructive cults and radical groups." Ross's interest in "cults" (q.v.) began in 1982, when his 83-year old grandmother was targeted by a group while in a Jewish nursing home. Ross's anticult (q.v.) work commenced within Jewish circles, and he was appointed to national committees for the Union of American Hebrew Congregations (Reform Movement). After serving from 1983 to 1985 in the Jewish Family Service, Ross decided to become a private consultant. He is particularly noted for being advisor to the ATF and FBI during the Waco (q.v.) siege in 1993. Formerly a leader of the old Cult Awareness Network (CAN) (q.v.), he is alleged to have been involved in several deprogrammings (q.v.). *See also* ANTICULT MOVEMENT.

RUHANI SATSANG. A Sikh (q.v.)-derived NRM, founded by Kirpal Singh (1896-1974) in Delhi in 1951. In 1917 Kirpal Singh had a vision which he took to be of Guru Nanak, but, on meeting Sawan Singh of the Radhasoami (q.v.) movement in Beas, he realized that Sawan had been the object of the vision. Kirpal stayed with the Radhasoami movement for 24 years, until Sawan's death; on failing to become Sawan's successor, he moved off to found his own independent Sawan Ashram, which formally became the Ruhani Satsang in 1951. Meanwhile, T. S. Khanna, one of Kirpal's followers, took his teachings to Toronto and subsequently Virginia, forming Ruhani Satsang groups. Kirpal visited the United States in 1955 and 1963, establishing various loosely related groups connected by the umbrella name "Divine Science of the Soul." In 1972 Kirpal merged these groups into Ruhani Satsang–Divine Science of the Soul, with Khanna as its board's chair. Kirpal initiated seekers from all religious traditions, attempting to foster interreligious understanding. After Kirpal's death, further divisions occurred within the movement, leading to the formation of the Sawan Kirpal Ruhani Mission (q.v.), under the leadership of Darshan Singh, Kirpal's son, and the Ruhani Satsang Divine Science, which recognized no one as Kirpal's successor. *See also* KIRPAL RUHANI SATSANG; SANT BANI ASHRAM.

RUSSELL, CHARLES TAZE (1852-1916). Founder-leader of the Watchtower Bible and Tract Society (q.v.), later known as the Jehovah's Witnesses (q.v.). Born in Allegheny, Pennsylvania, Russell came from a Presbyterian background, but particularly disliked the doctrines of predestination and eternal punishment. He encountered several Second Adventists and found a rapport with their doctrines, including conditional immortality (the view that the self is inherently mortal, only gaining immortality as a divine gift) and Christ's spiritual—not physical—*parousia* (presence). Russell wrote a pamphlet entitled *The Object and Manner of Our Lord's Return,* which was published in 1877, and, with Nelson H. Barbour, coauthored *Three Worlds, and the Harvest of This World* in the same year.

Russell broke with Barbour in 1878, following a dispute regarding the atonement. In July 1879 he commenced the publication of his own periodical, *Zion's Watch Tower and Herald of Christ's Presence,* which quickly achieved a circulation of 6,000. Russell wrote prolifically, his best-known writing being *The Divine Plan of the Ages,* which was the first of six volumes in the series *Millennial Dawn* (subsequently called *Studies in the Scriptures).* Russell's writings claimed to demonstrate from biblical prophecy and chronology that the year 1914 marked the end of the Gentile times and the inception of Christ's invisible rule. The year 1914 witnessed the assassination of Archduke Francis Ferdinand of Austria-Hungary and the outbreak of World War I. Although, of course, this did not bring earthly affairs to an end, Russell was nonetheless able to claim that "kings have had their day" and that Christ's invisible rule had begun in heaven. Russell's book *The Finished Mystery,* which completes the *Studies in the Scriptures* series, was published posthumously in 1917. He was succeeded by Joseph Franklin Rutherford (q.v.) (1869-1941).

RUTHERFORD, JOSEPH FRANKLIN (1869-1941). Often known as "Judge Rutherford," having obtained an attorney's license in 1892, J. F. Rutherford succeeded Charles Taze Russell (q.v.) in 1916 as leader of the International Bible Students Association (IBSA), subsequently known as the Jehovah's Witnesses (q.v.). Under Rutherford's leadership a number of important developments took place. It was in his period of office that the Witnesses' door-to-door work commenced. Important, too, was a convention at Columbus, Ohio, which Rutherford chaired in 1931, at which attendees adopted the resolution giving themselves the new name Jehovah's Witnesses (taken from Isaiah 43:10). Rutherford developed the Witnesses' antiwar stance, commended in Russell's posthumous *The Finished Mystery.*

Rutherford is particularly known for his *Millions Now Living Will Never Die!* (1920), which offered an interpretation of history, past and future, setting out a number of key dates in providential history. Present-day Jehovah's Witnesses concede that Rutherford's analysis may initially have been wrong about some matters, but point out that Russell and Rutherford were not prophets, only Bible students who were fallible like other human beings.

-S-

SACRED NAME MOVEMENT. A term collectively referring to a number of Christian organizations that insist on using the supposedly authentic Hebrew names for God and Jesus, such as "Yahweh" and "Yashua." The Sacred Name congregations emerged from the Seventh Day Church of God in Arkansas, originally under the leadership of Elder Lorenzo Snow (b. 1913) and his wife Icie Lela Paris Snow (b. 1912). The largest Sacred Name organization is the Assemblies of Yahweh (2, q.v.) (originally the Assembly of Yhwh), founded in 1939 in Holt, Michigan, by C. O. Dodd. Slightly different versions of the Hebrew for "God" and "Jesus" are found in different Sacred Name groups. Thus, Dodd's Assemblies of Yahweh favors "Yahweh" and "Elohim" as the divine names, and "Yahshua" for Jesus, while the Assembly of Yhwhhoshua prefers "Yhwh" and "Yhwhhoshua." The Assemblies of the Called Out Ones of Yah, founded in 1974 by Sam Surratt (d. 1990) insist that "Yah" and "Yeshuah" are the true versions of the names.

The Sacred Name organizations tend to regard the Old Testament as the definitive Scripture, in the light of which the New Testament is to be interpreted. God is regarded as a unity rather than a trinity. Jewish festivals—Passover, Weeks, Tabernacles, and Hanukah—are observed, together with Jewish dietary laws and tithing. Organizationally, the movement emphasizes the practices of the early Church, with admission by means of baptism—normally total immersion. Some Sacred Name organizations lay emphasis on receiving the Holy Spirit.

Sacred Name organizations, in addition to those mentioned above, include the Institute of Divine Metaphysical Research (founded by Dr. Henry Clifford Kinley in 1931); the Assembly of Yahvah (founded by L. D. Snow and E. B.

Adam in 1949); the Scripture Research Association (founded by A. B. Traina, 1950); the Assemblies of Yahweh (1, q.v.), also known as the "Bethel Assembly," founded in Bethel, Pennsylvania, in 1969 by Jacob O. Meyer; and the Bible Study Association (founded in 1980 by David B. Northnagel, Sr.). *See also* BRITISH ISRAEL; CHRISTIAN IDENTITY CHURCH; MESSIANIC JEWS.

SAHAJA YOGA. The movement's founder-leader, Her Holiness Shri Mataji Nirmala Devi Srivastava, was born in 1923 in Chindwara, India, of wealthy Christian parents. She claims to have been born in a self-realized state and to have had various childhood spiritual experiences. In her youth she was an active supporter of Mahatma Gandhi, and was personally known to him. She studied medicine and married Chandrika Prasad Srivastava, a top-ranking United Nations official from 1974 to 1989. Shri Mataji began teaching Sahaja Yoga in 1970. It is explained that "saha ja" means "inborn" or "spontaneous," indicating that union with the divine is something that all are born with and can be expected to realize—not a remote goal afforded to a privileged few. Shri Mataji claims the ability to awaken the divine within her followers, through the practice of kundalini yoga (q.v.). Self-realization is said to correct imbalances within oneself and others: accordingly, adepts have the ability to heal. Followers are instructed to practice Sahaja Yoga in the early hours of the morning and again in the evening; they also attend a Sunday puja. There is a code of ethics, prescribing nonattachment, and instructing members about family life. Alcohol and recreational drugs are disallowed. Shri Mataji draws on Christian as well as Hindu ideas, claiming to be the Adi Shakti (the primal feminine form of divinity) and also the Holy Ghost, the Christ, and the fulfillment of biblical prophecies. The movement claims 20,000 members in over 60 countries and 100,000 sympathizers.

SANDERS, ALEXANDER (1926-1988). Originally a follower of Gerald Gardner (q.v.), Sanders, together with Maxine

Sanders and Sybil Leek, broke away from Gardner's tradition of witchcraft and founded his own school. On Gardner's death in 1964, Sanders appropriated Gardner's title "king of the witches." The Alexandrian (Sanders's) tradition abandoned the Gardnerian practice of being "sky clad" during rituals and employed ceremonial robes. Sanders's interests in ritual magic (q.v.) found expression in his version of witchcraft, to a much greater degree than with Gardner. In common with the Gardnerian tradition, Alexandrian witches acknowledge three successive degrees of initiation: acceptance to the coven, becoming an accomplished witch, and finally the "Great Rite" of initiation to the priesthood. Unlike the Gardnerians, all members of the coven are permitted to attend ceremonies for all three levels of initiation, whereas in the Gardnerian tradition only second and third degree witches attend the second and third initiatory rites.

SANGHARAKSHITA. Born Dennis Lingwood in 1925, he gained an initial interest in Eastern ideas by reading H. P. Blavatsky's (q.v.) *Isis Unveiled,* and subsequently committed himself to Buddhism (q.v.) after reading the Diamond Sutra and the *Sutra of Hui Neng* at age 16. During World War II, Lingwood served as a signals officer in India, Ceylon, and Singapore. In 1946 he destroyed his papers and traveled through India as a world-renouncer. He took up residence within several Buddhist groups, receiving ordination, first as a Theravadin bhikkhu and subsequently in Mahayana traditions. From 1950 to 1964 Sangharakshita lived in Kalimpong, working among untouchables. Invited back to England by the English Sangha Trust, Sangharakshita briefly served as head of the vihara at Hampstead, but, after controversy with the trustees, he founded his own religious organization, the Friends of the Western Buddhist Order (FWBO) in 1967. The FWBO aims to be a new expression of Buddhism, particularly suited to Westerners. Sangharakshita was fiercely critical of the previous generation of Western Buddhists, whom he accused of merely treating Buddhism as an intellectual hobby: Sangharakshita aimed to make Buddhism affect one's

lifestyle and spiritual practice. Now in retirement, Sangharakshita has been succeeded by a "College of Preceptors"—
senior members of the order who are entrusted with the task
of upholding the Buddhist precepts. *See also* WESTERN BUD-
DHIST ORDER, FRIENDS OF THE.

SANNYASIN. A Hindu (q.v.) world renouncer. Traditionally,
the sannyasin is the fourth stage of the *ashramas*—the stages
of life which, theoretically, one is supposed to observe, according to the *Dharma Shastras*. When one reaches the final
stage of one's life, defined by the birth of grandchildren, one
"takes sannyasa," renouncing the world as a wandering celibate who casts off the sacred thread and all family ties and
relies on alms for subsistence as a holy man. The renunciate
aims to devote his life to meditation (q.v.) in order to achieve
the final state of *moksha* (liberation). Although defined as the
fourth stage, it is possible to become a sannyasin earlier in
life. Acceptance of such a religious responsibility is com-
paratively rare, however, at any age. The role of the sannyasin occurs in a number of Hindu-related NRMs, the best-
known of which is the International Society for Krishna Consciousness (ISKCON) (q.v.), and also in Osho (q.v.).

   Prabhupada (q.v.), the founder-leader of ISKCON, was
himself initiated as a sannyasin in 1959. While initiation as a
sannyasin is possible within ISKCON, few devotees have undertaken it, on account of the serious commitments it entails.
Most prefer to assume the role of the celibate *brahmachari* or
brahmacharini (q.v.) or else the *grihastha* (married householder). A number of ISKCON sannyasins are members of
ISKCON's Governing Body.

   Because of Osho's world-affirming nature, the term *sannyasin* is applied to anyone who resides at one of its ashrams.
There are no restrictions, since Osho taught the importance of
not being governed by communal religious rules, and the necessity of enjoying life's pleasures, including those of sex.

SANT BANI ASHRAM. Situated in Franklin, New Hampshire,
the Sant Bani Ashram was originally part of Kirpal Singh's

Ruhani Satsang—Divine Science of the Soul and was responsible for much of its publishing. Following Kirpal Singh's death, New Hampshire leader Russell Perkins was opposed to the likely succession of Darshan Singh, championing Ajaib Singh as the successive guru (q.v.). Perkins was also supported by leader Arran Stephens, but Stephens subsequently left the movement, accusing Ajaib of contradicting Kirpal's original teachings. *See also* KIRPAL RUHANI SATSANG; RUHANI SATSANG; SAWAN KIRPAL RUHANI MISSION.

SANTERIA. An African diaspora religion that pervades Latin America. It is syncretistic, combining African Yoruba religion with Iberian Roman Catholicism. Belief in spirits is a dominant feature, and it has been described as a form of voodoo. There are three million followers in Cuba, and a further 800,000 in the United States. *See also* CANDOMBLÉ; MACUMBA; UMBANDA; WINTI.

SANT NIRANKARI MANDAL. Arising from the Nirankari (q.v.), the movement's origins are attributed to Baba Buta Singh (1873-1943), although Baba Avtar Singh (1900-1969) established it as an organization in Delhi in 1948. Avtar Singh emphasized *satsang* (communal worship), *simran* (repetition of the name of God, "Nirankar" meaning "formless God"), and *sewa* (service to humanity). The Nirankari hold that God is to be found in all religious traditions, and they seek to promote peace, nonviolence, and universal brotherhood, which extends beyond the Sikh (q.v.) tradition. They respect and use scriptures of numerous world traditions. Such syncretism, however, together with their exaltation of Buta as a human guru (q.v.), arouses hostility from Khalsa Sikhs.

Avtar Singh was succeeded by Baba Gurbachan Singh (1930-1980), and currently Gurbachan Singh's son Baba Hardev Singh (b. 1953) heads the organization, which has 1,000 branches in India, as well as branches in the United States, Canada, Great Britain, and Australia.

SATANISM. Not be equated with witchcraft, wicca (q.v.), or Paganism (q.v.), Satanism involves acknowledgment of Satan, either as one to whom homage is due, or else acceptance of values that are believed to be enshrined in the concept of Satan. While some adherents hold that the origins of Satanism lie in the lost culture of Atlantis or in ancient Egyptian mythology, the figure of Satan as the opponent of God probably emerged from Zoroastrian theology, which was subsequently taken up within Judaism (q.v.) around the first century B.C.E. and also in Christianity (q.v.). The image of the devil as a figure with horns, cloven hooves, and a pitchfork has largely been the creation of medieval Christianity. The present-day interest in Satanism is not great, but it can be traced back to the 19th-century revival of the occult, stemming from Eliphas Levi. Of the recent exponents of Satanism, the best known is Anton Szandor LaVey (q.v.) (1930-1997), author of *The Satanic Bible.*

J. Gordon Melton's *Encyclopedia of American Religions* (1996) distinguishes between three different kinds of Satanist activity. There are small groups of psychopaths who dabble in the occult, using it as a front for committing felonies such as grave robbing, sexual assault, bloodletting, and other sadomasochist activities, but who lack systematic teachings about Satan. Second, there are Satanic groups who do work out a Satanic theology and organize themselves institutionally: the best-known examples are LaVey's own Church of Satan (q.v.), the Temple of Set (q.v.), and in England the Order of the Nine Angles and Dark Lily. Graham Harvey's "Satanism in Britain Today" (1995) also mentions the Northern Order of the Prince and the Church of Satanic Liberation, although little appears to be known about these groups. Third, there have allegedly been those who have practiced ritual "satanic abuse," supposedly using Satanism as a rationale for sexually abusing young children. This "Satanist scare" began in the United States in the 1980s, and similar allegations were made in Great Britain in the early 1990s, especially in Cleveland and Orkney. Although children were taken into care, no arrests were made, and government inquiries in Europe and the U.S. have failed to find any firm evidence of such practices.

Estimates of Satanist activity vary widely. Some 20,000 Satanists were estimated to exist in the United States in 1998, while other reckonings suggest that there are no more than 3,000 practicing Satanists at any one time. *See also* PROCESS CHURCH OF THE FINAL JUDGMENT.

SATCHIDANANDA. Born C. K. Ramaswamy Grounder in 1914, Ramaswamy took up the spiritual life after his wife's untimely death, becoming a *brahmachari* (q.v.). After entering the Ramakrishna Mission in 1946, he went on to meet Ramana, Aurobindo, and finally Sivananda (qq.v.), who gave him the name Satchidandana, meaning "being, consciousness and bliss." In 1951 Satchidananda traveled throughout India and Ceylon, establishing branches of Sivananda's Divine Life Society. Satchidananda was concerned with achieving reconciliation between the Sinhalese and Tamils. The year 1966 saw the start of a world tour, as a result of which Satchidananda founded the Integral Yoga Institute (IYI) in the United States. Satchidananda was the first Indian spiritual master to gain a permanent entry visa to the U.S. (1968), eventually becoming a U.S. citizen (1976).

Satchidananda taught a combination of yogas (q.v.): hatha yoga (physical exercises), karma yoga (deeds), raja yoga (q.v.) (concentration), japa yoga (use of mantras [q.v.] or sounds), bhakti yoga (devotion to God), and jnana yoga (insight into the nature of the self). He believed that a combination of physical health, clarity and training of the mind, strength of will, love, peace, and joy led to the highest spiritual goal, which was the recognition of unity behind diversity. Satchidananda taught the oneness of God, who is beyond name, form, place, and gender and who could be approached through many paths. Accordingly, Satchidananda did much to achieve interreligious understanding and cooperation. He gained audiences with Popes Paul VI and John Paul II and with the Dalai Lama. One of his principal achievements was the setting up in 1986 of LOTUS (Light of Truth Universal

Shrine) in a 750-acre site called Yogaville in Virginia, which remains the headquarters of the Integral Yoga Institute International.

SATYA SAI BABA. Born Satyanarayana Rajuin in 1926, Satya Sai Baba—usually referred to as "Sai Baba"—is famed as a miracle worker and held to be "God incarnate" by his followers. His miracle-working powers are believed to have existed from childhood. In 1940 he claimed to be the incarnation of Shirdi Sai Baba (q.v.) (1838-1918). Satya Sai Baba's miracles typically involve materializations—of rings and necklaces, of murtis and lingams, and of vibhuti, a gray ash which is believed to have miraculous powers such as healing. His movement grew in India in the 1950s, and two large ashrams now exist at Prasanthi Nilayama (a town in its own right since 1967) and in Whitefield, near Bangalore. Although Sai Baba has never visited the United States, his popularity grew from the 1970s onward, as a result of lectures given by Indra Devi at Santa Barbara, California, in 1967.

Satya Sai Baba's life is sometimes said to fall into three stages. His childhood and adolescent years (1926-1942) are marked by his using his miraculous powers for childish pranks, such as making clocks run backward. From 1942 until 1958 he was famed for his *mahimas* ("glorious activities," meaning the materializations). The final stage consists of *upadesh,* teaching humanity. Sai Baba's teachings rest on four fundamental principles: *satya* (truth), *dharma* (duty), *shanti* (peace), and *prema* (divine love). Dharma does not include caste obligation, since Sai Baba rejects caste, extending the principle of equality to all. Men and women are said to have equal status within the movement. Western seekers tend to be attracted by the movement's emphasis on meditation (q.v.), vegetarianism, and Sai Baba's presumed paranormal powers.

Sai Baba's followers regard him as divine, claiming that he is an avatar of Shiva, as well as Kalki, the final avatar for the *kali yuga* (the dark age). The fact that his followers talk about him "giving *darshan*"—a term usually attributed to the viewing of a form of deity—indicates the divine status that is accorded to him. He has told his followers that he will remain in human form until 2022, after which he will incarnate again as Sri Prema Sai Baba, who will be an avatar of Shakti. Sai Baba claims some 10 million followers (1999).

SAWAN KIRPAL RUHANI MISSION. Formed after the death of Kirpal Singh in 1974, this mission derives from his Ruhani Satsang—Divine Science of the Soul. When the Ruhani Satsang (q.v.) board declined to nominate a successor, Darshan Singh (b. 1921), Kirpal's son, established his own branch of the movement, together with other leaders. Darshan Singh traveled to the United States in 1978, and in the same year established the Kirpal Ashram in Delhi, which offers *langar* (communal food) to all, as well as meditation (q.v.). Like his father, Darshan endeavors to promote interfaith relations. His writings include *The Secret of Secrets* (1978). *See also* KIRPAL RUHANI SATSANG; RADHA-SOAMI SATSANG; SANT BANI ASHRAM.

SCHOOL OF ECONOMIC SCIENCE (SES). Founded in 1937 by Andrew MacLaren (1883/4-1975), this organization was originally devoted to the study of economics and philosophy; it does not consider itself to be a religion. Andrew MacLaren was a member of Parliament for most of the period 1922-1945 and was particularly interested in social justice and tax reform. His son Leon (Leonardo da Vinci) MacLaren (q.v.) (1910-1994) shared his father's concern for social justice, but believed that changing the laws governing human nature was an essential prerequisite of justice. After meeting the Maharishi Mahesh Yogi (q.v.) in 1960 and subsequently traveling to India where he met Sri Shantanand Saraswati (more usually referred to as "the Shankaracharya"), Leon MacLaren introduced their ideas to SES.

SES's predominant interest is philosophy, although it defines the subject somewhat differently from conventional Western universities: philosophy is studied for practical living, and SES's fundamental concern is the nature of the self.

SES draws on the teachings of G. I. Gurdjieff and P. D. Ouspensky (qq.v.), as well as the Hindu (q.v.) Vedantic tradition, Socrates and Plato, and elements of Judaism and Christianity (qq.v.). The self is equated with *brahman*, the Absolute, but needs awakening, being asleep. Awakening is achieved by means of a mantra (q.v.), the same for every student, which is given during the second-year course on meditation (those who have practiced Transcendental Meditation [TM] [q.v.] are permitted to continue using their TM mantra). Essential to living one's life are the laws of "measure": knowing when to begin and end activities such as waking and sleeping, fasting and eating, working and resting. Accordingly, students are encouraged to rise early, to meditate daily, to engage for a certain period in mundane manual labor, to eat moderately, and to follow a vegetarian diet. The school claims to be non-dogmatic, inviting students neither to accept nor reject, but to test ideas against their own experience. SES values are traditional: male and female roles are distinguished from one another, with men in authority, and it disapproves of premarital and homosexual sexual relationships. It does not involve itself with the occult.

There are SES branches worldwide, in the Great Britain, the United States, Canada, Australia, New Zealand, and elsewhere. There are autonomous independent organizations that teach its philosophy, known by names such as the School of Philosophy and the School of Practical Philosophy. *See also* HUMAN POTENTIAL MOVEMENT.

SCIENTOLOGY. Founded by L. Ron Hubbard (q.v.) (1911-1986), whose supporters established the first Church of Scientology in Los Angeles on 18 February 1954. Churches of Scientology and Scientology Missions can now be found worldwide.

Scientology claims to be a bona fide religion, in contrast with Dianetics (q.v.), which prepares the "thetan" (the self or soul) for its teachings by means of ridding it of "engrams"—its records of physical pain and unconscious states. Scientology teaches that there are a total of eight "dynamics" that can be successively addressed in Scientology training: self, creativity, group survival, species, life forms, physical universe, spiritual dynamic, and infinity. Dianetics addresses the first of these dynamics, after which one can progress to successive levels of "Operating Thetan" (OT). There are currently 15 OT levels available, although to date no Scientologist has ever passed beyond OT8. The teachings that pertain to these levels are strictly confidential, although on occasion a few ex-Scientologists have attempted to divulge them. Scientologists have insisted that such disclosures are travesties of their true teachings.

Theoretically, the Operating Thetan aims to free itself from the physical encumbrances of the universe, some of which relate to a major incident that took place on this planet some 75 million years previously. Once freed from such encumbrances, one can experience "ultimate salvation."

The Church of Scientology avers that it is possible to pursue Scientology without abandoning one's previous religious faith. The ideal of freedom is central to Scientology's ideals, and its creed affirms the equal rights of all, irrespective of race, color and creed. Insistent that "man is a spiritual being," the Church of Scientology continues actively to campaign against modern psychiatric methods, particularly those that aim to alter the chemical balance within a patient's brain, thus treating him or her as merely as a physical entity.

Membership statistics vary, ranging from one million to eight million. The church's own 1998 estimate of 5.6 million active Scientologists seems a reasonable one, with 11,310 full-time staff (1997). *See also* ERHARD SEMINAR TRAINING; HUMAN POTENTIAL MOVEMENT; SELF RELIGIONS; TWITCHELL, PAUL.

SEDEVACANTISTS. A worldwide network of ultraconservative neo-Catholic groups who claim that the popes from John XXIII onward have been overliberal and hence forfeited their right to the papal see, which they regard as now lying vacant. Such groups are normally nonviolent, although the Movement for the Restoration of the Ten Commandments of God (q.v.) in Uganda may have been connected to them. They are frequently anticult, accusing the Roman Catholic Church of failing to take a sufficiently strong stance against NRMs; some groups are anti-Semitic.

SEICHO-NO-IE. *A.k.a.: Truth of Life.* Literally "the home of infinite light, wisdom, and abundance" this is a Japanese New Thought (q.v.) group, founded in 1930 by Dr. Masaharu Taniguchi (1893-1987). Taniguchi joined Omoto when at Waseda University, but left in 1921. He maintained an interest in psychic phenomena, and in 1928 read *The Law of Mind in Action* by Fenwicke Holmes (brother of Ernest S. Holmes [q.v.]). He attributed subsequent financial success, his daughter's recovery from ill health, and a mystical experience to the application of its teachings. Material from a regular journal was collated into a 40-volume publication, *Seimei No Jisso* ("Reality in Life"). In 1931 Taniguchi published the *Holy Sutra: Nectarean Shower of Holy Doctrine,* which forms the basis of *shinsokan* practice—prayerful meditation (q.v.), done at home or in small groups, which aims to clear the mind. From 1938 onward the movement was progressively introduced to Japanese Americans on the West Coast of the United States, largely due to the work of Masaharu Matsuda, Tsuruta Yojan, and Taneko Shimaza. Some 7,000 members were reported in 1974.

SELF-REALIZATION FELLOWSHIP (SRF). The term *self-realization* is said to have been originally coined by Samuel Taylor Coleridge around 1795 and is now used widely as a term in philosophy and as a spiritual goal. The Self-Realization Fellowship was established by Swami Paramahansa Yogananda (q.v.) (1893-1953): originally the Yagoda Satsanga Society, set up in India in 1917, it was incorporated in the United States as the SRF in 1935. The SRF propagates *kriya yoga,* the precise details of which are confidential to practitioners. To embark on its program the seeker must first undergo a six-stage tuition course which leads to *diksha* (initiation) into the practice of kriya yoga.

After Yogananda's death, James J. Lynn (Rajarsi Janakananda)—a wealthy benefactor to the organization—assumed the leadership. When he died in 1955, Sri Daya Mata took over, and he continues to head the organization. There were 500 units in 1996.

SELF RELIGIONS. A term devised by Paul Heelas to denote a group of religions and self-improvement organizations that aim to develop the "self." Several stemmed from Mind Dynamics, which evolved from Silva Mind Control (q.v.)—for example Erhard Seminar Training (*est*—subsequently The Forum and Landmark) (q.v.), PSI World and PSI Mind Development (PSI stands for "People Searching Inside"), the School of Economic Science (q.v.), and Lifespring (founded in 1974 by John Harley), which gave rise to Insight (q.v.) (founded in 1978 by John-Roger Hinkins) and Movement of Spiritual Inner Awareness (q.v.). Other similar organizations include Actualizations (founded in 1975 by Stewart Emery and Carol Augustus), Exegesis (q.v.) (founded in 1977—now Programmes Ltd), Self-Transformation (founded in 1979 by Walter Bellin in Australia), Samuri (founded in the mid-1980s), Lifestream Seminars (Jim Quinn), the Living Game (Thomas Gregory), isa (Ole Larsons), i am (Pat Grove), and Life Training.

On superficial acquaintance such organizations may seem to have little by way of a specifically religious character, emphasizing techniques for personal efficiency and business success (specifically for activities like telephone sales in the case of Exegesis). However, they offer goals of personal enlightenment, and Werner Erhard, leader of *est*, compared the experience of "getting it," which his controversial seminars offered, with Zen (q.v.) *satori*. Not all scholars or self-improvement organizations agree that Heelas's term is satisfactory. Transcendental Meditation (q.v.), for example, denies being a religion at all, while the Church of Scientology (q.v.) insists that it develops the self as only one of a number of "dynamics." Other writers have used terms such as *Human Potential Movement* (q.v.)—although this term covers a wide range of therapies and spiritualities—*para-religions*, or *therapy cults*. Heelas (1996) reckons that, from the 1970s onward, some five million people have completed seminars from these organizations. *See also* AMWAY; SILVA METHOD.

SEMJASE SILVER STAR CENTER. The American name for Freie Interessengemeinschaft für Grenz- und Geisteswissenschaften und Ufologie-Studien (Free Community of Interest in the Border and Spiritual Sciences and UFO Studies), founded in the late 1970s by Eduard ("Billy") Meier (b. 1936). Meier claims to have received UFO experiences from 1942, when he was in telepathic contact with a being called "Sfath." After studying the psychical and spiritual for many years, his first claimed flying saucer contact was in 1975, when he encountered Semjase, from the Pleiades. Semjase declared that the universe is about to enter the "Waterman" (Aquarian) era, and that humans should observe "Twelve Bids," which bear some resemblance to the Jewish-Christian Ten Commandments. The movement's headquarters is in Hinterschmidrutri, Switzerland. *See also* UFO-RELIGIONS.

SETH. A spirit entity, channeled (q.v.) principally by Jane Roberts (q.v.) (1929-1984). Seth is described as "an energy personality essence." Roberts claimed to have established his identity as that of a deceased English teacher, whom she pseudonymously named Frank Withers. Withers claimed various existences throughout history, originating as a Lemurian before the world's creation, and having lived in Atlantis before assuming numerous human lives at different periods of history, in different cultures, and in both genders.

Seth's teachings are that we create our own reality as a result of our thinking, feelings, and the way in which we anticipate the future. A person is a multidimensional whole and is essentially a spirit which progresses through successive bodies. Seth also reveals teachings about the world's creation, time and space, the nature of God and Christ, and health and wholeness. Seth has predicted that Christianity will collapse through fragmentation and that it will be replaced by a new system of thought by 2075.

In order to disseminate Seth's teachings, Dr. Maude Caldwell (d. 1992) established the Austin Seth Center, whose headquarters moved to Eugene, Oregon, in 1992, after Caldwell's death. The Human Journeys Project is an attempt to spread Seth's teachings worldwide, mainly by literature distribution and translation.

Following Roberts, a number of channelers have claimed contact with Seth. The next best known is Thomas Massari, a former musician who taught ESP in Milwaukee in the 1970s and subsequently founded the Parapsychology Center there. After moving to Los Angeles in 1977 he established the Seth-Hermes Foundation there, giving lectures and consultations, as well as organizing classes and retreats.

SEVENTH-DAY ADVENTISM (SDA). A Christian denomination noted for its belief in the imminent return of Jesus Christ and for its insistence that the Jewish sabbath (Friday evening to Saturday evening) is the appropriate day for Christian worship. Adventism initially gained momentum through the teaching of William Miller (q.v.) (1782-1849), who predicted that Christ would return in 1843, subsequently revised to 1844. Following the 1844 "Great Disappointment," his follower Hiram Edson claimed to have received a revelation that the date of 1844 was correct, but that it marked a different event, namely, the beginning of Christ's heavenly rule. The authenticity of this revelation was confirmed by Ellen G. White (q.v.) (1827-1915), who came to be regarded as a prophet within Adventism. The name "Seventh-day Adventists" dates from 1861, and their first Annual Convention was held in 1863.

SDA doctrines are firmly based on the Bible, which it accepts as inerrant. Although the organization has published various summaries of its faith—the first being a "Synopsis of Our Faith" in 1872 by the Adventist Press in Michigan, setting out 25 "propositions"—it acknowledges that such formulations are subservient to the Bible, which sets out

Christianity's true creed. SDA is conservative but orthodox in its theology, affirming the doctrines of the Trinity, the Incarnation, and a substitutionary theory of atonement. It regards the Jewish system of sacrifices and festivals ("annual sabbaths"), prescribed in the Old Testament, as having been superseded by Christ's advent, but sabbath observance, being explicitly enjoined in the Mosaic decalogue, remained obligatory after Christ's first coming. SDA retains a belief in Christ's imminent return, but does not specify any date.

SDA is a lay organization, practicing adult baptism by total immersion, and celebrating the Lord's Supper (its preferred term for Holy Communion). Members are committed to a simple and healthful lifestyle, involving modest attire and chastity. In its early years SDA gained a particular reputation for its promotion of health, and the Kellogg brothers of Battle Creek, Michigan, are especially famous for their pioneering of health foods, particularly cereals.

Although numerous writers have treated SDA as a cult (q.v.) or a "Christian deviation," it is doubtful whether the organization should be considered as a new religious movement. It is no longer new, and in recent times it has gained recognition by various national Councils of Churches. Nonetheless, it significantly influenced the rise of the Jehovah's Witnesses (q.v.), and the Branch Davidians (q.v.) are an important branch of Adventism. There are currently some 10 million Seventh-day Adventists worldwide. *See also* MILLENNIALISM; NEW WORLD ORDER.

SHAH, IDRIES (1924-1996). Born in Simla, India, into an Afghan family who were connected to the Naqshbandi branch of Sufism (q.v.), Shah claimed descent from the prophet Muhammad and is sometimes accorded the title "Grand Sheikh." He was one of the leading exponents of Sufism in the West from the 1950s, working principally through his writings, rather than by attracting disciples. In line with the Sufi tradition, many of his writings present Sufi teachings in story form, the best known of which are the now-famous stories of Nasiruddin, which proved particularly popular with

1960s seekers. Of his 35 volumes, 20 are on Sufism, the most influential of which are *The Sufis* (1964) and *The Way of the Sufi* (1991), which present Sufism more historically and systematically. In 1965, together with J. G. Bennett, he founded the Institute for Cultural Research, which is based at Langton House, a 50-acre site in Kent, England.

Shah taught that Sufism entails four "journeys": *fana* (annihilation), in which the notion of self diminishes and one becomes intoxicated with divine love; *baqa,* when a Sufi becomes a *qutub* (local teacher), subordinating everything to God's will; becoming the Perfect Man ("man" here including both genders), a spiritual guide to all; and finally becoming the Perfect Man who guides others at the moment of physical death to the next stage of their spiritual development. Shah opposed external manifestations of Sufi identify, however, and his work promotes Sufism as part of a universal quest for truth, rather than a form of Islam (q.v.). Shah can thus be regarded as an exponent of Universal Sufism (q.v.).

SHAMANISM. A folk religion, originally practiced by a number of nomadic preliterate societies, which continues in Siberia, Finland, Lapland, and Korea and also among American and Canadian Indians. A *shaman* is a kind of religious oracle, who is deemed to be capable of gaining access to the spirit world, contacting the dead by traveling into the heavens and the hells. Such journeys are made in a trance state, sometimes as a result of imbibing mind-altering substances that yield out-of-body experiences accompanied by telepathic and other psychic powers. The shaman's role is often hereditary and is frequently heralded by "possession sickness"—indeterminate debilitating symptoms which disappear once the acolyte has assumed the role of shaman. The shaman is held to have special healing powers and can allow consultees to communicate with the dead, allaying malevolent spirits and laying wandering souls who perhaps have died in unfortunate circumstances, such as an unexpected accident, and who have been unable to receive appropriate rites of passage at the time of death.

Some NRMs have been significantly influenced by shamanism, for example, the Unification Church and the Cao Dai (qq.v.) of Vietnam. However, since the 1960s an interest has grown among Westerners of reviving and practicing shamanic rites. An important pioneer of Western shamanism is Michael Harner (q.v.), who has organized shamanic workshops in Europe, the United States, and the former Soviet Union. Shamanism also gained publicity through the writings of Carlos Castaneda (q.v.) around the same time. Shamans who have taught the art to Western seekers include Lynn Andrews, Black Elk (q.v.) (1863-1950), Lusiah Teish, Brooke Medicine Eagle, and Sun Bear (q.v.) (b. 1929). *See also* POWER ANIMAL.

SHILOH. Part of the 1960s/1970s Jesus Movement (q.v.), Shiloh was originally founded in 1968 by John J. Higgins, Jr. (b. 1939), as the House of Miracles, a Jesus People commune in Pleasant Hill, Oregon. Higgins was a former drug addict who had converted to fundamentalist Christianity (qq.v.) through reading the Bible. The organization grew rapidly in 1969 and became incorporated as the Oregon Youth Revival Centers, later Shiloh Youth Revival Centers. There were 163 centers in 1974, after which a number of Shiloh Fellowships (churches) were set up to accommodate those who did not seek full-time commitment. The Shiloh organization experienced severe upheaval when Higgins was dismissed in 1978 for his authoritarian leadership style. Higgins then became a pastor with the Calvary Chapel (q.v.), leaving a few remnant groups to struggle on. By 1986 none were left, and following a series of court cases relating to taxation, the organization formally disbanded in 1988.

SHINCH'ON-GYO. A Korean NRM resulting from a split within the Tonghak movement. Its founder-leader claimed to be the reincarnation of Ch'oe Cheu, the Tonghak's founder. *See also* CH'ONDOGYO.

SHINREIKYO. *A.k.a.: Goreigen (Divine Maxim).* Founded by Master Kanichi Otsuka after World War II, Shinreikyo teaches Kami-no-michi—the Way of God—which it regards as the only true teaching. This way is the universal law governing the past, present, and future, and it leads to prosperity; resistance to it leads to destruction. Healing is an important aspect of Shinreikyo. Otsuka is regarded as the great sage who is expected when spirituality is at an ebb and religious teachings lose their power. The movement was brought to the United States in 1963, and its literature in English is distributed by the Metaphysical Science Institute.

SHIRDI SAI BABA (1838-1918). An Indian holy man, said to have been an incarnation of Kabir (trad. 1398-1518). He settled in Shirdi, India, in 1872. His mission aimed at the reconciliation of Hindus and Muslims. A miracle worker, he is believed to have possessed the full range of siddhic powers and is particularly noted for a miracle in which he apparently enabled temple lamps to burn after filling them with water instead of oil. This association of Shirdi Sai Baba with fire may be connected with the phenomenon of *vibhuti* (sacred ash that spontaneously materializes and multiplies): his statue, erected by devotees in 1952 at his Shri Sai Samadhi Mandir, is said to generate vibhuti. Shirdi Sai Baba predicted that he would incarnate again eight years after his death, and the present-day Sai Baba (Satya Sai Baba [q.v.]) is believed to be his reincarnation (q.v.), possessing many of Satya Sai Baba's miraculous powers. Although less well known in the West than Satya Sai Baba, Shirdi Sai Baba remains a popular and independent focus of devotion, particularly in India.

SHIVABALAYOGI. *A.k.a.: Balayogi* (b. 1935). Born of a poor family in Adivarapupeta in Andhra Pradesh, India, Shivabalayogi at the age of 14 had an intense religious experience, which consisted of seeing divine light, hearing the sound of Om, and receiving a vision of Jangam Shiva (a form of deity). Shivabalayogi entered a state of samadhi, from which he emerged only in 1961 after 12 years, assuming the life of a

sadhu. Shri Shivabalayogi Maharaj offers no specific teachings, but gives *darshan* (appearance) to his followers, who
are offered *dhyana diksha* (initiation into meditation [q.v.]),
in which *vibhuti* (sacred ash) is generated. Importance is attached to knowledge from within, and world peace is said to
be attainable through individual inner peace. Shivabalayogi is
famed for his healing powers. Ashrams have been established
in India, two of which are in Bangalore. In the 1980s the
movement became international, with a center established in
London. Other centers have subsequently arisen in Portland,
Oregon; Raleigh, North Carolina; and Santa Barbara, California. *See also* SATYA SAI BABA.

SIDDHA YOGA DHAM ASSOCIATES FOUNDATION.
Established in 1975 by Swami Muktananda Paramahansa
(q.v.) (1908-1982), the movement teaches a form of yoga
(q.v.) entailing shaktipat initiation—a system leading to enlightenment through the activation of kundalini (q.v.) energy.
The appearance *(darshan)* of the guru (q.v.) himself is particularly important in this spiritual path, which is known as
guru-kripa yoga: shakti (usually conceived of as the female
form of divinity in the Hindu tradition) is the spiritual energy
of the guru, which attracts followers and induces the appropriate meditative state. Accordingly, devotion to one's guru,
which mediates the guru's grace, awakens the kundalini, enabling the follower to progress toward the realization of the
Inner Self, which is to be identified with Shiva. The guru's
presence, being an embodiment of the realized self, is more
important than the actual technique of meditation (q.v.) and
contemplation. Chanting is particularly important in the
movement, including chanting the guru's name and the use of
the Guru Gita. Service *(sewa)* is encouraged, one's work being offered to the guru. Hatha yoga is also used, but merely as
an auxiliary discipline. *See also* NITYANANDA.

SIKHISM. An Indian reform movement inaugurated by Guru
Nanak (1469-1539), arising from the Sant tradition and attracting both Hindu and Muslim followers. Nanak com-

menced a line of 10 human gurus (q.v.), ending in Guru Gobind Singh (1666-1708), who gave Sikhs the five khalsa
symbols, known as the "five Ks" *(kes*—uncut hair, *kangha*—
comb, *kirpan*—dagger, *kara*—bracelet, *kachh*—long shorts).
Not all Sikhs are Khalsa Sikhs, however, other types being
Kes dhari and Sahaj dhari Sikhs. Gobind Singh declared that
the succession of gurus should thereafter reside in the Guru
Granth Sahib (the Sikh holy book) and the Guru Panth (the
Sikh community). Sikhism teaches monotheism and dependence on divine grace, and in common with the Hindu (q.v.)
religions teaches *karma* and *samsara.* It is essentially a lay
movement, emphasizing work and service *(sewa)* to humanity, expecting a *grihastha* (householder) lifestyle rather than
an ascetic one.

Conventional Sikhism tends to view unfavorably claimants to the status of human guru after Gobind Singh; hence
Sikh movements deriving from a new guru have tended to be
marginalized. One such leader was Ravi Das (15th/16th century), from whose influence the Ravidasi (q.v.) (a.k.a. Ad
Dharm) movement emerged. The various Radhasoami groups
have drawn on Ravi Das's teachings, as well as those of
Kabir, Nanak, and Tulsi Singh. Following disputes about the
leadership, various schisms emerged, with the largest Radhasoami Satsang (q.v.) remaining at Beas, near Amritsar. Influenced by this group, Kirpal Singh founded his own Ruhani
Satsang (q.v.) in Delhi in 1951. Again, divisions emerged after Sawan Singh's death. The Nirankaris and Namdaris
(qq.v.) both claim to have living gurus in the present age.

The fact that Sikh NRMs have typically appealed to those
of Indian descent is largely attributable to their distinctive
dress code. A few leaders have attempted to introduce Sikh-
derived spirituality to Westerners, notably Harbhajan Singh
Khalsa Yogiji (b. 1929), who established the Healthy Happy
Holy (3HO) (q.v.) movement in Los Angeles in 1969, with a
largely white following. Paul Twitchell (q.v.) is one of the
few Westerners to have drawn largely on Sikhism in the form
of Eckankar (q.v.).

SILVA METHOD. *A.k.a.: Psychorientology (formerly Silva Mind Control).* Devised by José Silva of Laredo, Texas, who began his experiments in 1944, this technique forms part of the Human Potential Movement (q.v.). It involves alphagenetics—the stimulation of alpha waves in the brain, lowering brainwave frequency and leading to greater relaxation and meditative states. Professed results include the enhanced mental power, higher IQ, improved learning ability, greater creativity, and healing powers. The last of these enables the student to undertake "case working"—diagnosing others' state of health. The method includes relaxation, meditation (q.v.), and visualization. The meditation is termed "dynamic meditation," although it does not involve any physical movement, but enables understanding, creativity and autosuggestion. In visualization one receives images of "counselors," otherwise known as spirit guides (q.v.) or guardian angels (q.v.). "Going into alpha" is also said to lead to Christ awareness, cosmic awareness, and enlightenment. The Silva Method draws on the work of Norman Vincent Peale and Christian Science (q.v.), as well as Couéism and biofeedback. By 1989 some six million students are said to have undertaken the 48-hour course.

SINGER, MARGARET THALER (b. 1920?) A clinical psychologist and formerly adjunct professor at the University of California, Berkeley, Singer has served on the Advisory Boards of the Cult Awareness Network (CAN) and the American Family Foundation (AFF) (qq.v.). An ardent opponent of "cults," Singer is a leading advocate of the brainwashing (q.v.) theory, on which she has lectured and written. Her best-known work is *Cults in Our Midst: The Hidden Menace in Our Everyday Lives.* Singer has made many court appearances in her professional capacity, the first of which was at the Patty Hearst trial in 1978. In 1987 Singer led a "task force" investigating "deceptive and indirect methods of persuasion and control" and submitted a report to the American Psychological Association's Board of Social and Ethical Responsibility for Psychology. The board did not accept the report, claiming that it lacked scientific rigor. In several subsequent court hearings, Singer's status as an expert witness was successfully challenged, since her views on "mind control" are not generally accepted among other psychologists and psychiatrists.

SIVANANDA SARASWATI, SWAMI (1887-1963). Founder of the Divine Life Society. Sivananda trained as a doctor and in 1913 departed for Malaysia to offer medical care to Indian rubber plantation workers. Depressed at the effects of materialism, he decided in 1923 to take up *parivrajaka*—the life of the wandering ascetic. In 1924 he arrived in Rishikesh in the Himalayas, where he was initiated by Swami Viswananda Saraswati as a Shankaracharya. The practice taught by Sivananda incorporated yogic practice with study of Indian philosophy and service to one's fellow living beings. The Sivananda Ashram which he founded at Rishikesh incorporated a publishing house, a hospital, and a yoga (q.v.) training center. A prolific writer, Sivananda authored more than 300 publications. He is also renowned for his training of a substantial number of prominent Hindu teachers, notably Swami Jyotirmayananda (b. 1931), Satchidananda (q.v.) (initiated in 1949), Sivalingam, Chidananda, Venkatesananda, and Vishnu-devananda. Satchakrananda claimed a mystical initiation by Sivananda; Sylvia Hellma (of the Yasodhara Ashram Society) saw his face as a vision, and Alice Christensen (of the American Yoga Society) was inspired by him after a visionary experience.

SNAKE HANDLING. A practice carried out mainly by "Signs Pentecostals"—Pentecostalists (q.v.) in the Tennessee area and the southern United States who regard the ability to handle snakes with impunity as one of signs of the Holy Spirit. Snake handling congregations normally cite Mark 16:17-18: "And these signs shall follow them that believe . . . they shall take up serpents; and if they drink any deadly thing, it shall not hurt them . . ." The practice can be traced back to George Went Hensley in 1909, when some men are said to have emptied a box of rattlesnakes in front of him as he was preaching: Hensley, it is reported, continued undaunted. In 1914 Ambrose J. Tomlinson invited Hensley to demonstrate the practice to the Church of God's annual assembly, and from there the practice spread. Snake handling is characteristically done in an ecstatic trance-like state, which may serve to explain the relatively low incidence of accidents (there have been fewer than 100 deaths since its inception).

After one practitioner, Garland Defries, received a near-fatal bite, there was some reappraisal of the practice, and in 1928 the Church of God forbade the practice. Some Pentecostalist groups, such as the Original Pentecostal Church of God, have argued that Jesus' words imply immunity from snakebites if they occur accidentally, and that snakes should not be deliberately handled. After Lewis Ford of Dolly Pond Church of God with Signs Following experienced a fatal snakebite, the state of Tennessee passed legislation to outlaw the practice. Hensley himself died from a snakebite in 1955. A few Signs Pentecostalists have attempting drinking strychnine in order to experience protection against drinking poison, which is also suggested in Mark's gospel: this also led to a Tennessee ban in 1975 when two believers died.

Although snake handling has attracted much unfavorable criticism, the American Civil Liberties Union has defended it as an aspect of religious freedom. The Church of God with Signs Following had a membership of 5,000 in 1997, but only a few hundred actually handle snakes.

SNAPPING. A term proposed by Flo Conway and Jim Siegelman to characterize the process of sudden conversion to religious groups or ideologies. Conway and Seigelman's *Snapping: America's Epidemic of Sudden Personality Change* (1978) was written in the wake of Patty Hearst's sudden allegiance to the Symbionese Liberation Army, which they explain in terms of a brainwashing (q.v.) process, in which external authorities take control of one's thinking, bringing about radical personality change. Conway and Siegelman particularly apply this theory to conversion to

NRMs and claim to identify a number of tactics used by their leaders, including "love bombing" (q.v.), isolation techniques, induced fatigue, and threats. Despite its popular appeal, such theories are not supported by the majority of academic researchers on religious conversion.

SOCIETY OF JOHREI. Founded in 1971, the Society of Johrei is a splinter group of the Church of World Messianity (q.v.), claiming that the latter's teachings have departed from those of its founder, Mokichi Okada. Its followers are mainly from Brazil and Korea.

SOCIETY OF THE INNER LIGHT. A British esoteric movement founded by Dion Fortune (q.v.) (1890-1946), which seeks "expansion of consciousness" and acquaintance with the "ground of all being." Teachings and practices are based on Fortune's two principal texts, *The Mystical Qabalah* and *Cosmic Doctrine,* and combine Kabbalism (q.v.), biblical teachings, and Celtic and Arthurian mythology (q.v.), expressing these in ritual and meditation (q.v.). The society has also been influenced by Alice Bailey (q.v.) and notions of Ascended Masters. Seekers are offered three paths: the mystical, the hermetic, and the "Path of the Green Ray": the first aims at union with the divine, the third with seeking God in nature, while the second combines looking upward toward God with viewing the physical world. Distinctively British in character, members who undertake its four-year course must be born and reared in Great Britain, with knowledge of British traditions, folklore, and history, together with "a love of all things British." Former members of the society have included psychics W. E. Butler and Gareth Knight.

SOKA GAKKAI. A lay Buddhist movement in the Nichiren (q.v.) tradition, established by Tsunesaburo Makiguchi (1871-1944) and Josei Toda (1900-1958). The name Soka Gakkai literally means "Value Creation Society." Following Toda's death the movement has been headed by Daisaku Ikeda (b. 1928). The movement follows the teachings of Nichiren (1222-1282), who insisted that the Lotus Sutra contained the entire essence of Buddhism (q.v.).

The principal practice of the Soka Gakkai is the chanting of the mantra (q.v.) *Nam myoho renge kyo,* which literally means, "Homage to the ineffable law of the lotus teaching." The mantra is said to enable the practitioner to acquire material benefits and to be instrumental for attaining world peace. It is chanted privately for 20 minutes twice daily and collectively at *gongyo,* a ceremony in which selected extracts of the Lotus Sutra (parts of the "Hoben" and "Juryo" chapters) are recited. This is done in front of a *gohonzon,* a scroll on which the mantra is inscribed and which is framed within a wooden container known as a *butsudan.* When not in use, the gohonzon must be concealed. After *gongyo* the group will discuss a theme relating to Nichiren Buddhism or hear testimonies about the efficacy of the chant.

Originally, the Soka Gakkai was the lay counterpart to the Nichiren Shoshu (q.v.), which is presided over by a priesthood, with their high priest overseeing the Taiseki-ji Temple at the foot of Mount Fuji. Following a succession of disputes between Soka Gakkai's lay leaders and the Taiseki-ji priests, the high priest formally excommunicated Daisaku Ikeda and all other Soka Gakkai members in 1992, barring them from entering the main temple and refusing to issue them with further gohonzons. Part of the dispute between the two groups involved the question of the laity's status, and Ikeda had previously been accused of claiming equal status for the laity and the priests. The split has entailed the taking over of some of the priestly functions by the laity, principally the conduct of marriages and funerals. Reported membership in 1998 was 12 million.

SOLAR LIGHT RETREAT (formerly Solar Light Center). Founded in Oregon in 1965 by Marianne Francis (name legally changed to Aleuti Francesca in 1975), this group combines ideas from Theosophy (q.v.) and UFOlogy. Francesca claims to have access to advanced Space Beings who have put an end to war, disease, poverty, famine, and even taxation. These beings are associated with a Great White Brotherhood (q.v.), headed by Jesus. This brotherhood has sent avatars to earth, most notably Krishna, the Buddha, and Jesus. They send light to uplift the earth, enabling the progressive evolution of humanity. Reincarnation (q.v.) is a central belief, and the movement offers regression therapy, enabling followers to understand and deal with their past karma. It is further held that the earth is coming to the end of a 26,000-year cycle, which is marked by an increase of light energy, heralding a new Golden Age of Light, in which Christ will return and inaugurate a new heaven and a new earth. *See also* UFO-RELIGIONS.

SOLAR TEMPLE. A religious group in the neo-Templar (q.v.) tradition that gained notoriety in 1994 by virtue of 53 members simultaneously losing their lives in mysterious circumstances in Canada and Switzerland. The group was led jointly by Luc Jouret (1947-1994) and Joseph Di Mambro (qq.v.) (1920-1994). Jouret founded the International Order of Chivalry Solar Tradition (OICST) in 1984, and this formed the inner core of three organizations, the others being the Amenta Club and the Archédia Club, into which one received initiation before progressing to OICST.

The Solar Temple had no formally defined belief system. Interests encompassed ancient Egyptian death rituals, alternative medicine, reincarnation (q.v.), the Great White Brotherhood (q.v.), the New Age Movement (q.v.), and astrology. Jouret apparently taught that humanity was at the threshold of the dawning Age of Aquarius. Selected Solar Temple members were afforded "visions" of Ascended Masters or other sacred beings and objects, which appeared by means of hologrammatic images, skillfully created by an experienced electrician, but believed to be genuine. A strong ritual element included the enactment of "cosmic marriages," in which previous incarnations of existing members were ceremonially bonded in matrimony. It is claimed that Di Mambro encouraged members to practice "sex magic" (q.v.). Cosmic weddings were held to enable the participants to become part of a communion of souls who would survive the imminent apocalypse by being transported to the planet Sirius. Although the causes of the final catastrophe are unknown, it has been speculated that Di Mambro encouraged members to commit suicide to make this transition, and that, when they proved unwilling to act on his instruction, they were murdered by Jouret. Estimates of the remaining membership range from 140 to 500 (1998).

SOLOMON'S TEMPLE. An apocalyptic Christian fundamentalist (q.v.) group, led by Solomon Ben-David. Born in Jamaica, Ben-David settled in New York and subsequently led his followers to Jerusalem to witness Christ's second coming. He and his followers were arrested by Israeli authorities and repatriated in 1999.

SPANGLER, DAVID (b. 1945). New Age Movement (q.v.) author and lecturer. Born in Columbus, Ohio, Spangler spent part of his childhood in Morocco, where he had a memorable out-of-body experience. After returning to the United States in 1959 he was introduced to channeler (q.v.) Neva Dell Hunter and spoke at one of her conferences in 1964. This was the first of many lecturing engagements that Spangler undertook. In the same year Spangler enrolled as a genetics student at Arizona State University, but dropped out, preferring to give lectures and offer counseling on New Age themes, in association with Myrtle Glines. In 1965 Spangler claimed to have been contacted by "John," a spirit who communicated regularly with him—not as a channeled being, but in a manner akin to ordinary conversation. John and several other associates were in contact with him until 1985.

In 1970 Spangler visited the Findhorn (q.v.) community in Forres, Invernesshire, Scotland, and was instrumental in shaping its semester program. After returning to the United States in 1973, Spangler gave courses at the University of Milwaukee and founded the Lorian Association, which served as a focus for publishing, education, and promotion of the arts. From 1984 until 1991 he spent most of his time focusing on his writing.

Although essentially Christian, Spangler believed that the Church had lost its vitality and that spirituality was not to be found in institutional religion. He predicted that the present civilization would give way to a new culture, affording self-discovery, self-development, an integration of the individual with the environment, and service to the community. An important theme for Spangler is "planetary sensibility": the coming birth of a planetary mind and soul will mark a new stage of evolution in the life of the universe. Service is also an important theme in Spangler's thought: motivation and work will lead to a transformed future, in which there will be humane and abundant living. Spangler's books include *Revelation: Birth of a New Age* (1997), *Emergence: The Rebirth of the Sacred* (1984), and *A Critique of the New Age, Science and Popular Culture* (1991), co-authored with William Irwin Thompson. *See also* GAIA HYPOTHESIS.

SPEAKING IN TONGUES (Glossolalia). Particularly experienced within the Pentecostalist (q.v.) movement, in which believers spontaneously utter seemingly meaningless sounds during worship, this phenomenon is identified with the experience of Jesus' early disciples at Pentecost (Acts 2:1-13), in which they appeared to speak in a language that was not readily intelligible. Although it gained momentum in the late 19th and early 20th centuries, there are a few recorded instances among the 17th-century Huguenots, 18th-century Quakers, the Catholic Apostolic Church, and the Holiness Churches.

In 1875 the Rev. P. B. Swan's followers were known as "the Gift People"—a reference to the gifts of the Holy Spirit. At first the phenomenon was not particularly associated with the Pentecost experience; it was first identified thus in 1879 by Jethro Walthall, who founded the Assemblies of God (q.v.). From 1901 onward Agnes Ozman and Charles F. Parham (1873-1929) spread the phenomenon, which continued mainly within the Holiness movement until 1914. On 9 April

1906 a meeting at Azusa Street, Los Angeles, experienced glossolaliation and brought it into prominence, particularly associating it with an earthquake, contending that these were signs of the world's imminent end. In 1914 a meeting of various interested parties in the Grand Opera House, Hot Springs, Arkansas, brought the somewhat fragmented Pentecostalist movement into greater organization and resulted in the formation of the Assemblies of God. Other emergent Pentecostalist organizations were the Pentecostal Holiness Church and the Church of God (Cleveland, Tennessee). *See also* CHURCH OF THE LIVING WORD; MARANATHA CHRISTIAN CHURCHES.

SPIRIT GUIDE. A popular idea in New Age (q.v.) thinking, the spirit guide is one who offers help and guidance in life to an individual. It was referred to as a *daimon* in ancient culture (Socrates, for example, had his daimon), although this term now has negative connotations, being associated with the word *demon*. A spirit guide may be an angel (q.v.), an evolved being such as an Ascended Master, or a spirit of the dead. It is usually not an animal, except in the magical or shamanic (qq.v.) traditions. The spirit guide may communicate with the individual through dreams, one's "inner voice," or clairaudience. Some altered states of consciousness have been believed to be instrumental in achieving contact with one's guide, for example, through hallucinogenic drugs or ecstatic dancing.

Spirit guides differ from spirit helpers, who are lesser powers and have specialized functions, such as fending off illness or securing material prosperity. *See also* POWER ANIMAL; SILVA METHOD.

SPIRITISM. A term sometimes substituted for *spiritualism* (q.v.) by evangelical Christians, who dislike the possible implication that its practices are "spiritual." More widely, the term can simply refer to belief in spirits, or to religious movements in which belief in spirits is particularly significant, for example, shamanism (q.v.). Specifically, *spiritism* has come to be associated with Kardecism—the beliefs and practices that stem from the teachings of Allan Kardec (q.v.).

Some 15 million are reckoned to belong to spiritist groups (1998), and Kardec is believed to have had four million followers in 1991. *See also* CANDOMBLÉ; CAO DAI; SANTERIA; TEMPLE OF UNIVERSAL LAW; UMBANDA; WINTI.

SPIRITUALISM. The popular interest in Spiritualism is generally traced to the Fox sisters (q.v.) of Hydesville, New York, in 1848. Precursors of Spiritualism can be found in Emanuel Swedenborg, who claimed to have visited the spirit realms, and in Franz Anton Mesmer, who developed the art of trance induction. Mention should also be made of Andrew Jackson Davis (q.v.), "the Poughkeepsie Seer," who claimed contact with Swedenborg in 1847 and who became a prominent exponent of Spiritualism during the 1850s.

Spiritualism is often regarded as having three aspects: mental mediumship, spiritual healing, and physical mediumship. The first embraces altered states of consciousness and paranormal mental activities, such as trance induction, automatism (e.g., automatic writing), psychometry, and clairvoyance. The second is carried out either by physical contact (such as the laying on of hands) or by "absent healing." Physical mediumship is now rare: it involves the manifestation of visual, audible, or tangible material from the spirit world (ectoplasm, rappings, "apports") or psychokinetic moving of objects (such as table raising). Spiritualism enjoyed its heyday in the 1850s, but then went into decline, being marred by accusations of fraud, particularly up to the 1880s.

Spiritualism's tenets are frequently affirmed in a number of principles: these typically affirm the "fatherhood of God," the "brotherhood of man," belief in communication with spirits and angels (q.v.), the continued existence of the soul, a law of "cause and effect"—similar to karma—whereby one is compensated for good and evil deeds, and belief in the soul's eternal progress. Spiritualists have been divided on the question of reincarnation (q.v.), as well as the status of Jesus Christ. Some Spiritualist churches consider themselves to be Christian, while others do not. The National Spiritualist Association of Churches (NSAC), founded in Chicago in 1893, affirms the authority of the Bible. More recent "channelers" (q.v.) are less inclined to regard the Bible as authoritative, having in some cases drawn on the authority of channeled writings.

In addition to the NSAC, other organizing bodies include the General Assembly of Spiritualists (founded 1897) and the International General Assembly of Spiritualists (incorporated 1936). The Spiritualists' National Union (SNU) (founded 1901) and the Spiritualist Association of Great Britain (founded 1960, being a continuation of the 1892 Marylebone Spiritualist Association) are overseeing bodies in Great Britain. *See also* AQUARIAN FOUNDATION; ASTARA; BAILEY, ALICE; HOLY ORDER OF MANS; UNIVERSAL CHURCH OF THE MASTER; WHITE EAGLE LODGE.

SPIRITUAL SCIENCE CHURCH. *A.k.a.: Spiritual Science Mother Church.* Founded in 1923 by "Mother" Julia O. Forrest and Dr. Carl H. Pieres, this church derives from Christian Science (q.v.), to which Forrest formerly belonged. However, although healing is practiced, greater emphasis is given to communication from other realms, thus making the church more spiritualist (q.v.) oriented. Importance is also attached to preaching and to "intelligent prayer," which is believed to have a "cleansing" function. The church is Trinitarian in theology, but believes in reincarnation (q.v.). Its headquarters are in New York.

STAR-BORNE UNLIMITED. A New Age (q.v.) spiritual group, founded in 1986, emphasizing teachings about angels (q.v.) and based on the teachings of founder-leader Solara Antara Amaa-Ra. Solara was born in California and introduced to a variety of alternative spiritual groups in her early years. After buying a cabin in a secluded mountain canyon in Arizona, Solara wrote her first two books, *Invoking Your*

Celestial Guardians and *The Legend of Altazar: A Fragment of True History of Planet Earth.* The former gives instructions for contacting and embodying one's "Golden Solar Angel" or "starry Overself," and on receiving one's "angelic" or "starry" name, which is a prelude to achieving contact. The latter tells of the last days of Atlantis and Lemuria. Solara's third book, *The Star-Borne: A Remembrance for the Awakened Ones* (1989), is reckoned to be her most important, dealing with the "next level of planetary service." In order to gain full empowerment, one must pass through "the Door." However, this cannot be achieved individually, but only in solidarity with others, recognizing that all constitute the One. The opening of the Door, enabling mass ascension, began on 11 November 1992 and will be completed in 2011. Numerics are important in determining key events, and the numbers 11:11, relating to the 11 November date, were judged to be particularly significant. The stars assume a profound significance in Solara's angelology, and her fourth work, *EL*AN*RA,* identifies key points within the galaxy that keep our universe in position. World membership was estimated at 800 in 1992.

STARHAWK. The assumed name of Miriam Simos (b. 1951), a peace campaigner, feminist, and wiccan high priestess. Starhawk is one of a number of feminist wiccans who belong to Susan B. Anthony's Covenant of the Goddess (q.v.) (founded in 1975) and seek to establish a woman-centered form of wicca (q.v.), with exclusively female covens, focused on the goddess Diana. Starhawk is particularly known for *The Spiral Dance: A Rebirth of the Ancient Religion of the Great Goddess* (1979), which sets out an extensive set of rituals for the practice of witchcraft and magic (q.v.).

STEINER, RUDOLF (1861-1925). Writer, educationalist, and founder of Anthroposophy (q.v.). Born in Kraljevic—then in Hungary, now in Bosnia—Steiner reported clairvoyant experiences from early childhood. He entered the University of Vienna in 1879 to study science and developed a keen interest in J. W. von Goethe, as well as the philosophy of Immanuel Kant, J. G. Fichte, and G. W. F. Hegel, and literature and the arts more widely. At the age of 23 he was entrusted with the task of editing Goethe's scientific writings. He completed his doctorate at the University of Rostock in 1891.

Steiner took up meditation (q.v.) in early adulthood and joined the Rite of Memphis and Misraim. He may also have belonged to Ordo Templi Orientis (q.v.), although this is uncertain. Around 1900 the Theosophical Society invited him to lecture on Goethe; he became a member, subsequently becoming general secretary of the German branch in 1902. Steiner was critical of the Theosophists (q.v.) on several counts, particularly concerning the high regard that their leaders Annie Besant and Charles W. Leadbeater held for Krishnamurti (qq.v.): Steiner would not allow German Theosophists to belong simultaneously to Krishnamurti's Order of the Star of the East. In 1912 affairs came to a head when Besant revoked the charter of the German Theosophical Society, whereupon Steiner assumed control of 55 of Germany's 65 lodges, which he organized into the Anthroposophical Society in 1913.

As well as being a spiritual leader, Steiner is particularly noted for his Waldorf Schools, the first of which was established in 1919 for children of workers in the Waldorf-Astoria cigarette factory. There are currently 500 Waldorf Schools, employing Steiner's educational principles. Steiner was also interested in theater, and he developed the art of eurythmy— the use of bodily movements to express the deeper meaning of words and music—with Marie von Sievers, his second wife. He also pioneered bio-dynamics—a form of organic farming and gardening—and holistic medicine. His interest in Goethe's "Theory of Color" led to his own techniques of color therapy. *See also* AKASHIC RECORDS; ANGELS.

STUDY SOCIETY. Founded in England by Dr. Francis Roles in the 1930s and formerly known as the Society for the Study of Normal Psychology, this organization draws on the ideas of G. I. Gurdjieff and P. D. Ouspensky (qq.v.), as well as Indian Vedantism. Members of the Study Society supported the Maharishi Mahesh Yogi's (q.v.) lectures when he visited London in 1960 and 1961, and Roles was subsequently prompted to visit India and be taught by Sri Shantanand Saraswati, who, in common with the Maharishi, had been a student of Guru Dev (1869-1953). The Study Society attracted the interest of Leon MacLaren (q.v.) (1910-1994), who used many of its ideas in the development of the School of Economic Science (q.v.).

SUBUD. A spiritual movement founded by Pak Subuh (q.v.) (Muhammad Sukarno Sumohadiwidjojo, 1901-1987) in Indonesia in 1932 that gained momentum as a worldwide movement from 1954 onward. *Subud* is an acronym for "Susila, Budhi, Dharma," which is understood to mean "good morals," "inner force," and "surrender." The similarity of the name to that of the founder-leader is purely coincidental. Although Subuh's own background was Islamic, Subud does not regard itself as a religion, but as a fellowship or spiritual movement that strengthens one's faith and spiritual practice within whatever religion its various members follow. The main practice of Subud is the *latihan* (q.v.), in which members simply stand and "wait to receive."

Subud imposes no creed upon its members, and Pak Subuh claimed to offer no teachings. Nonetheless, Subuh gave numerous talks, which were translated from Indonesian into English and which covered a range of themes, including personal relationships, business, politics, and education. In particular, Subuh taught a theory of "seven powers," otherwise known as "the seven great spheres of universal life," coupled with a theory of seven levels of spiritual development. The seven powers are material power, vegetative power, animal power, human power, the power of the complete man, the power of compassion, and the power of the Supreme Lord.

Subud's practices are essentially aimed at ordinary individuals who pursue a conventional lifestyle outside the latihan. Subud rejects asceticism and is opposed to the manifestation of paranormal, occultist, and magical (q.v.)

practices, which it believes further the self-aggrandizement of their practitioners rather than facilitating spiritual progress. Largely due to the activities of Husein Rofé and John G. Bennett (q.v.), Subud's teachings and practices were disseminated beyond Indonesia after 1954, and in 1998 Subud reported some 385 groups and 12,000 members worldwide.

SUBUH, PAK (1901-1987). Founder of Subud (q.v.). Born into a Muslim family in Kedungjati, Java, Subuh's given name was Muhammad Sukarno Sumohadiwidjojo. He is better known to his followers as Subuh, Bapak ("father"), or by these two names combined as Pak Subuh. Subuh had an inaugural experience in 1924 in which his body and chest experienced violent shaking. He interpreted this as his first "opening," or *latihan kejiwaan* ("spiritual exercise," or "training of the spirit"), the first of several that occurred between 1924 and 1928. Subuh did not immediately gather disciples, but engaged in conventional life, marrying, having children, and continuing in secular employment.

As time passed, however, some of Subuh's acquaintances came to regard him as having special spiritual insight, and in 1932 Subuh held the first public *latihan* (q.v.). He quit his job in 1933, devoting his life to spreading the practice of the latihan. In 1954 Subuh met Husein Rofé, a British Muslim. Rofé received the "opening" from Subuh and subsequently visited Turkey and Cyprus, spreading Subuh's message. On returning to England, Rofé invited Subuh to join him at Coombe Springs, where John Bennett (q.v.) was introduced to him. Bennett was then a follower of G. I. Gurdjieff (q.v.), but became increasingly drawn to Subud and subsequently wrote *Concerning Subud* (1958), which became the standard introduction to the movement. Subuh made no claims about his own person, and his followers do not regard him as a prophet, a saint, or even a teacher. Subuh described himself as a *mogol*—a Muslim who has little knowledge of Islamic writings.

SUFI MOVEMENT. A form of Universal Sufism (q.v.), established in 1927 by Hazrat Inayat Khan (q.v.) (1882-1927). The movement's professed aims are to spread the unity of religion, to eradicate "bias" from existing religions, to develop mystical powers within human beings, and to promote a universal brotherhood, spanning East and West. The movement's international headquarters are in Geneva, Switzerland. The Sufi Cultural Centre in East London was established in 1971, and its activities include lectures on Sufism (q.v.), literature distribution, the organization of work camps in England and The Netherlands, healing and nutrition, and especially music, following the Sufi tradition of whirling dervishes.

After Khan's death the Sufi Movement was taken over by Hidayat Inayat Khan, his second son. However, his leadership is disputed by the Sufi Order International (q.v.), who claim that Hazrat Khan appointed his 10-year-old eldest son, Vilayat Inayat Khan (q.v.) (b. 1916), as his successor.

SUFI ORDER INTERNATIONAL. Originally founded in England in 1910 as the Sufi Order of the West (q.v.) by Hazrat Inayat Khan (1882-1927), this organization is also known as the Zenith Institute in Germany. It promotes a version of Universal Sufism (q.v.), regarding Sufi teachings as transcending Islam (q.v.), and drawing on a variety of religious traditions. The Sufi Order International claims that Sufism (q.v.) predates Islam, having originated from Zoroastrian Magi, who transmitted their knowledge to Islamic esotericists. Fundamental to its teachings are the unity of humankind with God and the desirability of the divinity that inhabits each individual. The religion that emerges thus becomes a "religion of the heart," transcending the individual religious traditions that exist throughout the globe. The movement draws on Hindu (q.v.) and Islamic meditation (q.v.) and does much to promote interfaith worship, employing Christian (q.v.), Buddhist (q.v.), and Hindu devotion as well as Islamic piety. The order emphasizes personal transformation, service to humanity, and acquaintance with esoteric truths. It is a healing order, and also stresses *ziraat* (Sufism and planetary consciousness).

SUFI ORDER OF THE WEST. Brought originally to England by Hazrat Inayat Khan (q.v.) (1882-1927) as the Sufi Movement (q.v.), the Sufi Order of the West promotes a form of Universal Sufism (q.v.), which is held to transcend Islam (q.v.). After Khan's death, the movement was led by his eldest son, Vilayat Inayat Khan (q.v.) (b. 1916), who founded the Sufi Order of the West. It teaches a common ground of all religions, aiming to transmit spiritual truth for modern Western culture that spans both Eastern and Western traditions. This common ground is expressed in forms of worship that Khan has devised and that find expression in the Universal Worship of the Church of All, which he established. Meditation (q.v.) using breath control and the use of *wazifa* (Sufi mantras [q.v.]) are employed by initiates. During the late 1960s and early 1970s, the practice of Shahabuddin Iless (Sufi dancing) was introduced, and the order is especially renowned for its "Dances of Universal Peace," created by Samuel L. Lewis (q.v.) (1896-1971) and influenced by Zen (q.v.), yogic and Hasidic traditions, and Sufism (q.v.). The movement's headquarters are in France; in the United States the central organization is located at the Abode of the Message, near Lebanon Springs, New York. The organization is now known as the Sufi Order International.

SUFISM. Traditionally regarded as the mystical branch of Islam (q.v.), possibly originating in the eighth and ninth centuries C.E. Various etymological explanations exist for the name; for example, *suf* meaning "wool-clad," referring to the world-renouncer's attire or the name may derive from *safa* (purity) or *en sof* (Hebrew for "divine"). Sufis are traditionally ascetic, and the movement is based on a teacher-disciple relationship, centering on a *tariqa* (a formally constituted order). The Sufi's aim is to attain oneness with the absolute (or God), which is achievable through a number of spiritual practices, most notably *dhikr* ("recitation," usually of God's names), and *sama* (meditation [q.v.]). These are used to bring about states of trance and ecstasy, in which nothing but God is perceived to exist. Sufism has also come to be associated with poetry, music, and perhaps most especially its dances that are performed by the "whirling dervishes." Although Sufism is often presented as distinct from "mainstream" Islam, between 50 and 75 percent of Muslims worldwide are associated with a tariqa with varying degrees of commitment. The Islamic philosopher Al-Ghazali (d. 1111) contended that mystical practices were consistent with traditional observance of the *shar'iah* (Islamic law).

While some Sufi teachers seek to direct their disciples toward Islam, others perceive the notion of divine union as transcending all religions. Some scholars have therefore distinguished between Islamic Sufism and "Universal Sufism" (q.v.), the latter drawing on teachings and practices that are associated with several of the world's religious traditions. Universal Sufism is usually, but not invariably, the form that is followed by Westerners: it was first brought into prominence by Hazrat Inayat Khan (q.v.) (1882-1927), and it exercised a marked influence on G. I. Gurdjieff (q.v.) (c. 1874-1949). There are 400 major Sufi orders worldwide. *See also* ARICA; BAWA MUHAIYADDEEN FELLOWSHIP; BENNETT, J. G.; BESHARA; SUFI MOVEMENT; SUFI ORDER INTERNATIONAL; SUFI ORDER OF THE WEST; SUFISM REORIENTED; SUFI SOCIETY.

SUFISM REORIENTED. Originally a Sufi (q.v.) group led by Hazrat Inayat Khan (q.v.), who founded the Sufi Movement (q.v.). Khan's successor Rabia Martin (whose leadership was not accepted in Europe, since she was a woman) entered into correspondence with Meher Baba (q.v.) and became convinced that he was the Qutb (the central being of the universe), and she transferred ownership of some Sufi property to Meher Baba. Martin did not actually meet Meher Baba, but her successor, Murshida Ivy Oneita Duce, did when he visited Myrtle Beach, South Carolina, and brought back a document entitled "Chartered Guidance from Meher Baba for the Reorientation of Sufism as the Highway to the Ultimate Universalized." Sufism Reorientated remains a distinctive group within the Meher Baba organization.

SUFI SOCIETY. A small group dedicated to Universal Sufism (q.v.), under the leadership of Dr. Sufi Aziz Balouch. Balouch was born near the Persia-Pakistan border and trained as a Muslim imam. He was variously a cultural attaché in Madrid's Pakistan embassy and a flamenco singer in Spain. After studying Islamic philosophy at a number of universities, he moved to England in 1947, where he established the Sufi Society. The society aims to promote Sufism (q.v.) through lectures and especially through music. It distributes books on Sufism and Sufi music and also has a keen interest in healing, which incorporates alternative medicine and medical astrology.

SUMMIT LIGHTHOUSE. Founded by Mark L. Prophet in 1958, this organization was incorporated as the Church Universal and Triumphant (CUT) (q.v.) in 1974, following Prophet's death. His wife, Elizabeth Clare Prophet, continues to lead the organization. The publications and educational wing of the movement is now designated Summit Lighthouse, leaving the liturgical aspects to CUT. Summit Lighthouse publishes the teachings of the Ascended Masters and produces a weekly journal entitled *Pearls of Wisdom. See also* GREAT WHITE BROTHERHOOD.

SUN BEAR (b. 1929). Founder-leader and medicine chief of the Bear Tribe Medicine Society. Born Gheezis Mokwa, he assumed the name of "Sun Bear" following an instruction from the Great Spirit in a vision. He was employed as part of a native studies program at the University of California, where he established the society in 1970. The present headquarters is in Vision Mountain, 35 miles from Spokane, Washington, where Sun Bear teaches "practical spirituality," which he has summarized as "Walk in balance on the Earth Mother." Sun Bear teaches harmony with the earth, drawing on Native

American prophecies warning of an imminent cataclysm. His following consists mainly of white Westerners, some 10,000 of whom visit Vision Mountain each year. (From 1970 onward Sun Bear has taught that his teachings should expand beyond American Indians.) This self-sufficient community teaches a blend of Native American shamanism and New Age (qq.v.) teachings, and it offers apprentice programs, medicine wheel gatherings, retreats, and "vision quests," which consist of fasting, prayer, and cleansing in sweat lodges. Sun Bear now proves popular as an author and lecturer: he has traveled to Great Britain, Germany, the Netherlands, India, and Australia. His principal writings are *At Home in the Wilderness, Buffalo Hearts* (1976), *The Medicine Wheel: Earth Astrology* (coauthored with his wife, Wabun, 1980), and *The Bear Tribe's Self-Reliance Book* (coauthored). His autobiography *Sun Bear, The Path of Power* appeared in 1984.

SYNANON CHURCH. Originally established as the Synanon Foundation in 1958 by Charles Dederich (1914?-1997) in Santa Monica, California, the organization's purpose was to help alcoholics and drug addicts. It was organized into several communes, the membership of which grew to 1,400 by the late 1960s. At its inception it did not regard itself as a religion, particularly since many residents came from a nonreligious background. However, internal discussions concerning its putative religious character caused it to declare itself a religion in 1974, and in 1980 the name Synanon Church was adopted. Its ideas draw on Buddhism (q.v.) and Taoism, together with the teachings of Western mystics and writers such as Ralph Waldo Emerson (q.v.). The organization attracted negative publicity on account of a number of lawsuits, including accusations of conspiracy to murder, following an incident in 1978. In the early 1970s it had 15,000 members (mainly in California), but by 1988, there were only 860 adherents. It disbanded in 1991.

SZEKELY, EDMOND BORDEAUX (1915-1980). Born in Hungary, Szekely was particularly important in the 20th-century revival of the Essenes (q.v.). Szekely claimed to have visited the Vatican library, where he discovered an ancient manuscript written in Aramaic by the apostle John. He reportedly translated this in the late 1920s, publishing part of the text in 1937 as *The Essene Gospel of Peace*. The Nazi regime caused Szekely to leave Europe in 1939; he took up residence at Tecate, Mexico, where he opened his Essene School. In 1959 a second Essene center was established in Escondido, California. The Essene School was later renamed the First Christians' Essene Church, which attracted around 1,000 members worldwide by 1987. Together with Romain Rolland, Szekely set up the International Biogenic Society and the Academy of Creative Living: both organizations were concerned with applying Essene principles to simple and sustainable living. The remainder of Szekely's translated manuscript was published in three further volumes starting in 1971.

-T-

TEMPLARISM. Original a military monastic order, the Templars were founded in 1118 by Hugh de Payens and Geoffrey de Saint-Omer and gained the support of Cistercian Abbot Bernard of Clairvaux (1090-1153). Their work entailed the protection of pilgrims traveling to Jerusalem and was supported by the King of Jerusalem and the Pope. The Templars were formally disbanded in 1312, although some continued to exist in small pockets, mainly in Portugal.

Following the French Revolution there was a revival of Templarism, largely due to the influence of Bernard-Raymond Fabré-Palaprat (1773-1838), who reconstituted the order with himself as the grand master. He also founded the Johannite Church, consecrating Ferdinand-François Chatre (1795-1857) as bishop. The Templar movement is thus associated with the Liberal Catholic Church (q.v.) and the ordination of irregular bishops.

Templarism exerted an important influence on Freemasonry and Rosicrucianism (q.v.). Julien Origas (1920-1983) was important for his founding of the Renewed Order of the Temple (ORT) as well as for his involvement in the Ancient Mystical Order of the Rosy Cross (AMORC) (q.v.). Templar practices found further expression in the Ordo Templi Orientis (q.v.), the Ordo Novi Templi, and the Solar Temple (q.v.), notorious for its mass deaths in 1994.

TEMPLE OF SET. A Satanist (q.v.) group, founded in California in 1975 by Michael Aquino. Originally a breakaway group of the Church of Satan (q.v.), Aquino, its high priest, sought a new mandate from Set, which is enshrined in *The Book of Coming Forth by Night.* The Temple of Set holds that Christianity (q.v.) progressively distorted Set, originally an Egyptian deity, to create the Christian concept of Satan. Set is not viewed as evil, but stands in contrast to the inanimate universe and aims to help humanity achieve its potential for higher evolution. Set is not worshipped as a god, but is nonetheless viewed as a real being who serves as a model for humanity: "As Set was, we are; as Set is, we will be." The aims of "individual transcendence" and evolutionary progress are made by the Black Flame, which means the gift of the intellect. The process of "becoming," by which one achieves this, is known as *xeper* and involves work and learning, including the ability to work magic (q.v.). The Temple of Set advocates black rather than white magic, since it is the former that is self-beneficial. The organization's teachings on magic are enshrined in Aquino's *Black Magic in Theory and Practice* (1992). The group distinguishes between "lesser black magic," which aims to effect changes in the objective universe, and "greater black magic," which seeks to change the individual's subjective universe. Although there are no universally prescribed rituals for practicing this magic, *Black Magic in Theory and Practice* provides an example of one such ritual, and the Temple of Set has devised various ceremonies for specific occasions.

Organizationally, the Temple of Set is headed by a Council of Nine, from which a high priest and an executive director are elected. Several "Orders" exist for particular specialist interests (e.g., Nietzsche, the Germanic tradition, Merlin) and local groups are known as "Pylons." Some Pylons operate by correspondence, rather than geography. There are six degrees of initiation: Setian, Adept, Priest/Priestess, Magister/Magistra, Magus/Maga, Ipsissimus/Ipsissima; however, initiates are normally expected merely to advance to the stage of Adept, which involves competence in black magic. The other degrees are for specialized purposes. The Temple of Set exists in the United States and Great Britain and had 2,000 members in 1998.

TEMPLE OF UNIVERSAL LAW. A Spiritualist (q.v.) organization, founded in 1936 by the Rev. Charlotte Bright (d. 1989) and currently led by her son, the Rev. Robert E. Martin. Teachings contain substantial Christian (q.v.) elements: members are Trinitarian, observe the Lord's Supper (communion) monthly, and use the Bible, although they also draw on other world religious traditions. They also believe themselves to have contact with the Great White Brotherhood (q.v.). In 1988 some 200 members were reported.

TEMPLE OV PSYCHICK YOUTH, THEE (TOPY). Founded in 1981 by pop singer Genesis P. Orridge, TOPY is provocatively antiestablishment, emphasizing the need for its "collaborators" (it avoids the terms "members" and "followers") to question everything and to accept responsibility for intuitively finding their own values. Its main practice is "sigil magick," a form of sex magick (q.v.) derived from Aleister Crowley (q.v.). Other influences include Paganism (q.v.) and some elements of Buddhism (q.v.), as well as surrealism and anarchism. The movement has no hierarchical structure (unusual for a magical group) and has no dogmas, rules, official leaders, or formal membership. TOPY exists in the United States, London, and elsewhere in Europe, although there are very few collaborators (only 12 in London in 1993).

TENRIKYO. The largest of the pre-Meiji (1889 Japanese constitution) religions in Japan, founded by Miki Nakayama (1798-1887), who experienced trance states from 1838 onward, in which she is said to have been possessed by the Shinto deity Tenri-o-no-mikoto (Lord of divine wisdom). Her followers gained recognition as a Shinto sect in 1908, although since the 1970s Tenrikyo prefers not to regard itself as Shinto. The organization acknowledges the Shinto pantheon, regarding all the gods as essentially one. One's body is on loan from Oya-gami (God the parent): while the human self is essentially good, it collects *hokori* ("dust") in the form of anger, selfishness, greed, and the like, which needs to be swept away through prayer. One's aim is to realize *yokigurashi* (salvation). The sacred ceremony *tsutome* for removing "dust" can only be performed at the movement's headquarters in Tenri. Nakamaya has been succeeded by a succession of male family members, who are accorded the title *shinbashira* ("true pillar"). In 1927 Tenrikyo was introduced to the United States, where over 3,000 members were reported in 1987. Japanese membership is currently around 2,350,000 (1999). *See also* KONKOKYO.

THELEMIC MAGICK. A form of sex magick, so named by Aleister Crowley (q.v.) (1875-1947). Crowley drew on the ideas of Theodore Ruess, a German occultist who first introduced Crowley to sex magick, and also on Pascal Beverly Randolph (1825-1875), founder of the Fraternitas Rosea Crucis. The word *thelemic* means "pertaining to the will" and alludes to Crowley's dictum, "'Do what thou wilt' shall be the whole of the law." While the sex magic of Randolph involved conventional sex between marriage partners, Crowley's version included sex with prostitutes—his "scarlet women"—and adulterous relationships.

THEOSOPHY. Founded in New York in 1875 by Helena Petrovna Blavatsky (q.v.) (1831-1891), Henry Steel Olcott (1832-1907), and William Q. Judge (1851-1896). Theosophy's principal aims included the establishment of a universal brotherhood that made no distinctions on the grounds of creed, caste, race, or gender; investigation of "unexplained laws of nature" and paranormal powers inherent in individuals; and the study of "comparative religion, philosophy, and science." Particularly in its earlier years, the Theosophical Society largely drew on Blavatsky's own teachings and tended to attract those who were convinced of the authenticity of paranormal phenomena, thus precluding more objective investigation. The study of world religions was largely influenced by Blavatsky's notion, expressed in her major work *The Secret Doctrine,* that there is a common hidden core underlying all the world's religious traditions. However, the society makes no credal requirements of its members, demanding nothing more than a commitment to these three principal aims. After the deaths of Blavatsky and Olcott, Annie Besant (q.v.) (1847-1933) assumed control of the organization, assisted by Charles W. Leadbeater (q.v.) (1854-1934).

The society is organized into numerous lodges worldwide, which meet for lectures and discussions on religion, the occult, and the work of Theosophy's founder-leaders. Of particular importance to Theosophists is religious practice, and most lodges offer meditation (q.v.) as well as study.

Although Theosophy appears currently to be in decline (34,000 members worldwide in 1998, compared with 100,000 in 1907), it has been particularly influential in the development of alternative forms of spirituality. Among the best-known alternative religious and spiritual systems that have developed from Theosophy are Rudolf Steiner's Anthroposophy (qq.v.) and Krishnamurti (q.v.) (who was discovered as a boy and adopted by Besant and Leadbeater). Buddhism (q.v.) in Great Britain gained momentum through the establishment of a Buddhist Lodge within the Theosophical Society, headed by Christmas Humphreys. It did much to attract Western interest in this religion, which until then was relatively unknown. *See also* BAILEY, ALICE; FORTUNE, DION.

THOMAS, JOHN (1805-1871). Founder-leader of the Christadelphians (q.v.). Born in England, Thomas emigrated to

America in 1832, becoming a physician in Richmond, Virginia. He associated initially with the Campbellites, but had a number of disagreements with them, particularly on the subject of whether understanding of the faith should precede baptism. In 1844 he finally broke with them, establishing his own *ecclesia* (congregation), and his followers assumed the name Christadelphians in 1848. Thomas's book *Elpis Israel* (Hope of Israel) (1849) remains one of the movement's principal texts. Thomas returned to Great Britain on several occasions, preaching and eliciting conversions. The movement seeks to return to New Testament beliefs and practices, as set out in the Bible. He was succeeded by Robert Roberts, author of the Christadelphians' second principal text, *Christendom Astray.*

TKACH, JOSEPH W. (1927-1995). Second leader of the Worldwide Church of God (q.v.), in succession to founder Herbert W. Armstrong (q.v.), from 1986 to 1995. In response to constant criticism of the church by Christian evangelicals, Tkach led the church in a more mainstream direction, initiating a major doctrinal review in 1987 which resulted in a revised Statement of Beliefs. Under Tkach's leadership the movement affirmed the doctrine of the Trinity, abolished "triple tithing," and denied that sabbath observance and the keeping of Jewish festivals and dietary laws were means of salvation, which came from faith alone. Tkach denied that the Worldwide Church of God was the "remnant" mentioned in Old Testament prophecy. Still committed to biblical inerrancy, Tkach remained highly critical of the theory of evolution. His reforms led to a withdrawal of roughly a third of Armstrong's following, resulting in financial problems and a number of splinter organizations. Following his death he was succeeded by his son Joseph W. Tkach, Jr. *See also* CHURCH OF GOD INTERNATIONAL; GLOBAL CHURCH OF GOD; UNITED CHURCH OF GOD.

TORONTO BLESSING. An outpouring of the Spirit, experienced in the Airport Vineyard Church in Toronto in 1994.

The church belongs to the Vineyard Ministries International (q.v.) movement, headed by John Wimber. Members of the congregation experienced being "slain in the Spirit," which had various physical manifestations, including falling to the ground as if unconscious, uncontrollable laughter, involuntary muscle and limb spasms, and copious weeping. Less commonly, some recipients of the Blessing uttered prophecies, saw visions, received "pictures," and, in a few cases, reported angelic (q.v.) visitations. The Toronto Blessing was subsequently brought to other Christians, particularly those of charismatic (q.v.) and, particularly, Pentecostalist (q.v.) leanings, spreading through Canada, the United States, and Europe. Although the origins of the Blessing are attributed to Toronto, there is evidence of earlier similar manifestations within the Vineyard movement in Europe (especially Scandanavia), Argentina, the United States, Canada, and New Zealand. Although many charismatic Christians have welcomed the spiritual renewal which they believe accompanies the Toronto Blessing, other Christian evangelicals have reserved judgment, and some have even suggested that it could be the work of Satan rather than God.

TRANSCENDENTALISM. Sometimes regarded as the American counterpart of the European Romantic movement, Transcendentalism emerged in New England, largely from Puritan and Quaker backgrounds. Largely inspired by Ralph Waldo Emerson (q.v.) (1803-1882), it was a reaction against the rationalism of the Enlightenment. Emerson himself had been a Unitarian (q.v.) minister, but had left the movement as a result of his personal inability to accept the sacrament of communion. After visiting Europe and making the acquaintance of Samuel Taylor Coleridge, William Wordsworth, and Thomas Carlyle, Emerson returned to America in 1834 and founded the Transcendentalist Club two years later. Supporters included Frederick Henry Hedge, Margaret Fuller, George Ripley, Convers Francis, Theodore Parker, Bronson Alcott, James Clarke, and Orestes Brownson, and the movement deeply influenced Henry David Thoreau, Walt Whitman,

Nathaniel Hawthorne, Emily Dickinson, and Herman Melville.

The Transcendentalist movement was essentially monistic, emphasizing the essential unity of all things and the individual's oneness with nature and with God. Nature was the true teacher, not religious or academic authorities, and intuitive insight was regarded as superior to rational thought. Individuality and self-enlightenment were encouraged, and a high degree of importance was attached to inner experience as a source of revelation. Nature did not exist independently of the mind, but as a set of ideas within it. Somewhat eclectic in character, Transcendentalism drew from the teachings of Emanuel Swedenborg and Jakob Böhme, the neo-Platonists, and Indian and Chinese spiritual classics which had only recently become available in English.

The movement was largely against the trend of 18th-century Western thinking, and it had a profound effect on a number of disparate areas of intellectual thought, spirituality, and society. Transcendentalism's affirmation of the worth of the individual and the value of human nature contributed to the Abolitionist Movement in America, educational innovations, the development of feminism, and—much later—the rise of the New Age Movement (q.v.). It has been claimed that Transcendentalist ideas also had an effect on the British Labour Party, Mahatma Gandhi, and Martin Luther King, Jr. The Free Religions also drew on Transcendentalist ideas, and, notwithstanding Emerson's personal break with the Unitarian Church, Unitarians have frequently viewed Transcendentalism as an important corrective to the rationalism with which Unitarianism is often associated. *See also* AQUARIAN FOUNDATION.

TRANSCENDENTAL MEDITATION (TM). Devised by the Maharishi Mahesh Yogi (q.v.) (b. 1917?), TM is said to be a revival of an ancient technique taught in the Yoga Sutras of Patanjali, in an updated and modified form. Practitioners insist that it is not a religion, but a technique that is capable of improving not only its practitioners but also society and the world at large. The organization began in 1957 as the Spiritual Regeneration Movement in Madras, becoming the American Foundation for the Science of Creative Intelligence in the United States in the mid-1960s. The latter was specifically targeted at the worlds of business and education, with the International Meditation Society being aimed at the wider public, and the Students International Meditation Society (SIMS) established in 1965.

After an initiation ceremony in which the guru (q.v.) gives the student a mantra (q.v.), he or she meditates (q.v.) on the mantra for two 20-minute periods each day. The guru selects the mantra in accordance with the student's personality and needs: it is transmitted orally and should be kept secret. TM does not recommend the use of mantras that are found in textbooks on Hinduism and Buddhism (qq.v.), claiming that these are for the monastic life, whereas TM mantras are for the "householder" *(grihastha)*. TM cites numerous scientific studies which claim that the practice induces a drop in one's metabolic rate and an increase in the brain's alphawaves, thus inducing calmness. TM practitioners are said to have fewer accidents, less frequent hospitalizations, and fewer medical disorders and to achieve greater confidence, significant improvements in personal efficiency, and indeed self-realization. The practice is initially expensive, costing around $750 at the time of writing.

TM claims that, when the square root of 1 percent of an area's population practices TM, numerous social benefits accrue: reduction in crime, greater life expectancy, improved economic prosperity, and even better weather and increased land productivity. It is believed that, at a global level, TM could bring about world peace if practiced in sufficient numbers.

From 1976 onward TM developed the "siddhi program." This attracted controversy when the media showed the practitioners demonstrating "yogic flying." Alleged powers of levitation were only one aspect of the program, which is said to enable participants to develop psychic and other paranormal powers more generally. A further recent development in

TM was the formation of the Natural Law Party in 1992, which contested many elections in the United States and in Europe. The therapeutic aspects of TM have been further promoted by the development of Maharishi Ayur-Ved, a traditional Indian healing method. This method finds expression in the work and writings of Deepak Chopra, among others. Estimates of practitioners vary widely, ranging from 50,000 to 3,000,000 (1999). *See also* HUMAN POTENTIAL MOVEMENT; SCHOOL OF ECONOMIC SCIENCE.

TREVELYAN, SIR GEORGE (1906-1996). Author and lecturer, and founder of the Wrekin Trust. Trevelyan has been described as the "grandfather of the New Age in England." Born of agnostic parents, his interest in spirituality was kindled by a lecture he attended in 1942, which prompted him to study Anthroposophy (q.v.). After World War II he was appointed warden, and subsequently principal, of Attingham Park in Shropshire, a residential adult education center whose courses included alternative forms of spirituality. When Trevelyan retired in 1971 he founded the Wrekin Trust as a means of keeping his interests alive. The Wrekin Trust is a New Age (q.v.) group whose interests include transpersonal psychology, Anthroposophy, health and healing, astrology, and various other forms of spirituality. In 1982 Trevelyan's work for the Wrekin Trust earned him a Right Livelihood Award, sometimes referred to as "the Alternative Nobel Prize"—established by Jakob von Uexkull, author and former member of the European Parliament (the prize is presented annually at the Swedish Parliament, the day before the Nobel Prize). Trevelyan was instrumental in the development of the Soil Associaton, the Findhorn (q.v.) Trust, the Teilhard de Chardin Society, and the Essene (q.v.) Network. He authored several books: *A Vision of the Aquarian Age* (1977), *Operation Redemption* (1981), *Summons to a High Crusade* (1985), and *Exploration into God* (1991).

TRUNGPA, CHOGYAM. *A.k.a.: Shambhala; Trungpa Rinpoche* (1939-1987). Born in Tibet, Trungpa was identified as the 11th Trungpa *tulku* (an incarnate lama) in the Kargyupa tradition. He left Tibet in 1959, following the Chinese invasion, and came to England in 1963, where he became a student at St. Anthony's College, Oxford. In 1967 he established the Samye-Ling Monastery in Dumfriesshire, Scotland—the first Tibetan Buddhist monastery outside Tibet. A serious car accident in 1969 left Trungpa partially paralyzed, and the following year he disrobed, married, and departed for the United States. There he traveled, lectured, and established Vajradatu—an umbrella organization coordinating Tibetan studies. Trungpa also founded the Karme Choling ("Tail of the Tiger") Meditation Center and the Naropa Institute in Boulder, Colorado (1974). The Naropa Institute has offered undergraduate and postgraduate degrees since 1977.

Trungpa was a charismatic figure, but proved himself to be controversial on account of his meat-eating, alcohol consumption, and relationships with some of his female students. (It is not true, however, that he used drugs.) A prolific writer, Trungpa did much to make the complexities of Tibetan Buddhism (q.v.) intelligible to Westerners. His principal writings include his autobiographical *Born in Tibet* (1966), *Meditation in Action* (1969), and *Cutting through Spiritual Materialism* (1973).

TWITCHELL, PAUL (1909-1971). Founder of Eckankar (q.v.). Twitchell claimed to have learned the art of "soul travel"—a fundamental technique of the movement—at the age of three. His decisive experience was in 1944, when he claimed to have met Rebazar Tarzs, a former ECK master who was born in Tibet in 1461. This experience occurred on a spiritual plane, and Rebazar Tarzs passed on to Twitchell the "rod of power," thus making him the 971st Mahanta, or living ECK master of the Vairagi order. Twitchell did not found the Eckankar movement immediately, but sought out other spiritual groups. From 1950 to 1955 he belonged to Swami Premananda's Self-Revelation Church of Absolute Monism but was expelled. He then joined the Church of Scientology (q.v.), becoming one of its first "clears." He was also simultaneously associated with Ruhani Satsang (q.v.) (in the Sant Math tradition). It has sometimes been alleged that Twitchell's encounters with these movements have caused undue borrowing of ideas: in particular, David C. Lane's *The Making of a Spiritual Movement* (1983) accused Twitchell of plagiarism, particularly from the writings of Scientology. Eckankar's response to such charges is that all religions teach fragments of Eckankar, which is the root and indeed the totality of all religion.

Since his death, Twitchell is believed to be working at higher spiritual levels, aiding souls to make further progress toward Sugmad—the Ocean of Love and Mercy, the final supreme goal. He was succeeded by Darwin Gross (q.v.) and later by Harold Klemp (q.v.), the current living ECK master.

TWO BY TWOS. *A.k.a.: Blacksocks; Christian Fellowship; Cooneyites; Disciples of Jesus; Friends; Go Preachers; People on the Way; Tramp Preachers.* Founded in Ireland by William Irvine (1863-1947), the movement is so called on account of its sending out of preachers in twos, in accordance with the practice described in Mark 6:7. The pejorative name "Cooneyites" relates to preacher Edward Cooney, who became coleader with Irvine in 1901, but shortly afterward broke away to form his own movement in the United States, now virtually defunct. From 1903 onward Irvine's followers were asked to renounce their personal belongings and former life and to subject themselves to poverty, chastity, and obedience. Their missionary work enabled the movement to spread worldwide, reaching Australasia, South Africa, South America, China, and the rest of Europe.

Two by Twos use the Bible as their sole source of authority and have developed no statement of belief apart from Scriptures. They celebrate the Lord's Supper (communion) weekly and practice believer's baptism, rebaptizing new members. Their lifestyle includes modesty of appearance, avoidance of worldly activities such as watching television, and usually pacifism. Organizationally, the movement works in "fields" with an overseer (also called "senior servant" or "elder brother"), with house churches that have between 10 and 20 members, overseen by a "bishop."

Irvine predicted that the world would end in 1914. In the final years of his lifetime the movement split, and Irvine ended his days in Jerusalem. Membership statistics are uncertain: estimates for U.S. membership (probably a third of the world membership) range from 10,000 to 100,000 (1998).

-U-

UFO-RELIGIONS. Collective name for new religious movements have arisen from the phenomenon of unidentified flying objects (UFOs). UFOs first came to public attention in 1947, largely as a result of an alleged sighting by American pilot Kenneth Arnold and the Roswell incident in New Mexico in the same year, when an alien spacecraft was said to have crashed, from which five bodies of extraterrestrials were supposedly recovered, one still alive.

Of the UFO-religions, the most prominent are the Aetherius Society, the Raëlian Church, Unarius, and Heaven's Gate (qq.v.). Erich von Daniken's writings suggested that belief in God arose as a result of extraterrestrials who had visited the planet several millennia previously. This notion is endorsed by the Raëlians, who attribute the earth's origins to inhabitants of a planet almost one light year distant from the earth. Some UFO-religions, such as the Raëlian Church and Heaven's Gate, have superimposed belief in extraterrestrials with detailed exegesis of Judeo-Christian scriptures.

The psychologist Carl G. Jung suggested that "flying saucers" were examples of modern myths, since tales of their existence seem to rely on rumors that lack firm evidence in objective reality. He contended that, whether or not they are "real," belief in them is based on the psychic projections of individuals. Descriptions of them make use of "archetypal symbols": one popular form of UFO is round, and the circle signifies eternity. It is therefore unsurprising that these groups have linked UFO sightings with religious belief. *See also* CHEN TAO; SEMJASE SILVER STAR CENTER; SOLAR LIGHT RETREAT; UNIVERSE SOCIETY CHURCH.

UMBANDA. A Brazilian spiritist (q.v.) religion that began in 1904, becoming more formally established in the 1920s. The possible derivation of the name is from the Sanskrit *aum ghanda* (divine principle), and the movement draws on Hindu and Buddhist (qq.v.) ideas, combined with African religion, Roman Catholicism, and Native American religion (q.v.). It is essentially spiritist, with spirits acting as intermediaries between humans and the *oshiras* (gods), who can be called upon for protection. There is a belief in reincarnation (q.v.): spirits can assume physical forms by subsequent birth in relation to their obedience to the oshiras. Healing is a dominant concern, again effected through contact with the ancestral spirits. The movement has 200,000 adherents.

UNAMENDED CHRISTADELPHIANS. A branch of Christadelphianism (q.v.) that refused in 1898 to accept the amended text of the Christadelphian statement of faith. The controversy related to "resurrectional responsibility"—the issue of who would be called upon to account for their lives at the final judgment day. The amendment affirmed that while both classes—those who would gain God's approbation and those who did not—would be resurrected, there would be some who would not be raised for judgment at all. This category would consist of those whom God had not chosen, and who would therefore not be accountable for their deeds but would continue to sleep undisturbed. Those who did not gain God's approval would be subjected to some after-death punishment, but not eternal torment, and would revert back to sleep since their souls and bodies would remain mortal. The Unamended Christadelphians insisted that all classes would stand judgment and withdrew from the movement. The Amended Christadelphians form the vast majority within the movement, and Unamended Christadelphians are now rarely found outside North America.

UNARIUS—SCIENCE OF LIFE. *A.k.a.: Unarius Educational Foundation.* A UFO-religion (q.v.), founded in 1954 in El Cajon, California, by Ernest L. Norman (d. 1971). Unarius is an acronym for Universal Articulate Interdimensional Understanding of Science. Norman professedly started his mission on Lemuria and Atlantis, claiming to have been in previous incarnations the Archangel Raphael who was supposedly incarnated as Jesus of Nazareth, Pharaoh Akhenaton (Amenhotep), and Anaxagoras. Norman claimed to have contact with "Space Brothers" from Venus, Mars, Hermes, Eros, Orion, and Muse, from whom he channeled (q.v.) several books, principally on spiritual growth and healing, which is effected by "ray-booms"—light beams from other planets. After his death, his wife Ruth (d. 1993) took over the leadership and apparently negotiated the earth's joining of an Intergalactic Confederation on 14 September 1973. It is believed that in 2001, 1,001 space scientists will arrive from Planet Myton (in the Pleiades) to assist humankind. The organization is currently led by Charles L. Spiegel and consists largely of correspondence courses, mainly on the psychology of consciousness and self-mastery.

UNIFICATION CHURCH (UC). Founded in 1954 by Sun Myung Moon (q.v.) in Seoul, South Korea, as the Holy Spirit Association for the Unification of World Christianity (HSA-UWC), this church's members acquired the nickname "Moonies," by which they are popularly known. In 1997 the organization officially changed its name to the Family Federation for World Peace and Unification (FFWPU) (q.v.). When its missionaries came to Europe and the United States in the late 1960s and early 1970s, the organization came to prefer the name Unification Church. The HSA-UWC combined elements of Protestant Christianity (q.v.) with Korea's folk shamanism (q.v.), and both elements continue to prevail.

In the 1970s and 1980s members engaged in diligent evangelization, and the UC's principal text, *Divine Principle* (q.v.), was expounded systematically at two-day, seven-day, and 21-day seminars. After joining, members were encouraged to participate in the Blessing Ceremony (called "mass weddings" by the media). There are now three categories of member: full-time missionaries, associate members, and home members. Associate members belong to the church, but frequently combine their allegiance with full-time secular employment or raising a family, while home members are those outside the UC who support common values. As the 1990s progressed, the UC taught that membership was of secondary importance, emphasizing the Blessing as the means of salvation, since only blessed couples will enter the Kingdom of Heaven. The Blessing can now be offered to nonmembers, who are not required to participate in the large ceremony, but merely sign a brief declaration of commitment to family values.

Worship in the Unification Church follows the Free Church tradition in the West, consisting of biblical readings, prayers, and hymns (Unificationists also include their own "holy songs"). The traditional Christian festivals are observed, on which are superimposed the UC's own festivals: Parents' Day, Children's Day, the Day of All Things, and God's Day, as well as a number of minor festivals. The "Pledge" ceremony is performed daily in the early morning at Family Federation centers: this consists of affirming one's allegiance to the Rev. and Mrs. Moon.

The UC has sponsored a large number of projects, ostensibly aimed at unifying humanity's different religions and cultures. Two major umbrella organizations, the International Cultural Foundation (ICF) and the International Religious Foundation (IRF), envelop a cluster of organizations: the ICF supported a number of "ICUS" (International Conference for the Unity of the Sciences) conferences and the Professors' World Peace Academy (PWPA), among other ventures. The IRF included New ERA (New Ecumenical Research Association), the Council for the World's Religions, and the Assembly of the World's Religions, all of which brought together clergy, academics involved in the study of religion, and at times politicians and diplomats. A recent economic crisis in Korea has had a harmful effect on Moon's investments, and many of activities of these organizations have now ceased. See also CARP; CAUSA; CHARISMATIC LEADERSHIP; HEAVENLY DECEPTION; KUNDIONA, CLEOPUS; MILLENNIALISM.

UNITARIAN UNIVERSALISM (UUism). The Unitarian Universalist Association (UUA) was formed in 1961, as a result of a merger between Unitarians and Universalists in the United States and Canada. (In Canada, the merged denominations are simply called Unitarians.) Originally Unitarianism taught the oneness of God, as opposed to doctrines of the Trinity and the deity of Christ, while Universalists affirmed the salvation of all humanity, with none consigned to eternal punishment. Unitarian Universalists (UUs) now affirm the freedom of religion and inquiry, imposing no credal demands as conditions of membership. Some congregations emphasize their Christian roots, while others are influenced by other world religions, by humanism, or by "earth-centered spirituality." There are some 600,000 adult members in the United States and Canada. UUs would no doubt deny being a new religious movement, since Unitarianism was brought to America by Joseph Priestley in 1794 and Universalism was introduced by John Murray in 1779; the 1961 union has not heralded any abrupt changes in the member congregations. Notwithstanding its long history, Unitarianism still features in anticult literature, particularly of the Christian evangelical variety.

UNITED CHURCH OF GOD. Founded in 1995 as a breakaway group from the Worldwide Church of God (q.v.), the United Church of God aims to restore the teachings of Herbert W. Armstrong (q.v.), founder and first leader of the Worldwide Church of God, in the wake of the major doctrinal changes initiated by his successor. The movement is an association of linked congregations, numbering 20,000 members in all, in the Americas, Europe, South Africa, and Australia.

UNITED NATIVE AFRICAN CHURCH. The first African Independent Church (q.v.), founded in 1891 in Lagos by W. E. Cole. It was the first of a number of organizations seeking a distinctively African expression of Christianity (q.v.), regarding the faith of the white Christian missionaries as not being wholly suited to black Africans. The church retains an Anglican liturgy, but uses the Yoruba language. It permits polygamy, in common with indigenous African practice. Baptism is by total immersion, not affusion, but is administered to infants as well as adults.

UNITY SCHOOL OF CHRISTIANITY. An organization in the New Thought (q.v.) tradition, founded by Charles Fillmore (q.v.) (1854-1948) and Myrtle Fillmore (1845-1931). After studying briefly under Emma Curtis Hopkins, the Fillmores founded Unity in 1891. It was incorporated in 1903 as the Unity School of Practical Christianity, becoming the Unity School of Christianity in 1914.

The term *Unity* is intended to imply an openness to ideas from all religions. No specific beliefs are demanded of members, although in practice the Unity School's tenets tend to be Christian-centered. It affirms the Jewish-Christian Scriptures, but claims that they are to be interpreted "metaphysically." Particular emphasis is given to healing: followers are encouraged to use "affirmations" as well as prayer; other misfortunes, such as poverty, are also addressed by such methods. "Absent healing" is effected by groups of members meeting together to attend to voluminous prayer requests that are sent to the school: there are currently 2.5 million each year. A 24-hour-a-day prayer vigil is maintained at the school's headquarters in Unity Village. The final goal is the complete purification of the body from earthly imperfections; this, according to Charles Fillmore, is only achievable through a series of reincarnations (q.v.).

Being a school rather than a church, its activities focus on training and on practice, rather than on worship and ritual. The school offers weekend courses, local study classes, prayer groups, and a postal library containing tapes as well as books. It is an umbrella organization, encompassing Silent Unity (one of two original components of the 1914 organization, the second being the Unity Tract Society), the Unity School for Religious Studies, the Village Chapel, and the school's publishing wing. Regular publications include *Unity* and *Daily Word,* which is now translated into 13 languages and distributed in 50 countries. After Charles Fillmore's death, the chain of succession passed to his offspring; the current leader is Connie Fillmore Bazzy, the Fillmores' great-granddaughter.

UNIVERSAL CHURCH OF THE MASTER (UCM). A spiritualist (q.v.) organization in the United States founded by the Rev. B. J. Fitzgerald (d. 1966) in 1908 and incorporated in 1918. Teachings are based on Fitzgerald's *A New Text of Spiritual Philosophy and Religion* and Levi Dowling's *The Aquarian Gospel of Jesus the Christ;* they are a blend of liberal Christianity and other world religious traditions. In 1995 there were 9,837 members, including 850 ministers.

UNIVERSAL LIFE (UNIVERSELLES LEBEN). Founded in 1975 by Gabrielle Wittek (b. 1931) and incorporated in 1984. From 1970 Wittek claimed to have received visions and heard voices from God, Jesus, and angels (q.v.). Universal Life, of which she is the "teaching prophetess," promotes meditation (q.v.) and healing, emphasizing holistic medicine. The Inner Spirit-of-Christ Churches, with branches in the United States, Italy, Spain, Israel, South Africa, and Australia, stem from Wittek's organization.

UNIVERSAL LIFE CHURCH. Founded in 1962 by Kirby J. Hensley (b. 1911) in Modesto, California, this organization provides free ordination by mail order or on the Internet to anyone who seeks it. The church has no official doctrines, although Hensley has his own somewhat eclectic teachings, blending Eastern ideas of karma with universalist Christianity (he was a self-taught Baptist minister). Following media publicity in the late 1960s, Hensley was invited to address college classes, where he conducted mass ordinations. Of six million ordinands in 1977, it is estimated that some 25,000 formed their own congregations. The church also offers a Doctor of Divinity degree for $20. Following a prohibition by the State of California on awarding unaccredited degrees, the church's Department of Education moved to Phoenix, Arizona. Hensley formed the People's Peace Prosperity Party and has run for the governorship of California and the U.S. Presidency. Membership estimates vary from five million to 18 million (1998), although the Universal Life Church states that "every conscious being is a member." *See also* CYBER-CHURCHES

UNIVERSAL LIFE CHURCH (BRYTHONIC). A "meso-Pagan" group, founded in Portland, Oregon, in 1985 by David Brock, who is its "magister" and high priest. The church combines ideas from Zoroastrianism, Kabbalism (q.v.), and wicca (q.v.) (professedly in Celtic and pre-Celtic varieties). Its members are white and antihomosexual. *See also* PAGANISM.

UNIVERSAL SUFISM. The name sometimes used by academics and others to designate a form of Sufism (q.v.) that lies outside the Islamic (q.v.) tradition, and which is often claimed to transcend Islamic Sufism, incorporating elements from a variety of religious traditions such as Buddhism, Hinduism, Christianity (qq.v.), Hermeticism, and occasionally Jewish Kabbalism (q.v.). Like Islamic Sufism, Universal Sufism emphasizes the mystical path, relying on techniques such as *dhikr* (recitation of God's names) and *sama* (meditation) in order to attain oneness with God. Much use is made of music and dance, following the Sufi tradition of whirling dervishes. Since mystical union with God is a state that transcends all religions, Universal Sufism has done much to encourage interfaith worship, claiming to recognize a common core in all religions. This form of Sufism has grown steadily in the United States, Canada, and Europe during the 20th century, but is by no means confined to the West. Its principal Western exponents have been Hazrat Inayat Khan (1882-1927) and Idries Shah (1924-1996) (qq.v.).

UNIVERSE SOCIETY CHURCH (UNISOC). A UFO-religion (q.v.), founded in 1951 by Hal Wilcox (b. 1932) as the Institute of Parapsychology (a.k.a. Universe Society). After having numerous psychic experiences as a child, Wilcox and some friends learned of the Great White Brotherhood (q.v.) and claimed to have gained contact with The Ancient Brotherhood of Fhasz (TABOF), an extraterrestrial who is said to inhabit the planet Narvon in Altair. Wilcox claims to channel (q.v.) his teachings, which are somewhat cryptic and expressed in obscure symbolism. Fhasz teaches that the universe is governed by two forces: light *(hal)* and the creative force *(shel)*. Shel enables contacts with UFOs—of which there have been many, particularly during the period 1951-1961—which are spacecraft carrying extraterrestrials. Fhasz has instructed Wilcox's follower to construct a temple to receive Anahsz and "one at his right hand"—an "opposite number" or mirror image of himself. Wilcox claims to have received other "past covenants" with extraterrestrials, one of which involved the then-new Japanese religion Tenrikyo (q.v.) in 1838. In 1988 there was only one center of the church, in Hollywood, California.

URANTIA. *The Urantia Book* is a "channeled" (q.v.) collection of writings, purportedly of composite celestial authorship and transmitted through an unnamed human channel between 1934 and 1935. It was authorized by the Ancients of Days, a council of beings who administer Orvonton, which is "one of seven evolutionary superuniverses of time and space." The collected volume, which consists of 196 papers and runs to 2,097 pages, was first published in 1955 by the Urantia Foundation, Chicago. The book relates a history of the universe, going back some 987 billion years, and of the Earth's (Urantia's) position in it. According to *The Urantia Book,* each inhabited planet develops a Garden of Eden, into which a Material Son and a Material Daughter are placed to be "uplifters." In time a Paradise Son appears to complete the evolutionary process, eliminating sickness, war, and moral decadence.

In *Urantia* Andon and Fonta are the primal human beings, arriving more than nine million years before Adam and Eve. During the intervening period Lucifer and Satan organize a rebellion, and the Planetary Prince Caligastia (the devil) is deposed. Adam and Eve attempt to improve humanity, but are constantly opposed by Lucifer, Satan, and Caligastia. In time Jesus arrives, and the book details the life of Jesus, in many respects paralleling the New Testament account, but with additional details about Jesus' childhood and travels. The book is divided into four principal sections: cosmology; an account of the local galaxy and its evolution toward perfection; the origin and history of Urantia; and the life of Jesus.

The Urantia Foundation (founded in 1955) aims to disseminate the book (now via the Internet as well as in traditional form) and to encourage the formation of study groups. The Urantia Brotherhood became an independent organization in 1989, but was prohibited from using the name "Urantia" or its associated symbols, and thus became the Fifth Epochal Fellowship in 1989 (*The Urantia Book* is the revelation of the Fifth Epoch). The International Urantia Association disseminates Urantia material at an international level, by means of literature. There are 368 Fellowships of Urantia Book readers in 10 countries.

-V-

VAILALA MADNESS. One of the cargo cults (q.v.), arising in the Gulf area of Papua New Guinea. It originated in 1919 when a prophet, Evara, went into trance states and predicted the arrival of a steamer bearing European goods, accompanied by the return of ancestral spirits. The movement was anti-white, but simultaneously claimed that the ways of traditional Pacific culture were inadequate. Preparation for the coming new age included moral reform (asceticism, Sunday observance, physical cleanliness, and simplicity of appearance), the erection of shrines and flagpoles, feasts for ancestors, and various rituals, including dances. By 1931 the movement had died out.

VAMPIRE CULTS. At its height in the 18th century, chiefly in Eastern Europe and in Slavonic and Baltic countries, vampirism entailed the belief in a body of "undead" people who haunted their victims and imbibed their blood. The undead were often thought to be suicide victims, or those who had experienced violent death, and they were believed to possess the characteristics of hating light, garlic, iron, running water, and—most especially—the sign of the cross. The belief that they drank blood may be connected with the idea of imbibing the life force of another individual through his or her blood, an idea that continues to be manifested in the Christian eucharist. Interest in vampirism had a revival in the late 19th and early 20th centuries with the appearance of *Dracula* (1897) by novelist Bram Stoker (1847-1912), whose principal character was probably based on Vlad the Impaler. In more recent times it has been alleged, principally by Christian evangelicals, that there has been a revival of vampire cults, evidenced by television series on vampires, video games, and comics: evangelicals view these as unwarranted and dangerous dabbling in the occult. Whatever the justification of such claims, there is no evidence that alleged "vampire cults" involve specifically religious obligations or constitute an organized movement that remotely approaches a religion. *See also* KARDEC, ALLAN; SATANISM.

VEDANTA SOCIETY. The only Hindu (q.v.) organization to become established in the West before 1900, derived from the teachings of Ramakrishna and Vivekananda (qq.v.). The teachings of Vedanta are deemed to be of greater importance that the gurus (q.v.) who propound them, and they are based on the Upanishads, the Bhagavad Gita, and Patanjali's Yoga Sutras. The first Western Vedanta organization was the Vedanta Society of New York (founded in 1896), followed by branches in San Francisco and Boston. Western followers of Vedanta have included Aldous Huxley (1894-1963), Gerald Heard (1889-1971), and Christopher Isherwood (1904-1986). In 1998 there were 13 Vedanta Societies and 125 centers run by the Ramakrishna Order.

VINEYARD MINISTRIES INTERNATIONAL. Founded by John Wimber in California, this organization originated from a coalition of Pentecostalist (q.v.) churches in the Los Angeles area in the 1970s. The Vineyard Christian Fellowship was developed by Kenn Gullikson in 1974, and Wimber's own group began as a Bible study group in Yorba Linda, California, and in 1982 assumed the name of the Vineyard Christian Fellowship of Yorba Linda. After experiencing remarkable growth in the 1980s (Wimber attracted 4,000 each Sunday, reaching 6,000 in 1992), the Association of Vineyard Churches was formed in 1986, and Gullikson's and Wimber's churches merged to form Vineyard Ministries International. Wimber emphasizes church growth and evangelism, the Christian life, and divine healing. Estimates of membership vary from 50,000 to 100,000, with between 200 and 315 congregations in 1999, spanning the United States, Canada, Mexico, South America, Europe, and South Africa. *See also* FIRE BAPTISM.

VIPASSANA. A form of Theravada Buddhist meditation (qq.v.), vipassana meditation contrasts with samatha meditation. The latter calms the mind, whereas vipassana ("insight meditation") aims at the cultivation of *prajna* (wisdom), leading to enlightenment. The vipassana practitioner meditates on the Buddhists' three "marks of existence"—*anatta* (no self), *anicca* (impermanence), and *dukkha* (unsatisfactoriness)—which characterize all constitutents of the universe.

Although vipassana is an ancient form of Buddhist meditation, reputedly taught by Gautama the Buddha himself, the anti-cult movement (q.v.) has frequently regarded vipassana as a cult, (q.v.) possibly on account of certain financial irregularities and sexual scandals that occurred in a few vipassana organizations during the 1980s.

Although the practice is ancient, it virtually died out by the 14th century, since a somewhat conservative Buddhist Sangha in Ceylon (modern Sri Lanka), Burma, and Thailand were more concerned with following the monastic precepts than in meditation. This meant that the laity, who had previously been permitted to practice vipassana, were deprived of it.

Vipassana experienced a revival starting in the 1950s. It was initially rediscovered in 1914 by the Ven. Ledi Sayadaw (1856-1923), who wrote a treatise on vipassana "for the benefit of European Buddhists." This was written in Burmese, however, and made little impact. Other Buddhist monks who helped to revive the practice in Burma and Thailand included U Narada (1868-1955) and U Kyaw Din (1878-1952). They were responsible for a second generation of vipassana teachers, most notably U Ba Kin (1899-1971), who in turn taught S. N. Goenka (a well-known teacher of Western pupils) and Maharsi Sayadaw (1904-1982). Sayadaw taught Jack Kornfield, Joseph Goldstein, and Sharon Salzburg, who jointly founded the Insight Meditation Society (q.v.) in Barre, Massachusetts, in 1976. Kornfield also studied under Ajahn Chah (1918-1992), whose pupil the Ven. Sumedo—an American— now heads the English Sangha Trust, in which vipassana is an important meditative practice. Another prominent vipassana center is the Dhiravamsa Foundation (formerly the Vipassana Fellowship of America).

The effects of the Western uptake of vipassana have included its practice by a significantly high proportion of women. A number of vipassana teachers are lay practitioners, in contrast with the traditional convention whereby the

Sangha taught Buddhist meditation. A further innovation is the commitment of vipassana practice to writing: the more-ancient tradition was that of oral teaching. There are 51 vipassana centers worldwide.

VIVEKANANDA, SWAMI (1863-1902). The first Hindu (q.v.) swami to bring Vedanta to the West. Born Narendranath Datta in Calcutta in 1863, Vivekananda initially pursued his spiritual quest as a follower of Brahmo Samaj. He met Ramakrishna (q.v.) in 1881 and almost instantly abandoned his aspirations of a law career in order to pursue life as a sannyasin (q.v.). Vivekananda was invited to speak at the World's Parliament of Religions at Chicago in 1893, where his speech aroused considerable comment. Vivekananda introduced his audience to Vedanta and proclaimed that all spiritual paths led to the same goal. This led to the inception of the Ramakrishna movement outside the Indian subcontinent.

In 1897 Vivekananda returned to India, where, together with a number of Ramakrishna's disciples, he founded the Ramakrishna Mission. From 1899 to 1900 Vivekananda traveled and taught in the United States and Europe, addressing the Paris Congress of Religions in 1900. Vivekananda's teachings were based on the Vedas and Upanishads, affirming *brahman* as the one primordial reality, and its identity with *atman* (the soul). Vivekananda codified Ramakrishna's spiritual practices, teaching a combination of karma, jnana, raja (q.v.) and bhakti yogas (q.v.).

Margaret E. Noble (1867-1911), also known as Nivedita, joined the movement and played a major role in editing and disseminating Vivekananda's writings, including his biography, as well as initiating much charitable work.

-W-

WACO. Waco, Texas, was the site of the New Mount Carmel Center, home of the Branch Davidians (q.v.), a Seventh-day

Adventist (q.v.) group led by David Koresh (q.v.) (Vernon Howell). The old Mount Carmel Center was purchased by Victor T. Houteff (1885-1955), who led an Adventist group known as the Shepherd's Rod (also known as the Rod [q.v.]). The old Mount Carmel site was sold, and a new site of some 400 acres was purchased. Florence Houteff progressively sold off land from this site, until only 77 acres remained, forming the site on which Koresh's Waco community was established.

Adventists of different kinds arrived at Mount Carmel in 1959 to witness the final end of the world, which of course did not occur. The community had become bankrupt, and Ben Roden, a former bricklayer who claimed to be the returned Elijah, collected sufficient money, buying the compound to found the Branch Davidians. After Roden's death in 1978, the group was led by his widow Lois, whose leadership was challenged by her son George. Howell, who had recently arrived at Waco, also staked a claim to be leader, but was ordered off the territory by George Roden. Returning in 1988, however, Howell (later David Koresh) established himself as leader of the Branch Davidians. He and 92 other members were burned to death in the compound in 1993, following a confrontation with the FBI.

WATCHTOWER BIBLE AND TRACT SOCIETY. Originally established by Charles Taze Russell (q.v.) (1852-1916) as Zion's Watch Tower Tract Society in 1881, this organization became known as the Watchtower Bible and Tract Society in 1884, after becoming legally chartered in Pennsylvania. It was the precursor of the Jehovah's Witnesses (q.v.), whose publishing house it remains. From 1909 its headquarters have been based in Brooklyn, New York. It is best known to the public for its monthly magazine *The Watchtower,* which is regularly studied, in conjunction with the Bible, at Jehovah's Witnesses' Kingdom Halls. The magazine *Awake!,* also published monthly, deals with matters of topical interest as well as biblical interpretation.

At its inception the Watchtower Society produced and disseminated Russell's writings and subsequently J. F. Rutherford's (q.v.). Under the leadership of Nathan H. Knorr (1905-1977), however, who took office in 1942, production widened substantially, and the society has since produced numerous books and booklets on a variety of religious themes, defining the Jehovah's Witnesses' stance on them. Since 1942 authorship has generally been anonymous, on the ground that only God should be given credit for religious truth, not individual human authors. The board of directors is drawn from the Governing Body of the Jehovah's Witnesses, thus ensuring that all publications reflect the official and agreed teachings of the Watchtower organization.

WATTS, ALAN (1915-1973). Writer and exponent of Zen Buddhism (qq.v.). Watts emigrated from Great Britain to the United States in 1938 and served as an Anglican priest from 1944 to 1950. Although Watts denied being a Zen Buddhist, he was deeply influenced by the writings of D. T. Suzuki and did much to popularize Zen and—to a lesser degree—Taoism for a Western audience. A prolific writer, he wrote extensively on Buddhism's relationship with the arts and with psychotherapy. Having an interest in Eastern as well as Western psychology, much of his writing owes a debt to Carl Jung. Watts distinguished between "Square Zen" and "Beat Zen," the latter being the interpretation of Zen taken up by the Californian counterculture and encapsulated in writings such as Jack Kerouac's *The Dharma Bums*. Although critical of the counterculture's uptake of Zen, Watts was influenced by the psychedelic revolution of the 1960s, recommending the use of drugs as a means of attaining altered states of consciousness. Watts was a visiting lecturer in various U.S. universities and toward the end of his life became dean of the American Academy of Asian Studies. Among his many writings, *The Way of Zen* (1957) did much to popularize Zen. *See also* AVATARA ADI DA.

WAY INTERNATIONAL, THE. Founded in 1942 as Vesper Chimes by Victor Paul Wierwille (1916-1985), this organization began as a radio ministry aimed at college students, incorporating as the Chimes Hour Youth Caravan in 1947. The name was changed to The Way in 1955 and subsequently to The Way International in 1974.

Wierwille was ordained as a pastor in the Evangelical and Reformed Church at Paine, Ohio, after obtaining a Master of Theology degree. In 1951 he began to speak in tongues (q.v.), followed by a claimed ability to faith-heal. The Way emphasizes the gifts of the Spirit, espousing a form of ultradispensationalism. Wierwille regarded history as falling into nine periods of divine "administration," placing humanity in a period of Grace, pending the final personal reign of Christ which awaits his Second Coming. The period of Grace is not completely coextensive with the New Testament era: the founding of the Church did not occur until Pentecost, leaving a brief timespan between Jesus' birth and the Church's inception—a period that was characterized by water baptism rather than the baptism of the Spirit and its resultant "gifts." The Way affirms the inerrancy of Scripture; however, while it affirms Jesus' status as Son of God and savior, it denies his divinity—a position which was set out in Wierwille's book *Jesus Christ Is Not God* (1975). The Holy Spirit is regarded not as a person, but as divine power. Wierwille is also noteworthy for his belief that the New Testament was originally written in Aramaic, the language Jesus spoke—a view derived from George M. Lamsa, who compiled *The Holy Bible from Ancient Eastern Manuscripts* and whom Wierwille had personally met.

Inquirers are introduced to the Way through the Power for Abundant Living courses, which Wierwille started in 1953. Members meet in home fellowships, since the Way does not own premises dedicated to worship. During the 1970s the organization achieved rapid expansion as a result of the Jesus People movement (q.v.), and in 1971 the Way hosted a Rock of Ages Festival aimed at the youth culture. Following Wierwille's death, the movement is now led by L. Craig Martin-dale (b. 1948). Its headquarters remain in New Knoxville, Ohio, and its message continues to be propagated through *The Way Magazine* (first published in 1954). Membership estimates vary widely, ranging from 10,000 to 100,000 (1998).

WEST, LOUIS JOLYON (1924-1999). Formerly chief of psychiatry at the University of California, Los Angeles, and medical director of the Neuro-Psychiatric Institute, "Jolly" West (as he was commonly known) was a member of the American Family Foundation's Advisory Board. He published and lectured extensively on "destructive cults," subscribing to the brainwashing (q.v.) theory. West propounded a "medical model" of "cults" (q.v.) claiming that they were like malignant cancers among healthy cells and hence had to be eradicated. West also proved controversial on account of a number of "mind control" experiments carried out in the 1950s. Subsequent experiments in the 1970s at Oklahoma University are said to have been sponsored by the Central Intelligence Agency.

WESTERN BUDDHIST ORDER, FRIENDS OF THE (FWBO). Founded in Great Britain in 1967 by the Ven. Sanghrakshita (b. 1925 as Dennis Lingwood), the FWBO endeavors to be a practical expression of Buddhism (q.v.), appropriate for Westerners, while drawing on the traditions of the Theravada, Mahayana, and Vajrayana. Essentially a lay movement, it emphasizes right livelihood rather than the monastic life and was innovative in establishing a number of small business ventures to finance itself. A supporter is known as *mitra* (friend), while one who seeks a higher degree of commitment can become a *dharmachari* or *dharmacharini* (the male and female terms, respectively). Critical of the previous generation of Western Buddhists, whom they allege treated Buddhism as an intellectual hobby, importance is attached to meditation (q.v.), the principal forms being the Mindfulness of Breathing and the *metta bhavana* (awareness of compassion). Vegetarianism and avoidance of alcohol are also expected. Many of the *dharmacharis* and *dhar-macharinis* live in single-sex communities, where heterosexual relationships are disallowed. There are over 1,500 members worldwide, 459 of whom were reported in 1999 as *dharmachari(ni)s*.

WHITE, ELLEN G. (1827-1915). Born as Ellen Gould Harmon in Gorham, Maine, Ellen G. White was one of the founder-leaders of Seventh-day Adventism (q.v.). When William Miller (q.v.) lectured in Portland, Maine, from 1840 until 1842 the Harmon family came to accept his teachings about the endtimes and were expelled from their Methodist congregation as a consequence.

Following the Great Disappointment of 1844, when Miller's predictions were unrealized, Ellen Harmon began to receive visions. Her decisive vision was of Jesus entering the Holy of Holies, revealing the sacred Ark and the Ten Commandments, the fourth of which (the one requiring sabbath observance) was surrounded by a halo. This vision confirmed the teachings of Hiram Edson and Joseph Bates, two other early pioneers of Adventism (Edson had taught that the "cleansing of the sanctuary," referred to in Daniel—*pace* William Miller—signified the beginning of Christ's heavenly, not earthly, rule; Bates had insisted that the seventh day was the appropriate day for rest and worship). In 1846 Harmon married James White, an Adventist preacher.

White wrote prolifically on a variety of subjects: biblical exegesis, doctrine, salvation, temperance, family and social life, and church organization. She progressively attracted a following, rivaling the Millerites, who were fatally damaged by the Great Disappointment. The Seventh-day Adventists attach particular importance to White, regarding her as a prophet and viewing prophecy as one of the gifts of the Spirit and a mark of the true "remnant church" on earth.

WHITE EAGLE LODGE. A Spiritualist (q.v.) organization, originating from medium Grace Cooke (q.v.) (1892-1979). Founded in 1936 as the White Eagle Brotherhood, its name was changed to the White Eagle Lodge in 1945, with new headquarters at New Lands, Liss, in Hampshire, England. Cooke claimed to contact a "Red Indian" by the name of White Eagle in the spirit world, who offered teachings, guidance, and healing. White Eagle taught gentleness, and harmony with the laws of life. His five "cosmic laws" included reincarnation (q.v.); the law of "cause and effect" whereby one ultimately reaped the fruits of one's actions; all events in life as constant sets of opportunities; correspondence between the physical and spirit worlds ("as above, so below"); and a law of "equilibrium" (entailing that no state, such as joy or sorrow, can continue indefinitely, but will eventually be pulled back toward its opposite). The body is one's outer garment, with the soul as the true self, or "Christ spirit." Sickness, White Eagle teaches, is caused by imbalance or disharmony. Healing focuses divine power on the sick soul and is accomplished either by "contact," where healers lay on hands, or by "absent healing," in which a group of six healers gathers to mediate healing at a distance. A third kind of healing is "lone healing," where some 36 healers focus simultaneously on an absent sick person.

There are three categories of membership. After being an ordinary member for at least a year, one may progress to the status of Outer Brother. A further initiation leads to becoming an Inner Brother, capable of channeling White Eagle himself, as well as a Star Brotherhood. Followers of White Eagle aim at the "Christing" of the self, the healing of nations, and healing the "soul of the world."

WINTI. *A.k.a.: Alfodré.* An African diaspora religion, practiced by the Creole in Surinam and also by emigrants to the Netherlands. It is syncretistic, combining elements of African religion with Christianity. Central to its worldview are the *winti* (spirits) and ancestral spirits, who must be placated in order to avoid misfortune and sickness. This is effected by mediums who enter a state of spirit possession. *See also* CANDOMBLÉ; MACUMBA; SANTERIA; UMBANDA.

WICCA. The term relating to the Old English *wiccecraeft* (witchcraft), but generally preferred by its practitioners, on account of the negative connotations associated with "witchcraft." Historically the witch was a wise woman who offered counsel in matters relating to health and love. Witchcraft incurred persecution by the Christian Church, where it was often wrongly assumed that witches had pacts with the devil, formally renounced Christ, or acted as mediums. Various official Church documents outlawed the witches' practices, the best known of which is *Malleus Maleficarum* (1486), formulated by the Inquisitors Kraemer and Sprengler. Margaret Murray's *The Witch-Cult in Modern Europe* (1921) was the first academic study to question the prevalent view that witches were devil worshippers, and Murray argued that witchcraft belonged to Europe's pre-Christian religious heritage. This latter claim, however, no longer finds acceptance among scholars.

Witchcraft experienced a revival in Great Britain in the 1950s, and in the United States a decade later. Much of the revival of witchcraft owes its existence to Gerald Gardner (q.v.) (1884-1964), the fountainhead of the Gardnerian tradition. The other main tradition is the Alexandrian, founded by Alexander Sanders (q.v.) (1926-1988), whose followers broke away from Gardner.

Several other traditions of witchcraft exist. Some have a cultural focus, such as Celtic, Norse (q.v.), Druid (q.v.), or Egyptian. The goddess Diana serves as a focal devotional figure for other wiccans. "Hedge witches" practice witchcraft alone, independent of any coven. Most covens organize their rituals in accordance with the lunar calendar, celebrating quarter days; eight main festivals associated with solstices and equinoxes are also marked. Instructions for these rites are set out in a "Book of Shadows"—normally a handwritten and unpublished manuscript which is distinctive for the particular coven. *See also* BUDAPEST, ZSUZSANNA EMESE; COVENANT OF THE GODDESS; COVENANT OF UNITARIAN UNIVERSALIST PAGANS; DIANIC WICCA; FELLOWSHIP OF ISIS; STARHAWK.

WON BUDDHISM. The "Buddhism of Unity," a reformist Buddhist movement originating in Korea, founded by Chungbin Pak (1891-1943), usually called "the Sot'aesan" ("Great Master") by his followers. The Sot'aesan gained enlightenment in 1916 and founded the Won Buddhist order in 1924. Won Buddhism is a reformist movement in several ways. It seeks to be a distinctively Korean form of Buddhism (q.v.), believing that prior forms of Buddhism have been overreliant on Chinese and Indian texts and phraseology. The movement also seeks to purge Buddhism of shamanic (q.v.) elements. It aims to make Buddhism available for the majority, and not merely the few (such as monks, who are generally male and live an austere lifestyle in remote locations). The movement seeks to reconcile different Buddhist factions, believing that each only teaches a part of the Buddhist dharma. Most important, Won Buddhists use no images of the Buddha, preferring instead to address their devotion to the Irwonsang, the symbol of the circle which represents enlightenment and the Dharmakaya (the absolute body of the Buddha, which is shared by all buddhas). Before his death the Sot'aesan transcribed his teachings in the *Chongchon,* a compilation of Won Buddhist scriptures, now translated into English. He was succeeded by the Ven. Chongsan (1900-1962) and the Ven. Taesan (b. 1914). In 1996 there were 140,000 members in North Korea and 400 temples in South Korea. *See also* CH'ONDOGYO.

WORD-FAITH MOVEMENT. A Protestant Christian evangelical Pentecostalist (q.v.) movement, emphasizing the achievement of prosperity, in the form of physical and mental health and—perhaps more especially—of financial well-being. The movement spans of a number of Christian evangelical organizations and is particularly associated with Kenneth Hagin, Kenneth Copeland, Charles Capps, and Frederick F. C. Price. Other "faith" teachers include John Avanzini, Marilyn Hickey, Robert Tilton, and Morris Cerullo (q.v.). Ulf Ekman, leader of the Word of Life Church (q.v.) in Uppsala, Sweden, is often regarded as belonging to this school. The ideas of the movement lie in the teachings of E. W. Kenyon (1867-1948) and William Branham (q.v.) (1909-1965) and are associated with the Manifest Sons of God and Latter-Rain (q.v.) movements.

Essentially "word faith" is based on the creative power of words and the importance of using verbal affirmations, as well as the faith of one's heart, in order to secure benefits from God. Just as God's word was the agent of creation, so the believer's words positively require God to answer. Followers are encouraged to use verbal affirmations to become debt-free, to acquire money, to achieve promotion at work, or indeed to attain whatever physical benefit they feel they need. "Name it and claim it" is a slogan frequently used by such believers. One technique frequently employed within the Word-Faith movement is "seed faith": this involves giving a donation to the organization, having been told that it is a token of faith and will secure a tenfold return. Such recommendations are believed to be scriptural: Avanzini points out that the prophet Samuel's mother Hannah, who was childless, obtained her boon from God by making a vow (using the power of words), presenting her request, and—importantly—making a gift to God (1 Samuel 1).

The movement has attracted much criticism, even from Christian evangelicals, who question the orthodoxy of its theology. Kenyon, for example, claimed that since human beings were created in God's image, Jesus was not God's unique incarnation. He also taught that humankind's atonement was not achieved through Jesus' death on the cross, but through his three-day descent to hell, where he was tormented by Satan and his demons. It has also been suggested, with justification, that Word-Faith owes much to New Thought (q.v.) as well as to the Bible: Kenyon studied New Thought and has been accused of incorporating ideas from Christian Science and the Unity School of Christianity (qq.v.). *See also* PROSPERITY THEOLOGY.

WORD OF LIFE CHURCH. Led by Ulf Ekman in Uppsala, Sweden, the Word of Life Church belongs to the Word-Faith movement (q.v.). Claiming that prayer is always answered, the church stresses the reality of healing miracles and the use of prayer to attain material and financial prosperity. The Bible's statement that Jesus had come "to preach good news to the poor" (Luke 4:18) is taken to mean that Jesus offers the possibility of becoming rich. Ekman's book *Financial Freedom* was published in 1989. The organization has been accused of unorthodox teachings on several counts. Ekman implies that Jesus only became God at his baptism, thus espousing a form of "adoptionism," and he claims that all Christ's followers became divine after Pentecost.

WORLD COMMUNITY SERVICE. Founded in Madras in 1958 by Yogiraj Vethathiri Maharishi (b. 1911), who was influenced by Swami Paranjoti—founder of the Temple of Universal Peace—whom he met in the 1940s, the World Community Service aims at the realization of world peace through the individual's attainment of peace. This is attained through the practice of simplified kundalini yoga (q.v.) (SKY), which is accessible to householders and Westerners rather than world-renouncers. A number of distinctive yogas are employed: shanti yoga is used to control one's kundalini energy; turiya yoga fully arouses the energy, leading to a state of tranquility and bliss; finally, turiyateetha yoga leads to the final merging of individual and universal consciousness. The organization's headquarters moved to Guduvancheri, India, Vethathiri's home town, in 1961. Vethathiri visited the United States in 1972, gaining a Western following, particularly from Indians living in America. His writings include *Yoga for Modern Age, Karma Yoga,* and *World Peace.*

WORLD MESSAGE LAST WARNING CHURCH. A church founded in Uganda in 1999 by Wilson Bushara, who claimed to be God's final prophet. Members engaged in communal living, having handed over the proceeds from the sale of all possessions. The movement was disbanded in 2000, following accusations of sexual misconduct by Bushara.

WORLDWIDE CHURCH OF GOD (WCG). Founded by Herbert W. Armstrong (q.v.) (1892-1986) in Eugene, Oregon, in 1933 as the Radio Church of God, this organization assumed its present name in 1968. It has been particularly noted for Armstrong's broadcasts "The World Tomorrow" and for the publication of *The Plain Truth,* which achieved a circulation of nearly six million by 1988. The church's beliefs and practices are clearly divisible into two periods: the Armstrong period and the Tkach period.

In common with the Seventh-day Adventist (q.v.) movement, of which he was a part, Armstrong accepted a doctrine of scriptural inerrancy, but held that scripture did not support the mainstream doctrine of the Trinity. Armstrong taught the need for observance of the Old Covenant as well as the New, which entailed works as well as faith, and the keeping of the Jewish festivals—Passover, Pentecost, Trumpets, the Day of Atonement, Tabernacles, and the first and last Great Day of the year—as well as the Jewish dietary laws proscribing pork and shellfish. Festivals such as Christmas and Easter were essentially pagan in character. Tithing was prescribed (sometimes double and triple). The WCG does not advertise its worship publicly and does not own distinctive places of worship.

Faced with the Christian evangelicals' constant characterization of the WCG as a "cult (q.v.)," Armstrong's successor Joseph W. Tkach (q.v.) introduced radical changes, which effectively reversed Armstrong's distinctive teachings. In 1987 Tkach ordered a doctrinal review, which resulted in a new Statement of Beliefs. Armstrong's own writings were progressively withdrawn, including his popular Bible correspondence course. *The Plain Truth* focused increasingly on the Bible, rather than current affairs. From 1994 onward there were even further moves in the direction of mainstream Christianity (q.v.): the doctrine of the Trinity was affirmed, triple tithing was abolished, and sabbath observance, the festivals, and dietary laws were reappraised: although not actually abolished, it is now taught that these are not the means of salvation.

As a result of these changes, about a third of the membership left, forming their own splinter organizations. This, coupled with the abolition of triple tithing, caused serious financial hardship, and at one point it was feared that *The Plain Truth* might cease publication. Following Tkach's death in 1995, his son Joseph W. Tkach, Jr., leads the movement and continues his father's reforms. In 1993 there were 140,000 weekly attendees and 97,000 baptized members; by 1996 the number of members had diminished to 75,000. *See also* CHURCH OF GOD INTERNATIONAL; GLOBAL CHURCH OF GOD; UNITED CHURCH OF GOD.

-Y-

YOGA. Derived from the Sanskrit word *yuj,* meaning "yoke," the term denotes the spiritual path with which the seeker is associated. A feature of Indian religious traditions, it is found principally in Hinduism, as well as Buddhism (qq.v.), Jainism, and certain forms of Sikhism (q.v.). Patanjali's Yoga Sutras (2nd-3rd c. B.C.E.) identify eight "limbs" of yoga, for the attainment of *moksha* (final liberation): *yama* (external control of one's senses), *niyama* (control of one's mind), *asana* (physical postures), *pranayama* (control of one's breathing), *pratyahara* (internal sense control), *dharana* (meditation), *dhyana* (concentration or contemplation), and *samadhi* (ultimate rest). Hatha yoga—popularly known simply as "yoga"—combines Patanjali's third and fourth steps and is principally aimed at physical health. Yoga's ultimate aim is *moksha,* but its forms are also used for attaining higher levels of consciousness, healing, and the attainment of paranormal powers *(laya yoga).*

The Bhagavad Gita—probably written somewhere between 500 B.C.E. and 250 C.E.—teaches three forms of yoga: *karma yoga* (the yoga of actions), *jnana yoga* (the yoga of inner awareness), and *bhakti yoga* (the yoga of devotion). Bhakti is particularly emphasized by the ISKCON and the Gaudiya Math (qq.v.) movement, which uses the Gita as a principal text for teaching devotion to Krishna. The Vedanta tradition adds a fourth kind of yoga to this trio, namely *raja yoga* (q.v.), which seeks to achieve mental and psychic control. Various gurus have combined these types of yoga in an assortment of ways. Ramakrishna and Vivekananda (qq.v.) taught the Gita's three types, while others, such as Aurobindo (q.v.) added a fourth "yoga of self perfection," calling his system "Integral Yoga," a name also used by his erstwhile disciple Sachidandana (q.v.) to describe his own distinctive practice. Kundalini yoga (q.v.) aims at arousing spiritual energy through one's *chakras* (q.v.)—points in the body pertaining to an occult anatomical system.

Recent Western interest in yoga was initially aroused by Ramakrishna and Vivekananda, while Yogananda (q.v.) was the first Indian guru to bring it to the West in his distinctive form of *kriya yoga* to the United States. *See also* BRAHMA KUMARIS; HEALTHY, HAPPY, HOLY; RAMANA; SELF-REALIZATION FELLOWSHIP; SIDDHA YOGA DHAM; SIVANANDA.

YOGANANDA, SWAMI PARAMAHANSA (1893-1953). One of the earliest Hindu swamis to visit the West and founder of the Self-Realization Fellowship (q.v.), Yogananda claims a lineage *(parampara)* of teachers going back to Mahavatar Babaji, who revived the practice of kriya yoga through Lahiri Mahasaya (1828-1895) and Sri Yukteswar (1855-1936), whom he met in 1910. In 1914 Yogananda joined Yukteswar's swami order and set up the Yagoda Satsanga Society in India in 1917. In 1920 he was sent to Boston as a delegate to the International Congress of Religious Liberals. This event led to the establishment of an ashram near Boston in 1922 and to the establishment of a Western branch of the Yagoda Satsanga Society, which became incorporated as the Self-Realization Fellowship (SRF) in 1935. Yogananda toured the United States and later the world, disseminating his teachings and attracting record crowds.

Yogananda's best-known writings include his address "The Science of Religion," originally delivered on 6 October

1920. His *Autobiography of a Yogi* (1946) was translated into 18 languages and has become a spiritual classic. It draws heavily on Judeo-Christian Scripture as well as Hindu teachings since Yogananda taught the harmony of all religions. Although it does not set out the practices of kriya yoga themselves (since these are confidential to their practitioners), the book describes Yogananda's experience of *samadhi* and his gaining access to subtle spiritual laws that afford visions and miracles. Being a science, the practice of religion is empirical and experiential, and practitioners of kriya yoga claim direct religious experience in the form of love, serenity, and control over their lives. Kriya yoga involves breath control, withdrawal of the senses, and meditation (q.v.), and its highest realization affords recognition of the physical world as *maya* (illusion) and of the divinity of the self. Although Yogananda's teachings, being neo-Vedanta, are essentially monistic, Yogananda taught that the Absolute can be conceived of as personal or impersonal, thus allowing room for *bhakti* (devotion) to personal forms of divinity.

Followers claim that, when Yogananda died in 1953, his body showed no signs of decay for the 20 days in which it lay prior to his burial, thus evidencing his supreme spiritual qualities. He is believed to be ever-living, and followers can become united with him. *See also* BREATHARIANS.

-Z-

ZELL, TIM. Founder of the Church of All Worlds (q.v.). Together with Lance Christie, Zell founded Atl at Westminster College, Fulton, Missouri, which became the Atlan Foundation at the University of Oklahoma in the mid-1960s. Zell was the first to adopt the term "neo-Pagan." He founded the Church of All Worlds in 1968. He also edited *The Green Egg,* then the best-known journal which enabled emergent Pagan and wiccan (qq.v.) groups to network. In 1976 Zell moved to California, relinquishing the leadership of the church and the editorship of *The Green Egg.* He changed his name to Otter G'Zell, as a result of a vision and went on to engage in a number of research projects. One of these was a quest to propagate unicorns from goats—a project for which he claimed success, exhibiting a few specimens publicly and producing a journal entitled *Unicornews* from 1980 to 1982. In the 1990s Zell organized the Universal Federation of Pagans, with the purpose of establishing a worldwide network.

ZEN. A form of Buddhism (q.v.), said to have been introduced into China by Bodhidharma in 520 C.E. Known as Ch'an in China, meaning "meditation" (q.v.), the word was transposed to "Zen" when it migrated to Japan. Zen combines philosophical Taoism with Indian Buddhism, emphasizing the ultimate inexpressibility of its teachings and the notion and the aim of finding one's buddha-nature by means of meditative practices combined with spontaneous intuitive insight. Zen became popular in the West principally through the writings of Daisetz Teitaro Suzuki (1870-1966), who came from Japan to the United States and wrote prolifically on the subject. In Great Britain Christmas Humphreys (1901-1983), the founder of the Buddhist Society, wrote much to popularize Buddhism in general and Zen in particular.

Zen in itself is a traditional form of Buddhism, and not a new religious movement, although some anti-cult (q.v.) literature has included Zen and made a critique of it. However, because of Zen's emphasis on spontaneity and on finding one's own buddha-nature, elements of America's youth culture in the 1960s—principally the beatniks and hippies—claimed to have taken up Zen, interpreting it as entailing unlimited spontaneity and freedom, with a do-as-you-please philosophy. This Western interpretation of Zen has come to be known as "Beat Zen": its principal leaders included novelist Jack Kerouac (1922-1969), renowned for his novel *The Dharma Bums,* which describes autobiographically the uptake of Beat Zen by a group from the 1960s American counterculture. Other exponents were poets Allen Ginsburg and Gary Snyder. Alan Watts (q.v.), a former Anglican clergyman, became interested in Zen and wrote a considerable amount of popular material on its more philosophical ideas. *See also* ARICA; AVATARA ADI DA; OSHO.

ZIONIST CHURCHES. A group of some 2,500 black South African churches, principally in Zululand and Swaziland, which have sought to find a distinctively indigenous African expression of Christianity (q.v.). Traditional African elements feature in worship, and importance is attached to prophecy, speaking in tongues (q.v.), and healing. Many Zionist churches reject all medicine—indigenous or Western—believing solely in prayer-healing. Baptism is by total immersion. Some Zionist churches observe Saturday (being the Jewish sabbath) as the appropriate day of worship, rather than Sunday. Many Zionist churches permit polygamy, in accordance with traditional African practice.

The name "Zionist" originally derived from the Christian Catholic Apostolic Church, founded in Zion City, Illinois, by J. A. Dowie (1847-1907), but "Zion" now tends to have more spiritual connotations and is often—but by no means always—used as part of the official name of individual churches within the movement. The Zionist Christian Church (ZCC) had three million members in 1994. *See also* AFRICAN INDEPENDENT CHURCHES.

Glossary

The following religious terminology is used in the text but may not be understood by the nonspecialist reader. However, they are not themselves concepts directly relating to new religious movements. The bracketed initials at the end of some entries indicate the religion to which they belong (B = Buddhism; C = Christianity; H = Hinduism; I = Islam; J = Judaism; N = New Age Movement; S = Sikhism).

acharya. Revered teacher (H, B, Jain).

amrit. Ceremony in which one is initiated into Khalsa Sikhism.

animal magnetism. New Thought theory, deriving from Franz Mesmer, that the body was encircled by a magnetic field or fluid, an imbalance in which could cause illness.

Ark. (1) Ark of the Covenant: the portable shrine in which the stone tablets containing the Ten Commandments were believed to have been carried in ancient times. (2) Cupboard at the front of a synagogue, in which the Torah scrolls reside (J).

Ascended Masters. Great White Brotherhood.

ashram. Center for meditation and instruction (H).

atman. Self, or soul (H, B).

Avalokiteshvara. Literally, "the Lord who looked down": the bodhisattva of compassion (B).

avatar. "Descent" of God into physical form (H).

Bhagavad Gita. A spiritual classic, part of the Mahabharata, involving a dialogue between Krishna and Arjuna. Its date is uncertain, possibly around 200 B.C.E. (H).

bhakti. Devotion (H).

bhikkhu. Theravadin monk (B).

biofeedback. A range of techniques for gain feedback about one's physical state in order to control one's body. Principal uses are for relaxation and meditation (N).

bodhisattva. In the Theravadin tradition, a buddha-to-be. In the Mahayana, one who postpones his or her final nirvana in order to help other living beings (B).

chela. Follower (H).

Chenrezig. Tibetan name of Avalokiteshvara (B).

darshan. Literally "appearance"; usually applied to a deity or a human guru to whom deity is ascribed, when followers are permitted to have sight of him or her (H).

deliverance. A term used especially in the Pentecostalist/charismatic traditions for casting out demons (C).

deva. A god (H) or nature spirit (N).

Dhammapada. A short Theravada Buddhist scripture, propounding Buddhism's fundamental teachings (B).

Dharma. Literally "essence." One's obligation or path to follow in life (H, B).

dhikr (zhikr). Repetition of God's name and attributes (I).

diksha. First initiation (H).

enneagram. System devised by G. I. Gurdjieff for understanding human nature by identifying nine personality types.

Five Ks. Symbols worn by Khalsa Sikhs at the behest of Guru Gobind Singh (*kes*—uncut hair, *kangha*—comb, *kirpan*— dagger, *kara*—bracelet, *kachh*—long shorts) (S).

glossolaliation. "Speaking in tongues"; uttering sounds during worship that do not belong to any known human language (C).

Great Awakening. Controversial revivalist movement in North America (1720-1750), led by Calvinist preacher George Whitefield (1714-1770).

Great Tribulation. A short but intense period of persecution of Christians, mentioned in the Book of Revelation. This has variously been thought to refer to the Fall of Jerusalem (70 C.E.) or a three-and-a-half-year period preceding the Battle of Armageddon.

gurdwara. Sikh temple (S).

handfasting. Pagan marriage ceremony.

Holy of Holies. The innermost part of the former Jerusalem Temple, which only the high priest was permitted to enter, on the Day of Atonement (J, C).

jnana. Wisdom (H, B).

Kabir. Hindu-Sufi mystic, poet and sage (trad. 1398-1518) in the Sant tradition.

Kalki. Final avatar of Vishnu, still to arrive, who will wind up the present yuga.

karma. Action, deeds, or effects of one's deeds that necessarily require expiation (H, B, S).

khalsa. Often translated as "brotherhood," the community of men and women who have undergone amrit and assumed the "five Ks" of Guru Gobind Singh (S).

kirtan. Public worship with singing (H, S).

Lemuria. Legendary ancient lost city.

Maharishi. Great seer (H).

maya. Illusion (H, B, S).

Mesmerism. Theories derived from Franz (Friedrich) Anton Mesmer (1734-1815), combining electrical discoveries with occultist ideas, and applied to the human body and mind.

mind cure. New Thought theory that cure can be effected by powers of the mind.

moksha. Release from samsara, the gaining of enlightenment (H).

neuro-linguistic programming (NLP). A method of communication and motivating others (N).

parampara. Disciplic succession (H).

post-Catholic. A term used for certain Roman Catholic-derived New Christian groups, who cannot accept the authority of any pope after Pius XII.

psychic surgery. A set of paranormal techniques to remove pathogenic objects painlessly from the body, originating from the Philippines.

Puranas. Hindu texts, recounting Krishna's deeds (H).

remnant. A small number of faithful Jews who would survive the Babylonian exile. The term has subsequently been applied by some Christians to those who would survive the Great Tribulation.

sadhu. Holy man (H).

Saivite. Of the tradition that venerates Shiva (H).

samadhi. Literally "rest." The term can refer to death (H), or to the result of meditation (as in the final point of the Eightfold Path) or to enlightenment itself (B).

samsara. Cycle of birth and rebirth (H, B, S).

sanctification. The process of becoming purer, as a result of the Holy Spirit's work after conversion, or "justification" (C).

Sant. Indian mystical movement, combining Vashnavite Hinduism with Nath yoga and possibly Sufism, and reacting against the outward manifestations of religiosity.

sat c(h)it ananda. Being, consciousness, and bliss (H).

satori. Zen term for enlightenment (B).

satsang (sangat or **sadhsangat).** Local group or congregation (S).

shakti. Feminine form of deity (H).

shaman. A kind of medium, who is held to be capable of journeying into the world of the dead on behalf of the living.

sidhhis. Miraculous powers, cultivated by spiritual adepts (H).

substitutionary theory of Atonement. Doctrine that Christ died as a substitute or surrogate victim, in place of humanity, in order to accept their due punishment for sin (C).

tetragrammaton. The Hebrew four-letter, unpronounced name for God (YHWH), sometimes rendered as "Yahweh."

Theravada. Conservative school of Buddhism, which claims to be closest to the teachings of the historical Buddha.

typology. (1) Method of classification. (2) Method of interpreting Scripture, designed to demonstrate that Old Testament events foreshadow those of the New (e.g., Noah's ark, being made of wood, is the "type" foreshadowing Christ's cross) (C).

Upanishads. Philosophical-religious writings, probably compiled around 800 B.C.E. (H).

Vaishnavite. Follower of Vishnu (H).

Vedas. Four ancient Hindu texts (Rig Veda, Sama Veda, Atharva Veda, Yajur Veda); can be extended to include the Upanishads and other writings deemed to be directly revealed (H).

visualization. Form of meditation, in which use is made of pictorial images (B).

Yahweh. Divine name, which Jews may not pronounce (J).

yogi. A spiritual adept (H, B).

yuga. Age, of which the world's duration is divided into four, of progressively deteriorating quality (H).

Bibliography

Contents

Introduction

The publisher's original brief was that this volume should contain a "comprehensive bibliography." This, of course, is impossible: indeed, entire volumes exist on new religious movements (NRMs) devoted to bibliography alone, and they still do not achieve anything approaching comprehensiveness. What follows, therefore, aims to be a representative bibliography rather than a comprehensive one.

Literature on NRMs comes from a variety of sources, and this is reflected in what follows. For the new religions themselves, the written word has been one of the principal vehicles of propagating their message. As followers begin to perceive a more lasting significance in a founder-leader's words, they may become available in written form. Since the production of books is expensive, and since initial contactees may not have sufficient interest and motivation to read entire books, transcripts of talks, lecture notes, tracts, pamphlets, short booklets, and in-house magazines typically become an NRM's initial pieces of writing.

There are a few exceptions: the Church of Jesus Christ of Latter-day Saints began with *The Book of Mormon*, and it is of the essence of channeling that the channeler is able to transcribe extended messages from his or her channel, resulting in books like *Oahspe,* the Seth books, and *A Course in Miracles.* Tracts, pamphlets and—particularly early and often amateurishly produced—magazines tend to have a somewhat ephemeral existence, making it difficult for the researcher to gain access to this type of literature.

A similar problem of accessibility exists with countercult literature. In the early stages of an NRM's development, Christianity, with its history of weeding out heresy and its emphasis on sound doctrine, felt constrained to publish critiques of emergent spiritual groups. In order to make these widely available, much of this material has taken the form of short publications. "Cult critiques" in the form of entire books began in the later parts of the 19th century and grew in modest proportions until shortly after World War II. The new wave of NRMs that swept across the United States during the 1960s and 1970s—largely due to increasing globalization and the youth counterculture—elicited more than a Christian critique.

With the progress of secularization, the public in general became less interested in theological matters like critiques of the Jehovah's Witnesses' views on the Trinity. As NRMs came to be perceived as a societal threat rather than as Christian heresies, issues such as brainwashing, fundraising, and living conditions gave rise to countercult literature with a somewhat different focus. Such societal changes have in turn been reflected in the writings of the new religions: Jehovah's Witnesses' apologetic literature now rarely seeks to correct mainstream Christian Trinitarianism and instead aims to demonstrate that there is a remedy for societal ills that Jehovah's Witnesses and others might commonly agree to exist.

Academic studies have tended to lag behind the more popular and sensationalist cult critiques. This is partly explained by the time it takes to produce serious academic research, in stark contrast with hack journalists and self-styled "cult experts," who are often under pressure to meet a public demand for fast information on topical events, in particular disasters such as Jonestown, Waco, the Solar Temple, and Heaven's Gate. Another factor, however, that has caused the relative slowness of academic writing relates to the history of religious studies as a subject. A century previously, students of religion were subjected almost entirely to Christian theology and related subjects such as biblical studies. The late 1950s and 1960s saw a greater emphasis on the study of the major world religions, with minor and emergent religions being generally perceived as unworthy of serious study.

At first, academic writings tended to be predominantly sociological. In addition to the increasing public interest in new religions as social phenomena, NRMs provided researchers with an opportunity to investigate human behavior within a microcosm—an opportunity afforded particularly by NRMs that engaged in community living, apart from the world at large. While sociological study tends to remain predominant, an increasing number of scholars of religion have begun to examine NRMs as systems of belief and practice, offering serious answers to fundamental questions about human existence: where life came from, how it ought to be lived, what kind of future human beings have on this planet, and how to deal with rites of passage for life-cycle events.

In the case of some new religions, they have themselves experienced developments of doctrine. Founder-leaders have proliferated new writings, at times adapting their teachings to new situations and sometimes retracting previous pronouncements. As founder-leaders died, and a second generation of followers assumed control, new sets of writings have emerged, either as commentaries on the founder-leader and his or her teachings (for example, on L. Ron Hubbard) or else to take the movement in a new direction (as with the Worldwide Church of God).

Without producing an annotated bibliography, which is infeasible here, it is not possible to indicate precisely the nature of the writings listed below. The broad classifications, together with the relevant dictionary entries, should suffice to indicate which writings are apologetic and which are critical or hostile. Inevitably, classifying literature in this highly complex field raises problems to which there is no entirely satisfactory solution. I have avoided introducing the category of scriptures in the scheme below: unlike religions such as Christianity and Buddhism it is not always clear whether certain key texts are "scripture" or not. There are differences of opinion, for example, among Unification Church members as to whether their key text *Divine Principle* is scriptural: some Unificationist leaders contend that it is no more than an important theological treatise, at times comparing it to the writings of St. Augustine or John Calvin in Christianity. The Church of Scientology only began to use the term "scripture" from around 1997, finally defining it as the totality of L. Ron Hubbard's writings on Dianetics and Scientology (in other words, excluding his science-fiction). Other NRMs use the writings of their related mainstream tradition, for example, Jehovah's Witnesses and ISKCON, although both organizations prefer their own distinctive translations.

Other categories, such as "primary" and "secondary" source material have also proved problematic. Some writings may be very poor secondary sources on NRMs themselves, and yet prove to be excellent primary source material about the anticult movement. Other tempting distinctions are between "insider" and "outsider," "academic" and "popular," and "objective" and "critical." Although such categories are not without use in this area, they are enormously problematic. For example, is J. G. Bennett a Subud "insider" or an "outsider," having written enthusiastically as a member but subsequently leaving the organization? The vast majority of scholars are thoroughly aware of the problem of claiming to aspire to "objectivity," and indeed there are a number who are hostile to various NRMs. Scholars can also have religious allegiance, and indeed a not insignificant number of academics are Pagans, Bahá'í, Soka Gakkai members, or followers of Indian gurus: indeed it is often their membership that has caused them to undertake academic study of their chosen faith. Although there is a broad distinction between apologetic literature, critical literature, and literature that seeks neutrality, such boundaries are neither clear nor universally agreed. Moreover, it is not necessarily the case that academic writing is measured, well researched, and impartial, in contrast to journalists and critics who are frequently accused of being hectic, scare-mongering, and jumping to conclusions. Regrettably, some academic work is shoddy, some is prejudiced, and some is both. Conversely, some journalists, such as David Shaw, David Barrett, and Shirley Harrison, are restrained and have researched their material well.

In what follows, I have divided the printed literature into 19 categories in all, in most cases with subdivision: (I) general introductions; (II) works providing historical background; (III) writings on NRMs originating in the 19th century; (IV) Theosophy-derived NRMs; (V) Jewish and Jewish-related NRMs; (VI) 20th-century New Christian NRMs; (VII) Islamic and Sufi movements; (VIII) Hindu-related NRMs; (IX) Sikh-related NRMs; (X) Buddhist and Buddhist-derived NRMs; (XI) Japanese religions (excluding Buddhism); (XII) NRMs originating in primal societies (principally African-Caribbean and shamanistic); (XIII) independent new religions (an assortment which cannot readily be fitted into other categories); (XIV) the Human Potential Movement (sometimes referred to as the "self religions"); (XV) wicca, witchcraft and paganism; (XVI) the New Age Movement; (XVII) UFO-religions; (XVIII) issues and themes in NRMs; and finally (XIX) misscellaneous other publications and works cited in the dictionary.

This categorization is neither neat nor unproblematic. Some readers may question the classification of Krishnamurti as Theosophy-derived, Essenes as New Christian, or Osho as Buddhist, or the treatment of Spiritualism, spiritism, and channeling as separate categories. It would be tedious to provide a defense of my methods of classification; suffice it to say that classification must be done somehow, and I have simply conjectured as to where readers are likely to look.

The inclusion of literature on this list should not be construed as the author's seal of approval. No doubt there are books that members of some NRMs would like to have seen removed: I know, for example, that Scientologists detest the writings of Atack and Miller, to the extent of taking legal action to ensure the withdrawal of their works. Again, I have endeavored to include a range of material, spanning NRMs' primary source material, emphatic discussion, critical evaluation, and countercult literature. With regard to certain NRMs, there is a distinct dearth of literature, and in a few cases I am not aware of the existence of literature specializing in that movement. Other NRMs prove to be the exact opposite: Aleister Crowley, L. Ron Hubbard, and Sir George King were so prolific that a complete list of their writings would swamp this bibliography. In such cases, I have itemized their most important works only, in the interests of ensuring that each NRM is represented as fairly as possible in the literature. Where a group is not explicitly listed, the reader is referred to the general literature.

One final point of detail relates to dates and editions used. The editions cited are those that proved most readily available, not necessarily the first or the latest editions. Ascertaining when and where a first edition was produced would be an inordinately difficult task. Some early NRM leaders initially circulated their teachings as notes or as amateurishly produced in-house publications, which are no longer readily available. Others wrote in a language other than English, and their works were translated at a later stage. The easiest solution, therefore, was to cite an edition that has recently been on sale, or which can found in the catalogues of institutions such as the Library of Congress or the British Library. There is little merit in providing citations which readers cannot subsequently find, if they wish to pursue their quest. The dictionary entries themselves provide information on the pedigree of NRMs' most important writings.

I. General

A. Other bibliographies

Arweck, Elisabeth, and Peter B. Clarke. *New Religious Movements in Western Europe: An Annotated Bibliography.* Westport, Conn.: Greenwood Press, 1997.

Beckford, J., and James Richardson. "A Bibliography of Social Scientific Studies of New Religious Movements." *Social Compass,* 30, no. 1 (1983).

Bergman, Jerry. *Jehovah's Witnesses and Kindred Groups: A Historical Compendium and Bibliography.* New York: Garland, 1985.

Bjorling, Joel. *The Bahá'i Faith: A Historical Bibliography.* New York: Garland, 1985.

Choquette, Diane. *New Religious Movements in the United States and Canada: A Critical Assessment and Annotated Bibliography.* Westport, Conn.: Greenwood Press, 1985.

Clarke, P. B. *Bibliography of Japanese New Religions.* Richmond, Surrey: Japan Library, 1999.

Collins, William P. *Bibliography of English Language Works on the Babi and Bahá'í Faith, 1845-1985.* Wilmette, Ill.: Bahá'í Publishing Trust, 1991.

Driscoll, J. Walter. *Gurdjieff: An Annotated Bibliography.* New York: Garland, 1985.

DuPree, Sherry Sherrod. *African American Holiness Pentecostal Charismatic: Annotated Bibliography.* New York: Garland, 1992.

Earhart, H. Byron. *The New Religions of Japan: A Bibliography of Western-Language Materials.* Ann Arbor: Center for Japanese Studies, University of Michigan, 1983.

Eberhart, George M. *UFOs and the Extraterrestrial Contact Movement: A Bibliography.* 2 vols. Metuchen, N.J.: Scarecrow Press, 1986.

Guignette, Jean-Paul. *Bibliography of Biographical Studies on Helena Petrovna Blavatsky (1831-1891).* London: Theosophical History Centre, 1987.

Melton, J. Gordon. *A Bibliography of Buddhism in America, 1880-1940.* Santa Barbara, Calif.: Institute for the Study of American Religion, 1985.

Melton, J. Gordon, and Robin Martin. *A Bibliography of American Communalism.* Evanston, Ill.: Institute for the Study of American Religions, n.d.

Melton, J. Gordon, and Isotta Poggi. *Magic, Witchcraft and Paganism in America: A Bibliography.* New York: Garland, 1992.

Mitchell, R. C., and Harold W. Turner. *A Comprehensive Bibliography of Modern African Religious Movements.* Evanston, Ill.: Northwestern University Press, 1966.

Pritchett, W. Douglas. *The Children of God, Family of Love: An Annotated Bibliography.* New York: Garland, 1985.

Shields, Steven L. *The Latter Day Saint Churches: An Annotated Bibliography.* New York: Garland, 1987.

Turner, Harold W. *Bibliography of New Religious Movements in Primal Societies.* Boston: G. K. Hall, 1992.

Yorke, Gerald. *Bibliography of the Works of Aleister Crowley.* N.p.: Black Lodge Publishing, 1991.

B. General Reference Works on NRMs

Annett, Stephen. *The Many Ways of Being.* London: Abacus, 1976.

Beit-Hallahmi, Benjamin. *The Illustrated Encyclopedia of Active New Religions, Sects, and Cults.* New York: Rosen Publishing Group, 1993.

Bowden, Henry Warner. *Dictionary of American Religious Biography.* Westport, Conn.: Greenwood Press, 1993.

Bromley, David G., and Jeffrey K. Hadden. *The Handbook on Cults and Sects in America.* Greenwich, England: Jai Press, 1993.

Goring, Rosemary. *Larousse Dictionary of Beliefs and Religions.* Edinburgh: Larousse, 1992.

Guiley, Rosemary Ellen. *Harper's Encyclopedia of Mystical and Paranormal Experience.* New York: HarperCollins, 1991.

Harris, I., S. Mews, P. Morris, and J. Shepherd, eds. *Contemporary Religions: A World Guide.* Harlow, Essex: Longman, 1992.

Melton, J. Gordon. *Encyclopedia of American Religions.* 5th ed. Detroit: Gale, 1996.

———. *Encyclopedic Handbook of Cults in America.* New York: Garland, 1992.

———. *Religious Bodies in the United States: A Directory.* New York: Garland, 1992.

————. *Religious Leaders of America.* Detroit: Gale, 1991.

C. Methodological and Theoretical Issues

Becker, Howard. *Systematic Sociology on the Basis of the Beziehungslehre and Gebildelehre of Leopold von Wiese.* New York: Wiley, 1932.

Berner, Ulrich. "Reflections upon the Concept of 'New Religious Movement.'" *Method and Theory in the Study of Religion* 12, nos. 1-2 (2000): 267-276.

Clarke, Peter. *The Study of Religion: Traditional and New Religions.* London: Routledge, 1991.

Hill, Michael. "Sect"; in M. Eliade, *Encyclopedia of Religion,* vol. 13. New York: Simon and Schuster Macmillan, 1995.

Hill, Michael, ed. *A Sociological Yearbook of Religion in Britain: 5.* London: SCM, 1972.

Troeltsch, E. *The Social Teachings of the Christian Church.* London: Macmillan, 1931.

Turner, H. W. "A New Field in the Study of Religions." *Religion* 1 (1971): 15-23.

Yinger, J. M. *Religion in the Struggle for Power: A Study in the Sociology of Religion.* Durham, N.C.: Duke University Press, 1961.

————. *The Scientific Study of Religion.* London: Collier-Macmillan, 1970.

D. General Academic Introductions

Bainbridge, W. S. *The Sociology of Religious Movements.* London: Routledge, 1997.

Barker, Eileen. *New Religious Movements: A Practical Introduction.* London: H.M.S.O., 1989.

Barker, Eileen, ed. *New Religious Movements: A Perspective for Understanding Society.* New York: Edwin Mellen, 1982.

Barker, Eileen, James A. Beckford, and Karel Dobbelaere. *Secularization Rationalism and Sectarianism: Essays in Honour of Bryan R. Wilson.* Oxford: Clarendon Press, 1993.

Barker, Eileen, and Margit Warburg, eds. *New Religions and New Religiosity.* Aarhus, Denmark: Aarhus University Press, 1998.

Beckford, J. ed. *New Religious Movements and Rapid Social Change.* London: Sage, 1986.

Bednarowski, Mary Farrell. *New Religions and the Theological Imagination in America.* Bloomington: Indiana University Press, 1989.

Chryssides, George D. *Exploring New Religions.* London: Cassell, 1999.

Ellwood, Robert, Jr. *Alternative Altars: Unconventional and Eastern Spirituality in America.* Chicago: University of Chicago Press, 1979.

Ellwood, Robert S., and Harry B. Partin. *Religious and Spiritual Groups in Modern America.* 2d ed. Englewood Cliffs, N.J.: Prentice Hall, 1988.

Fichter, Joseph H., ed. *Alternatives to American Mainline Churches.* Barrytown, N.Y.: Unification Theological Seminary, 1983.

Fuss, Michael A., ed. *Rethinking New Religious Movements.* Rome: Pontifical Gregorian University Research Center on Cultures and Religions, 1998.

Glock, Charles Y., and Robert N. Bellah, eds. *The New Religious Consciousness.* Berkeley: University of California Press, 1975.

Hexham, Irving. *Understanding Cults and New Religions.* Grand Rapids, Mich.: Eerdmans, 1986.

Hexham, Irving, and Karla Poewe. *New Religions as Global Cultures: Making the Human Sacred.* Boulder, Colo.: Westview Press, 1997.

Meldgaard, Helle, and Johannes Aagaard, eds. *New Religious Movements in Europe.* Aarhus, Denmark: Aarhus University Press, 1997.

Melton, J. Gordon. *American Religious Creeds.* 3 vols. New York: Triumph Books, 1991.

————. "Modern Alternative Religions in the West." In J. Hinnells, *A New Handbook of Living Religions.* Harmondsworth: Penguin, 1998: 594-617.

Melton, J. Gordon, and Robert L. Moore. *The Cult Experience: Responding to the New Religious Pluralism.* New York: Pilgrim Press, 1982.

Miller, Timothy, ed. *America's Alternative Religions.* Albany: State University of New York Press, 1995.

Needleman, Jacob. *The New Religions.* New York: Doubleday, 1970.

Needleman, Jacob, and George Baker, eds. *Understanding the New Religions.* New York: Seabury, 1981.

Nelson, Geoffrey K. *Cults, New Religions, and Religious Creativity.* London: Routledge and Kegan Paul, 1987.

Rawlinson, Andrew. *The Book of Enlightened Masters: Western Teachers in Eastern Traditions.* Chicago: Open Court, 1997.

Rothstein, Michael, ed. *Belief Transformations.* Aarhus, Denmark: Aarhus University Press, 1996.

Saliba, John. *Perspectives on New Religious Movements.* London: Geoffrey Chapman, 1995.

Stark, R., ed. *New Religious Movements: Genesis, Exodus, and Numbers.* New York: Rose of Sharon Press, 1985.

Stark, R., and W. S. Bainbridge. *Religion, Deviance, and Social Control.* New York: Routledge, 1996.

Storr, Anthony. *Feet of Clay: A Study of Gurus.* London: HarperCollins, 1996.

Towler, Robert, ed. *New Religions and the New Europe.* Aarhus, Denmark: Aarhus University Press, 1995.

Wallis, Roy. *The Elementary Forms of Religious Life.* London: Routledge and Kegan Paul, 1984.

————. "The Sociology of the New Religions." *Social Studies Review* 1, no. 1 (September 1985): 3-7.

Wilson, Bryan. "An Analysis of Sect Development." *American Sociological Review* 24 (1959): 3-15.

————. *The Social Impact of New Religious Movements.* New York: Rose of Sharon Press, 1983.

Wilson, Bryan, and J. Cresswell, eds. *New Religious Movements: Challenge and Response.* London: Routledge, 1999.

Zaretsky, Irving I., and Mark P. Leone. *Religious Movements in Contemporary America.* Princeton, N.J.: Princeton University Press, 1974.

E. Popular

Bancroft, A. *New Religious World.* London: Macdonald, 1985.
————. *Twentieth-Century Mystics and Sages.* London: Arkana, 1989.
Barrett, David V. *The New Believers: Sects, "Cults," and Alternative Religions.* London: Cassell, 2001.
Brown, Mick. *The Spiritual Tourist: A Personal Odyssey through the Outer Reaches of Belief.* London: Bloomsbury, 1998.
Harrison, Shirley. *"Cults": The Battle for God.* London: Christopher Helm, 1990.
Shaw, David. *Spying in Guru Land: Inside Britain's Cults.* London: Fourth Estate, 1994.

F. Countercult Literature and Cult Critiques

Ankerberg, John, and John Weldon. *Encyclopedia of Cults and New Religions.* Eugene, Oreg.: Harvest House Publishers, 1999.
Appel, Willa. *Cults in America: Programmed for Paradise.* New York: Holt, Rinehart and Winston, 1983.
Atkins, Gaius Glenn. *Modern Cults and Religious Movements.* Old Tappan, N.J.: Fleming H. Revell, 1923.
Braden, Charles S. *These Also Believe: A Study of Modern American Cults and Minority Religious Movements.* New York: Macmillan, 1960.
Crabtree, Herbert. *Some Religious Cults and Movements of Today and Their Contribution to the Religion of To-morrow.* London: Lindsey Press, 1932.
Davies, Horton. *Christian Deviations: The Challenge of the New Spiritual Movements.* London: SCM, 1965.

Enroth, Ronald. *A Guide to Cults and New Religions.* Downers Grove, Ill.: InterVarsity Press, 1983.

————. *The Lure of the Cults.* Chappaqua, N.Y.: Christian Herald Books, 1979.

————. *What Is a Cult?* Downers Grove, Ill.: InterVarsity Press, 1982.

————. *Youth, Brainwashing, and Extremist Cults.* Grand Rapids, Mich.: Zondervan, 1977.

Evans, Christopher. *Cults of Unreason.* London: Harrap, 1973.

Ferguson, Charles W. *The New Books of Revelations: The Inside Story of America's Astounding Religious Cults.* Garden City, N.Y.: Doubleday, 1929.

Gomes, Alan W. *Unmasking the Cults.* Carlisle, England: OM Publishing, 1995.

Gruss, Edmond C. *Cults and the Occult.* 3d ed. Phillipsburg, N.J.: Presbyterian and Reformed Publishing, 1994.

Harris, Doug. *Cult Critiques.* Richmond, Surrey: Reachout Trust, 1995.

Hassan, S. *Combatting Cult Mind Control.* Wellingborough, England: Aquarian, 1990.

Haworth, Ian. "Cult Concerns: An Overview of Cults and Their Methods in the UK." *Assignation* 11, no. 4 (July 1994): 31-34.

Hoekema, Anthony A. *The Four Major Cults: Christian Science, Jehovah's Witnesses, Mormonism, Seventh-day Adventism.* Exeter, England: Paternoster, 1963.

Irvine, William C. *Heresies Exposed.* Neptune, N.J.: Loizeaux, 1955.

Kyle, Richard. *The Religious Fringe: A History of Alternative Religions in America.* Downers Grove, Ill.: InterVarsity Press, 1993.

Larson, Bob. *Larson's New Book of Cults.* Wheaton, Ill.: Tyndale House, 1989.

Lindsey, Hal. *Satan Is Alive and Well on Planet Earth.* Grand Rapids, Mich.: Zondervan, 1972.

Martin, Walter. *The Kingdom of the Cults.* Minneapolis, Minn.: Bethany House, 1985.

————. *The New Cults.* Ventura, Calif.: Vision House, 1980.

McDowell, Josh, and Don Stewart. *The Deceivers: What Cults Believe; How They Lure Followers.* Amersham, England: Scripture Press, 1992.

Petersen, William J. *Those Curious New Cults.* New Canaan, Conn.: Keats, 1975.

Ritchie, Jean. *The Secret World of Cults: Inside the Sects That Take over Lives.* London: Angus and Robertson, 1991.

Ross, Joan Carol, and Michael D. Langone. *Cults: What Parents Should Know.* Weston, Mass.: Carol Publishing Group and American Family Foundation, 1988.

Shapiro, Eli. "Destructive Cultism." *American Family Physician* 15, no. 2 (1977): 83.

Van Baalen, Jan Karel. *The Chaos of Cults: A Study in Present-Day Isms.* Grand Rapids, Mich.: Eerdmans, 1962.

Vosper, Cyril. *The Mind Benders.* London: Spearman, 1971.

II. Historical Background

A. Emanuel Swedenborg

Larsen, Robin, ed. *Emanuel Swedenborg: A Continuing Vision: A Pictorial Biography and Anthology of Essays and Poetry.* New York: Swedenborg Foundation, 1988.

Swedenborg, Emanuel. *Apocalypse Explained: According to the Spiritual Sense in Which the Arcana There Predicted but Heretofore Concealed are Revealed.* New York: Swedenborg Foundation, 1911-1912.

———. *The Apocalypse Revealed: Wherein Are Disclosed the Arcana There Foretold Which Have Hitherto Remained Concealed.* 18th ed. New York: Swedenborg Foundation, 1984.

———. *Arcana Coelestia: The Heavenly Arcana Contained in the Holy Scripture or Word of the Lord Unfolded, Beginning with the Book of Genesis.* New York: Swedenborg Foundation, 1905-1910.

———. *Heaven and Its Wonders and Hell.* London: Swedenborg Society, 1966.

————. *The True Christian Religion: Containing the Universal Theology of the New Church Foretold by the Lord in Daniel VII, 13, 14; and in Revelation XXI, 1, 2.* 23d ed. New York: Swedenborg Foundation, 1984.

Synnestvedt, Sig. *The Essential Swedenborg: Basic Religious Teachings of Emanuel Swedenborg.* New York: Swedenborg Foundation, 1984.

B. Ralph Waldo Emerson and Transcendentalism

Emerson, Ralph Waldo. *Essays.* London: Macmillan, 1911.

Gardner, John Fentress. *American Heralds of the Spirit: Emerson, Whitman, and Melville.* Hudson, N.Y.: Lindisfarne Press, 1992.

Geldard, Richard. *The Esoteric Emerson: The Spiritual Teachings of Ralph Waldo Emerson.* Hudson, N.Y.: Lindisfarne Press, 1993.

————. *The Vision of Emerson.* Shaftesbury, England: Element, 1995.

C. The World's Parliament of Religions

Barrows, J. H., ed. *The World's Parliament of Religions: An Illustrated and Popular Story of the World's First Parliament of Religions, Held in Chicago in Connection with the Columbian Exposition of 1893.* 2 vols. Chicago: Parliament Publishing Co., 1893.

Lancaster, Clay. *The Incredible World's Parliament of Religions at the Chicago Columbian Exposition of 1893: A Comparative and Critical Study.* Fontwell, England: Centaur, 1987.

Seager, Richard Hughes. *The World's Parliament of Religions: The East/West Encounter, Chicago, 1893.* Bloomington: Indiana University Press, 1995.

D. Christian Fundamentalism

Barr, James. *Fundamentalism*. Philadelphia: Westminster Press, 1978.

Gasper, Louis. *The Fundamentalist Movement*. The Hague: Mouton, 1963.

Gilles, Anthony E. *Fundamentalism: What Every Catholic Needs to Know*. Cincinnati: St. Anthony Messenger Press, 1984.

Keating, Karl. *Catholicism and Fundamentalism: The Attack on "Romanism" by "Bible Christians."* San Francisco: Ignatius Press, 1988.

Marsden, George M. *Fundamentalism and American Culture: The Shaping of Twentieth-Century Evangelicalism, 1870-1925*. Oxford: Oxford University Press, 1982.

Marty, Martin E. *Fundamentalisms Observed*. Chicago: University of Chicago Press, 1991.

O'Meara, Thomas F. *Fundamentalism: A Catholic Perspective*. New York: Paulist Press, 1990.

Packer, J. I. *Fundamentalism and the Word of God*. London: Inter-Varsity Fellowship, 1970.

III. NRMs Originating in the 19th Century

A. Theosophy

Alcyone (Jiddhu Krishnamurti). *At the Feet of the Master*. Adyar, Madras: Theosophical Publishing House, 1982.

Barker, A. T. *The Mahatma Letters: To A. P. Sinnett from the Mahatmas M. & K. H.* Adyar, Madras: Theosophical Publishing House, 1979.

Besant, Annie. *Beauties of Islam*. Adyar, Madras: Theosophical Publishing House, 1990.

———. *Esoteric Christianity; or, The Lesser Mysteries*. Adyar, Madras: Theosophical Publishing House, 1914.

———. *Jainism*. Adyar, Madras: Theosophical Publishing House, 1983.

———. *Theosophy*. London: T. C. & E. C. Jack, 1912.

Besant, Annie, and C. W. Leadbeater. *The Lives of Alcyone*. Adyar, Madras: Theosophical Publishing House, 1924.

———. *Thought-Forms*. London: Theosophical Publishing House, 1901.

Blavatsky, H. P. *Is Theosophy a Religion?* Adyar, Madras: Theosophical Publishing House, 1975.

———. *Isis Unveiled: A Master-Key to the Mysteries of Ancient and Modern Science and Theology*. Pasadena, Calif.: Theosophical University Press, 1976.

———. *The Secret Doctrine: The Synthesis of Science, Religion, and Philosophy*. Pasadena, Calif.: Theosophical University Press, 1977.

———. *Sunrise: Theosophic Perspectives*. Pasadena, Calif.: Theosophical University Press, 1991.

———. *The Voice of the Silence*. Adyar, Madras: Theosophical Publishing House, 1982.

Campbell, Bruce. *Ancient Wisdom Revived: A History of the Theosophical Movement*. Berkeley: University of California Press, 1980.

Carlson, Maria. *"No Religion Higher Than Truth": A History of the Theosophical Movement in Russia, 1875-1922*. Princeton, N.J.: Princeton University Press, 1993.

Chapman, Janine. *Quest for Dion Fortune*. York Beach, Maine: Samuel Weiser, 1993.

Cranston, Sylvia. *HPB: The Extraordinary Life and Influence of Helena Blavatsky, Founder of the Modern Theosophical Movement*. New York: Putnam, 1993.

Ellwood, Robert. *Theosophy*. Wheaton, Ill.: Theosophical Publishing House, 1986.

Fielding, Charles. *The Story of Dion Fortune*. Dallas, Tex.: Star and Cross, 1985.

Fortune, Dion. *The Cosmic Doctrine*. Wellingborough, England: Aquarian, 1988.

———. *Esoteric Orders and Their Work and the Training and Work of the Initiate*. Wellingborough, England: Aquarian, 1987.

———. *The Mystical Qabalah*. London: Ernest Benn, 1972.

————. *Psychic Self-Defence: A Study in Occult Pathology and Criminality.* Wellingborough, England: Aquarian, 1988.

Gomes, Michael. *The Dawning of the Theosophical Movement.* Wheaton, Ill.: Theosophical Publishing House, 1987.

Hanson, Virginia. *H. P. Blavatsky and the Secret Doctrine.* Wheaton, Ill.: Theosophical Publishing House, 1988.

Hodson, Geoffrey. *The Brotherhood of Angels and Men.* London: Theosophical Publishing House, 1927.

Johnson, Paul. *In Search of the Masters: Behind the Occult Myth.* South Boston, Mass.: Hedderly-Benton, 1990.

————. *Madame Blavatsky: The "Veiled Years."* London: Theosophical History Centre, 1987.

Judge, William Q. *The Ocean of Theosophy.* Covina, Calif.: Theosophical University Press, 1948.

Kingsland, William. *The Real H. P. Blavatsky: A Study in Theosophy, and a Memoir of a Great Soul.* London: Theosophical Publishing House, 1985.

Leadbeater, C. W. *The Devachanic Plane: Its Characteristic and Inhabitants.* London: Theosophical Publishing Society, 1896.

————. *A Textbook of Theosophy.* Adyar, Madras: Theosophical Publishing House, 1912.

————. *Vegetarianism and Occultism.* Adyar, Madras: Theosophical Publishing House, 1984.

Leslie-Smith, L. H. *One Hundred Years of Modern Occultism: A Review of the Parent Theosophical Society.* London: Theosophical History Centre, 1987.

Marvin Williams, Gertrude. *Priestess of The Occult: Madame Blavatsky.* New York: Alfred A. Knopf, 1946.

Mills, Joy. *A Hundred Years of Theosophy: A History of The Theosophical Society in America.* Wheaton, Ill.: Theosophical Publishing House, 1987.

Murphet, Howard. *When Daylight Comes: A Biography of Helena Petrovna Blavatsky.* Wheaton, Ill.: Theosophical Publishing House, 1975.

Neff, Mary K. *Personal Memoirs of H. P. Blavatsky.* New York: Dutton, 1937.

Nethercot, Arthur H. *The First Five Lives of Annie Besant.* London: Rupert Hart-Davis, 1961.

————. *The Last Four Lives of Annie Besant.* Chicago: University of Chicago Press, 1963.

Overton Fuller, Jean. *Blavatsky and Her Teachers: An Investigative Biography.* London: East-West Publications, 1988.

Ransom, Josephine. *The Seventy-Fifth Anniversary Book of the Theosophical Society.* Adyar, Madras: Theosophical Publishing House, 1950.

————. *A Short History of the Theosophical Society.* Adyar, Madras: Theosophical Publishing House, 1938.

Richardson, Alan. *Priestess: The Life and Magic of Dion Fortune.* Wellingborough, England: Aquarian, 1987.

Shearman, Hugh. *Charles Webster Leadbeater: A Biography.* London: St. Alban Press, 1980.

Taylor, Anne. *Annie Besant: A Biography.* Oxford: Oxford University Press, 1992.

Tillett, Gregory. *The Elder Brother: A Biography of Charles Webster Leadbeater.* London: Routledge and Kegan Paul, 1982.

Tingley, Katherine. *Theosophy: The Path of the Mystic.* Pasadena, Calif.: Theosophical University Press, 1977.

Wessinger, Catherine L. *Annie Besant and Progressive Messianism (1847-1933).* Lewiston, Ill.: Edwin Mellen, 1988.

B. Spiritualism and Spiritism

Brown, Slater. *The Heyday of Spiritualism.* New York: Hawthorn Books, 1970.

Cayce, Edgar. *My Life as a Seer: The Lost Memoirs.* New York: St. Martin's Press, 1999.

Cayce, Edgar, Gail Cayce Schwartzer, and Douglas G. Richards. *Mysteries of Atlantis Revisited.* San Francisco: Harper and Row, 1988.

Cayce, Hugh Lynn. *Venture Inward.* New York: Harper and Row, 1964.

Coll, Francisco. *Discovering Your True Identity.* Osceola, Iowa: American Leadership College, 1968.

Davis, Andrew Jackson. *The Harmonial Philosophy: A Compendium and Digest of the Works.* Milwaukee, Wisc.: National Spiritualist Association of Churches, n.d.

———. *The Magic Staff: An Autobiography.* New York: A. J. Davis.

———. *The Principles of Nature, Her Divine Revelations and a Voice to Mankind.* New York: S. S. Lyon and W. Fishbough, 1847.

Fitzgerald, B. J. *A New Text of Spiritual Philosophy and Religion.* San Jose, Calif.: Universal Church of the Master, 1954.

Ford, Arthur. *Why We Survive.* New York: Gutenberg Press, 1952.

Ford, Arthur, and Marguerite Harmon Bro. *Nothing So Strange.* New York: Harper and Row, 1958.

Hardinge, Emma. *Modern American Spiritualism.* New Hyde Park, N.Y.: University Books, 1970.

Kardec, Allan. *Experimental Spiritism: Book on Mediums; or, Guide for Mediums and Invocators.* Wellingborough, England: Aquarian, 1978.

———. *The Gospel According to Spiritism.* Chadwell Heath, England: Allan Kardec Publishing, 1993.

———. *Le Livre des Esprits.* (The book of spirits). Paris: Librarie Spirite, 1857.

Kerr, Howard. *Mediums, and Spirit-Rappers, and Roaring Radicals.* Urbana: University of Illinois Press, 1973.

Nelson, Geoffrey K. *Spiritualism and Society.* London: Routledge and Kegan Paul, 1969.

Newbrough, John. *Oahspe: A New Bible in the Words of Jehovah and His Angel Ambassadors.* New York: Oahspe Publishing Association, 1882.

Pearsall, Ronald. *The Table-Rappers.* New York: St. Martin's Press, 1972.

Stearn, Jess. *Edgar Cayce: The Sleeping Prophet.* New York: Doubleday, 1967.

C. New Thought

D'Andrade, Hugh. *Charles Fillmore: Herald of the New Age.* New York: Harper and Row, 1974.

Dresser, Annetta Gertrude. *The Philosophy of P. P. Quimby.* Boston: George H. Ellis, 1895.

Dresser, Horatio. *History of the New Thought Movement.* New York: T. Y. Crowell, 1919.

———. *The Quimby Manuscripts.* New York: Julian Press, 1961.

Evans, Warren Felt. *Esoteric Christianity and Mental Therapeutics.* Boston: H. H. Carter, 1866.

———. *Mental Medicine.* Boston: H. H. Carter, 1873.

Fillmore, Charles. *Christian Healing: The Science of Being.* London: Fowler, 1917.

Fillmore, Connie. *The Unity Guide to Healing.* Unity Village, Mo.: Unity, 1987.

———. *The Unity Guide to Prosperous Living.* Unity Village, Mo.: Unity, 1973.

Fillmore, Myrtle. *How to Let God Help You.* Lee's Summit, Mo.: Unity School of Christianity, 1956.

Holmes, Ernest. *Creative Mind.* New York: Putnam, 1997

———. *The Science of Mind.* London: A. M. Philpot, 1927.

Holmes, Fenwicke L. *Ernest Holmes: His Life and Times.* New York: Dodd, Mead, 1970.

———. *The Law of Mind in Action.* London: Routledge, 1921.

Hopkins, Emma Curtis. *High Mysticism.* Marina del Rey, Calif.: DeVorss, 1987.

———. *Scientific Christian Mental Practice.* Marina del Rey, Calif.: DeVorss, 1987.

James, Fannie B. *Divine Science: Its Principle and Practice.* Denver: Textbook of Divine Science, 1957.

Melton, J. Gordon. *New Thought: A Reader.* Santa Barbara, Calif.: Institute for the Study of American Religion, 1990.

Parker, Gail T. *Mind Cure in New England.* Hanover, N.H.: University Press of New England, 1973.

Quimby, Phineas Parkhurst. *The Complete Writings.* Marina del Rey, Calif.: DeVorss, 1988.

Unity School of Christianity. *Metaphysical Bible Dictionary.* Unity Village, Mo.: Unity School of Christianity, 1986.

————. *Unity: A Hundred Years of Faith and Vision.* Unity Village, Mo.: Unity Books, 1988.

Witherspoon, Thomas E. *Myrtle Fillmore: Mother of Unity.* Unity Village, Mo.: Unity Books, 1984.

D. Christian Science

Church of Christ, Scientist. *Christian Science: A Sourcebook of Contemporary Materials.* Boston: Christian Science Publishing Society, 1990.

Dakin, Edwin Franden. *Mrs. Eddy: The Biography of a Virginal Mind.* New York: Charles Scribner's, 1930.

Eddy, Mary Baker. *Prose Works: Other than Science and Health with Key to the Scriptures.* Boston: First Church of Christ, Scientist, 1953.

————. *Science and Health with Key to the Scriptures.* Boston: First Church of Christ, Scientist, 1994.

Gottschalk, Stephen. *The Emergence of Christian Science in American Religious Life.* Berkeley: University of California Press, 1978.

Milmine, Georgine. *The Life of Mary Baker Eddy and the History of Christian Science.* London: Hodder and Stoughton, 1909.

Peel, Robert. *Christian Science: Its Encounter with American Culture.* New York: Holt, 1958.

————. *Mary Baker Eddy: The Years of Authority, 1892-1910.* New York: Holt, Rinehart and Winston, 1980.

————. *Mary Baker Eddy: The Years of Discovery, 1821-1875.* Boston: Christian Science Publishing Society, 1966.

————. *Mary Baker Eddy: The Years of Trial, 1876-1891.* Boston: Christian Science Publishing Society, 1971.

E. New Christian groups

1. Christadelphians

Lippy, Charles H. *The Christadelphians in North America*. Lewiston, N.Y.: Edwin Mellen, 1989.

Roberts, Robert. *A Guide to the Formation and Conduct of Christadelphian Ecclesias*. Birmingham, England: Christadelphian, 1922.

———. *A Guide to the Formation and Conduct of the Christadelphians*. Quincy, Mass.: Christadelphian Advocate Publications, n.d.

———. *Christendom Astray from the Bible*. London: F. G. Jannaway, 1930.

Tennant, Harry. *The Christadelphians: What They Believe and Preach*. Birmingham, England: Christadelphian, 1988.

Thomas, John. *Elpis Israel: An Exposition of the Kingdom of God*. Birmingham, England: C. C. Walker, 1903.

2. Church of Jesus Christ of Latter-day Saints

Barrow, P. *Mormons and the Bible: The Place of the Latter-day Saints in American Religion*. Oxford: Oxford University Press, 1991.

Bennett, John C. *The History of the Saints; or, An Exposé of Joe Smith and Mormonism*. Boston, Mass.: Leland and Whiting, 1842.

Brodie, Fawn M. *No Man Knows My History: The Life of Joseph Smith, the Mormon Prophet*. New York: Alfred A. Knopf, 1985.

Bushman, Richard L. *Joseph Smith and the Beginnings of Mormonism*. Urbana: University of Illinois Press, 1984.

Cooley, Everett. *Diary of Brigham Young, 1857*. Salt Lake City: University of Utah Tanner Trust Fund, 1980.

Davies, Douglas, ed. *Mormon Identities in Transition*. London: Continuum, 1999.

Guers, Emilius. *Irvingism and Mormonism: Tested by Scripture.*
London: James Nisbet, 1854.

Ludlow, D. H., ed. *Encyclopedia of Mormonism.* New York:
Collier Macmillan, 1992.

Martin, Walter R. *The Maze of Mormonism.* Grand Rapids,
Mich.: Zondervan, 1962.

McConkie, Bruce R. *Mormon Doctrine.* Salt Lake City, Utah:
Bookcraft, 1979.

McKiernan, F. Mark. *The Restoration Movement: Essays in
Mormon History.* Lawrence, Kans.: Coronado Press, 1973.

Mullan, Bob. *The Mormons.* London: W. H. Allen, 1967.

Persuitte, David. *Joseph Smith and the Origins of the Book of
Mormon.* Jefferson, N.C.: McFarland, 1991.

Quinn, D. Michael. *The New Mormon History: Revisionist Essays on the Past.* Salt Lake City: Signature Books, 1992.

Shipps, Jan. *Mormonism: The Story of a New Religious Tradition.* Urbana: University of Illinois Press, 1985.

Smith, Joseph. *The Book of Mormon.* Manchester, England: Deseret Enterprises, 1972.

———. *The Doctrine and Covenants of the Church of Jesus
Christ of Latter-day Saints and The Pearl of Great Price.* Salt
Lake City, Utah: The Church of Jesus Christ of Latter-day
Saints, 1982.

———. *History of the Church of Jesus Christ of Latter-day
Saints.* Salt Lake City, Utah: Deseret, 1978.

Warner, J. *The Mormon Way.* Englewood Cliffs, N.J.: Prentice-
Hall, 1967.

3. Adventism

Houteff, Victor T. *The Great Controversy over "The Shepherd's
Rod."* Waco, Tex: Universal Publishing Association, 1954.

———. *The Shepherd's Rod Series.* Salem, S.C.: General Association of Davidian Seventh-day Adventists, 1990.

Land, Gary, ed. *Adventism in America: A History.* Grand Rapids,
Mich.: Eerdmans, 1986.

Weber, Timothy P. *Living in the Shadow of the Second Coming: American Pre-Millennialism, 1875-1925.* Oxford: Oxford University Press, 1979.

White, Ellen G. *The Great Controversy between Christ and Satan: The Conflict of the Ages in the Christian Dispensation.* Mountain View, Calif.: United Publishers, 1975.

————. *Patriarchs and Prophets; or, The Great Conflict between Good and Evil as Illustrated in the Lives of Holy Men of Old.* London: Pacific Press, 1892.

4. Branch Davidians: Waco group

Breault, Marc, and Martin King. *Inside the Cult.* New York: New American Library, 1993.

Lewis, J. R. *From the Ashes: Making Sense of Waco.* London: Rowman and Littlefield, 1994.

Tabor, James D., and Eugene V. Gallagher. *Why Waco? Cults and the Battle for Religious Freedom in America.* Berkeley: University of California Press, 1995.

Wright, Stuart A., ed. *Armageddon in Waco: Critical Perspectives on the Branch Davidian Conflict.* Chicago: University of Chicago Press, 1995.

5. Jehovah's Witnesses

Beckford, J. A. *The Trumpet of Prophecy.* Oxford: Blackwell, 1975.

Burganger, Karl. *The Watch Tower Society and Absolute Chronology: A Critique.* Lethbridge, Canada: Christian Koinonia International, 1981.

Cole, Marley. *Jehovah's Witnesses: The New World Society.* London: Allen and Unwin, 1956.

Crompton, R. *Counting the Days to Armageddon: The Jehovah's Witnesses and the Second Presence of Christ.* London: Lutterworth, 1996.

Gruss, Edmond Charles. *The Jehovah's Witnesses and Prophetic Speculation.* Phillipsburg, N.J.: Presbyterian and Reformed Publishing, 1972.

Horowitz, David. *Pastor Charles Taze Russell: An Early American Christian Zionist.* New York: Philosophical Library, 1986.

New World Bible Translation Committee. *New World Translation of the Holy Scriptures.* Brooklyn, N.Y.: Watch Tower Bible and Tract Society of Pennsylvania, 1961.

Penton, M. James. *Apocalypse Delayed: The Story of Jehovah's Witnesses.* Toronto: University of Toronto Press, 1985.

Reed, David A. *Jehovah's Witness Literature: A Critical Guide to Watchtower Publications.* Grand Rapids, Mich.: Baker Book House, 1993.

Russell, C. T. *The Finished Mystery.* Brooklyn, N.Y.: International Bible Students Association, 1917.

―――. *Studies in the Scriptures.* 6 vols. New York: International Bible Students Association, 1886-1904.

Rutherford, J. F. *Millions Now Living Will Never Die.* Brooklyn, N.Y.: International Bible Students Association, 1920.

Schnell, W. J. *Thirty Years a Watch Tower Slave: The Confessions of a Converted Jehovah's Witness.* Grand Rapids, Mich.: Baker Book House, 1959.

Stafford, Greg. *Jehovah's Witnesses Defended: An Answer to Scholars and Critics.* Huntington Beach, Calif.: Elihu Books, 2d ed, 2000.

Watchtower Bible and Tract Society. *Jehovah's Witnesses: Proclaimers of God's Kingdom.* Brooklyn, N.Y.: Watchtower Bible and Tract Society of New York, 1993.

―――. *2000 Yearbook of Jehovah's Witnesses.* Brooklyn, N.Y.: Watchtower Bible and Tract Society of New York, and International Bible Students Association, 2000.

―――. *Watchtower Library, 1999.* CD-ROM. Brooklyn, N.Y.: Watchtower Bible and Tract Society, 2000.

White, Timothy. *A People for His Name: A History of Jehovah's Witnesses and an Evaluation.* New York: Vantage Press, 1967.

6. Early Pentecostalism

Bartleman, Frank. *Azusa Street*. Plainfield, N.J.: Logos International, 1980.

Burgess, Stanley M. *Dictionary of Pentecostal and Charismatic Movements*. Regency Reference Library. Grand Rapids, Mich.: Zondervan Publishing House, 1988.

Burton, Thomas. *Serpent-Handling Believers*. Knoxville: University of Tennessee Press, 1993.

Cox, Harvey. *Fire from Heaven: The Rise of Pentecostal Spirituality and the Reshaping of Religion in the Twenty-First Century*. Reading, Mass.: Addison-Wesley, 1995.

Dallimore, Arnold. *The Life of Edward Irving: The Fore-Runner of the Charismatic Movement*. Edinburgh: Banner of Truth Trust, 1983.

Dayton, Donald W. *Theological Roots of Pentecostalism*. Grand Rapids, Mich.: Francis Asbury, 1987.

Drummond, Andrew Landale. *Edward Irving and His Circle: Including Some Consideration of the "Tongues" Movement in the Light of Modern Psychology*. Edinburgh: James Clarke, 1934.

Duffield, Guy P. *Foundations of Pentecostal Theology*. Los Angeles: LIFE Bible College, 1983.

Garrett, Clarke. *Spirit Possession and Popular Religion: From the Camisards to the Shakers*. Baltimore: John Hopkins University Press, 1987.

Hollenweger, Walter J. *Pentecostalism: Origins and Developments Worldwide*. Peabody, Mass.: Hendrickson, 1997.

———. *The Pentecostals*. London: SCM, 1976.

Hollenweger, Walter J., and Allan H. Anderson, eds. *Pentecostals after a Century: Global Perspectives on a Movement in Transition*. Sheffield, England: Sheffield Academic, 1999.

Jones, Charles Edwin. *A Guide to the Study of the Pentecostal Movement*. Metuchen, N.J.: Scarecrow Press, 1983.

Kimbrough, David L. *Taking up Serpents: Snake Handlers of Eastern Kentucky*. Chapel Hill: University of North Carolina Press, 1995.

Menzies, William W. *Anointed to Serve: The Story of the Assemblies of God.* Springfield, Mo.: Gospel Publishing House, 1988.

Nickel, Thomas R. *Azusa Street Outpouring, as Told to Me by Those Who Were There.* Hanford, Calif.: Great Commission International, 1986.

Oliphant, Margaret. *The Life of Edward Irving.* London: Harper and Brothers, 1862.

Poewe, Karla. *Charismatic Christianity as a Global Culture.* Columbia: University of South Carolina Press, 1994.

Poloma, Margaret M. *The Assemblies of God at the Crossroads: Charisma and Institutional Dilemmas.* Knoxville: University of Tennessee Press, 1989.

Riss, Richard M. *A Survey of Twentieth-Century Revival Movements in North America.* Peabody, Mass.: Hendrickson, 1988.

Slay, James L. *This We Believe.* Cleveland, Tenn.: Pathway Press, 1963.

Strachan, C. Gordon. *The Pentecostal Theology of Edward Irving.* London: Darton, Longman and Todd, 1973.

Synan, Vinson. *The Holiness-Pentecostal Movement in the United States.* Grand Rapids, Mich.: Eerdmans, 1987.

———. *The Twentieth-Century Pentecostal Explosion: The Exciting Growth of Pentecostal Churches and Charismatic Renewal Movements.* Altamonte Springs, Fla.: Creation House, 1987.

Worsfold, James E. *The Origins of the Apostolic Church in Great Britain with a Breviate of Its Early Missionary Endeavours.* Wellington, New Zealand: Julian Literature Trust, 1991.

F. Magickal Groups

1. General, Historical, and Early Leaders

Butler, E. M. *The Fortunes of Faust.* Cambridge: Cambridge University Press, 1979.

————. *The Myth of the Magus.* Cambridge: Cambridge University Press, 1980.

————. *Ritual Magic.* Cambridge: Cambridge University Press, 1980.

Cavendish, Richard. *The Encyclopedia of the Unexplained: Magic, Occultism, and Parapsychology.* London: Arkana, 1989.

Colquhoun, Ithell. *Sword of Wisdom: MacGregor Mathers and "The Golden Dawn."* New York: Putnam, 1975.

Hall, Manly P. *An Encyclopedic Outline of Masonic, Hermetic, Qabbalistic, and Rosicrucian Symbolical Philosophy.* Los Angeles: Philosophical Research Society, 1989.

King, Francis. *Modern Ritual Magic: The Rise of Western Occultism.* Bridport, Dorset: Prism and Unity Press, 1990.

Lévi, Eliphas. *Transcendental Magic: Its Doctrine and Ritual.* London: Bracken Books, 1995.

Mathers, S. L. MacGregor. *The Book of the Sacred Magic of Abra-Melin, the Mage.* London: J. M. Watkins, 1956.

McIntosh, Christopher. *Eliphas Lévi and the French Occult Revival.* London: Rider, 1972.

Thorndike, Lynn. *A History of Magic and Experimental Science.* New York: Columbia University Press, 1958.

Waite, A. E. *The Pictorial Key to the Tarot.* New York: Citadel Press, 1990.

Westcott, William Wynn. *The Science of Alchemy: Spiritual and Material.* Edmonds, Wash.: Alchemical Press, 1983.

2. P. B. Randolph, Thelemic Magick, and Ordo Templi Orientis

King, Francis. *The Secret Rituals of the O.T.O.* New York: Samuel Weiser, 1973.

McMurtry, G. L. *Poems: The Angels and the Abyss; Dark Space and Bright Stars.* London: Ordo Templi Orientis, 1986.

Randolph, P. B. *After Death: The Immortality of Man.* Quakertown, Pa.: Philosophical Publishing Co., 1970.

————. *Eulis! The History of Love: Its Wondrous Magic, Chemistry, Rules, Laws, Moods, Modes, and Rationale.* Toledo, Ohio: Randolph Publishing, 1874.

————. *The Immortality of Love.* Quakertown, Pa.: Beverly Hall Corporation, 1978.

————. *Magia Sexualis.* Rome: Mediterranee, 1987.

————. *Pre-Adamite Man: Demonstrating the Existence of the Human Race upon This Earth 100,000 Years Ago!.* Toledo, Ohio: Randolph Publishing. 1888.

————. *Ravalett: The Rosicrucian's Story.* Quakertown, Pa.: Philosophical Publishing Co, 1939.

————. *Seership: Guide to Soul Sight.* Quakertown: The Confederation of Initiates, 1930.

————. *Sexual Magic.* New York: Magickal Childe, 1988.

Shual, Katon. *Sexual Magick.* Oxford: Mandrake, 1989.

3. Aleister Crowley and the Hermetic Order of the Golden Dawn

Booth, Martin. *A Magick Life: The Life of Aleister Crowley.* London: Hodder and Stoughton, 2000.

Cammell, Charles Richard. *Aleister Crowley: The Man, the Mage, the Poet.* London: Richards, 1951.

Crowley, Aleister. *The Book of the Law.* York Beach, Maine: Samuel Weiser, 1987.

————. *The Complete Astrological Writings.* London: Star Books, 1987.

————. *The Confessions of Aleister Crowley.* London: Routledge and Kegan Paul, 1979.

————. *Enochian World of Aleister Crowley: Enochian Sex Magick.* Scottsdale, Ariz.: New Falcon, 1991.

————. *Magick in Theory and Practice.* New York: Magickal Childe Publishing, 1929.

————. *Thelema: The Holy Books of Thelema.* York Beach, Maine: Samuel Weiser, 1988.

Crowley, Amado. *The Secrets of Aleister Crowley.* Guildford, England: Diamond Books, 1991.

D'Arch Smith, Timothy. *The Books of the Beast: Essays on Aleister Crowley, Montague Summers, Francis Barrett, and Others.* Wellingborough, England: Crucible, 1987.

Gilbert, R. A. *A. E. Waite: Magician of Many Parts.* Wellingborough, England: Crucible, 1987.

————. *The Golden Dawn: Twilight of The Magicians.* Wellingborough, England: Aquarian, 1983.

————. *The Golden Dawn and the Esoteric Section.* London: Theosophical History Centre, 1987.

————. *The Golden Dawn Companion.* Wellingborough, England: Aquarian, 1986.

Grant, Kenneth. *Remembering Aleister Crowley.* London: Skoob Books, 1991.

Green, Marian. *Quest Witchcraft Anthology.* London: Quest, 1982.

Heindel, Max. *The Rosicrucian Cosmo-Conception.* Oceanside, Calif.: International Headquarters Rosicrucian Fellowship and L. N. Fowler.

Howe, Ellic. *The Magicians of the Golden Dawn: A Documentary History of a Magical Order, 1887-1923.* Wellingborough, England: Aquarian, 1985.

Hyatt, Christopher S. *An Interview with Israel Regardie: His Final Thoughts and Views.* Phoenix, Ariz.: Falcon Press, 1985.

Kerr, Howard. *The Occult in America: New Historical Perspectives.* Urbana: University of Illinois Press, 1986.

King, Francis X. *The Magical World of Aleister Crowley.* London: Arrow Books, 1987.

Regardie, Israel. *The Eye in the Triangle: An Interpretation of Aleister Crowley.* Phoenix, Ariz.: Falcon Press, 1986.

————. *The Legend of Aleister Crowley.* Phoenix, Ariz.: Falcon Press, 1983.

————. *What You Should Know about the Golden Dawn.* Phoenix, Ariz.: Falcon Press, 1987.

Robertson, Sandy. *The Aleister Crowley Scrapbook.* York Beach, Maine: Samuel Weiser, 1988.

Symonds, John. *The Great Beast: The Life of Aleister Crowley.* St. Albans, England: Mayflower, 1973.

——. *The King of the Shadow Realm: Aleister Crowley, His Life and Magic.* London: Duckworth, 1989.

——. *The Magic of Aleister Crowley.* London: Frederick Muller, 1958.

Torrens, R. G. *The Inner Teachings of the Golden Dawn.* London: Neville Spearman, 1969.

Zalewski, Pat. *The Equinox and Solstice Ceremonies of the Golden Dawn.* Saint Paul, Minn.: Llewellyn Publications, 1992.

——. *Golden Dawn Enochian Magic.* Saint Paul, Minn.: Llewellyn Publications, 1994.

——. *The Secret Inner Order Rituals of the Golden Dawn.* Phoenix, Ariz.: Falcon Press, 1988.

——. *Z-5 Secret Teachings of the Golden Dawn.* Saint Paul, Minn.: Llewellyn Publications, 1992.

4. Templarism and Rosicrucianism

Clymer, R. Swinburne. *The Book of Rosicruciae.* Quakertown, Pa.: Philosophical Publishing, 1949.

——. *Manual Order of Service and Ritual Church of Illumination.* Quakertown, Pa.: Philosophical Publishing, 1952.

Lewis, H. Spencer. *The Mystical Life of Jesus.* San Jose, Calif.: Supreme Grand Lodge of AMORC, 1988.

——. *Rosicrucian Manual.* San Jose, Calif.: Rosicrucian Press, 1941.

McIntosh, Christopher. *The Rosicrucians: The History and Mythology of an Occult Order.* Wellingborough, England: Aquarian, 1980.

Melton, J. Gordon. *Rosicrucianism in America.* New York: Garland, 1990.

Parsons, John Whiteside. *Freedom Is a Two-Edged Sword and Other Essays.* Phoenix, Ariz.: Falcon Press, 1989.

Vaughan, Thomas. *The Fraternity of the Rosy Cross and a Short Declaration of Their Physical Work.* Edmonds, Wash.: Alchemical Press, 1983.

Waite, A. E. *The Brotherhood of the Rosy Cross.* London: Rider, 1924.

Westcott, W. W. *The Rosicrucians, Past and Present, at Home and Abroad.* Edmonds, Wash.: Sure Fire Press, 1989.

5. Solar Temple

Introvigne, Massimo. "Ordeal by Fire: The Tragedy of the Solar Temple." *Religio,* 25 (1995): 267-283.

Mayer, Jean-François. "Les Chevaliers de l'Apocalypse: L'Ordre du Temple Solaire et ses adeptes" (The knights of the Apocalypse: The Order of the Solar Temple and its adepts]; in Françoise Champion, and Martine Cohen, eds., *Sectes et démocratie.* Paris: Editions du Seuil, 1999: 205-223.

————. *Les Mythes du Temple Solaire.* (The myths of the Solar Temple). Geneva: Georg, 1996.

————. "'Our Terrestrial Journey Is Coming to an End': The Last Voyage of the Solar Temple." *Nova Religio,* no. 2 (April 1999): 172-196.

Palmer, Susan J. "Purity and Danger in the Solar Temple." *Journal of Contemporary Religion,* 11, no. 3 (1996): 303-318.

6. Other Recent Magickal Movements

Bonewits, P. E. I. *Real Magic.* Berkeley, Calif.: Creative Arts Book Co., 1979.

Burton, Tina. *"Intuitive Magick"? A Study of the Temple Ov Psychick Youth, 1981-1989.* London: n.p. 1989.

Green, Marian. *Magic for the Aquarian Age.* Wellingborough, England: Aquarian, 1983.

Robertson, Olivia. *The Isis Wedding Rite: Liturgy of The Fellowship of Isis.* Enniscorthy, Ireland: Cesara Publications, 1983.

Savage, Adrian. *An Introduction to Chaos Magick.* New York: Magickal Childe, 1988.

IV. Theosophy-derived NRMs

1. Alice Bailey and the Arcane School / Lucis Trust

Bailey, Alice A. *The Destiny of the Nations.* New York: Lucis Publishing Co., 1974.

———. *Discipleship in The New Age.* New York: Lucis Publishing Co., 1979.

———. *From Bethlehem to Calvary: The Initiations of Jesus.* New York: Lucis Publishing Co., 1937.

———. *Letters on Occult Meditation.* New York: Lucis Publishing Co., 1974.

———. *The Reappearance of the Christ.* New York: Lucis Publishing Co., 1984.

———. *Telepathy And The Etheric Vehicle.* New York: Lucis Publishing Co., 1975.

———. *A Treatise On Cosmic Fire.* New York: Lucis Publishing Co., 1989.

———. *The Unfinished Autobiography of Alice A. Bailey.* New York: Lucis Publishing Co., 1987.

Overton Fuller, Jean. *The Comte de Saint-Germain: Last Scion of the House of Rakoczy.* London: East-West Publications, 1988.

2. Rudolf Steiner and Anthroposophy

Easton, Stewart C. *Rudolf Steiner: Herald of a New Epoch.* New York: Anthroposophic Press, 1980.

King, Francis X. *Rudolf Steiner and Holistic Medicine.* London: Rider, 1986.

Steiner, R. *Aspects of Human Evolution.* New York: Anthroposophic Press, 1983.

———. *Deeper Insights into Education.* New York: Anthroposophic Press, 1983.

———. *Rudolf Steiner: An Autobiography.* New York: Anthroposophic Press, 1997.

Wilson, Colin. *Rudolf Steiner: The Man and His Vision.* Wellingborough, England: Aquarian, 1985.

3. Krishnamurti

Bhatt, M. *Krishnamurti: A Life.* New York: Viking, 1992.
Jayakar, Pupal. *Krishnamurti: A Biography.* San Francisco: Harper and Row, 1986.
Krishnamuri, Jiddhu. *The Awakening of Intelligence.* London: Gollancz, 1973.
————. *Commentaries on Living.* 3 vols. London: Gollancz, 1956, 1959, 1960.
————. *Freedom from the Known.* London: Gollancz, 1983.
————. *The Future Is Now: Last Talks in India.* London: Gollancz, 1988.
————. *The Krishnamurti Reader.* London: Penguin, 1970.
————. *Krishnamurti's Journal.* London: Gollancz, 1982.
————. *Think on These Things.* New York: Harper and Row, 1964.
Lutyens, Mary. *Krishnamurti: The Open Door.* London: Murray, 1988.
————. *Krishnamurti: The Years of Awakening.* London: Rider, 1984.
————. *Krishnamurti: The Years of Fulfilment.* London: Rider, 1985.

4. Church Universal and Triumphant/Summit Lighthouse

Lewis, James R. *Church Universal and Triumphant in Scholarly Perspective.* Stanford, Calif.: Center for Academic Publication, 1994.
Prophet, Elizabeth Clare. *The Great White Brotherhood.* Malibu, Calif.: Summit University Press, 1983.
Prophet, Mark L., and Elizabeth Clare Prophet. *Climb the Highest Mountain: The Path of the Higher Self.* Los Angeles: Summit Lighthouse.

————. *The Lost Teachings of Jesus.* Livingston, Mont.: Summit University Press, 1993.

————. *The Lost Years of Jesus.* Livingston, Mont.: Summit University Press, 1993.

York, Michael. "The Church Universal and Triumphant." *Journal of Contemporary Religion* 10, no. 1 (1995): 71-82.

5. I AM Movement

Ballard, Guy, and Edna Ballard. *I AM Adorations and Affirmations.* Chicago: Saint Germain Press, 1936.

————. *The Magic Presence.* Chicago: Saint Germain Press, 1935.

————. *Unveiling Mysteries.* Chicago: Saint Germain Press, 1934.

I Am Religious Activity. *The Saint Germain Series.* Edited by Godfré Ray King (Guy W. Ballard). Schaumburg, Ill.: Saint Germain Press, 1987.

————. *The Voice of the I Am.* Edited by Godfré Ray King (Guy W. Ballard). Chicago: Saint Germain Press, 1985.

King, Godfré Ray (Guy W. Ballard). *Unveiled Mysteries.* Chicago: Saint Germain Press, 1935.

————. *The Magic Presence.* Chicago: Saint Germain Press, 1935.

Saint Germain Foundation. *"I Am" Decrees for the Violet Consuming Flame.* Chicago: Saint Germain Press, 1987.

6. White Eagle Lodge

Cooke, Grace. *The Illuminated Ones.* Liss, England: White Eagle Publishing Trust, 1966.

————. *The Jewel in the Lotus.* Liss, England: White Eagle Publishing Trust, 1993.

————. *Meditation.* Liss, England: White Eagle Publishing Trust, 1955.

————. *Sun Men of the Americas.* Liss, England: White Eagle Publishing Trust, 1975.
Lind, Ingrid. *The White Eagle Inheritance.* Wellingborough, England: Turnstone Press, 1984.
White Eagle Lodge. *Wisdom from White Eagle.* Liss, England: White Eagle Publishing Trust, 1987.

7. Christ Maitreya

Creme, Benjamin. *Maitreya's Mission.* Amsterdam: Share International Foundation, 1993.
————. *The Reappearance of Christ and the Masters of Wisdom.* London: Tara, 1980.

V. Jewish and Jewish-derived NRMs

1. Kabbalism

Ashlag, Yehuda. *Kabbalah: A Gift of the Bible.* Jerusalem: Research Center of Kabbalah, 1994.
Berg, Philip S. *Kabbalah for the Layman.* 3 vols. Jerusalem: Research Center of Kabbalah, 1981-1988.
Roland, Paul. *Kabbalah.* London: Piatkus, 1999.

2. Liberal, Reform, and Progressive Judaism

Cronbach, A. *Reform Movements in Judaism.* New York: Bookman Associates, 1963.
Daily Sabbath and Occasional Prayers, 7th ed. London: Reform Synagogue of Great Britain, 1997.
Forster, Brenda. *Jews by Choice: A Study of Converts to Reform and Conservative Judaism.* New York: Ktav, 1991.
Philipson, D., and F. Philipson. *The Reform Movement in Judaism.* New York: Ktav, 1967.

Rausch, David A. *Messianic Judaism: Its History, Theology, and Polity.* New York: Edwin Mellen, 1982.

Rayner, J. *Jewish Religious Law: A Progressive Perspective.* New York: Berghahn, 1988.

Rayner, J., and B. Hooker. *Judaism for Today.* London: Union of Liberal/Progressive Synagogues, 1978.

Schochet, Jacob Immanuel. *Mashiach: The Principle of Mashiach and the Messianic Era in Jewish Law and Tradition.* New York: S.I.E., 1991.

3. Lubavitch

"'I' and 'Not I': A Lubavitch Story." *Parabola—Myth, Tradition and the Search for Meaning* 22, no. 3 (Fall 1997): 65.

Morris, B. J. "The Childrens-Crusade: The Tzivos-Hashem-Youth-Movement as an Aspect of Hasidic Identity and the So-Called Chabad Movement of Lubavitch Hasidism." *Judaism* 40, no. 3 (1991): 333-343.

Nadler, A., and E. Hoffman. "Despite All Odds: The Story of Lubavitch." *New Republic,* 206, no. 18, 4 May 1992: 23.

Shaffir, W. "Jewish Messianism, Lubavitch-Style: An Interim-Report." *Jewish Journal of Sociology,* 35, no. 2. (December 1993): 115-128.

4. Messianic Jews

Cohn-Sherbok, D. *Messianic Judaism.* London: Continuum, 2000.

Feher, Shoshanah. *Passing over Easter: Constructing the Boundaries of Messianic Judaism.* Walnut Creek, Calif.: AltaMira Press, 1998.

Harris-Shapiro, Carol. *Messianic Judaism: A Rabbi's Journey through Religious Change in America.* Boston: Beacon Press, 1999.

Rausch, David A. *Messianic Judaism: Its History, Theology, and Polity.* New York: Edwin Mellen, 1982.

VI. New Christian NRMs

1. Black Pentecostalism

Anderson, Allan. *The Faith of African Pentecostals in South Africa.* Praetoria: University of South Africa, 1993.
Dupree, S. S. *Biographical Dictionary of African-American, Holiness-Pentecostals 1880-1990.* Washington D.C.: Middle Atlantic Reigional Press, 1989.
Sanders, Cheryl J. *Saints in Exile: The Holiness-Pentecostal Experience in African American Religion and Culture.* New York: Oxford University Press, 1996.

2. Branham, William

Branham, William Marrion. *As the Eagle Stirreth Her Nest.* Jeffersonville, Ind.: Spoken Word Publications, 1985.
————. *The Eleventh Commandment.* Jeffersonville, Ind.: Spoken Word Publications, n.d.
————. *The Great Shining Light.* Jeffersonville, Ind.: Voice of God Recordings, 1989.
————. *The Revelation of the Seven Seals.* Jeffersonville, Ind.: Spoken Word Publications, 1967.
Lindsay, Gordon. *William Branham: A Man Sent from God.* Jeffersonville, Ind.: William Branham, 1950.
Weaver, C. Douglas. *The Healer-Prophet, William Marrion Branham: A Study of the Prophetic in American Pentecostalism.* Macon, Ga.: Mercer University Press, 1987.

3. Brethren

Cambell, R. K. *Reunited Brethren: A Brief Historical Account Including a Brief Statement of Some Vital Principles of Faith.* Danville, Ill.: Grace and Truth, 1990.
Cousins, Peter. *The Brethren.* Oxford: Pergamon Press, 1982.
Darby, John Nelson. *The Collected Writings.* 35 vols. Oak Park, Ill.: Bible Truth Publishers, 1971.

Durnbaugh, Donald F. *The Brethren Encyclopedia.* Oak Brook, Pa.: The Brethren Encyclopedia, 1983-1984.

Neatby, W. B. *A History of the Plymouth Brethren.* London: Hodder and Stoughton, 1901.

Weremchuk, Max S. *John Nelson Darby: A Biography.* Neptune, N.J.: Loizeaux, 1992.

4. Bruderhof

The Bruderhof: A Christian Community. Rifton, N.Y.: Plough Publishing House, 1985.

5. Christian Identity (including Ku Klux Klan and British Israel)

Aho, J. A. *The Politics of Righteousness: Idaho Christian Patriotism.* Seattle: University of Washington Press, 1990.

Allen, J. H. *Judah's Sceptre and Joseph's Birthright.* Boston: A. A. Beauchamp, 1930.

Bushart, H. L., J. R. Craig, and M. Barnes. *Soldiers of God: White Supremacists and Their Holy War for America.* New York: Kensington Books, 1998.

Coates, James. *Armed and Dangerous.* New York: Hill and Wang, 1987.

The Covenant People. Merrimac, Mass.: Destiny Publishers, 1966.

Gale, William P. *Racial and National Identity.* Glendale, Calif.: Ministry of Christ Church, n.d.

Gayer, M. H. *The Heritage of the Anglo-Saxon Race.* Haverhill, Mass.: Destiny Publishers, 1941.

Haberman, Frederick. *Tracing Our White Ancestors.* Phoenix, Ariz.: Lord's Covenant Church, 1979.

Hate Groups in America. New York: Anti-Defamation League of B'nai B'rith, 1982.

Kaplan, J., ed. *Nation and Race: The Developing Euro-American Racist Subculture*. Boston.: Northeastern University Press, 1998.

The Pattern of History. Merrimac, Mass.: Destiny Publishers, 1961.

Rand, Howard B. *Digest of Divine Law*. Haverhill, Mass.: Destiny Publishers, 1943.

Schwartz, Alan, and Gail L. Gans. "The Identity Churches: A Theology of Hate." *ADL Facts* 28, no 1 (Spring 1983).

Smith, Gerald L. K. *The Cross and the Flag*. Serial 1st ed. 1942.

Stadsklev, C. O. *Our Christian Beginnings*. Hopkins, Minn.: America's Hope Broadcasts, n.d.

————. *Personal Salvation*. Hopkins, Minn.: America's Hope, n.d.

————. *What Happened at Calvary*. Hopkins, Minn.: America's Hope, n.d.

Swift, Wesley A. *God, Man, Nations, and the Races*. Hollywood, Calif.: New Christian Crusade Church, n.d.

————. *Testimony of Tradition and the Origin of Races*. Hollywood, Calif.: New Christian Crusade Church, n.d.

6. Churches of Christ

Hughes, Richard T. *Reviving the Ancient Faith: The Story of Churches of Christ in America*. Grand Rapids, Mich.: Eerdmans, 1996.

McAllister, Lester G., and William E. Tucker. *Journey in Faith: A History of the Christian Church (Disciples of Christ)*. Saint Louis, Mo.: Bethany Press, 1975.

Wookey, Steve. *As Angels of Light: The Teaching and Practice of the Central London Church of Christ*. Narrowgate: n.p., 1990.

7. Church of God International

Armstrong, Garner Ted. *Europe and America in Prophecy*. Tyler, Tex.: Church of God International, 1984.
————. *Some Fishy Stories about an Unproved Theory*. Pasadena, Calif.: Ambassador College Press, 1971.
————. *Sunday—Saturday . . . Which?* Tyler, Tex: Church of God International, 1982.
————. *Where Is the True Church?* Tyler, Tex: Church of God International, 1982.

8. Church of Jesus Christ at Armageddon (Love Israel)

Allen, S. *Beloved Son.* Indianapolis, Ind.: Bobbs-Merrill, 1982.
Israel, Love. *Love.* Seattle: Church of Armageddon, 1971.

9. Essenes and Esoteric Christian Groups

Blighton, Paul and Ruth Blighton. *The Golden Force.* San Francisco: Holy Order of MANS, 1967.
King, C. W. *The Gnostics and Their Remains, Ancient and Mediaeval.* Minneapolis, Minn.: Wizards Bookshelf, 1973.
Nier, Susan. *The Discovery.* Homestead, Fla.: OmniTouch, 1993.
Ouseley, Gideon Jasper. *The Gospel of the Holy Twelve (The Essene New Testament).* London: Watkins, 1956.
Szekeley, E. B. *The Essene Gospel of Peace.* San Diego, Calif.: Academy Books, 1977.
————. *The Essene Way: Biogenic Living.* Cartago, Costa Rica: International Biogenic Society, 1978.
————. *The Gospel of the Essenes: The Unknown Books of the Essenes and Lost Scrolls of the Essene Brotherhood, the Original Hebrew and Aramaic Texts.* London: Daniel, 1976.
————. *The Teachings of the Essenes from Enoch to the Dead Sea Scrolls.* London: Daniel, 1978.

Weddell, George, Mary Weddell, and Miriam B. Willis. *Creative Colour.* Hermet, Calif.: Fellowship of Peace, 1989.

10. The Family

Davis, Deborah (Lind Berg). *The Children of God: The Inside Story.* Grand Rapids, Mich.: Zondervan, 1984.

Family, The. "Our Statements: The Fundamental Beliefs and Essential Doctrines of the Fellowship of Independent Missionary Communities Commonly Known as the Family." Zurich: World Services, 1992.

—————. "Position and Policy Statement." Zurich: World Services, 1992.

Hamilton, Alastair. *The Family of Love.* Edinburgh: James Clarke, 1981.

Lewis, James R., and J Gordon Melton. *Sex, Slander, and Salvation: Investigating the Family/Children of God.* Stanford, Calif.: Center for Academic Publication, 1994.

Moses, David. *The MO Letters.* Hong Kong: Gold Lion Publishers, 1977.

van Zandt, David E. *Living in the Children of God.* Princeton, N.J.: Princeton University Press, 1991.

Wallis, Roy. "Fishing for Men." *The Humanist* 38, no. 1 (1978): 14-16.

—————. "Observations on the Children of God." *Sociological Review* 24 no. 4 (1976): 807-828.

Wangerin, Ruth. *The Children of God: A Make-Believe Revolution?* Westport, Conn.: Bergin and Garvey, 1993.

Williams, Miriam. *Heaven's Harlots: My Fifteen Years as a Sacred Prostitute in the Children of God Cult.* New York: Eagle Brook, 1998.

11. Father Divine's Peace Mission

Baker, George. *The Condescension of God: As Revealed by Father Divine to Dr. Lewi Pethrus of Sweden.* Woodmont, Pa.: Peace Mission, 1957.

Burnham, Kenneth E. *God Comes to America: Father Divine and the Peace Mission Movement.* Boston: Lambeth Press, 1979.

Divine, M. J. (Mother Divine). *The Peace Mission Movement.* Philadelphia: Imperial Press, 1982.

Harris, Sara. *Father Divine: Holy Husband.* Garden City, N.Y.: Doubleday, 1953.

Hoshor, John. *God in a Rolls-Royce: The Rise of Father Divine: Madman, Menace, or Messiah?* New York: Hillman-Curl, 1936.

Pethrus, Lewi. *The Consdescension of God.* Gladwyn, Pa.: Peace Mission, n.d.

Watts, Jill. *God, Harlem, U.S.A.: The Father Divine Story.* Berkeley: University of California Press, 1992.

Weisbrot, Robert. *Father Divine.* Boston: Beacon Press, 1983.

12. Focolare

Gallagher, Jim. *A Woman's Work: Chiara Lubich.* London: Fount, 1997.

Lubich, Chiara. *The Living Presence: Experiencing Jesus in the Word, the Eucharist, and Our Midst.* London: New City, 1996.

Robertson, E. H. *The Fire of Love.* London: New City, 1989.

13. Gnosticism

Burke, Abbot George. *Robe of Light: A Gnostic Christian Cosmology.* Oklahoma City, Okla.: St. George Press, 1985.

Guthrie, K. S. *The Dawn of Civilization and the Giving of Fire: According to the Popol Vuh.* Edmonds, Wash.: Sure Fire Press, 1990.

Oeller, Stephan A. *The Mystery and Magic of the Eucharist.* Hollywood, Calif.: Gnostic Press, 1990.

Singer, June. *A Gnostic Book of Hours: Keys to Inner Wisdom.* San Francisco: HarperSanFrancisco, 1992.

14. Holy Order of MANS

Lucas, Phillip C. *The Odyssey of a New Religion: The Holy Order of MANS from New Age to Orthodoxy.* Bloomington: Indiana University Press, 1995.

15. House Church Movement

Walker, Andrew. "The House Church Movement: Not an Aspect of 'Charismatic Renewal' but a New Sectarianism." *Religion Today* 1, no. 1 (1984): 6-7.

―――. *Restoring the Kingdom: The Radical Christianity of the House Church Movement.* 2d ed. London: Hodder and Stoughton, 1988.

16. Jesus Fellowship Church and the Jesus Army

Cooper, Simon, and Mike Farrant. *Fire in Our Hearts: The Story of the Jesus Fellowship.* Northampton, England: Multiply Publications, 1997.

Jesus Fellowship Church. *Jesus, the Name; Jesus, the Foundation.* Nether Heyford, Northants, England: Jesus Fellowship Church, 1992.

418   *Bibliography*

17. Jesus People Movement

Ellwood, Robert S. *The Sixties Spiritual Awakening: American Religion Moving from Modern to Postmodern.* New Brunswick, N.J.: Rutgers University Press, 1994.
Moody, Jess. *The Jesus Freaks.* Waco, Tex.: Word Books, 1971.
Gaskin, Stephen. *The Caravan.* New York: Random House, 1972.
————. *Haight-Ashbury Flashbacks.* Berkeley, Calif.: Ronin, 1990.
————. *Monday Night Class.* Santa Rosa, Calif.: Book Farm, 1970.

18. Latter-Rain Movement

Grubb, Paul N. *The End-Time Revival.* Memphis, Tenn.: Voice of Faith Publishing House, n.d.
Hoekstra, Raymond G. *The Latter Rain.* Portland, Oreg.: Wings of Healing, 1950.
Riss, Richard Michael. *The Latter Rain Movement of 1948 and the Mid-Twentieth Century Evangelical Awakening.* M.A. thesis, Regent College, Vancouver, B.C., 1979.
Rogers, Adrian. *The Power of His Presence.* Wheaton, Ill.: Crossway Books, 1995.
Wimber, John, and Kevin Springer. *Power Healing.* London: Hodder and Stoughton, 1986.

19. Liberal Catholicism

Cooper, Irving Steiger. *Ceremonies of the Liberal Catholic Rite.* Ojai, Calif.: St. Alban Press, 1964.
Hodson, Geoffrey. *The Inner Side of Church Worship.* Wheaton, Ill.: Theosophical Press, 1948.
Leadbeater, C. W. *The Inner Side of Christian Festivals.* London: St. Alban Press, 1973.

————. *The Science of the Sacraments.* Adyar, Madras: The Theosophical Publishing House, 1980.

Tillett, Gregory. *The Elder Brother.* London: Routledge and Kegan Paul, 1982.

20. Local Church

Duddy, Neil T. *The God-Men: An Inquiry into Witness Lee and the Local Church.* Downers Grove, Ill.: InterVarsity Press, 1981.

Lee, Witness. *An Autobiography of a Person in the Spirit.* Anaheim, Calif.: Living Stream Ministry, 1986.

————. *Elders' Training.* 8 vols. Anaheim, Calif.: Living Stream Ministry, 1985-1986.

————. *The Recovery of God's House and God's City.* Anaheim, Calif.: Living Stream Ministry, 1980.

————. *Truth Lessons.* 2 vols. Anaheim, Calif.: Living Stream Ministry, 1985-1986.

Melton, J. G. *The Experts Speak Concerning Witness Lee and the Local Churches.* Anaheim, Calif.: Living Stream Ministry, 1995.

————. *An Open Letter Concerning the Local Church, Witness Lee, and the God-Men Controversy.* Santa Barbara, Calif.: Institute for the Study of American Religion, 1985.

21. Metropolitan Churches

Enroth, Ronald M., and Gerald E. Jamison. *The Gay Church.* Grand Rapids, Mich.: Eerdmans, 1974.

Perry, Troy D. *Don't Be Afraid Anymore: The Story of Reverend Troy Perry and the Metropolitan Community Churches.* New York: St. Martin's Press, 1992.

————. *The Lord Is My Shepherd and He Knows I'm Gay.* New York: Bantam Books, 1978.

22. Moral Re-Armament

Buchman, Frank N. D. *Remaking the World*. Washington, D.C.: Mackinac Press, n.d.

Gordon, Anne Wolrige. *Peter Howard: Life and Letters*. London: Hodder and Stoughton, 1969.

Howard, Peter. *Britain and the Beast*. London: Heinemann, 1963.

————. *Frank Buchman's Secret*. London: Heinemann, 1961.

————. *That Man Frank Buchman*. London: Blandford Press, 1946.

Lean, Garth. *On the Tail of a Comet: The Life of Frank Buchman*. Colorado Springs, Colo.: Helmers and Howard, 1988.

Williamson, Geoffrey. *Inside Buchmanism: An Independent Inquiry into the Oxford Group Movement and Moral Re-Armament*. London: Watts, 1954.

23. Oneness ("Jesus Only") Pentecostalism

Beisner, E. Calvin. *"Jesus Only" Churches*. Grand Rapids, Mich.: Zondervan, 1998.

Boyd, Gregory A. *Oneness Pentecostals and the Trinity*. Grand Rapids, Mich.: Baker Book House, 1992.

24. Opus Dei

Gavey, J. J. M. *Parents' Guide to Opus Dei*. New York: Sicut Dixit, 1989.

Hutchison, Robert. *Their Kingdom Come: Inside the Secret World of Opus Dei*. London: Doubleday, 1997.

Messori, Vittorio. *Opus Dei: Leadership and Vision in Today's Catholic Church*. Washington, D.C.: Regnery, 1997.

O'Connor, William. *Opus Dei: An Open Book: A Reply to* The Secret World of Opus Dei *by Michael Walsh*. Dublin: Mercier Press, 1991.

Salvador, Bernal. *Msgr. Josemaría Escrivá de Balaguer: A Profile of the Founder of Opus Dei.* London: Scepter, 1977.

Walsh, Michael J. *Opus Dei: An Investigation into the Secret Society Struggling for Power within the Roman Catholic Church.* New York: HarperSanFrancisco, 1992.

————. *The Secret World of Opus Dei.* London: Grafton, 1989.

West, W. J. *Opus Dei: Exploding a Myth.* Crows Nest, Australia: Little Hills Press, 1987.

25. Peoples Temple

Barker, Eileen. "Religious Movements: Cult and Anticult since Jonestown." *Annual Review of Sociology,* vol 12 (1996): 329-346.

Chidester, David. *Salvation and Suicide: An Interpretation of the Peoples Temple and Jonestown.* Bloomington: Indiana University Press, 1988.

Church of Scientology. "Jonestown: The Big Lie." *Freedom* 27, no. 2 (1995): 24-27.

Hall, John. *Gone from the Promised Land: Jonestown in American Cultural History.* New Brunswick, N.J: Transaction Books, 1987.

Kerns, Phil, and Doug Wead. *People's Temple, People's Tomb.* Plainfield, N.J.: Logos International, 1979.

Melton, J. Gordon. *The Peoples Temple and Jim Jones: Broadening Our Perspective.* New York: Garland, 1990.

Moore, Rebecca. *In Defense of Peoples Temple.* Lewiston, N.Y.: Edwin Mellen, 1988.

————. *A Sympathetic History of Jonestown: The Moore Family Involvement in Peoples Temple.* Lewiston, N.Y.: Edwin Mellen, 1985.

Moore, Rebecca, and Fielding McGehee III, eds. *New Religious Movements, Mass Suicide, and Peoples Temple: Scholarly Perspectives on a Tragedy.* Lewiston, N.Y.: Edwin Mellen, 1989.

Reiterman, Tim R. *The Untold Story of The Rev. Jim Jones and His People.* New York: Dutton, 1982.

Weightman, Judith Mary. *Making Sense of the Jonestown Suicides: A Sociological History of Peoples Temple.* Lewiston, N.Y.: Edwin Mellen, 1983.

26. Promise Keepers

Hicks, Robert. *The Masculine Journey: Understanding the Six Stages of Manhood.* Colorado Springs, Colo.: NavPress, 1993.
Keen, Sam. *Fire in the Belly: On Being a Man.* New York: Bantam Books, 1992.
McCartney, Bill, et al. *What Makes a Man? Twelve Promises That Will Change Your Life.* Colorado Springs, Colo.: NavPress, 1992.

27. Religious Science (including Divine Science)

Brooks, Louise McNamara. *Early History of Divine Science.* Denver: First Divine Science Church, 1963.
Divine Science Church and College. *Divine Science: Its Principle and Practice.* Denver: Divine Science Church and College, 1957.
Gregg, Irwin. *The Divine Science Way.* Denver: Divine Science Federation International, 1975.

28. Sacred Name Movement

Meyer, Jacob O. *Exploding the Inspired Greek New Testament Myth.* Bethel, Pa.: Assemblies of Yahweh, 1978.
———. *The Memorial Name—Yahweh.* Bethel, Pa.: Assemblies of Yahweh, 1978.
Snow, E. D. "A Brief History of the Name Movement in America." *Faith* 45 (January-February 1982).

29. Snake Handling

Covington, Dennis. *Salvation on Sand Mountain: Snake Handling and Redemption in Southern Appalachia.* Reading, Mass.: Addison-Wesley, 1994.
La Barre, Weston. *They Shall Take up Serpents.* New York: Schocken, 1969.

30. Toronto Blessing

Beverley, James A. *Revival Wars: A Critique of Counterfeit Revival.* Toronto: Evangelical Research Ministries, 1997.
Boulton, Wallace. *The Impact of "Toronto."* Crowborough, England: Monarch, 1995.
Chevreau, Guy. *Catch the Fire: The Toronto Blessing, an Experience of Renewal and Revival.* London: HarperCollins, 1994.
Howard, Roland. *Charismania: When Christian Fundamentalism Goes Wrong.* London: Mowbray, 1997.
Hunt, Stephen. "The 'Toronto Blessing': A Rumour of Angels?" *Journal of Contemporary Religion.* 10, no. 3, (October, 1995): 257-272.
Poloma, Margaret M. *By Their Fruits: A Sociological Assessment of the "Toronto Blessing."* Akron, Ohio: University of Akron, 1996.
———. *Inspecting the Fruit: A 1997 Sociological Assessment of the Toronto Blessing.* Akron, Ohio: University of Akron, 1997.

31. Two by Twos

Paul, William E. *They Go About "Two by Two."* Denver: Impact Publications, 1977.

32. Unification Church

Primary sources
CAUSA Institute. *CAUSA Lecture Manual*. New York: CAUSA Institute, 1985.
Eu, Hyo Won. *Divine Principle*. New York: Holy Spirit Association for the Unification of World Christianity, 1973.
Holy Spirit Association for the Unification of World Christianity. *Exposition of Divine Principle*. New York: HSA-UWC, 1996.
Kwak, Chung Hwan. *Outline of the Principle Level 4*. New York: HSA-UWC, 1980.
———. *The Tradition*. New York: Rose of Sharon Press, 1985.
Kwak, Chung Hwan, Kwang Yol Yoo, and Joong-Hyun Choe, eds. *Footprints of the Unification Movement*. 2 vols. Seoul: HSA-UWC, 1996.

Writings by Unification Church members
Biermans, John T. *The Odyssey of New Religions Today: A Case Study of the Unification Church*. New York: Edwin Mellen, 1988.
Breen, Michael. *Sun Myung Moon: The Early Years, 1920-1953*. Hurstpierpoint, West Sussex: Refuge Books, 1997.
Durst, Mose. *To Bigotry, No Sanction: Reverend Sun Myung Moon and the Unification Church*. Chicago: Regnery Gateway, 1984.
Kim, Won Pil. *The Path of a Pioneer: The Early Days of Reverend Sun Myung Moon and the Unification Church*. London: HSA-UWC, 1986.
Kim, Young Oon. *Unification Theology*. New York: HSA-UWC, 1980.
———. *Unification Thought*. New York: Unification Thought Institute, 1973.
Lee, Sang Hun. *Communism: A Critique and Counter Proposal*. Washington, D.C.: Freedom Leadership Foundation, 1973.
———. *Life in the Spirit World and on Earth*. New York: Family Federation for World Peace and Unification, 1998.

Independent academic studies

Barker, Eileen. *The Making of A Moonie.* Oxford: Blackwell, 1984.

Bromley, David G. *"Moonies" in America: Cult, Church, and Crusade.* Beverly Hills, Calif.: Sage, 1979.

Bryant, M. Darrol. *A Time for Consideration: A Scholarly Appraisal of the Unification Church.* New York: Edwin Mellen, 1978.

Bryant, M. Darrol, and Susan Hodges, eds. *Exploring Unification Theology.* Barrytown, N.Y.: Unification Theological Seminary, 1978.

Chryssides, George D. *The Advent of Sun Myung Moon: The Origins, Beliefs, and Practices of the Unification Church.* London: Macmillan, 1991.

Fichter, Joseph H. *The Holy Family of Father Moon.* Kansas City, Mo.: Leaven Press, 1985.

Introvigne, Massimo. *The Unification Church.* Turin, Italy: Signature Books, 2000.

Lofland, John. *Doomsday Cult: A Study of Conversion, Proselytization, and Maintenance of Faith.* Englewood Cliffs, N.J.: Prentice-Hall, 1966.

Matczak, S. A. *Unificationism.* New York: Edwin Mellen, 1982.

Mignot, Edward. "CARP: Spreading the 'Gospel' of Unificationism: A Report from the 1987 CARP Convention in Berlin." *Areopagus* 4, nos. 3-4 (Winter 1987): 49-51.

Sherwood, Carlton. *Inquisition: The Persecution and Prosecution of the Reverend Sun Myung Moon.* Washington, D.C.: Regnery Gateway, 1991.

Sontag, Frederick. *Sun Myung Moon and the Unification Church.* Nashville, Tenn.: Abingdon, 1977.

Ex-member accounts and countercult literature

Bjornstad, James. *The Moon Is Not the Son.* Minneapolis, Minn.: Bethany Fellowship, 1976.

Durham, Deanna. *Life among the Moonies: Three Years in the Unification Church.* Plainfield, N.J.: Logos International, 1981.

Heftmann, Erica. *Dark Side of the Moonies.* Harmondsworth, England: Penguin, 1983.

Hong, Nansook. *In the Shadow of the Moons.* New York: Little, Brown, 1998.

Owen, R. J. *The Moonies: A Critical Look at a Controversial Group.* Thetford, Norfolk: Ward Lock Educational, 1982.

Williams, Jacqui, and David Porter. *The Locust Years.* London: Hodder and Stoughton, 1987.

Yamamoto, J. Isamu. *The Puppet Master: An Inquiry into Sun Myung Moon and the Unification Church.* Downers Grove, Ill.: InterVarsity Press, 1977.

33. Word-Faith Movement

Allen, A. A. *My Cross.* Miracle Valley, Ariz.: Allen Revivals, n.d.

Allen, A. A., and Walter Wagner. *Born to Lose, Bound to Win.* Garden City, N.Y.: Doubleday, 1970.

Avanzini, John. *It's Not Workin', Brother John! Twenty-five Things That Close the Windows of Heaven.* Tulsa, Okla.: Harrison House, 1992.

———. *Thirty, Sixty, Hundred Fold: Your Financial Harvest Released.* Tulsa, Okla.: Harrison House, 1989.

———. *War on Debt: Breaking the Power of Debt.* Hurst, Tex.: HIS Publishing, 1990.

Cerullo, Morris. *The Miracle Book.* 3d ed. San Diego, Calif.: Morris Cerullo World Evangelism, 1992.

———. *Two Men from Eden.* San Diego, Calif.: Morris Cerullo World Evangelism, 1991.

Copeland, Kenneth. *The First Thirty Years: A Journey of Faith.* Fort Worth, Tex.: Kenneth Copeland Publications, 1997.

———. *The Laws of Prosperity.* Fort Worth, Tex.: Kenneth Copeland Publications, 1992.

Stewart, Don. *How You Can Have Something Better through God's Master Plan.* Phoenix, Ariz.: Don Stewart Evangelical Association, 1975.

Stewart, Don, and Walter Wagner. *The Man from Miracle Valley.* Long Beach, Calif.: Great Horizons, 1971.

Wagner, C. Peter. *The Third Wave of the Holy Spirit: Encountering The Power of Signs and Wonders Today.* Ann Arbor, Mich.: Servant Publications, 1988.

————. *Warfare Prayer: How to Seek God's Power and Protection in the Battle to Build His Kingdom.* Ventura, Calif.: Regal Books, 1992.

34. The Way International

Lamsa, George M. *The Holy Bible from Ancient Eastern Manuscripts: George M. Lamsa's Translations from the Aramaic of the Peshitta.* San Francisco: Harper and Row, 1985.

MacCollam, Joel A. *The Way of Victor Paul Wierwille.* Leicester, England: InterVarsity Press, 1978.

Wierwille, Victor Paul. *Jesus Christ Is Not God.* New Knoxville, Ohio: American Christian Press, 1975.

————. *Receiving the Holy Spirit Today.* New Knoxville, Ohio: American Christian Press, 1976.

Williams, J. L. *Victor Paul Wierwille and The Way International.* Chicago: Moody Press, 1979.

35. Worldwide Church of God

Armstrong, Herbert W. *The Autobiography.* Pasadena, Calif.: Ambassador College Press, 1967.

————. *The Incredible Human Potential.* New York: Everest House, 1978.

————. *Mystery of the Ages.* New York: Dodd, Mead, 1985.

————. *The United States and Britain in Prophecy.* Pasadena, Calif.: Worldwide Church of God, 1986.

————. *The Wonderful World Tomorrow: What Will It Be Like?* New York: Everest House, 1979.

Benware, Paul N. *Ambassador of Armstrongism: An Analysis of the History and Teachings of the Worldwide Church of God.* Fort Washington, Pa.: Christian Literature Crusade, 1984.

Chambers, Roger R. *The Plain Truth about Armstrongism.* Grand Rapids, Mich.: Baker Book House, 1988.

Kroll, Paul. *Is There Life after Death?* Pasadena, Calif.: Worldwide Church of God, 1988.

Robinson, David. *Herbert Armstrong's Tangled Web.* Tulsa, Okla.: John Hadden Publishers, 1980.

Tkach, Joseph. *Transformed by Truth.* Sisters, Oreg.: Multnomah, 1997.

VII. Islamic and Sufi Movements

1. G. I. Gurdjieff and P. D. Ouspensky

Anderson, Margaret. *The Unknowable Gurdjieff.* London: Routledge and Kegan Paul, 1962.

Bennett, J. G. *Gurdjieff: Making a New World.* London: Coombe Springs Press, 1973.

———. *Idiots in Paris: Diaries of J. G. Bennett and Elizabeth Bennett, 1949.* York Beach, Maine: Samuel Weiser, 1991.

———. *Needs of a New Age Community: Talks on Spiritual Community and Fourth Way Schools.* Santa Fe, N. Mex: Bennett Books, 1990.

———. *Talks on Beelzebub's Tales.* York Beach, Maine: Samuel Weiser, 1988.

———. *Witness: The Autobiography of John G. Bennett.* Charles Town, W. Va.: Claymont Communications, 1983.

Butkovsky-Hewitt, Anna. *With Gurdjieff in St. Petersburg and Paris.* London: Routledge and Kegan Paul, 1978.

Byrd, Rudolph P. *Jean Toomer's Years with Gurdjieff: Portrait of an Artist, 1923-1936.* Athens: University of Georgia Press, 1990.

Gurdjieff, G. I. *Beelzebub's Tales to His Grandson: An Objectively Impartial Criticism of the Life of Man.* London: Arkana, 1992.

———. *The Herald of Coming Good.* Edmonds, Wash.: Sure Fire Press, 1988.

———. *Life Is Real Only Then, When "I Am."* London: Arkana, 1991.

———. *Meetings with Remarkable Men.* London: Arkana, 1985.

Kherdian, David. *On a Spaceship with Beelzebub: By a Grandson of Gurdjieff.* New York: Globe Press Books, 1991.

Moore, James. *Gurdjieff: The Anatomy of a Myth.* Shaftesbury, England: Element, 1991.

Nicoll, Maurice. *Psychological Commentaries on the Teaching of G. I. Gurdjieff and P. D. Ouspensky.* 5 vols. London: Stuart and Watkins, 1970-1976.

Nott, C. S. *Teachings of Gurdjieff: The Journal of a Pupil. An Account of Some Years with G .I. Gurdjieff and A. R. Orage in New York and at Fontainebleau-Avon.* London: Routledge and Kegan Paul, 1984.

Ouspensky, P. D. *The Fourth Way: A Record of Talks and Answers to Questions Based on the Teachings of G. I. Gurdjieff.* London: Routledge and Kegan Paul, 1984.

———. *In Search of the Miraculous: Fragments of an Unknown Teaching.* London: Routledge and Kegan Paul, 1984.

———. *Letters from Russia, 1919.* London: Arkana, 1978.

———. *A New Model of the Universe: Principles of the Psychological Method in Its Application to Problems of Science, Religion, and Art.* Mineola, N.Y.: Dover Publications, 1997.

———. *The Psychology of Man's Possible Evolution.* London: Routledge and Kegan Paul, 1984.

———. *Talks with a Devil.* Wellingborough, England: Thorsons, 1983.

———. *Tertium Organum: The Third Canon of Thought, a Key to the Enigmas of the World.* New York: Vintage Books, 1970.

Pogson, Beryl. *Maurice Nicoll: A Portrait.* New York: Fourth Way Books, 1987.

Popoff, Irmis B. *Gurdjieff Group Work with Wilhem Nyland.* York Beach, Maine: Samuel Weiser, 1986.

Reyner, J. H. *Ouspensky: The Unsung Genius.* London: Allen and Unwin, 1981.

Riordan Speeth, Kathleen. *The Gurdjieff Work.* Los Angeles: Jeremy P. Tarcher, 1989.

Teachings of Gurdjieff: The Journal of a Pupil. London: Routledge and Kegan Paul, 1961.

Waldberg, Michel. *Gurdjieff: An Approach to His Ideas.* London: Arkana, 1989.

Walker, Kenneth. *A Study of Gurdjieff's Teaching.* London: Jonathan Cape, 1957.

———. *Venture with Ideas: Meetings with Gurdjieff and Ouspensky.* New York: Pellegrini and Cudahy, 1952.

2. Universal Sufism

Arberry, A. J. *Sufism.* London: Allen and Unwin, 1956.

Geaves, Ron. *The Sufis of Britain: An Exploration of Muslim Identity.* Cardiff, Wales: Cardiff Academic Press, 2000.

Haeri, S. F. *The Elements of Sufism.* Shaftesbury, England: Element, 1995.

Khan, Vilayit Inayit. *The Message in Our Time.* San Francisco: Harper and Row, 1978.

Knysh, Alexander. *Islamic Mysticism: A Short History.* Leiden: Brill, 2000.

Lings, Martin. *What Is Sufism?* Cambridge: Islamic Texts Society, 1995.

Shah, Idries. *The Diffusion of Sufi Ideas in the West.* Boulder, Colo.: Keysign, 1972.

———. *The Sufis.* London: Octagon, 1984.

———. *The Way of the Sufi.* London: Arkana, 1990.

Williams, L. F. R. *Sufi Studies: East and West.* New York: Dutton, 1974.

Wittevene, H. J. *Universal Sufism.* Shaftesbury, England: Element, 1997.

3. Ahmadiyya

Ali, Muhammad. *The Founder of the Ahmadiyya Movement.* Newark, Calif.: Ahmadiyya Anjuman Ishaat Islam, Lahore, 1994.

Dard, A. R. *Life of Ahmad.* Lahore, Pakistan: Tabshir, 1948.

Faruqui, N. A. *Ahmadiyyat in the Service of Islam.* Newark, Calif.: Ahmadiyya Anjuman Ishaat Islam, Lahore, 1983.

Khan, Muhammad Zafrulla. *Ahmadiyyat: The Renaissance of Islam.* London: Tabshir, 1978.

Nafwi, S. Abul Hasan Ali. *Oadianism: A Critical Study.* Lucknow, India: Academy of Islamic Research and Publications, 1974.

4. Bawa Muhaiyaddeen Fellowship

Muhaiyaddeen, M. R. Guru Bawa. *Truth and Light.* Philadelphia: Guru Bawa Fellowship of Philadelphia, 1974.

5. Nation of Islam

Clark, J. H., ed. *Malcolm X: The Man and His Times.* New York: Macmillan, 1969.

El-Amin, Mustafa. *The Religion of Islam and The Nation of Islam: What Is the Difference?* Newark, N.J.: El-Amin Productions, 1991.

Evanzz, K. *The Messenger: The Rise and Fall of Elijah Muhammad.* New York: Pantheon, 1999.

Gardell, M. *Countdown to Armageddon: Louis Farrakhan and the Nation of Islam.* London: Hurst, 1996.

Goldman, P. L. *The Death and Life of Malcolm X.* Urbana: University of Illinois Press, 1979.

Lee, Martha. *The Nation of Islam.* New York: Syracuse University Press, 1996.

Lincoln, C. E. *The Black Muslims in America.* Boston: Beacon Press, 1961.

Marsh, Clifton. *From Black Muslims to Muslims: The Transition from Separatism to Islam, 1930-1980.* Metuchen, N.J.: Scarecrow Press, 1984.

———. *The Lost-Found Nation of Islam in America.* Lanham, Md.: Scarecrow Press, 2000.

Muhammad, Elijah. *Message to the Blackman in America.* Chicago: Muhammad Mosque of Islam, No. 2, 1965.

Muhammad, Silis. *In the Wake of the Nation of Islam.* College Park, Ga.: Silis Muhammad, 1985.

Muhammad, Warith Deem. *As a Light Shineth from the East.* Chicago: WDM Publishing, 1980.

Waugh, E. H., B. Abu-Laban, and R. Qureshi, eds. *The Muslim Community in North America.* Edmonton: University of Alberta Press, 1983.

6. Subud

Bennett, John G. *Concerning Subud.* London: Hodder and Stoughton, 1958.

———. *Exploring Aspects of the Subud Experience.* New York: Dharma Book Co., 1961.

Geels, Antoon. *Subud and the Javanese Mystical Tradition.* Richmond, Surrey: Curzon, 1997.

Lyle, Robert. *Subud.* Tunbridge Wells, England: Humanus, 1983.

Rieu, Dominic C. H. *A Life with a Life: An Introduction to Subud.* Tunbridge Wells, England: Humanus, 1983.

Sumohadiwidjojo, Muhammad Subuh. *Susila Budhi Dharma: The Way of Submission to the Will of God, Subud.* Jakarta: Publikasi Subud Indonesia, 1990.

von Bissing, Ronimund. *Songs of Submission: On the Practice of Subud.* Greenwood, S.C.: Attic Press, 1962.

VIII. Hindu-Related NRMs

1. Ananda Marga

Ananda Marga. *The Spiritual Philosophy of Shrii Shrii Ananda-murti.* Denver: Ananda Marga Publications, 1981.
Anandamurti. *The Great Universe: Discourses on Society.* Los Altos Hills, Calif.: Ananda Marga Publications, 1973.

2. Aurobindo

Aurobindo, Sri. *The Life Divine.* New York: India Library Society, 1965.
———. *Sri Aurobindo.* New York: Dutton, 1971.
———. *Sri Aurobindo Birth Centenary Library.* 30 vols. Pondicherry, India: Sri Aurobindo Birth Centenary Library, 1970-1973.
McDermott, Robert, ed. *The Essential Aurobindo.* New York: Schocken Books, 1973.
Minor, Robert Neil. *Sri Aurobindo: The Perfect and the Good.* Columbia, S.C.: South Asia Books, 1978.

3. Baba Ram Dass (Richard Alpert)

Alpert, Richard (Baba Ram Dass). *Be Here Now.* Boulder, Colo.: Hanuman Foundation, 1992.
———. *Grist for the Mill.* Santa Cruz, Calif.: Unity Press, 1977.
———. *Miracle of Love: Stories about Neem Karoli Baba.* New York: Dutton, 1979.
———. *The Only Dance There Is.* New York: J. Aronson, 1976.

4. Brahma Kumaris

Brahma Kumaris. *Brahma Baba: Who Started a Unique Spiritual Revolution.* Pandav Bhavan, Mount Abu, India: Prajapita Brahma Kumaris, n.d.

————. *Inner Beauty: A Book of Virtues.* Pandav Bhawan, Mount Abu, India: Brahma Kumaris World Spiritual University, 1994.

————. *Power and Effect of Thoughts.* Pandav Bhawan, Mount Abu, India: Brahma Kumaris World Spiritual University, n.d.

————. *Raja Yoga Meditation: A General Introduction.* Pandav Bhawan, Mount Abu, India: Raja Yoga Centre for the Brahma Kumaris International Spiritual University. n.d.

————. *Vision of a Better World.* Pandav Bhawan, Mount Abu, India: Brahma Kumaris World Spiritual University, n.d.

Gill-Kozul, Carol, ed. *Living Values: A Guidebook.* London: Brahma Kumaris World Spiritual University, 1995.

Hassija, B. K. Jagdish Chander. *Development of Self; or, Human Resource Development for Success in Management through Spiritual Wisdom and Meditation.* Delhi: Brahma Kumaris Centre, n.d.

————. *Self-transformation, Universal-transformation, and Harmony in Human Relations.* Delhi: Brahma Kumaris Centre, n.d.

Hodgkinson, Liz. *Peace and Purity: The Story of the Brahma Kumaris: A Spiritual Revolution.* London: Rider, 1999.

Shubow, Robert. *The Voyagers: The True Story of a Race of Beings Far More Intelligent than Us.* London: Brahma Kumaris World Spiritual University, 1988.

Walliss, John. "From World Rejection to Ambivalence: The Development of Millenarianism in the Brahma Kumaris." *Journal of Contemporary Religion* 14, no. 3 (1999): 375-386.

Whaling, Frank. "The Brahma Kumaris." *Journal of Contemporary Religion* 10, no. 1 (1995): 3-28.

5. Brunton, Paul

Brunton, Paul. *The Notebooks of Paul Brunton.* 16 vols. Burdett, N.Y.: Larson, 1984-1988.
———. *A Search in Secret India.* New York: Dutton, 1935.
———. *The Secret Path: A Technique of Self-Discovery.* New York: Dutton, 1935.

6. Chinmoy

Chinmoy, Sri. *Arise! Awake!* New York: Frederick Fell, 1972.
———. *One Spirit: A Journey to the Heart of America.* Forest Hills, N.Y.: Peace Runs International, 1997.
———. *A Sri Chinmoy Primer.* Forest Hills, N.Y.: Vishma Press, 1974.
Madhuri (Nancy Elizabeth Sands). *The Life of Sri Chinmoy.* Jamaica, N.Y.: Sri Chinmoy Lighthouse, 1972.

7. Cohen, Andrew

Cohen, Andrew. *Autobiography of an Awakening.* Corte Madera, Calif.: Moksha Foundation, 1992.
———. *Enlightenment Is a Secret.* Corte Madera, Calif.: Moksha Foundation, 1991.
———. *In Defense of the Guru Principle.* Lenox, Mass.: Moksha Press, 1999.
———. *My Master Is My Self.* Corte Madera, Calif.: Moksha Foundation, 1989.
———. *An Unconditional Relationship to Life.* Larkspur, Calif.: Moksha Press, 1995.

8. Elan Vital (Formerly Divine Light Mission)

Cameron, Charles, ed. *Who is Guru Maharaj Ji?* New York: Bantam, 1973.

Maharaji. *Listen to the Cry of Your Own Heart. Something Wonderful Is Being Said.* Los Angeles: Visions International, 1995.

————. *The Living Master.* Denver: Divine Light Mission, 1978.

9. Integral Yoga (B. K. S. Iyengar)

Iyengar, B. K. S. *The Art of Yoga.* London: Unwin, 1985.

————. *Light on Yoga: Yoga Dipika.* New York: Schocken Books, 1977.

10. International Society For Krishna Consciousness (ISKCON)

Bromley, David G., and Larry D. Shinn. *Krishna Consciousness in the West.* Lewisburg, Pa.: Bucknell University Press, 1989.

Brooks, Charles R. *The Hare Krishnas in India.* Delhi: Motilal Banarsidass, 1992.

Gelberg, Steven, ed. *Hare Krishna, Hare Krishna.* New York: Grove Press, 1983.

Hayagriva Dasa. *The Hare Krishna Explosion: The Birth of Krishna Consciousness in America, 1966-1969.* New Vrindaban, W. Va.: Palace Press, 1985.

Hubner, John, and Lindsey Gruson. *Monkey on a Stick.* San Diego, Calif.: Harcourt Brace Jovanovich, 1988.

Judah, J. Stillson. *Hare Krishna and the Counter Culture.* New York: Wiley, 1974.

Knott, Kim. *My Sweet Lord: The Hare Krishna Movement.* Wellingborough, England: Aquarian, 1986.

Poling, Tommy H. *The Hare Krishna Character Type: A Study of the Sensate Personality.* Lewinston, N.Y: Edwin Mellen, 1986.

Prabhupada, A. C. Bhaktivedanta Swami. *Bhagavad-Gita as It Is.* New York: Bhaktivedanta Book Trust, 1984.

————. *Coming Back: The Science of Reincarnation.* New York: Bhaktivedanta Book Trust, 1982.

————. *Krsna: The Supreme Personality of Godhead.* Boston: ISKCON Press, 1970.

————. *Perfect Questions, Perfect Answers.* New York: Bhaktivedanta Book Trust, 1983.

————. *Sri Caitanya-caritamrta.* 9 vols. New York: Bhaktivedanta Book Trust, 1996.

————. *Srimad Bhagavatam.* 12 vols. New York: Bhaktivedanta Book Trust, 1986.

Rochford, E. Burke, Jr. *Hare Krishna in America.* New Brunswick, N.J.: Rutgers University Press, 1991.

Satsvarupa Dasa Goswami. *Prabhupada.* Los Angeles: Bhaktivedanta Book Trust, 1983.

Shinn, Larry D. *The Dark Lord: Cult Images and the Hare Krishnas in America.* Philadelphia: Westminster Press, 1987.

11. Ishvara (Lifewave)

Rawlinson, Andrew. "The Rise and Fall of Lifewave." *Religion Today* 4 nos. 1-2 (1987): 11-14.

12. Kripalu Yoga

Desai, Yogi Amrit. *Kripalu Yoga: Meditation in Motion.* 2 vols. Lenox, Mass.: Kripalu Publications, 1985.

13. Kundalini Yoga

Irving, Darrel. *Serpent of Fire: A Modern View of Kundalini.* York Beach, Minn.: Samuel Weiser, 1995.

Krishna, Gopi. *The Awakening of Kundalini.* New York: Dutton, 1975.

14. Kriya Yoga

Premananda, Swami. *Light on Kriya Yoga.* Washington, D.C.: Swami Premananda Foundation, 1969.

15. Master Da (Franklin Jones)

Da Avabhasa (Franklin Jones). *The Hymn of the True Heart-Master: The New Revelation-Book of the Ancient and Eternal Religion of Devotion to the God-Realized Adept.* Clearlake, Calif.: Dawn Horse Press, 1992.
————. *What Are True and False Religion, Spirituality, and Meditation.* Naitauba, Fiji: Sri Love-Anandashram, 1991.
Da Free John (Franklin Jones). *The Bodily Location of Happiness: On the Incarnation of the Divine Person and the Transmission of Love-Bliss.* Clearlake, Calif.: Dawn Horse Press, 1982.
————. *The Dawn Horse Testament of Heart-Master Da Free John.* Clearlake, Calif.: Dawn Horse Press, 1985.
————. *I Am Happiness.* Clearlake, Calif.: Dawn Horse Press, 1982.
John, Bubba Free (Franklin Jones). *Love of the Two-Armed Form.* Clearlake, Calif.: Dawn Horse Press, 1978.
————. *The Paradox of Instruction: An Introduction to the Esoteric Spiritual Teaching of Bubba Free John.* Clearlake, Calif.: Dawn Horse Press, 1977.
Jones, Franklin. *The Knee of Listening.* Clearlake, Calif.: Dawn Horse Press, 1973.

16. Mother Meera

Goodman, Martin. *In Search of the Divine Mother.* London: Thorsons, 1998.
Harvey, Andrew. *Hidden Journey.* London: Bloomsbury, 1991.
————. *Return of the Mother.* Berkeley, Calif.: Frog, 1995.
Mother Meera. *Answers.* Ithaca, N.Y.: Meeramma, 1991.

17. Ramana

Osborne, Arthur. *Ramana Maharshi and the Path of Self-Knowledge*. London: Rider, 1973.

18. Sahaja Yoga

Coney, Judith. *Sahaja Yoga: Socializing Processes in a South Asian New Religious Movement*. Richmond, Surrey: Curzon, 1999.
Nirmala Devi, Shri Mataji. *Sahaja Yoga*. Delhi: Nirmala Yoga, 1982.

19. Satchidananda

Bordow, Sita, et al. *Sri Swami Satchidananda: Apostle of Peace*. Yogaville, Va.: Integral Yoga Publications, 1986.
Satchidananda, Sri Swami. *Integral Hatha Yoga*. New York: Holt, Rinehart and Winston, 1970.
————. *Living Yoga*. New York: Interface Books, 1977.
Weiner, Sita. *Swami Satchidananda*. New York: Bantam Books, 1972.

20. Siddha Yoga Dham

Muktananda, Swami. *Guru*. New York: Harper and Row, 1981.
————. *I Am That: The Science of Hamsa from Vijnana Bhairava*. South Fallsburg, N.Y.: SYDA Foundation, 1978.
————. *Play of Consciousness*. New York: Harper and Row, 1974.

21. Sivananda

Sivananda, Swami. *Sadhana.* Sivanandanagar, India: Divine Light Society, 1967.
Sivananda Yoga Center. *The Sivananda Companion to Yoga.* New York: Simon and Schuster, 1983.

22. Swami Rama

Rama, Swami. *The Art of Joyful Living.* Honesdale, Pa.: Himalayan International Institute of Yoga Science and Philosophy of the U.S.A., 1989.
———. *Exercise without Movement.* Honesdale, Pa.: Himalayan Institute of Yoga Science and Philosophy of the U.S.A, 1984.
———. *Lectures on Yoga.* Arlington Heights, Ill.: Himalayan International Institute of Yoga Science and Philosophy of the U.S.A., 1986.
———. *Living with the Himalayan Masters.* Honesdale, Pa.: Himalayan International Institute of Yoga Science and Philosophy of the U.S.A., 1978.
———. *Path of Fire and Light.* Honesdale, Pa.: Himalayan International Institute of Yoga Science and Philosophy of the U.S.A., 1986.
———. *Perennial Psychology of the Bhagavad Gita.* Honesdale, Pa.: Himalayan Institute of Yoga Science and Philosophy of the U.S.A., 1985.

23. Ramakrishna and Vivekananda

Gupta, Mahendraneth. *The Gospel of Sri Ramakrishna.* San Francisco: San Francisco Vedanta Society, 1912.
Isherwood, Chrisopher. *Ramakrishna and His Disciples.* New York: Simon and Schuster, 1965.
———. *Vedanta for the Western World.* New York: Viking, 1945.
Johnson, Clive, ed. *Vedanta.* New York: Bantam Books, 1974.

Rolland, Romain. *The Life of Vivekananda and the Universal Gospel.* Calcutta: Advaita Ashrama, 1970.

24. Satya Sai Baba

Bowen, D. *The Sathya Sai Baba Community in Bradford.* Leeds, England: University of Leeds Monographs, 1988.

Haraldsson, E. *Modern Miracles: An Investigative Report on Psychic Phenomena Associated with Sathya Sai Baba.* New York: Fawcett-Columbine, 1987.

Murphet, Howard. *Sai Baba, Man of Miracles.* Chennai: Macmillan India, 1997.

Osborne, Arthur. *The Incredible Sai Baba.* Bashir Bhag, Hyderabad, India: Orient Longman, 1985.

Ruhela, S. P. *Sri Sathya Sai Baba and the Future of Mankind.* New Delhi: Vikas, 1994.

Srinivas, Smriti. "The Brahmin and the Fakir: Suburban Religiosity in the Cult of Shirdi Sai Baba." *Journal of Contemporary Religion* 14, no. 2 (May 1995): 245-262.

25. Shirdi Sai Baba

Kamth, M. V. and V. B. Kher. *Sai Baba of Shirdi: A Unique Saint.* Bombay, India: Jaico Publishing House, 1991.

Thayee, Shivamma. *My Life with Sri Shirdi Sai Baba.* Faridabad, India: Sai Age Publications, 1992.

26. Shivabalayogi

Bala Yogi Maharaj, Shri Shiva. *Life and Spiritual Ministration.* Bangalore, India: Shri Shivabalayogi Maharaj Trust, n.d.

———. *Spiritual Essence and Luminescence.* Bangalore, India: Shri Shivabalayogi Maharaj Trust, n.d.

27. Transcendental Meditation (TM)

Allan, John. *TM: A Cosmic Confidence Trick.* Leicester, England: Inter-Varsity Press, 1980.

Bloomfield, Harold H. *TM: Discovering Inner Energy and Overcoming Stress.* New York: Delacorte Press, 1978.

Denniston, Denise. *The TM Book: How to Enjoy the Rest of Your Life.* Fairfield, Iowa: Fairfield Press, 1997.

Forem, Jack. *Transcendental Meditation: Maharishi Mahesh Yogi and the Science of Creative Intelligence.* London: Allen and Unwin, 1974.

Jefferson, William. *The Story of the Maharishi.* New York: Pocket Books, 1976.

Kroll, Una. *TM: A Signpost for the World.* London: Darton, Longman and Todd, 1976.

Maharishi Mahesh Yogi. *On the Bhagavad-Gita: A New Translation and Commentary: Chapters 1-6.* Harmondsworth, England: Penguin, 1976.

———. *Science of Being and Art of Living: Transcendental Meditation.* Harmondsworth, England: Penguin, 1995.

Roth, Robert. *Maharishi Mahesh Yogi's Transcendental Meditation.* New York: Donald I. Fine, 1994.

Russell, Peter. *The TM Technique.* London: Penguin, 1978.

28. Yogananda

Walters, J. Donald (Swami Kriyananda). *The Path: One Man's Quest on the Only Path There Is.* Nevada City, Calif.: Crystal and Clarity, 1996.

Yogananda. *Autobiography of a Yogi.* Los Angeles: Self-Realization Fellowship, 1990.

———. *The Science of Religion.* Los Angeles: Self-Realization Fellowship, 1987.

IX. Sikh-Derived NRMs

1. Historical Background and Sant Tradition

Fripp, Peter. *The Mystic Philosophy of Sant Math*. London: Neville Spearman, 1964.
McLeod, W. H. *Historical Dictionary of Sikhism*. Lanham, Md.: Scarecrow Press, 1995.

2. Eckankar

Eckankar. *Eckankar: An Introduction*. Minneapolis, Minn.: Eckankar, 1988.
Gross, Darwin. *Awakened Imagination*. Oak Grove, Oreg.: SOS Publishing, 1987.
Klemp, Harold. *The Book of Eck Wisdom*. Minneapolis, Minn.: Eckankar, 1988.
————. *Child in the Wilderness*. Minneapolis, Minn.: Eckankar, 1989.
————. *Journey of Soul*. Minneapolis, Minn.: Eckankar, 1988.
————. *Soul Travelers of the Far Country*. Minneapolis, Minn.: Eckankar, 1988.
————. *The Temple of Eck*. Minneapolis, Minn.: Eckankar, 1991.
————. *A Wind of Change*. Menlo Park, Calif.: IWP Publications, 1980.
Lane, David Christopher. *The Making of a Spiritual Movement: The Untold Story of Paul Twitchell and Eckankar*. Del Mar, Calif.: Del Mar Press, 1983.
Steiger, Brad. *In My Soul I Am Free*. Minneapolis, Minn.: Eckankar, 1991.
Twitchell, Paul. *The Drums of Eck*. San Diego, Calif.: Illuminated Way Press, 1975.
————. *Eckankar Dictionary*. Minneapolis, Minn.: Eckankar, 1991.
————. *The Eck-Vidya: Ancient Science of Prophecy*. Minneapolis, Minn.: Eckankar, 1982.

———. *The Key to Eckankar.* Minneapolis, Minn.: Eckankar, 1988.
———. *The Shariyat-Ki-Sugmad, Book One.* Minneapolis, Minn.: Eckankar, 1988.
———. *The Shariyat-Ki-Sugmad, Book Two.* Minneapolis, Minn.: Eckankar, 1991.

3. Healthy Happy Holy (3HO)

Sahib Harbhajan Singh (Yogi Bhajan). *The Experience of Consciousness.* Pomona, Calif.: KRI Publications, 1977.
———. *The Teachings of Yogi Bhajan.* New York: Hawthorn Books, 1977.

4. Kirpal Ruhani Satsang

Singh, Kirpal. *Morning Talks.* Franklin, N.H.: Sant Bani Ashram, 1974.
———. *The Way of the Saints.* Sanbornton, N.H.: Sant Bani Ashram, 1976.
Singh, Kirpal, Ajaib Singh, and Sawan Singh. *The Message of Love.* Sanbornton, N.H.: Sant Bani Ashram, n.d.

5. Movement of Spiritual Inner Awareness

Hinkins, John-Roger. *The Christ Within.* New York: Baraka Press, 1976.
———. *The Spiritual Family.* New York: Baraka Press, 1976.

6. Nirankari

Nirankari Baba Avtar Singh. *Sampuran Avtar.* Delhi: Sant Nirankari Mandal, 1996.

7. Radhasoami

Johnson, Julian. *The Path of the Masters.* Punjab, India: Radhasoami Satsang Beas, 1988.

Lane, David Christopher. *Radhasoami Parampara in Definition and Classification.* M.A. thesis, University of California Graduate Theological Union, Berkeley, Calif.: 1981.

————. *The Radhasoami Tradition: A Critical History of Guru Successorship.* New York: Garland, 1992.

Singh, Huzur Maharaj Sawan. *Philosophy of the Masters.* 5 vols. Beas, India: Radhasoami Satsang Beas, 1963-1967.

8. Sawan Kirpal Ruhani Mission

A Brief Biography of Darshan Singh. Bowling Green, Va.: Sawan Kirpal Publications, 1983.

Chadda, H. C., ed. *Seeing Is above All.* Bowling Green, Va.: Sawan Kirpal Publications, 1977.

Singh, Darshan. *The Secret of Secrets.* Bowling Green, Va.: Sawan Kirpal Publications, 1978.

X. Buddhist and Buddhist-derived NRMs

1. Development of Buddhism in the west

Chryssides, G. D. "Buddhism Goes West". *World Faiths Insight* 20 n.s. (October 1988): 37-45.

————. *The Path of Buddhism.* Edinburgh: St Andrew Press, 1988.

Fields, Rick. *How the Swans Came to the Lake: A Narrative History of Buddhism in America.* Boston: Shambhala, 1986.

Furlong, Monica. *Genuine Fake: A Biography of Alan Watts.* London: Unwin, 1987.

Humphreys, Christmas. *Both Sides of the Circle: The Autobiography of Christmas Humphreys.* London: Allen and Unwin, 1978.

———. *Buddhism.* Harmondsworth, England: Penguin, 1951.

———. *Sixty Years of Buddhism in England.* London: Buddhist Society, 1968.

Oliver, Ian. *Buddhism in Britain.* London: Rider, 1979.

Prebish, Charles S. *American Buddhism.* North Scituate, Mass.: Duxbury, 1979.

Trungpa, Chögyam. *Born in Tibet.* London: Unwin, 1987.

———. *Cutting through Spiritual Materialism.* Boston: Shambhala, 1973.

———. *Meditation in Action.* Boston: Shambhala, 1969.

2. Engaged Buddhism

Kotler, Arnold. *Engaged Buddhist Reader: Ten Years of Engaged Buddhist Publishing.* Berkeley, Calif.: Parallax Press, 1996.

Nhat Hanh, Thich. *Being Peace.* Berkeley, Calif: Parallax Press, 1987.

———. *Living Buddha, Living Christ.* New York: Simon and Schuster, 1996.

———. *The Miracle of Mindfulness: A Manual on Meditation.* Boston: Beacon Press, 1987.

———. *Peace Is Every Step: The Path of Mindfulness in Everyday Life.* New York: Bantam Books, 1991.

———. *Touching Peace: Practicing the Art of Mindful Living.* Berkeley, Calif.: Parallax Press, 1992.

Queen, Christopher S., ed. *Engaged Buddhism in the West.* Boston: Wisdom Publications, 2000.

Queen, Christopher S., and Sallie B. King. *Engaged Buddhism: Buddhist Liberation Movements in Asia.* Albany: State University of New York Press, 1996.

Sivaraksa, Sulak. *A Socially Engaged Buddhism.* Bangkok: Thai Inter-Religious Commission for Development, 1988.

3. New Kadampa Tradition

Gyatso, Geshe Kelsang. *Heart Jewel: A Commentary to the Essential Practice of the New Kadampa Tradition of Mahayana Buddhism.* London: Tharpa, 1991.

―――. *Introduction to Buddhism.* London: Tharpa, 1992.

―――. *Joyful Path of Good Fortune: The Complete Buddhist Path to Enlightenment.* London: Tharpa, 1997.

―――. *The Meditation Handbook.* London: Tharpa, 1996.

Lopez, Donald S., Jr. "An Interview with Geshe Kelsang Gyatso." *Tricycle: The Buddhist Review.* (Spring 1988): 70-76.

―――. "An Interview with Thubten Jigme Norbu." *Tricycle: The Buddhist Review.* (Spring 1998): 77-82.

―――. "Two Sides of the Same God." *Tricycle: The Buddhist Review.* (Spring 1998): 67-69.

Williams, Paul. "Dorje Shugden." *Middle Way* 71, no. 2 (August 1996): 130-132.

4. Rajneesh/Osho

Appleton, Sue. *Was Bhagwan Shree Rajneesh Poisoned by Ronald Reagan's America?* Cologne: Rebel Publishing House, 1991.

Carter, Lewis F. *Charisma and Control in Rajneeshpuram: The Role of Shared Values in the Creation of a Community.* Cambridge: Cambridge University Press, 1990.

Coney, Judith. "Recent Changes in Rajneeshism." *Religion Today* 2 no. 1 (1985): 8-9.

Heelas, Paul, and Judith Thompson. *The Way of the Heart.* Wellingborough, England: Aquarian, 1986.

Milne, Hugh. *Bhagwan: The God That Failed.* London: Caliban, 1986.

Mullan, Bob. *Life as Laughter: Following Bhagwan Shree Rajneesh.* London: Routledge, 1983.

Osho (Bhagwan Shree Rajneesh). *The Gateless Gate.* Bombay: Life Awakening Movement, 1971.

————. *God's Got a Thing about You.* Rajneeshpuram, Oreg.: Rajneesh Foundation International, 1983.

————. *The Goose Is Out.* Antelope, Oreg.: Rajneesh Foundation International, 1982.

————. *The Grass Grows by Itself: Bhagwan Shree Rajneesh Talks on Zen.* Poona, India: Rajneesh Foundation, 1979.

————. *The Greatest Challenge: The Golden Future.* New Delhi: Sterling, 1997.

————. *The Heart Sutra: Discourses on the Prajnaparamita Hridayam Sutra.* Shaftesbury, England: Element, 1994.

————. *Hsin Hsin Ming: The Book of Nothing Discourses on the Faith Mind of Sosan.* Rajneeshpuram, Oreg.: Ma Anand Sheela, Acharya Rajneesh Foundation International, 1983.

————. *I Celebrate Myself.* Cologne: Rebel Publishing House, 1989.

————. *The Mustard Seed: Discourses on the Sayings of Jesus from the Gospel According to Thomas.* Shaftesbury, England: Element, 1994.

————. *Only One Sky: On the Tantric Way of Tilopa's Song of Mahamudra.* New York: Dutton, 1976.

————. *Priests and Politicians: The Mafia of the Soul.* Cologne: Rebel Publishing House, 1987.

————. *Sex.* Woodland Hills, Calif.: Lear Enterprises, 1981.

————. *The Shadow of the Bamboo.* Rajneeshpuram, Oreg.: Rajneesh Foundation International, 1984.

————. *You Ain't Seen Nothin' Yet.* Rajneeshpuram, Oreg.: Rajneesh Foundation International, 1984.

Thompson, Judith. *The Way of The Heart: The Rajneesh Movement.* Wellingborough, England: Aquarian, 1986.

5. Rissho Kosei Kai

Niwano, Nikkyo. *Lifetime Beginner: An Autobiography.* Tokyo: Kosei, 1978.

————. *My Father, My Teacher.* Tokyo: Kosei, 1982.

6. Soka Gakkai and Nichiren Shoshu

Bocking, Brian. "Reflections on Soka Gakkai." *Scottish Journal of Religious Studies* 2 no.1 (1981): 38-52.

Causton, Richard. *Nichiren Shoshu Buddhism.* London: Rider, 1988.

Cowan, Jim. *The Buddhism of the Sun.* Richmond, Surrey: NSUK, 1982.

Ikeda, Daisaku. *Buddhism in Action.* Tokyo: Nichiren Shoshu International Center, 1989.

————. *The Flowers of Chinese Buddhism.* New York: Weatherhill, 1986.

————. *The Human Revolution.* 5 vols. New York: Weatherhill, 1976-1986.

————. *Unlocking the Mysteries of Birth and Death: Buddhism in the Contemporary World.* London: Macdonald, 1988.

Kirimura, Yasuji. *The Life of Nichiren Daishonin.* Tokyo: Nichiren Shoshu International Center, 1982.

————. *Outline of Buddhism.* Tokyo: Nichiren Shoshu International Center, 1986.

Lectures on the Sutra: The Hoben and Juryo Chapters. Rev. ed. Tokyo: Nichiren Shoshu International Center, 1984.

Metraux, Daniel. *The History and Theology of Soka Gakkai: A Japanese New Religion.* Lewiston, N.Y.: Edwin Mellen, 1988.

Nichiren Daishonin. *The Major Writings of Nichiren Daishonin.* Tokyo: Nichiren Shoshu International Center, 1979.

Wilson, Bryan, and Karel Dobbelaere. *A Time to Chant: The Soka Gakkai Buddhists in Britain.* Oxford: Clarendon Press, 1998.

7. Other Nichiren Groups

Fujii, Nichidatsu. *Buddhism for World Peace.* Tokyo: Japan-Bharat Sarvodaya Mitrata Sangha, 1980.

Guthrie, Stewart. *A Japanese New Religion: Rissho Kosei-Kai in a Mountain Hamlet.* Ann Arbor: Center for Japanese Studies, University of Michigan, 1988.

Hardacre, Helen. *Lay Buddhism in Contemporary Japan: Reiyukai Kyodan.* Princeton, N.J.: Princeton University Press, 1984.

Kubo, Katsuko. *Reflections: In Search of Myself.* Tokyo: Sangaku, 1975.

Kubo, Tsugunari. *Inner Trip: A Journey into Your Heart.* Tokyo: Sangaku, 1975.

Rissho Kosei-kai. *The Story of Rissho Kosei-kai.* Tokyo: Rissho Kosei-kai, 1982.

8. Vipassana

Goldstein, Joseph. *The Experience of Insight.* Boulder, Colo.: Shambhala, 1976.

Goldstein, Joseph, and Jack Kornfield. *Seeking the Heart of Wisdom.* Boston: Shambhala, 1987.

Hart, William. *The Art of Living: Vipassana Meditation as Taught by S. N. Goenka.* San Francisco: Harper and Row, 1987.

Kornfield, Jack. *Living Buddhist Masters.* Kandy, Sri Lanka: Buddhist Publication Society, 1977.

9. Western Buddhist Order

Sangharakshita, Maha Sthavira. *Buddhism and Blasphemy: Buddhist Reflections on the 1977 Blasphemy Trial.* London: Windhorse, 1978.

———. *The Ten Pillars of Buddhism.* Glasgow: Windhorse, 1989.

———. *The Thousand-Petalled Lotus: An English Buddhist in India.* London: Heinemann, 1976.

Subhuti, Dharmachari (Alex Kennedy). *Buddhism for Today: A Portrait of a New Buddhist Movement.* Salisbury, England: Element, 1983.

10. Won Buddhism

Chon, Pal Khn, trans. *The Scripture of Won Buddhism (Won Pulkyo Kyojun).* Iri, South Korea: Won Kwang, 1988.
Chung, Bongkil. *An Introduction to Won Buddhism: Wonbulgyo.* Iri, South Korea: Won Buddhist Press, 1994.
Wonbulgyo. *The Great Sage of Creation and Grace: Sot'aesan Taejongsa.* Iri, South Korea: Wongwang, 1991.
———. *Won Buddhism: A New Religion in the Era of Creation.* Iri, South Korea: Won Buddhist Press, 1995.

11. Zen

Herrigel, Eugen. *Zen in the Art of Archery.* London: Routledge and Kegan Paul, 1979.
Herrigel, Gustie L. *Zen in the Art of Flower Arrangement.* London: Routledge and Kegan Paul, 1979.
Humphreys, Christmas. *A Western Approach to Zen.* London: Allen and Unwin, 1971.
Kapleau, P. *Three Pillars of Zen: Teaching, Practice, and Enlightenment.* Garden City, N.Y.: Anchor Press, 1980.
———. *Zen: Dawn in the West.* Garden City, N.Y.: Anchor Press, 1979.
Keightley, Alan. *Into Every Life a Little Zen Must Fall: A Christian Philosopher Looks to Alan Watts and the East.* London: Wisdom Publications, 1986.
Kerouac, Jack. *The Dharma Bums.* New York: Viking, 1958.
———. *On the Road.* New York: Viking, 1957.
Reps, Paul. *Zen Flesh, Zen Bones.* Harmondsworth: Penguin, 1976.

Sangharakshita. *The Essence of Zen: Five Talks by the Ven. Maha Sthavira Sangharakshita.* London: Friends of the Western Buddhist Order, 1976.

Suzuki, D. T. *The Awakening of Zen.* Boston: Shambhala, 1987.

————. *Essays in Zen Buddhism.* 3 vols. London: Rider, 1970.

————. *Living by Zen: A Synthesis of the Historical and Practical Aspects of Zen Buddhism.* London: Rider, 1991.

Watts, Alan. *In My Own Way: An Autobiography, 1915-1965.* New York: Vintage Books, 1973.

————. *Square Zen, Beat Zen, and Zen.* San Francisco: City Lights Books, 1959.

————. *This Is It and Other Essays on Zen and Spiritual Experience.* New York: Vintage Books, 1973.

————. *The Way of Zen.* Harmondsworth, England: Penguin, 1976.

Wood, Ernest. *Zen Dictionary.* Harmondsworth, England: Penguin, 1977.

XI. Japanese NRMs

1. General

Bocking, Brian. *A Popular Dictionary of Shinto.* Richmond, Surrey, England: Curzon, 1997.

Clarke, P. B. and J. Somers, eds. *Japanese New Religions in the West.* Folkestone, Kent: Curzon Press, 1994.

Earhart, H. Byron. *Japanese Religion: Unity and Diversity.* Belmont, Calif.: Wadsworth, 1982.

————. *Religions of Japan: Many Traditions within One Sacred Way.* San Francisco: Harper and Row, 1984.

Ellwood, Robert S., Jr. *The Eagle and the Rising Sun: Americans and the New Religions of Japan.* Philadelphia: Westminster Press, 1974.

Lande, Assulv. "Japanese New Religions." *Update* 6 no. 4 (1982): 17-32.

McFarland, H. Neill. *The Rush Hour of the Gods: A Study of New Religious Movements in Japan.* New York: Macmillan, 1967.

Picken, Stuart D. B. *Historical Dictionary of Shinto.* Lanham, Md.: Scarecrow Press, 2001.

Reader, Ian. *Religion in Contemporary Japan.* Honolulu: University of Hawaii Press, 1991.

2. Aum Shinrikyo

Asahara, Shoko. *Disaster Approaches the Land of the Rising Sun.* Hitoana Fujuinimiya, Shizuyoko, Japan: Aum Shinrikyo, 1995.

———. *Tathagata Aabhidhamma: The Ever-Winning Law of the True Victors.* 2 vols. Hitoana Fujuinimiya, Shizuyoko, Japan: Aum Shinrikyo, 1991, 1992.

———. *The Teaching of Truth.* 5 vols. Hitoana Fujuinimiya, Shizuyoko, Japan: Aum Shinrikyo, 1991-1992.

Kaplan, David E., and Andrew Marshall. *The Cult at the End of the World.* New York: Crown, 1996.

Reader, Ian. *Religious Violence in Contemporary Japan: The Case of Aum Shinrikyo.* Honolulu: University of Hawaii Press, 2000.

3. Church of World Messianity (Johrei)

Okada, Mokichi. *Johrei: Divine Light of Salvation.* Kyoto: Society of Johrei, 1984.

Oyasato Research Institute, Tenri University. *The Theological Perspectives of Tenrikyo.* Tenri, Japan: Tenri University Press, 1986.

4. Konkokyo

Fukuda, Yoshiaki. *Outline of Sacred Teaching of Konko Religion.* San Francisco: Konko Missions of North America, 1955.
Hombu, Konkokyo, ed. *The Sacred Scriptures of Konkokyo.* Konko-cho, Japan: Konkokyo Hombu, 1933.
Konko Kyo's Fifty Years in America. San Francisco: Konko Churches of America, 1976.

5. Seicho-No-Ie

Taniguchi, Masaharu. *Holy Sutra, Nectarean Shower of Holy Doctrine.* Tokyo: Seicho-No-Ie Foundation, 1931.
———. *How We See God's Perfect World.* Tokyo: Seicho-No-Ie Center, 1995.
———. *Truth of Life.* Tokyo: Seicho-No-Ie Foundation, 1961.

6. Tenrikyo

Ellwood, Robert S., Jr. *Tenrikyo: A Pilgrimage Faith.* Tenri, Japan: Oyasato Research Institute, 1982.
Fukaya, Tadamasa. *A Doctrinal Study: The Truth of Origin.* Tenri, Japan: Tenrikyo Overseas Mission Department, 1983.
———. *The Fundamental Doctrines of Tenrikyo.* Tenri, Japan: Tenrikyo Overseas Mission Department, 1973.
Hardacre, Helen. *Kurozumikyo and the New Religions of Japan.* Princeton, N.J.: Princeton University Press, 1986.
Moroi, Yoshinori. *What Is Tenrikyo?* Tenri, Japan: Tenrikyo Church Headquarters, 1968.
Nakayama, Shozen Shimbashira. *On the Idea of God in the Tenrikyo Doctrine.* Tenri, Japan: Tenrikyo Church, 1962.
Nishiyama, Teruo. *Introduction to the Teachings of Tenrikyo.* Tenri, Japan: Tenrikyo Overseas Mission Department, 1981.

XII. NRMs in Primal Societies

A. African and Caribbean NRMs

1. General

Kiernan, J. P. *The Production and Management of Therapeutic Power in Zionist Churches within a Zulu City.* New York: Edwin Mellen, 1990.

Lincoln, C. E. and L. H. Mamiya. *The Black Church in the Afro-American Experience.* Durham, N.C.: Duke University Press, 1990.

Meiti, J. S. *African Religion and Philosophy.* Garden City, N.Y.: Praeger, 1970.

Prozesky, M., and John de Gruchy. *Living Faiths in South Africa.* Cape Town: David Philip, 1995.

Simpson, G. E. *Religious Cults of the Caribbean: Trinidad, Jamaica and Haiti.* Rio Piedras: Institute of Caribbean Studies, University of Puerto Rico, 1970.

Stuart, Ossie. "African Diaspora Religion." In J. Hinnells, *A New Handbook of Living Religions.* Harmondsworth, England: Penguin, 1998: 690-727.

Sundkler, B. G. M. *Zulu Zion and Some Swazi Zionists.* Cape Town: David Philip, 1975.

Turner, H. W. *Living Tribal Religions.* London: Ward Lock Educational, 1971.

————. "New Studies of New Movements: Some Publications on Independent Churches since 1973." *Journal of Religion in Africa* 11, no. 2 (1980): 121-133.

————. *Profile Through Preaching: A Study of Sermon Texts Used in a West African Independent Church.* London: Edinburgh House Press, 1965.

————. *Religious Innovation in Africa: Collected Essays on New Religious Movements.* Boston: G. K. Hall, 1979.

————. *Religious Movements in Primal Societies.* Elkhart, Ind: Mission Focus Publications, 1989.

Wilmore, G. S. *Black Religion and Black Radicalism.* Maryknoll, N.Y.: Orbis, 1983.

2. Brotherhood of the Cross and Star

Goring, R. *Something More than Gold: A European View of Brotherhood of the Cross and Star.* Lewes, England: B.C.S. Books, 1999.

Mbon, Friday M. "Lying Appropriately: The Ethics of Olumba Olumba Obu." *Religion Today* 3, no. 3 (1987): 9-11.

————. "Obu's Conflicting Opinions of the White Man and African Spiritual Leadership." *Update* 10 no. 3 (1986): 57-62.

————. "Olumba Olumba Obu and African Traditional Culture." *Update* 9 no. 3, (1985): 36-49.

3. Rastafarians

Barrett, Leonard E. *The Rastafarians: Sounds of Cultural Dissonance.* Boston: Beacon Press, 1988.

————. *Soul-Force: African Heritage in Afro-American Religion.* New York: Anchor Press, 1974.

Campbell, Horace. *Rasta and Resistance.* Dar es Salaam: Tanzania Publishing House, 1985

Cashmore, E. E. "The Decline of the Rastas?" *Religion Today* 1 no. 1 (1984): 3-4.

————. *The Rastafarians.* London: Minority Rights Group, 1982.

————. *Rastaman: The Rastafarian Movement in England.* London: Allen and Unwin, 1979.

Chevannes, Barry, ed. *Rastafari and Other African-Caribbean Worldviews.* New Brunswick, N.J.: Rutgers University Press, 1985.

Clarke, Peter B. *Black Paradise: The Rastafarian Movement.* Wellingborough, England: Aquarian, 1986.

Dix, Bob. *The Rastafarians.* Belfast: Breda Centre, 1985.

Faristzaddi, Millard. *Itations of Jamaica and I Rastafari.* Miami: Judah Anbesa Ihntahnahshinahl. 1987.

Morrish, Ivor. *Obeah, Christ, and Rastaman: Jamaica and Its Religion.* Cambridge: James Clarke, 1982.

Murrell, N. S. *Chanting down Babylon: The Rastafari Reader.* Philadelphia: Temple University Press, 1998.

Owens, Joseph. *Dread: The Rastafarians of Jamaica.* London: Heinemann, 1984.

B. Shamanism and Native American Religion

1. General

Covell, Alan Carter. *Folk Art and Magic: Shamanism in Korea.* Seoul: Hollym, 1986.

Drury, Nevill. *The Elements of Shamanism.* Shaftesbury, England: Element, 1989.

Eliade, Mircea. *Shamanism: Ancient Techniques of Ecstasy.* London: Arkana, 1989.

Harner, Michael J. *The Way of the Shaman: A Guide to Power and Healing.* San Francisco: Harper and Row, 1980.

Harner, Michael J., ed. *Hallucinogens and Shamanism.* New York: Oxford University Press, 1973.

Heinze, Ruth-Inge. *Shamans of the Twentieth Century.* New York: Irvington, 1991.

Huhm, Halla Pai. *Kut: Korean Shamanist Rituals.* Seoul: Hollym, 1982.

Lewis, I. M. *Ecstatic Religion: A Study of Shamanism and Spirit Possession.* London: Routledge, 1989.

2. Lynn Andrews

Andrews, Lynn V. *Medicine Woman.* New York: Perennial Library, 1981.

3. Black Elk

Black Elk. *Black Elk Speaks.* New York: W. Morrow, 1932.
Brown, Joseph Epes, ed. *The Sacred Pipe: Black Elk's Account of the Seven Rites of the Oglala Sioux.* Norman: University of Oklahoma Press, 1953.

4. Brook Medicine Eagle

Medicine Eagle, Brook. *The Last Ghost Dance: A Guide for Earth Mages.* New York: Ballantine Wellspring, 2000.

5. Carlos Castaneda and Peyote Religion

Aberle, David F. *The Peyote Religion among the Navaho.* New York: Wenner-Glen Foundation for Anthropological Reserarch, 1966.
Castaneda, Carlos. *Journey to Ixtlan: The Lessons of Don Juan.* Harmondsworth, England: Penguin, 1973.
———. *Tales of Power.* New York: Washington Square Press, 1976.
———. *The Teachings of Don Juan: A Yaqui Way of Knowledge.* Harmondsworth, England: Penguin, 1978.

6. Ghost Dance

LaBarre, W. *The Ghost Dance.* New York: Dell, 1972.
Miller, D. H. *Ghost Dance.* Lincoln: University of Nebraska Press, 1985.
Mooney, J. *The Ghost Dance Religion and Wounded Knee.* New York: Dover, 1973.
Thornton, R. *We Shall Live Again: The 1870 and 1880 Ghost Dance Movements as Demographic Revitalization.* New York: Cambridge University Press, 1986.

7. Sun Bear

Sun Bear. *Buffalo Hearts*. Spokane, Wash.: Bear Tribe Publication, 1976.

————. *Sun Bear, the Path of Power: As Told to Wabun and to Barry Weinstock*. Spokane, Wash.: Bear Tribe Publication, 1984.

Sun Bear and Wabun. *The Bear Tribe's Self-Reliance Book*. Spokane, Wash.: Bear Tribe Publication, 1977.

————. *The Medicine Wheel: Earth Astrology*. New York: Fireside Books, 1992.

8. Lusiah Teish

Teish, Lusiah. *Jambalaya: The Natural Woman's Book of Personal Charms and Practical Rituals*. San Francisco: HarperSanFrancisco, 1985.

C. Other NRMs Originating in Primal Societies

1. Cao Dai

Blagov, Sergei. *The Cao Dai: A New Religious Movement*. Moscow: Institute of Oriental Studies, 1999.

Cao Dai Sacerdotal Council. "Caodism: The Third Universal Amnesty of God." Information leaflet. North Potomac, Md.: Cao Dai Missionary, c.1999.

Oliver, Victor L. *Caodai Spiritism: A Study of Religion in Vietnamese Society*. Leiden, The Netherlands: E. J. Brill, 1976.

Thien-Ly Huong Do, Merdeka. *Cao Daiism: An Introduction*. Perris, Calif.: Cao Dai Temple Overseas, Center for Dai Dao Studies, 1994.

2. Cargo Cults

Lanternari, V. *The Religions of the Oppressed.* New York: Knopf, 1963.

Lindstrom, L. *Cargo Cult: Strange Stories of Desire from Melanesia.* Honolulu: University of Hawaii Press, 1993.

Maher, R. F. *New Men of Papua: A Study of Culture Change.* Madison: University of Wisconsin Press, 1961.

Trompf, G. W., ed. *Cargo Cults and Millenarian Movements: Transoceanic Comparisons of New Religious Movements.* Berlin: Mouton de Gruyter, 1990.

Whitehouse, H. *Inside the Cult: Religious Innovations and Transmission in Papua New Guinea.* Oxford: Clarendon Press, 1995.

Worsley, P. *The Trumpet Shall Sound: A Study of "Cargo" Cults in Melanesia.* New York: Schocken, 1968.

3. Ch'ondogyo

Weems, Benjamin B. *Reform, Rebellion, and the Heavenly Way.* Tucson: University of Arizona Press, 1964.

4. Huna

Glover, William R. *Huna: The Ancient Religion of Positive Thinking.* Vista, Calif.: Huna Research Association, 1988.

King, Serge. *Urban Shaman.* New York: Simon and Schuster, 1990.

Long, Max Freedom. *The Huna Code in Religions.* Vista, Calif.: Huna Research Publications, 1965.

————. *Introduction to Huna.* Sedona, Ariz.: Esoteric Publications, 1975.

————. *The Secret Science at Work.* Vista, Calif.: Huna Research Publications, 1953.

XIII. Independent New Religions

1. Bahá'í

'Abdu'l- Bahá. *Some Answered Questions.* Wilmette, Ill.: Bahá'í Publishing Trust, 1990.

Adamson, Hugh C., and Philip Hainsworth. *Historical Dictionary of the Bahá'í Faith.* Lanham, Md.: Scarecrow Press, 1997.

Amanat, Abbas. *Resurrection and Renewal: The Making of the Babi Movement in Iran, 1844-1850.* Ithaca, N.Y.: Cornell University Press, 1989.

Bahá'í International Community. *The Bahá'ís: A Profile of the Bahá'í Faith and Its Worldwide Community.* New York: Bahá'í International Community, 1992.

Balyuzi, H. M. *'Abdu'l-Bahá.* Oxford: George Ronald, 1987.

———. *Bahá'u'lláh: The King of Glory.* Oxford: George Ronald, 1980.

———. *The Báb: The Herald of the Day of Days.* Oxford: George Ronald, 1973.

Beckwith, Francis. *Bahá'í.* Minneapolis, Minn.: Bethany House Publishers, 1985.

Cole, Juan R., and Moojam Momen. *Studies in Bábí and Bahá'í History: From Iran East and West.* Los Angeles: Kalimát Press, 1984.

Effendi, Shoghi. *God Passes By.* Wilmette, Ill.: Bahá'í Publishing Trust, 1987.

Esslemont, J. E. *Bahá'u'lláh and the New Era.* London: Bahá'i Publishing Trust, 1974.

Hatcher, William S., and J. Douglas Martin. *The Bahá'í Faith: The Emerging Global Religion.* San Francisco: Harper and Row, 1986.

Kitab-i-Aqdas. Haifa, Israel: Bahá'í World Centre, 1992.

Martin, Douglas. *The Persecution of the Bahá'ís of Iran, 1844-1984.* Ottawa, Ont.: Association for Bahá'í Studies, 1984.

Momen, Moojan, ed. *The Bábí and Bahá'í Religions, 1844-1944: Some Contemporary Western Accounts.* Oxford: George Ronald, 1981.

———. *A Short Introduction to the Bahá'í Faith.* Oxford: Oneworld, 1997.

———. *Studies in Bábí and Bahá'í History.* Los Angeles: Kalimát Press, 1997.

Rabbani, Rúhíyyih. *The Guardian of the Bahá'í Faith.* London: Bahá'í Publishing Trust, 1988.

Sheppherd, Joseph. *The Elements of the Bahá'í Faith.* Shaftesbury, England: Element, 1992.

Smith, Peter. *The Bábí and Bahá'í Religions: From Messianic Shi'ism to a World Religion.* Cambridge: Cambridge University Press, 1987.

2. Breatharians (Jasmuheen)

Jasmuheen. *In Resonance.* Burgrain, Germany: KOHA-Verlag, 1995.

———. *Living on Light: The Source of Nourishment for the New Millennium.* Burgrain, Germany: KOHA-Verlag, 1997.

3. Falun Gong

Li Hongzhi, Master. *China Falun Gong.* Hong Kong: Falun Fo Fa, 1992.

———. *Zhuan Falun* (The revolving wheel of Dharma). Hong Kong: Falun Fo Fa, 1998.

4. Meher Baba

Meher Baba. *Discourses.* Myrtle Beach, S.C.: Sheriar Foundation, 1995.

———. *The Everything and the Nothing.* Sydney: Meher House, 1976.

Shepherd, Kevin. *Meher Baba: An Iranian Liberal.* Cambridge: Anthropographia, 1986.

5. Satanism

Aquino, Michael. *The Church of Satan*. Los Angeles: Michael Aquino, 1989.

———. *The Crystal Tablet of Set*. San Francisco: Temple of Set, 1984.

Bainbridge, W. S. *Satan's Power*. Berkeley: University of California Press, 1978.

Bugliosi, Vincent, and Curt Gentry. *Helter Skelter: The True Story of the Manson Murders*. New York: Bantam, 1975.

Carlson, Shawn. *Satanism in America*. Buffalo, N.Y.: CSER, 1989.

———. *Satanism in America: How the Devil Got Much More than His Due*. El Cerrito, Calif.: Gaia Press, 1989.

Clapton, Gary. *The Satanic Abuse Controversy: Social Workers and the Social Work Press*. London: University of North London Press, 1993.

Haining, Peter. *The Satanists*. London: Mayflower, 1971.

Harvey, Graham. "Satanism in Britain Today." *Journal of Contemporary Religion* 10, no. 3 (1995): 283-296.

La Fontaine, J. S. *The Extent and Nature of Organised and Ritual Abuse*. London: H.M.S.O., 1994.

Larson, Bob. *Satanism: The Seduction of America's Youth*. Nashville, Tenn.: Nelson, 1989.

LaVey, Anton Szandor. *The Devil's Notebook*. Portland, Oreg.: Feral House, 1989.

———. *The Satanic Bible*. New York: Avon Books, 1969.

———. *The Satanic Rituals*. New York: Avon Books, 1972.

———. *The Satanic Witch*. Portland, Oreg.: Feral House, 1989.

Lyons, Arthur. *Satan Wants You: The Cult of Devil Worship in America*. New York: Mysterious Press, 1988.

———. *The Second Coming: Satanism in America*. New York: Dodd, Mead, 1970.

Murray, Gilbert. *Satanism and the World Order*. London: Allen and Unwin, 1920.

Pengelly, J. and D. Waredale. *Something Out of Nothing: The Myth of "Satanic Ritual Abuse" and the Truth about Paganism and Witchcraft*. London: Pagan Federation, 1992.

Richardson, James T., Joel Best, and David Bromley. *The Satanism Scare*. New York: Aldine de Gruyter, 1991.

Sennit, Stephen. *The Process*. Mexborough, England: Nox Press, 1989.

Steffon, Jeffrey J. *Satanism: Is It Real?* Ann Arbor, Mich.: Servant Publications, 1992.

Stratford, Lauren. *Satan's Underground*. Eugene, Oreg.: Harvest House, 1988.

Swissler, Mary Ann. *Deliverance from Evil: Survivors of Ritualistic Abuse Speak Out*. Pasadena, Calif.: Pasadena Publishing Co., 1992.

Tate, Tim. *Children for the Devil: Ritual Abuse and Satanic Crime*. London: Methuen, 1991.

Victor, Jeffrey S. *Satanic Panic: The Creation of a Contemporary Legend*. Chicago: Open Court, 1993.

Zacharias, Gerhard. *The Satanic Cult*. London: Allen and Unwin, 1980.

6. Unitarian Universalism

Bolam, C. Gordon, et al. *The English Presbyterians from Elizabethan Puritanism to Modern Unitarianism*. London: Allen and Unwin, 1968.

Chryssides, George D. *The Elements of Unitarianism*. Shaftesbury, England: Element, 1998.

Chryssides, George D., ed. *Unitarian Perspectives on Contemporary Religious Thought*. London: Lindsey Press, 1999.

Gomes, Alan W. *Unitarian Universalism*. Carlisle, England: OM Publishing, 1998.

Goring, J., and R. Goring. *The Unitarians*. Exeter, England: Religious and Moral Education Press, 1984.

Hall, Alfred. *The Beliefs of a Unitarian*. London: Lindsey Press, 1932.

Hewett, Phillip. *The Unitarian Way*. Toronto: Canadian Unitarian Council, 1985.

Howe, Charles A. *The Larger Faith: A Short History of American Universalism*. Boston: Skinner House, 1993.

Parke, David B., ed. *The Epic of Unitarianism: Original Writings from the History of Liberal Religion.* Boston: Skinner House, 1985.

Reed, Cliff. *"Unitarian? What's That?": Questions and Answers about a Liberal Religious Alternative.* London: Lindsey Press, 1999.

Robinson, David. *The Unitarians and the Universalists.* Westport, Conn.: Greenwood Press, 1985.

Sias, John. *A Hundred Questions That Non-Members Ask about Unitarian Universalism.* Nashua, N.H.: Transition Publishing, 1995.

Tarrant, W. G. *The Story and Significance of the Unitarian Movement.* London: Philip Green, 1910.

Wigmore-Beddoes, Dennis G. *Yesterday's Radicals: A Study of the Affinity between Unitarianism and Broad Church Anglicanism in the Nineteenth Century.* Cambridge: James Clarke, 1971.

Wilbur, Earl Morse. *A History of Unitarianism: Socinianism and Its Antecedents.* 2 vols. Cambridge, Mass.: Harvard University Press, 1946, 1952.

Wright, Conrad. *A Stream of Light: A Short History of American Unitarianism.* Boston: Skinner House, 1989.

Wright, Conrad Edick. *American Unitarianism, 1805-1865.* Boston: Massachusetts Historical Society and Northeastern University Press, 1989.

XIV. Human Potential Movement and Self Religions

1. General

Drury, Nevill. *The Elements of Human Potential.* Shaftesbury, England: Element, 1989.

2. Emin

Leo. *Cobwebs and Tears.* London: Regal Print (Chelsea), 1982.

―――. *Dear Dragon*. London: Cobwebs Press, 1976.

―――. *Gemrod: A Study of the Great Renaissance (and the Blue Book Writings)*. London: Cobwebs Press, 1976.

―――. *Sayings of Leo: Towards Yourself*. London: Cobwebs Press, 1978.

3. *est*/Landmark Forum

Bartley, W. W., III. *Werner Erhard: The Transformation of a Man*. New York: Potter, 1978.

Finkelstein, P., B. Wenegrat, and I. Yalom. "Large Group Awareness Training." *Annual Review of Psychology* 33, (1982): 515-539.

Hargrove, Robert A. *est: Making Life Work*. New York: Dell, 1976.

Heelas, Paul. "Californian Self Religions and Socializing the Subjective." In E. Barker, ed., *New Religious Movements: A Perspective for Understanding Society*. New York: Edwin Mellen, 1982: 69-85.

―――. "Cults for Capitalism, Self Religions, Magic, and the Empowerment of Business." In P. Gee and J. Fulton, eds., *Religion and Power: Decline and Growth*. London: Chameleon Press, 1991: 27-41.

Weldon, John. *est (Erhard Seminars Training)*. Downers Grove, Ill.: InterVarsity Press, 1982.

4. Exegesis

Heelas, Paul. "Exegesis: Methods and Aims." In P. Clarke, ed., *The New Evangelists: Recruitment, Methods, and Aims of New Religious Movements*. London: Ethnographica, 1987.

5. Foundation of Human Understanding

Masters, Roy. *How to Conquer Suffering without Doctors.* Los Angeles: Foundation of Human Understanding, 1976.
————. *Your Mind Can Keep You Well.* Los Angeles: Foundation of Human Understanding, 1968.

6. School of Economic Science

Houname, Peter, and Andrew Hogg. *Secret Cult.* Tring, England: Lion, 1984.

7. Scientology

Atack, Jon. *A Piece of Blue Sky: Scientology, Dianetics, and L. Ron Hubbard.* New York: Lyle Stuart, 1990.
Braddeson, Walter. *Scientology for the Millions.* Los Angeles: Sherbourne Press, 1969.
Burrell, Maurice C. *Scientology: What It Is and What It Does.* London: Lakeland, 1970.
Church of Scientology. *The Background and Ceremonies of the Church of Scientology of California, World Wide.* Copenhagen: New Era Publications International, 1986.
————. *Scientology: Theology and Practice of a Contemporary Religion.* Los Angeles: Bridge Publications, 1998.
————. *The Scientology Handbook: Based on the Works of L. Ron Hubbard.* Hollywood, Calif.: Author Services Inc., 1994.
————. *What is Scientology?* Los Angeles: Bridge Publications, 1998.
Garrison, Omar V. *The Hidden Story of Scientology.* London: Arlington Books, 1974.
Hubbard, Corydon Bent. *L. Ron Hubbard: Messiah or Madman?* Secaucus, N.J.: Lyle Stuart, 1987.
Hubbard, L. Ron. *Axioms and Logics: The Axioms of Scientology, The Prelogics, The Logics, The Axioms of Dianetics.* Los Angeles: Bridge Publications, 1982.

————. *Dianetics: The Modern Science of Mental Health*. New York: Hermitage House, 1950.

————. *The Dynamics of Life*. Los Angeles: Bridge Publications, 1989.

————. *L. Ron Hubbard: The Man and His Work*. Los Angeles Calif.: Church of Scientology International, 1991.

————. *Science of Survival*. Los Angeles: Bridge Publications, 1989.

————. *Scientology 0-8: The Book of Basic*. Los Angeles Calif.: New Era Publications, 1983.

————. *Scientology 8-8008*. Los Angeles Calif.: Bridge Publications, 1989.

————. *Scientology 8-80*. Phoenix, Ariz.: Hubbard Association of Scientologists, 1952.

Kent, Stephen A. "Scientology's Relationship with Eastern Religious Traditions." *Journal of Contemporary Religion* 11, no. 1 (1996): 21-36.

Lamont, Stewart. *Religion, Inc.: The Church of Scientology*. London: Harrap, 1986.

Miller, Russell. *Bare-Faced Messiah: The True Story of L. Ron Hubbard*. London: Michael Joseph, 1987.

Wallis, Roy. *The Road to Total Freedom: A Sociological Analysis of Scientology*. New York: Columbia University Press, 1977.

————. "Scientology: Therapeutic Cult to Religious Sect." *Sociology* 9, no. 1, (1975): 89-100.

8. Silva Method

Silva, José. *The Silva Mind Control Method*. London: Grafton, 1980.

XV. Wicca, Witchcraft, and Paganism

Adler, Margot. *Drawing down the Moon: Witches, Druids, Goddess-Worshippers, and Other Pagans in America Today.* Boston: Beacon Press, 1986.

Budapest, Z. *The Holy Book of Women's Mysteries.* New York: Harper and Row, 1990.

Carr-Gomm, Philip. *The Elements of the Druid Tradition.* Shaftesbury, England: Element, 1999.

Crowley, Vivianne. *Wicca: The Old Religion in the New Age.* Wellingborough, England: Aquarian, 1989.

Faber, M. D. *Modern Witchcraft and Psychoanalysis.* London: Fairleigh Dickinson University Press and Associated University Presses, 1993.

Farrar, Janet, and Stewart Farrar. *The Life and Times of a Modern Witch.* Custer, Wash.: Phoenix, 1988.

———. *The Pagan Path.* Custer, Wash.: Phoenix, 1995.

Gardner, Gerald B. *The Meaning of Witchcraft.* New York: Magickal Childe, 1988.

———. *Witchcraft Today.* New York: Magickal Childe, 1982.

Guiley, Rosemary Ellen. *The Encyclopedia of Witches and Witchcraft.* New York: Facts on File, 1989.

Harvey, Graham. *Listening People, Speaking Earth.* London: Hurst, 1997.

Harvey, Graham, and Charlotte Hardman. *Paganism Today.* London: Thorsons, 1995.

Hawkins, Craig S. *Goddess Worship, Witchcraft, and Neo-Paganism.* Carlisle, England: OM Publishing, 1998

Holzer, Hans. *The New Pagans.* New York: Doubleday, 1972.

Leland, Charles G., ed. *Arcadia: Gospel of the Witches.* Llithfaen, Pwllheli, Wales: Deosil Dance Publications, 1991.

Lorimer, David. *The Circle of Sacred Dance.* Shaftesbury, England: Element, 1991.

Luhrmann, Tanya M. *Persuasions of the Witch's Craft.* Oxford: Blackwell, 1989.

Murray, Margaret. *The Witch-Cult in Western Europe: A Study in Anthropology.* Oxford: Clarendon, 1921.

Sanders, Alex. *The Alex Sanders Lectures*. New York: Magickal
Childe, 1984.
Starhawk. *The Spiral Dance: A Rebirth of the Ancient Religion
of the Great Goddess*. San Francisco: Harper and Row, 1979.
Stone, Merlin. *When God Was a Woman*. New York: Harcourt
Brace and Javonovich, 1976.
Valiente, Doreen. *The Rebirth of Witchcraft*. London: Robert
Hale, 1989.

XVI. The New Age Movement

1. General and Academic

Bloom, William, ed. *The New Age: An Anthology of Essential
Writings*. London: Rider, 1991.
Button, John, and William Bloom, eds. *The Seeker's Guide: A
New Age Resource Book*. London: Aquarian, 1992.
Campbell, Eileen, and James H. Brennan. *The Aquarian Guide
to the New Age*. Wellingborough, England: Aquarian, 1990.
————. *Dictionary of Mind, Body, and Spirit: Ideas, People and
Places*. London: Aquarian, 1994.
Drane, John. *What Is the New Age Saying to the Church?* London: Marshall Pickering, 1991.
Ferguson, Marilyn. *The Aquarian Conspiracy: Personal and
Social Transformation in Our Time*. New York: Putnam,
1987.
Hanegraaff, Wouter J. *New Age Religion and Western Culture:
Esotericism in the Mirror of Secular Thought*. Leiden, The
Netherlands: E. J. Brill, 1996.
Heelas, Paul. *The New Age Movement: The Celebration of the
Self and the Sacralization of Modernity*. Oxford: Blackwell,
1986.
Lash, John. *The Seeker's Handbook: The Complete Guide to
Spiritual Pathfinding*. New York: Harmony Books, 1990.
Perry, Michael. *Gods Within: A Critical Guide to the New Age*.
London: S.P.C.K., 1992.

Sadleir, Steven S. *The Spiritual Seeker's Guide: The Complete Source for Religions and Spiritual Groups of the World.* Costa Mesa, Calif.: Allwon, 1992.

Saliba, J. A. *Christian Responses to the New Age.* London: Cassell, 1999.

Sutcliffe, Steven, and Marion Bowman, eds. *Beyond New Age: Exploring Alternative Spirituality.* Edinburgh: Edinburgh University Press, 2000.

2. Channeling

General and early channeling

Alexander, Brooks. *Spirit Channeling.* Downers Grove, Ill.: InterVarsity Press, 1988.

Bjorling, Joel. *Channeling: A Bibliographic Exploration.* New York: Garland, 1992.

Klimo, Jon. *Channeling: Investigations on Receiving Information from Paranormal Sources.* Los Angeles: Jeremy P. Tarcher, 1987.

Oahspe. Los Angeles: Essenes of Kosmon, 1950.

Rueckert, Carla L. *A Channeling Handbook.* Louisville, Ky.: L/L Research, 1987.

Edgar Cayce

Bro, Harmon Hartzell. *Edgar Cayce: A Seer out of Season.* Wellingborough, England: Aquarian, 1990.

Cayce, Hugh Lynn, ed. *The Edgar Cayce Reader.* 2 vols. New York: Paperback Library, 1969.

Stearn, Jess. *Edgar Cayce: The Sleeping Prophet.* New York: Bantam Books, 1986.

Course in Miracles

Schucman, Helen. *A Course in Miracles.* Tiburon, Calif.: Foundation for Inner Peace, 1985.

―――. *The Gifts of God.* Tiburon, Calif.: Foundation for Inner Peace, 1988.

Singh, Tara. *Commentaries on* A Course in Miracles. Los Angeles: Life Action Press, 1986.

Wapnick, Kenneth. *Absence From Felicity: The Story of Helen Schucman and Her Scribing of* A Course in Miracles. Roscoe, N.Y.: Foundation for "A Course in Miracles," 1991.

————. *The Fifty Miracle Principles of A Course in Miracles.* Roscoe, N.Y.: Foundation for "A Course in Miracles," 1992.

————. *Forgiveness and Jesus.* Roscoe, N.Y.: Foundation for "A Course in Miracles," 1986.

Lazaris

Pursel, Jach (Lazaris). *Lazaris Interviews.* 2 vols. Beverly Hills, Calif.: Concept Synergy, 1988.

————. *The Sacred Journey: You and Your Higher Self.* Beverly Hills, Calif.: Concept Synergy, 1987.

————. *The Sirius Connection.* Palm Beach, Fla.: NPN, 1996.

Ramtha (J. Z. Knight)

Kerins, Deborah, ed. *The Spinner of Tales: A Collection of Stories as Told by Ramtha.* Yelm, Wash.: New Horizon, 1991.

Knight, J. Z. *A State of Mind: My Story.* New York: Warner Books, 1987.

Ramtha (J. Z. Knight). *I Am Ramtha.* Portland, Oreg.: Beyond Words, 1986.

Weinberg, Seven L. *Ramtha: An Introduction.* Eastsound, Wash.: Sovereignty, 1988.

Weinberg, Seven L., ed. *Ramtha.* Eastsound, Wash.: Sovereignty, 1986.

Seth (Jane Roberts)

Roberts Jane (Seth). *How to Develop Your ESP Power.* New York: Frederick Fell, 1966. Reprinted as *The Coming of Seth.* New York: Pocket Books, 1976.

————. *Seth Speaks: The Eternal Validity of the Soul.* New York: Bantam Books, 1985.

Watkins, Susan. *Conversations with Seth: The Story of Jane Roberts's ESP Class.* 2 vols. Englewood Cliffs, N.J.: Prentice-Hall, 1980, 1981.

Urantia
Renn, Ruth E. *Study Aids for Part IV of* The Urantia Book. Chicago: Urantia Foundation, 1975.
Urantia Foundation. *The Urantia Book.* Chicago: Urantia Foundation, 1955.
Westen, Robin. *Channelers: A New Age Directory.* New York: Perigee, 1988.

3. Damanhur

Merrifield, Jeff. *Damanhur: The Real Dream.* London: Thorsons, 1998.

4. Findhorn (Including Sir George Trevelyan and David Spangler)

Caddy, Eileen. *Choosing to Love: A Practical Guide for Bringing More Love into Your Life.* Forres, Scotland: Findhorn Press, 1993.
———. *Footprints on the Path.* Forres, Scotland: Findhorn Press, 1991.
———. *God Spoke to Me.* Rev. ed. Forres, Scotland: Findhorn Press, 1991.
Caddy, Eileen, and David E. Platts. *Bringing More Love into Your Life: The Choice Is Yours.* Forres, Scotland: Findhorn Press, 1992.
Findhorn Community, The. *The Findhorn Garden: Pioneering a New Vision of Humanity and Nature in Cooperation.* Forres, Scotland: Findhorn Press, 1988.
Maynard, Edwin, ed. *Faces of Findhorn: Images of Planetary Family, Findhorn Community.* Forres, Scotland: Findhorn Publications, 1980.
Spangler, David. *A Pilgrim in Aquarius.* Forres, Scotland: Findorn Publications, 1996.
———. *Revelation: Birth of a New Age.* Forres, Scotland: Findorn Publications, 1977.

Spangler, David, and William Irwin Thompson. *Emergence: The Rebirth of the Sacred.* New York: Dell, 1984.

──────. *Reimagination of the World: A Critique of the New Age, Science, and Popular Culture.* Santa Fe, N. Mex.: Bear and Co., 1991.

Trevelyan, George. *Operation Redemption: A Vision of Hope in an Age of Turmoil.* Wellingborough, England: Thorsons, 1983.

──────. *Summons to a High Crusade.* Forres, Scotland: Findhorn Press, 1985.

──────. *A Vision of the Aquarian Age.* 2d ed. London: Coventure, 1977.

5. Gaia and New Age Ecology

Lovelock, James. *The Ages of Gaia: A Biography of Our Living Earth.* Oxford: Oxford University Press, 1988.

──────. *Gaia: A New Look at Life on Earth.* Oxford: Oxford University Press, 1979.

──────. *Gaia: The Practical Science of Planetary Medicine.* New York: Oxford, 2000.

Thompson, William Irwin. *Gaia: A Way of Knowing.* Great Barrington, England: Lindisfarne Press, 1987.

Wright, Machaelle Small. *Behaving as if the God in All Life Mattered: A New Age Ecology.* Walpole, N.H.: Stillpoint, 1986.

6. Glastonbury

Hexham, Irving. "The 'Freaks' of Glastonbury: Conversion and Consolidation in an English Country Town." *Update* 8, no. 1 (1983): 3-12.

Howard-Gordon, Frances. *Glastonbury: Maker of Myths.* Glastonbury, England: Gothic Image Publications, 1997.

7. Solara (Star-Borne Unlimited)

Solara. *EL*AN*RA*. Charlottesville, Va.: Star-Borne Unlimited, 1991.

————. *How to Live Large on a Small Planet*. Whitefish, Mont.: Star-Borne Unlimited, 1996.

————. *Invoking Your Celestial Guardians*. Charlottesville, Va.: Star-Borne Unlimited, 1986.

————. *The Legend of Altazar, A Fragment of True History of Planet Earth*. Charlottesville, Va.: Star-Borne Unlimited, 1987.

————. *The Star-Borne—A Remembrance for the Awakened Ones*. Charlottesville, Va.: Star-Borne Unlimited, 1989.

8. Miscellaneous New Age Classics

Dowling, Levi H. *The Aquarian Gospel of Jesus the Christ*. Romford, Essex: Fowler, 1989.

Hay, Louise L. *You Can Heal Your Life*. Enfield: Eden Grove, 1984.

Kersten, Holger. *Jesus Lived in India: His Unknown Life before and after the Crucifixion*. Shaftesbury, England: Element, 1994.

Redfield, James. *The Celestine Prophecy*. New York: Warner Books, 1993.

————. *The Celestine Prophecy: An Experiential Guide*. New York: Warner Books, 1995.

————. *The Tenth Insight*. New York: Warner Books, 1996.

XVII. UFO-Religions

1. Background and General

Adamski, George. *Cosmic Philosophy*. Freeman, S. Dak.: Pine Hill Press, 1971.

Lewis, David Allen. *UFO: End-Time Delusion.* Green Forest, Ark.: New Leaf Press, 1992.

Lewis, James R., ed. *The Gods Have Landed: New Religions from Other Worlds.* New York: State University of New York Press, 1995.

Peters, Ted. *UFOs: God's Chariots? Flying Saucers in Politics, Science, and Religion.* Atlanta: John Knox Press, 1977.

Thompson, Keith. *Angels and Aliens: UFOs and the Mythic Imagination.* Reading, Mass.: Addison-Wesley, 1991.

University for Life. *Visitors from Other Planets.* Miami: Mark-Age, 1974.

von Daniken, Erich. *Chariots of the Gods? Unsolved Mysteries of the Past.* London: Corgi, 1976.

2. Aetherius Society

Aetherius Society. *The Aetherius Society Calendar, with the Annual Commemoration Dates for 1988.* Hollywood, Calif.: Aetherius Society, 1988.

———. *Temple Degree Study Courses.* Hollywood, Calif.: Aetherius Society, 1982.

King, George. *Contact Your Higher Self through Yoga.* Los Angeles: Aetherius Society, 1980.

———. *The Day the Gods Came.* Hollywood, Calif.: Aetherius Society, 1970.

———. *My Contact with the Great White Brotherhood.* Hollywood, Calif.: Aetherius Society, 1983.

———. *The Nine Freedoms.* Hollywood, Calif.: Aetherius Society, 1974.

———. *Operation Space Power: The Solution to the Spiritual Energy Crisis.* Hollywood, Calif.: Aetherius Society, 1987.

———. *The Practices of Aetherius.* Hollywood, Calif.: Aetherius Society, 1964.

———. *The Twelve Blessings: The Cosmic Concept for the New Aquarian Age as Given by the Master Jesus in His Overshadowing of George King.* Hollywood, Calif.: Aetherius Society, 1974.

————. *You Are Responsible!* London: Aetherius Press, 1961.
Wallis, Roy. "The Aetherius Society: A Case Study in the Formation of a Mystagogic Congregation." *Sociological Review* 22, no. 1 (1974): 27-44.

3. Chen Tao

Chen Tao. *God's Descending in Clouds (Flying Saucers) on Earth to Save People.* Garland, Tex.: Chen Tao, 1997.
————. *The Practical Evidence and Study of the World of God and Buddha.* Garland, Tex.: Chen Tao, 1996.

4. Heaven's Gate

Steiger, Brad, and Hayden Hewes. *Inside Heaven's Gate: The UFO Cult Leaders Tell Their Story in Their Own Words.* New York: Signet, 1997.

5. Raëlian Church

Chryssides, G. D. "Is God a Space Alien? The Cosmology of the Raëlian Church." *Culture and Cosmos* 4, no. 1 (2000): 36-53.
Raël (Claude Vorilhon). *Let's Welcome Our Fathers from Space: They Created Humanity in Their Laboratories.* Tokyo: AOM Corporation, 1992.
————. *The Message Given to Me by Extra-Terrestrials: They Took Me to Their Planet.* Tokyo: AOM Corporation, 1992.

6. Unarius

Norman, Ruth E. *Preview for the Spacefleet Landing on Earth in 2001 A.D.* El Cajon, Calif.: Unarius Academy of Science, 1987.

————. *The Unarius Educational Foundation: An Historical Biography.* El Cajon, Calif.: Unarius Educational Foundation, 1985.

XVIII. Issues and Themes in New Religious Movements

1. General

Beckford, James. *Cult Controversies: The Societal Response to New Religious Movements.* London: Tavistock, 1985.
Singer, M. T. *Crazy "Therapies": What Are They? Do They Work?* San Francisco: Jossey-Bass, 1996.
————. *Cults in Our Midst: The Hidden Menace in Our Everyday Lives.* San Francisco: Jossey-Bass, 1995.

2. Exit and Entry, Brainwashing and Deprogramming

Bjornstad, James. "Cults and Christian Conversion: Is there a Difference?" *Update* 6, no. 1 (1982): 50-59.
Conway, Flo and Jim Siegelman. *Snapping: America's Epidemic of Sudden Personality Change.* 2d ed. New York: Stillpoint Press, 1995.
Lifton, R. J. *Thought Reform and the Psychology of Totalism: A Study of Brainwashing in China.* Chapel Hill: University of North Carolina Press, 1989.
Patrick, Ted, and Tom Dulack. *Let Our Children Go!* New York: Dutton, 1976.
Robbins, T., J. Needleman, and D. Anthony, eds. *Conversion, Coercion, and Commitment in New Religious Movements.* New York: Crossroads, 1983.
————. *Cults, Converts, and Charisma: The Sociology of New Religious Movements.* London: Sage, 1988.
Singer, M. T. "Coming Out of the Cults." *Psychology Today* 12, 8 January 1979: 75-76, 79-80, 82.
Swatland, A., and S. Swatland. *Escape from the Moonies.* London: Hodder and Stoughton, 1982.

Whittle, Thomas G. *The Cult Awareness Network: Anatomy of a Hate Group.* Los Angeles: Church of Scientology, c.1995.
Wright, Stuart A. *Leaving Cults: The Dynamics of Defection.* Washington, D.C.: Society for the Scientific Study of Religion, 1987.

3. Millennialism

Mann, A. T. *Millennial Prophecies.* Shaftesbury, England: Element, 1992.
Olson, Theodore. *Millennialism, Utopianism, and Progress.* Toronto: University of Toronto Press, 1982.
Robbins, Thomas, and Susan J. Palmer. *Millennium, Messiahs, and Mayhem.* New York: Routledge, 1997.
Wessinger, Catherine. "How the Millennium Comes Violently: A Comparison of Jonestown, Aum Shinrikyo, Branch Davidians, and the Montana Freemen." *Dialog* 36, no. 4 (Fall 1997): 277-288.
———. *How the Millennium Comes Violently: From Jonestown to Heaven's Gate.* New York: Seven Bridges Press, 2000.
Wessinger, Catherine, ed. *Millennialism, Persecution, and Violence: Historical Cases.* Syracuse, N.Y.: Syracuse University Press, 2000.

4. Women in NRMs

King, U. *Women in the World's Religions Past and Present.* New York: Paragon, 1987.
Puttick, Elizabeth. *Women in New Religions: In Search of Community, Sexuality, and Spiritual Power.* London: Routledge, 1997.
Puttick, E., and P. B. Clarke, eds. *Women as Teachers and Disciples in Traditional and New Religions.* Lewiston, N.Y.: Edwin Mellen, 1993.

Wessinger, Catherine. *Women's Leadership in Marginal Religions: Explorations outside the Mainstream.* Urbana: University of Illinois Press, 1993.

5. Official Reports on NRMs

British Council of Churches, Committee for Relations with People of Other Faiths. *Secretary's Twentieth Informal Report.* London: British Council of Churches, 1985.

Catholic Truth Society. "Sects: The Pastoral Challenge" *Briefing 86* 16, no. 2 (1986): 142-152; Reprinted as *New Religious Movements: A Challenge to the Church.* London: Catholic Truth Society, 1986.

Church of England General Synod. *New Religious Movements: A Report by the Board for Mission and Unity.* London: General Synod of the Church of England, 1989.

Cottrell, Richard. *Report on the Activity of Certain New Religious Movements within the European Community.* Report to the European Parliament, Committee on Youth, Culture, Education, Information, and Sport. PE 82.322/fin, 22 March 1984.

Vivien, Alain. *Les sectes en France: Expressions de la liberté morale ou facteurs de manipulations? Rapport au Premier Ministre.* (The sects in France: Legitimate freedom of expression or manipulation? Report to the prime minister.) Paris: Documentation Française, 1985.

6. Legal issues

Bradney, Anthony. *Religions, Rights, and Laws.* New York: Leicester University Press, 1993.

"Interview: Richard Cottrell, M.E.P." *Update* 8 nos. 3-4 (1984): 30-34.

Turner, Harold W. "Reports on Practical Legislative Application (International): Great Britain." *Conscience and Liberty: In-*

ternational Journal of Religious Freedom 1, no. 1 (1989): 67-72.

XIX. Other Useful Publications and Works Cited in the Text

Bennett, J. G. *The Dramatic Universe.* 4 vols. London: Hodder and Stoughton, 1965-1966.

Huxley, Aldous. *The Perennial Philosophy.* New York: Harper and Row, 1944.

Kuhn, T. *The Structure of Scientific Revolutions.* Chicago: University of Chicago Press, 1962.

Leary, Timothy. *Flashbacks: An Autobiography.* Los Angeles: Houghton Mifflin, 1983.

———. *Psychedelic Prayers after the Tao Te Ching.* Kerhonkson, N.Y.: Poets Press, 1966.

———. *The Psychedelic Experience: A Manual Based on the Tibetan Book of the Dead.* New York: University Books, 1964.

Leary, Timothy, R. Alpert, and R. Metzner. *The Psychedelic Experience.* New York: Citadel Press, 1995.

Long, Barry. *Meditation: A Foundation Course.* London: Barry Long Books, 1995.

———. *The Way In: A Book of Self-Discovery.* Santa Rosa, Calif: Barry Long Books, 2000.

XX. Useful Web Sites

The Internet has now become a powerful research tool, one which scholars of religion can no longer afford to neglect. NRMs have particularly benefited from its presence, since the World Wide Web provides them with an opportunity to present their message directly to the public, unfiltered by media hostility or anticult prejudice. In its earlier years, material was simply placed by a few sympathizers who had the appropriate enthusiasm and technical expertise but not always good communication skills or sound understanding. They tended to be volatile: personal pages created by adherents from their work web site disappeared as soon as their employment terminated. They were also hard to find amidst the web's vast network of information. More recently, the vast majority of religious organizations have come to maintain professionally designed web sites that provide systematic exposition of their aims and tenets. With the increasing drive to purchase appropriate domain names, there is not only a tendency for their web addresses to be memorable and logical, but to have a more permanent presence on the web.

The list that follows consists principally of NRMs' official pages. In cases where there did not appear to be an official web presence, I have indicated where a sympathizer's web site can be found. Where there are good academic sources, these are also mentioned. Since it is assumed that readers will wish to use such sources for further study, I have not listed web sites that provide little more than a brief "thought for the day," are dedicated to selling goods and services, or can only be accessed by subscription.

As well as enabling NRMs to provide information, the World Wide Web equally affords the opportunity for critics to put their case. There are, of course, many such sites, and in many cases the information is unreliable. I have therefore elected to list the web sites of the principal countercult and cult monitoring organizations: these tend to be more comprehensive and often provide good hypertext links to critics of specific NRMs.

A. General Information

Adherents.com: extensive statistical information
    http://www.adherents.com
Ontario Consultants on Religious Tolerance
    http://www.religioustolerance.org
Skeptic's Dictionary
    http://www.skepdic.com
University of Calgary: sources for the study of cults, sects, new
    and contemporary religions
    http://www.ucalgary.ca/~nurelweb/

University of Virginia, Sociology Department
http://cti.itc.virginia.edu/~jkh8x/soc257/home.html
University of Wolverhampton, England: Religious Studies on
the Internet (hypertext links to many web sites listed below)
http://www.wlv.ac.uk/sed/rsnet.htm

B. Specific NRMs

3HO (Healthy, Happy, Holy)
http://www.3ho.org
http://www.yogibhajan.com
Adi Da Samraj (Bubba Free John; formerly Laughing Man Institute)
http://adidam.com
Aetherius Society
http://www.aetherius.org
African Initiated Churches
http://www.geocities.com/missionalia/aic.htm (academic)
http://www.ricsa.org.za (Research Institute on Christianity in
South Africa)
Ahmadiyya
http://www.ahmadiyya.com
Alamo
http://www.alamoministries.com
Aleph
http://www.aleph.to/index_e.html
Alevis
http://www.sahkulu.org/alevi/xalevis
AMORC
http://www.amorc.org
Amway
http://www.amway.com
Ananda Marga
http://www.anandamarga.org
Anthroposophy
http://www.anthroposophy.net

Asatru
   http://www.oingo.com/topic/54/54033.html
Assemblies of Yahweh
   http://www.assembliesofyahweh.com/aoy/index.html
   http://marvin.ecc.cc.mo.us/~rdimmett/aoy/ (unofficial)
Association for Research and Enlightenment
   http://www.are-cayce.com
Association of Unity Churches
   http://www.unity.org
Aum Shinrikyo
   http://www.dotco.com/t3/Aum.html (official police reports)
   http://www.conspire.com/aum.html (a report on the subway
      gassing)
Aurobindo
   http://www.miraura.org
   http://www.collaboration.org
Baba Ram Dass (Richard Alpert)
   http://ramdasstapes.org
Bahá'í
   http://www.bahai.org
   http://bahai-library.org (Baha'i Academics Resource Library)
Bawa Muhaiyaddeen Fellowship
   http://www.bmf.org/index.html
Black Elk
   http://iserver.saddleback.cc.ca.us/div/la/neh/blackelk.htm
Brahma Kumaris
   http://www.bkwsu.com
Brahmo Samaj
   http://www.chanda.freeserve.co.uk/brahmoframe.htm
   http://freeindia.org/biographies/roy (unofficial)
Branch Davidians
   http://www.branchdavidian.com
   http://www.sevenseals.com
   http://www.cia.com.au/serendipity/waco.html
   http://eserver.org/BS/36/shaw.html (unofficial)
Branham, William
   http://www.williambranham.com

Breatharians (Jasmuheen)
  http://www.selfempowermentacademy.com.au
  http://seasilver.threadnet.com/Preventorium/jasmuhen.htm
Brethren
  http://www.cob-net.org (Church of the Brethren)
  http://www.brethren.org
  http://www.caic.org.au/biblebase/brethren2.htm (Exclusive
    Brethren)
  http://www.mbconf.org (Mennonite Brethren)
British Israel
  http://www.british-israel.net (British Israel Church of God)
Brotherhood of the Cross and Star
  http://users.ntr.net/~brotherhood/text/western.html
Bruderhof
  http://www.bruderhof.org
Cao Dai
  http://www.caodai.org
Cayce, Edgar
  http://www.cayce.com
  http://www.edgarcayce.com
Cerullo, Morris
  http://www.prayerwatch.org
Channelling
  http://home.sol.no/~kjole/ncca/channel.html
Chen Tao
  http://www.watchman.org/profile/chentaopro.htm
  http://europe.cnn.com/US/9803/19/saucer.cult/index.html
  http://www.forteantimes.com/artic/109/chen.html
Chinmoy
  http://www.webcom.com/shambhu/welcome.html
  http://www.peacerun.com
  http://www.geocities.com/Athens/Aegean/5810/links.html
Christadelphians
  http://www.christadelphian.org.uk
  http://www.christadelphia.org
Christian Science
  http://www.tfccs.com
  http://www.csmonitor.com

http://www.religious-freedom.org
http://www.marybakereddy.org
http://www.tfccs.com/GV/CSPS/CSJ/csjrnl.html
Christ Maitreya (Benjamin Creme)
    http://www.shareintl.org
Churches of Christ
    http://www.intlcc.com
    http://www.icoc.org
Church of All Worlds
    http://www.caw.org
Church of Jesus Christ of Latter-day Saints
    http://www.lds.org
    http://www.mormon.com
    http://www.2think.org/hii/mormon.shtml
    http://www.restoration.org (traditional and splinter groups
        from LDS)
Church of Satan and Satanism
    http://www.churchofsatan.com
    http://www.satanism101.com
    http://www.in.net/~satan/
Church of Scientology
    http://www.scientology.org/home.html
    http://www.lronhubbard.org/lrhhome.htm
    http://www.dianetics.org/dnhome.html
    http://www.able.org
    http://www.narconon.org
    http://www.criminon.org
    http://www.thewaytohappiness.org
    http://www.freedommag.org
    http://www.hubbardcollege.org
    http://www.cchr.org
    http://www.battlefieldearth.com
    http://www.bridgepub.com
Church Universal and Triumphant
    http://www.tsl.org
Cohen, Andrew
    http://www.andrewcohen.org

Course in Miracles (Inner Peace Foundation)
http://www.spiritsite.com/writing/coumir/index.htm
Covenant of the Goddess
http://www.cog.org
Crowley, Aleister
http:// www.otohq.org
http://www.maroney.org
http://www.lsi.usp.br/usp/rod/magick/aleister_crowley.html
Davies, Andrew, Jr. ("Poughkeepsie Seer")
http://www.waymemorial.org/AndrewDavis.htm
Druidism: British Druid Order
http://www.druidorder.demon.co.uk
Eckankar
http://www.eckankar.org/home.html
Elan Vital
http://www.elanvital.org
http:// www.maharaji.org
Emerson, Ralph Waldo
http://www.rwe.org
Emissaries of Divine Light
http://www.geocities.com/athens/oracle/7642/serv03.htm
    (unofficial, neutral)
Engaged Buddhism
http://www.dharmanet.org/engaged.html
http://www.engaged-zen.org
http://www.engagedpage.com
Essene Church of Christ
http://www.essene.org
Falun Gong
http://www.clearwisdom.net
Family, The (formerly Children of God)
http://www.thefamily.org
Father Divine's Peace Mission
http://www.libertynet.org/fdipmm/
Findhorn Foundation
http://www.findhorn.org
Focolare
http://www.focolare.org

Gaia
    http://www.gaiabooks.co.uk/books
Gnosticism
    http://www.webcom.com/~gnosis/welcome.html
Gurdjieff, G. I.
    http://www.gurdjieff.org
Heaven's Gate
    http://www.trancenet.org/heavensgate/
Holy Order of MANS (Christ the Savior Brotherhood)
    http://se.unisa.edu.au/h.html (unofficial)
House Church Movement in China (Watchman Nee)
    http://www.xenos.org/essays/neeframe.htm
Inner Light Foundation
    http://www.innerlight.org
International Churches of Christ
    http://www.icoc.org
Ishvara (Lifewave)
    http://www.ishvara.org
ISKCON (International Society for Krishna Consciousness)
    http://www.iskcon.org
    http://www.iskcon.org.uk
Jehovah's Witnesses
    http://www.watchtower.org
    http://www.jehovah.to (unofficial)
Jesus Army (Jesus Fellowship Church)
    http://www.jesus.org.uk
Jews for Jesus
    http://www.jewsforjesus.org
Johrei
    http://www.johreifellowship.com
Korean new religions
    http://cinema.sangji.ac.kr/WINDOW/window/win00091.htm
Krishnamurti
    http://www.kfoundation.org
    http://www.jkrishnamurti.org
Kundalini Yoga
    http://www-cad.eecs.berkeley.edu/HomePages/keutzer/
    kundalini/kundabib-web.html (bibliography)

Landmark Education (formerly *est*)
    http://www.landmark-education.com
Latter Rain
    http://www.latter-rain.com
    http://www.latterrain.org
Lazaris
    http://www.lazaris.com
Lucis Trust
    http://www.lucistrust.org
Mahikari
    http://www.mahikari.org
Meher Baba
    http://www.avatarmeherbaba.org
Messianic Jews
    http://www.ifmj.org (International Federation of Messianic
        Jews)
    http://www.umjc.org (Union of Messianic Jewish Congrega-
        tions)
    http://www.kehilatariel.org (Kehilat Ariel Messianic Congre-
        gation)
Metropolitan Community Churches
    http://www.churchnet.org.uk/ukchurches/metro.shtml
Moral Rearmament (MRA)
    http://www.mra.org.uk/
    http://www.caux.ch/ (unofficial)
Mother Meera
    http://www.mothermeera.com
Movement of Inner Spiritual Awareness (MSIA)
    http://cti.itc.virginia.edu/~jkh8x/soc257/nrms/msia.html
        (academic)
    http://www.caic.org.au/miscult/jrmsia.htm (critical)
Naropa University
    http://www.naropa.edu
Nation of Islam
    http://www.noi.org
Native American Religion
    http://www.religioustolerance.org/nataspir.htm (unofficial)

Neo-Catechumenate
  http://ourworld.compuserve.com/homepages/esammut/
    interest.html
New Age web sites
  http://www.delphi.com/newage
  http://www.newage.com
  http://www.salemctr.com/newage
  http://www.chinesenewagesociety.org
  http://www.accessnewage.com
New Apostolic Church
  http://www.nak.org/home-gb.html
New Kadampa Tradition (NKT)
  http://www.kadampa.net
  http://www.manjushri.org.uk
  http://www.geocities.com/~manjushri_cntr/
Nichiren Shu
  http://www.nichirenshu.org
Nipponzan Myohoji
  http://www.oingo.com/topic/239/239153.html
Oahspe
  http://www.angelfire.com/in2/oahspe/links.html
Oneness Pentecostalism (United Pentecostal Church Interna-
    tional)
  http://www.upci.org/churches
Opus Dei
  http://www.opusdei.org
Ordo Templi Orientis
  http://www.otohq.org
Original Kleptonian Neo-American Church
  http://okneoac.com
Osho
  http://www.sannyas.net
  http://www.osho.com
Pagan Federation
  http://www.hexhus.a.se/pfint (Pagan Federation Interna-
    tional)
  http://www.paganfed.demon.co.uk (Pagan Federation [UK])

http://members.tripod.com/~TaraMiller/pagan.html
(unofficial)
Paganism: see witchcraft/wicca
Pentecostalism
http://www.leeuniversity.edu/library/dixon (Pentecostal Research Center)
Peoples Temple
http://www-rohan.sdsu.edu/~remoore/jonestown/
Process Church of the Final Judgement
http://religiousmovements.lib.virginia.edu/nrms/Process.html
Promise Keepers
http://www.promisekeepers.org
Radhasoami
http://www.angelfire.com/band/radhasoamisantmath/index.
html
http://www.mtsac.edu/~dlane/rsdeb.html (academic)
http://www.philtar.ucsm.ac.uk/encyclopedia/hindu/ascetic/
radha.html (academic)
Ramakrishna
http://www.ramakrishna.org
Ramana
http://www.ramana-maharshi.org
Rastafari
http://www.aspects.net/~nick/religion.htm
Ravidasi
http://www.gururavidassji.org.uk
Rebirthing
http://www.breathaware.com/links.html
Reform Judaism
http://www.rj.org
Reiyukai
http://www.kokugakuin.ac.jp/ijcc/wp/cpjr/newreligions/
komoto.html
http://www.crosswinds.net/~campross/Reiyukai.html
Religious Science, United Church of
http://www.religiousscience.org
Rissho Kosei-Kai
http://www.crosswinds.net/~campross/RKK.html

Sacred Name Movement
   http:// www.qumran.com/sacrednames
Sahaja Yoga
   http://www.sahajayoga.org/index.html
Santeria
   http://www.altarofmysoul.com
   http://www.hechicero.com
Sant Nirankari
   http://www.nirankari.org
Satchidananda
   http://www.yogaville.org
Satya Sai Baba
   http://www.sathyasai.org
   http://www.ozemail.com.au/~vsivasup/sai/noframes/
      index.html
School of Economic Science
   http://www.schooleconomicscience.org
Sedevacantists
   http://www.truecatholic.org
Seth (channeled by Jane Roberts)
   http://www.secretoflife.com/seth/index.html
Seventh-day Adventism
   http://www.breadoflife.simplenet.com/sbhn
   http://www.cuc.edu/sdaorg
   http://www.adventist.org.uk
Shamanism
   http://www.shamanism.org
Shinreikyo
   http://www.unification.net/ws/shinrei2.htm
Shirdi Sai Baba
   http://www.shirdisai.org
   http://www.sai.org
   http://www.saibaba.org
Shivabalayogi
   http://www.shiva.org/initiate.htm
Siddha Yoga Dham
   http://www.syda.org

Silva Method (formerly Silva Mind Control)
   http://www.silvamethod.com
   http://www.talamasca.org/avatar/silvahistory.html
   http://users.erols.com/dckeys/silva
Sivananda
   http://www.sivananda.org
Society of the Inner Light
   http://www.innerlight.org.uk/index.html
Soka Gakkai
   http://www.sgi-usa.org
   http://en.sokagakkai.or.jp/html3/index3.html
Spiritualism
   http://www.nsac.org (National Spiritualist Association of
     Churches [USA])
   http://www.fst.org/150home.htm (First Spiritual Temple—
     non-denominational Spiritualist)
Star-Borne Unlimited (Solara)
   http://www.nvisible.com
Subud
   http://www.subud.org
   http://www.raymondo.demon.co.uk
   http://www.subudusa.org
Sufism
   http://www.sufiorder.org
Summit Lighthouse (Church Universal and Triumphant)
   http://www.tsl.org
Temple of Set
   http://www.xeper.org
Tenrikyo
   http://www.tenrikyo.or.jp
Temple ov Psychick Youth (TOPY)
   http://www.eskimo.com/~carcosa/topy.html
Theosophy
   http://theosophy.org
   http://www.theosophy.com
Toronto Blessing
   http://www.tacf.org (Toronto Airport Fellowship Church)

Transcendentalism (Ralph Waldo Emerson)
    http://www.rwe.org
    http://www.watershed.online.ca/literature/Emerson/
        EMERSON.html
    http://www.geocities.com/~freereligion/1emerson.html
Transcendental Meditation (TM)
    http://www.tm.org
    http://www.tm-london.org.uk/set1.html
Trungpa, Chogyam
    http://www.shambhala.org
    http://dharma-haven.org/tibetan/teachings-chogyam-
        trungpa.html
Unamended Christadelphians
    http://www.texas-christadelphians.com
Unarius Academy of Science
    http://www.unarius.org
Unification Church/Family Federation
    http://www.ettl.co.at/unification
    http://www.ffwpu.org
    http://www.tparents.org
United Church of God
    http://www.ucg.org
Unity School of Christianity
    http://www.unity.org
    http://www.silentunity.org
Universal Church of the Master
    http://www.u-c-m.org
Universal Life Church (Kirby J. Hensley)
    http://ulc.org/ulc
Urantia
    http://www.urantia.org (Urantia Foundation)
    http://www.urantiabook.org (Urantia Book)
Vampires
    http://www.net1plus.com/users/vyrdolak/home.htm
    http://www.avia.darkrealm.net
Vedanta Society
    http://www.vedanta.org

Vineyard Ministries
    http://www.vineyardinternational.org
Vipassana
    http://www.dhamma.org
    http://vipassana.org
Vivekananda
    http://www.vivekananda.org
Watts, Alan
    http://www.alanwatts.com
Way International: no official web site at the time of writing
Western Buddhist Order, Friends of the
    http://www.fwbo.org
    http://www.westernbuddhistreview.com/index.html
White Eagle Lodge
    http://207.48.133.174/
Witchcraft /wicca
    http://www.wicca.com (Celtic Connection)
    http://www.witchcraft.org (Children of Artemis Witchcraft
        and Wicca)
    http://www.wicca.org (Church and School of Wicca)
    http://www.paganism.org (Paganism)
    http://www.pagans.org/wicca/welcom.htm (Paganism)
Won Buddhism
    http://users.erols.com/sanghyun
Word-Faith Movement
    http://tbm.org/faithmove.htm
    http://www.tbm.org/Faithlinks.htm
Word of Life Church
    http://www.wolc.com
Worldwide Church of God
    http://www.wcg.org
Yogananda
    http://www.ananda.org
    http://www.yogananda.org

C. Critical, Countercult, and Cult Monitoring Sites

American Family Foundation
 http://www.csj.org
Apologetics and Counter-Cult Resources for Research and Ministry (a Christian organization, providing an extensive index
 of organizations)
 http://www.gospelcom.net/apologeticsindex
CESNUR (Centre for the Study of New Religious Movements,'
 Italy)
 http://www.cesnur.org
Cult Awareness and Information Centre, Australia
 http://www.caic.org.au
Cult Awareness Network (CAN)
 http://www.cultawarenessnetwork.org
Cult Information Centre UK
 http://www.cultinformation.org.uk
Dialog Center International
 http:// www.dci.dk
Ex-Cult Resource Center
 http:// www.ex-cult.org
FAIR (Family Action Information and Resource)
 http://www.sar.bolton.ac.uk/fair/main.html
Freedom of Mind Institute
 http://www.freedomofmind.org
In Search of Truth
 http://www.truthquest.fsnet.co.uk
Research and Information Services
 http://www.workersect.org
Ross, Rick
 http://www.rickross.com
Spiritual Counterfeits Project
 http://www.scp-inc.org
Watchman Fellowship (special interest in Jehovah's Witnesses)
 http://www.watchman.org/watchman.htm

Index

Main entries and entries in the chronology are not included.

284, 298, 304, 308, 338, 344,
   356, 361
Karme Choling Meditation Center, 329
karmic counseling, 270
Kawate, Bunjiro, 191
Kellner, Karl, 13, 168, 247
Kelly, Galen, 102
Kenyon, E. W., 257, 353
Kerouac, Jack, 346, 259
Khan, Hidayat, 174, 187, 314
Khan, Hazrat Inayat, 8, 174, 314,
   315, 316, 339
Khan, Vilayat, 174, 187, 292, 314,
   315
Kibwetere, Joseph, 226
Kim, Young Oon, 109, 224
King, Sir George, 25
Kinley, Henry Clifford, 278
Kirpal Light Satsang, 189
Kirpal Singh, 9, 275-76, 281-82,
   286, 298
Kisser, Cynthia, 102
Klemp, Harold, 28, 114, 149-50,
   330
Kleps, Art, 202, 248
Knight, Gareth, 40, 302
Knight, J. Z., 13, 77
Knorr, Nathan, 175, 346
Korea, 10, 57, 71, 80-81, 109,
   110, 197, 224, 295, 297, 303,
   334-35, 302, 333, 335, 352
Koresh, David, 17, 59, 274, 345
Kornfield, Jack, 169, 343
Kosmon Bible, 243
Kosmon Church, 243-44
Kripalvananda, 193
Krishna, 25, 46, 49, 74-75, 80, 95,
   145, 158, 159, 172-73, 194,
   215, 218, 255, 262, 269, 304,
   357, 361
Krishnamurti, Jiddhu, 7, 53, 95,
   201, 311, 323
Ku Klux Klan, 91, 167
Kubo, Kakutaro, 270
Kuka, 228
Kundalini Research Institute, 154,
   196
kundalini yoga, 46, 76, 153, 154,
   189, 193, 214, 227, 228, 279,
   297, 354, 357

Lama Foundation, 265
Landmark Education Corporation,
   121, 164, 290
latihan, 312
Latter Rain Evangel, 200
Latter-day Saints, 2, 18, 141
Latter-Rain Movement, 19, 93,
   252, 353
Laughing Man Institute, 48
LaVey, Anton Szandor, 16, 91-92,
   256, 283
Laya yoga, 154, 196
Leadbeater, Charles, 7, 53, 194,
   203, 311, 323
League for Spiritual Discovery,
   201
Leary, Timothy, 247, 264
Lectorium Rosicrucianum, 275
Lee, Witness, 204-5
Lekhraj, Dada, 56-57
Levi, Eliphas, 185, 209, 274, 283
Lewis, Harvey Spencer, 31, 37
Lewis, Ralph M., 31
Lewis, Samuel L., 8, 187, 188,
   315
Liberal Catholicism, 171, 182,
   189, 201, 234, 319
Life Training, 290
Lifespring, 290
Lifestream Seminars, 290
Lifton, Robert Jay, 57-58, 102
Light of the Universe, 37
Lighthouse Ranch, 179
Lindsay, Gordon, 59
Lingwood, Dennis, 280-81, 348
Little, Malcolm, 213
Little Flock, 204
Living Game, 290
Living Stream Ministry, 204
Long, Max Freedom, 165
lost tribes, 39, 61-62, 144, 167,
   184
Lotus Sutra, 239-41, 270-71, 272,
   303
love bombing, 302
Love Israel, 90-91
Lovelock, James E., 142-43
Lubavitch, 183
Lubich, Chiara, 137
Lucis Trust, 38

Index

voodoo, 282
Vorilhon, Claude, 259
Vosper, Cyril, 126-27

Waco, 17, 59, 96, 192, 272-3, 275
Waite, A. E., 100, 157, 185, 250
Walk, The, 92
Walthall, Jethro, 306
Watchtower, 17, 19, 175, 276
Watts, Alan, 48, 359
Way International, The, xxiv
Weber, Max, 1, 77, 102
Wedgewood, James Ingall, 201, 203
Weeks, Eugene B., 133
Weiner, Bob, 216
Weishaupt, Adam, 168
West, Louis Jolyon, 102
Westcott, W. W., 156
Western Buddhist Order, 67, 152, 217, 280
White, Ellen G., 17, 85, 223, 238, 272, 292
White Eagle, 97
wicca, 14-15, 65-66, 78, 98, 101, 107, 133, 143, 148, 210, 251, 280, 283, 310, 339, 358
Wierwille, Victor Paul, vii, 347
Wilbur, Ken, 48
Wilcox, Hal, 339
Wilson, John, 61
Wilson, Robert Anton, 168
Wimber, John, 325, 342
Wingo, E. Otha, 165
Wings of Deliverance, 181, 253
Wise, Isaac M., 268
witchcraft. *See* wicca
Wittek, Gabrielle, 337
Wolcott, Louis Eugene, 231
Woodman, W. R., 156
Word of Life Church, xxix
Word-Faith Movement, 60, 257, 354
World Aryan Conference, 91
World Conference of Pentecostals, 19

World Goodwill, 207
World Messianity and Johrei Fellowship, 94, 212, 302
World Union for Progressive Judaism, 268
World's Christian Fundamentalist Association, 140-41
World's Parliament of Religions, 8-9, 11, 344
Worldwide Church of God, 20, 39, 85, 90, 147, 184, 324, 335
Wrekin Trust, 328
Wright, Machaelle Small, 33

Yagoda Satsanga Society, 358
Yahweh ben Yahweh, 232
Yali, 70
Yarr, John Herbert, 173
Yasodhara Ashram Society, 300
Yinger, J. M., 102
Yoga House Ashram, 31
Yoga Sutras, 122, 158, 174, 217, 326, 342,
yoga, 30, 38, 43, 44, 45, 46, 56, 57, 60, 76, 95, 113, 122, 134, 153, 154, 157, 158, 159, 160, 174, 185, 189, 190, 193, 196, 202, 214, 217, 227, 229, 242, 258, 260-61, 263, 264, 279, 284, 285, 289, 297, 300, 327, 342, 344, 354, 358, 364
Yogananda, 9, 60, 159, 171, 289-90, 357

Zablocki, Benjamin, 58
Zarephath-Horeb, 99
Zell, Tim, 88-89, 251
Zen, 38, 48, 67, 95, 119, 202, 217, 249, 261, 264, 290, 315, 346
Zenith Institute, 314
Zerby, Karen, 52
Zionist churches, 26
Zion's Watch Tower Tract Society, 345
Zoroastrianism, 32, 49, 77, 218, 243, 283, 314, 338

About the Author

George D. Chryssides studied philosophy and religion at the University of Glasgow and completed his doctorate at Oriel College, Oxford. He has taught philosophy and religious studies at several British universities and is currently senior lecturer in religious studies at the University of Wolverhampton, England. He has acted as consultant on new religious movements to the United Reformed Church in England, and he served for several years as chair of the board for the Centre for the Study of New Religious Movements at Selly Oak Colleges, Birmingham, England.

Dr. Chryssides has studied new and minority religious movements extensively since the mid-1980s and has contributed to numerous academic journals and international conferences. His books include *The Path of Buddhism* (Edinburgh: St. Andrew Press, 1988), *The Advent of Sun Myung Moon* (London: Macmillan, 1991), *The Elements of Unitarianism* (Shaftesbury, England: Element, 1998), and *Exploring New Religions* (London: Cassell, 1999).